Revolutions

As the centres of world capitalism struggle to overcome long-term stagnation and existential crisis, this book aims to recover the legacy of revolutions against capitalism and imperialism.

The capitalist world today faces pervasive crises of unprecedented depth. To economic and social crises that were already deepening as the neoliberal decades wore on, it added the ecological emergency and then a pandemic of historic proportions, both made worse by political and ideological paralysis. These crises also raise the threat of imperialist war.

The possibility of revolutionary change is increasingly in the air and this volume captures this extraordinary moment. Anticipating this situation, we at the Geopolitical Economy Research Group organized an international conference on Revolutions at the University of Manitoba, Canada, in 2017, to mark the centenary of the Russian Revolution, and this book stems from it. The editors' introduction interrogates the intimate relation of capitalism to revolutions, and scans the political horizon of the present conjuncture. The chapters that follow fill in this retrospect and prospect. The five keynote addresses provide the historical spine and they are supplemented by others from the conference and beyond. These chapters consider revolution from a variety of perspectives, including the revolutions in Russia, China and Venezuela but also the French and Haitian Revolutions; Marx's critical political economy and revolution; the long history of counter-revolution; revolution and indigenous peoples; the media and revolution and the importance of revolution at the grassroots.

The chapters in this book were originally published as a special issue of *Third World Quarterly*.

Radhika Desai is Professor of Political Studies at the University of Manitoba, Canada, the Director of the Geopolitical Economy and the President of the Society for Socialist Studies.

Henry Heller is Professor of History at the University of Manitoba, Canada.

ThirdWorlds

Edited by Shahid Qadir, *University of London, UK*

ThirdWorlds will focus on the political economy, development and cultures of those parts of the world that have experienced the most political, social, and economic upheaval, and which have faced the greatest challenges of the postcolonial world under globalisation: poverty, displacement and diaspora, environmental degradation, human and civil rights abuses, war, hunger, and disease.

ThirdWorlds serves as a signifier of oppositional emerging economies and cultures ranging from Africa, Asia, Latin America, Middle East, and even those 'Souths' within a larger perceived North, such as the U.S. South and Mediterranean Europe. The study of these otherwise disparate and discontinuous areas, known collectively as the Global South, demonstrates that as globalisation pervades the planet, the south, as a synonym for subalterity, also transcends geographical and ideological frontier.

The most recent titles include:

Studying the State
A Global South Perspective
Edited by Esteban Nicholls

Converging Social Justice Issues and Movements
Edited by Tsegaye Moreda, Saturnino M. Borras Jr., Alberto Alonso-Fradejas and Zoe W. Brent

Rising Powers in International Conflict Management
Converging and Contesting Approaches
Edited by Emel Parlar Dal

Rising Powers and State Transformation
Edited by Shahar Hameiri, Lee Jones and John Heathershaw

The Spatiality of Violence in Post-war Cities
Edited by Emma Elfversson, Ivan Gusic and Kristine Hoglund

Beyond the Gatekeeper State
Edited by Sara Rich Dorman

Citizen Aid and Everyday Humanitarianism
Development Futures?
Edited by Anne-Meike Fechter and Anke Schwittay

Decolonising Gender in South Asia
Edited by Nazia Hussein and Saba Hussain

Decolonising Curricula and Pedagogy in Higher Education
Bringing Decolonial Theory into Contact with Teaching Practice
Edited by Shannon Morreira, Kathy Luckett, Siseko H. Kumalo and Manjeet Ramgotra

Revolutions
Edited by Radhika Desai and Henry Heller

For more information about this series, please visit:
www.routledge.com/series/TWQ

Revolutions

Edited by
Radhika Desai and Henry Heller

LONDON AND NEW YORK

First published 2022
by Routledge
2 Park Square, Milton Park, Abingdon, Oxon OX14 4RN

and by Routledge
605 Third Avenue, New York, NY 10158

Routledge is an imprint of the Taylor & Francis Group, an informa business

Introduction, Chapters 1–6 and 8–11 © 2022 Global South Ltd
Chapter 7 © 2019 Julia Buxton. Originally published as Open Access.

With the exception of Chapter 7, no part of this book may be reprinted or reproduced or utilised in any form or by any electronic, mechanical, or other means, now known or hereafter invented, including photocopying and recording, or in any information storage or retrieval system, without permission in writing from the publishers. For details on the rights for Chapter 7, please see the chapter's Open Access footnote.

Trademark notice: Product or corporate names may be trademarks or registered trademarks, and are used only for identification and explanation without intent to infringe.

British Library Cataloguing in Publication Data
A catalogue record for this book is available from the British Library

ISBN: 978-1-032-01361-9 (hbk)
ISBN: 978-1-032-01364-0 (pbk)
ISBN: 978-1-003-17832-3 (ebk)

DOI: 10.4324/9781003178323

Typeset in Myriad Pro
by Newgen Publishing UK

Publisher's Note
The publisher accepts responsibility for any inconsistencies that may have arisen during the conversion of this book from journal articles to book chapters, namely the inclusion of journal terminology.

Disclaimer
Every effort has been made to contact copyright holders for their permission to reprint material in this book. The publishers would be grateful to hear from any copyright holder who is not here acknowledged and will undertake to rectify any errors or omissions in future editions of this book.

Printed in the United Kingdom
by Henry Ling Limited

Contents

Citation Information		vii
Notes on Contributors		ix

Introduction: Revolutions: a twenty-first-century perspective   1
Radhika Desai and Henry Heller

1   The Russian Revolution at 100: the Soviet experience in the mirror of
permanent counterrevolution   12
Kees van der Pijl

2   Colours of a revolution. Post-communist society, global capitalism and the
Ukraine crisis   29
Ruslan Dzarasov and Victoria Gritsenko

3   Building socialism: from 'scientific' to 'active' Marxism   46
David Lane

4   Culture and revolution: Bakhtin, Mayakovsky and Lenin (disalienation as
[social] creativity)   62
Aleksandr Buzgalin and Lyudmila Bulavka-Buzgalina

5   The Chinese Revolution and the Communist International   78
Enfu Cheng and Jun Yang

6   Marx's critical political economy, 'Marxist economics' and actually occurring
revolutions against capitalism   93
Radhika Desai

7   Continuity and change in Venezuela's Bolivarian Revolution   111
Julia Buxton

8   A political economy for social movements and revolution: popular media
access, power and cultural hegemony   128
Lee Artz

CONTENTS

9 Bush/revolution: theses on the challenges that gatherers and hunters pose
   to dominant structures   146
   Peter Kulchyski

10 The communitarian revolutionary subject: new forms of social transformation   161
   David Barkin and Alejandra Sánchez

11 Hegel, Haiti and revolution: the post-colonial moment   182
   Henry Heller

   Index   202

Citation Information

The chapters in this book were originally published in the *Third World Quarterly*, volume 41, issue 8 (2020). When citing this material, please use the original page numbering for each article, as follows:

Introduction
Revolutions: a twenty-first-century perspective
Radhika Desai and Henry Heller
Third World Quarterly, volume 41, issue 8 (2020), pp. 1261–1271

Chapter 1
The Russian Revolution at 100: the Soviet experience in the mirror of permanent counterrevolution
Kees van der Pijl
Third World Quarterly, volume 41, issue 8 (2020), pp. 1272–1288

Chapter 2
Colours of a revolution. Post-communist society, global capitalism and the Ukraine crisis
Ruslan Dzarasov and Victoria Gritsenko
Third World Quarterly, volume 41, issue 8 (2020), pp. 1289–1305

Chapter 3
Building socialism: from 'scientific' to 'active' Marxism
David Lane
Third World Quarterly, volume 41, issue 8 (2020), pp. 1306–1321

Chapter 4
Culture and revolution: Bakhtin, Mayakovsky and Lenin (disalienation as [social] creativity)
Aleksandr Buzgalin and Lyudmila Bulavka-Buzgalina
Third World Quarterly, volume 41, issue 8 (2020), pp. 1322–1337

Chapter 5
The Chinese Revolution and the Communist International
Enfu Cheng and Jun Yang
Third World Quarterly, volume 41, issue 8 (2020), pp. 1338–1352

Chapter 6

Marx's critical political economy, 'Marxist economics' and actually occurring revolutions against capitalism
Radhika Desai
Third World Quarterly, volume 41, issue 8 (2020), pp. 1353–1370

Chapter 7

Continuity and change in Venezuela's Bolivarian Revolution
Julia Buxton
Third World Quarterly, volume 41, issue 8 (2020), pp. 1371–1387

Chapter 8

A political economy for social movements and revolution: popular media access, power and cultural hegemony
Lee Artz
Third World Quarterly, volume 41, issue 8 (2020), pp. 1388–1405

Chapter 9

Bush/revolution: theses on the challenges that gatherers and hunters pose to dominant structures
Peter Kulchyski
Third World Quarterly, volume 41, issue 8 (2020), pp. 1406–1420

Chapter 10

The communitarian revolutionary subject: new forms of social transformation
David Barkin and Alejandra Sánchez
Third World Quarterly, volume 41, issue 8 (2020), pp. 1421–1441

Chapter 11

Hegel, Haiti and revolution: the post-colonial moment
Henry Heller
Third World Quarterly, volume 41, issue 8 (2020), pp. 1442–1461

For any permission-related enquiries please visit:
http://www.tandfonline.com/page/help/permissions

Notes on Contributors

Lee Artz, Department of Communication, Purdue University Northwest, Hammond, IN, USA.

David Barkin, Department of Economics, Universidad Autónoma Metropolitana, Xochimilco, Mexico City, Mexico.

Lyudmila Bulavka-Buzgalina, Department of Political Economy, Faculty of Economics, Lomonosov Moscow State University, Moscow, Russia.

Julia Buxton, School of Public Policy, Central European University, Budapest, Hungary.

Aleksandr Buzgalin, Department of Political Economy, Faculty of Economics, Lomonosov Moscow State University, Moscow, Russia.

Enfu Cheng, Division of Marxism Studies, Chinese Academy of Social Sciences, Beijing, China.

Radhika Desai, Department of Political Studies and Geopolitical Research Group, University of Manitoba, Winnipeg, MB, Canada.

Ruslan Dzarasov, Research Center Economic Theory, Plekhanov Russian University of Economics, Moscow, Russia; Macroeconomics, Central Economics and Mathematics Institute of Russian Academy of Sciences, Moscow, Russia.

Victoria Gritsenko, Plekhanov Russian University of Economics, Moscow, Russia.

Henry Heller, Department of History, University of Manitoba, Winnipeg, MB, Canada.

Peter Kulchyski, Department of Native Studies, University of Manitoba, Winnipeg, MB, Canada.

David Lane, Emmanuel College, Cambridge University, Cambridge, UK.

Alejandra Sánchez, Doctoral Programme in Economic Sciences, Universidad Autónoma Metropolitana, Xochimilco, Mexico City, Mexico.

Kees van der Pijl, School of Global Studies, University of Sussex, Brighton, UK.

Jun Yang, Department of Communist Party of China History and Party Building, Party School of Shanghai Committee of Communist Party of China, Shanghai, China.

Introduction

Revolutions: a twenty-first-century perspective

Radhika Desai and Henry Heller

ABSTRACT

We held the 'Revolutions' conference in 2017 to commemorate the Russian Revolution and redeem the actual record of revolutions in the Third World for the left. A quarter-century after the demise of the USSR, we found liberal capitalist triumphalism unwarranted. Two of the most important expectations to which it gave rise – that the world had become 'unipolar' and that it would enjoy a 'peace dividend' – remained unfulfilled. Instead, the world became multipolar and the West, led by the United States, engaged in unprecedented economic and military aggression against countries that contested its power. If this were not enough, social unrest and explosions in the First World as well as the Third underlined the relevance of revolutions. To trace their lineage, we recall capitalism's intimate relation with revolution. It has needed revolutions to usher it into history and to usher it out. In addition to revolutions against developed capitalism, we also underline how important and necessary revolutions against nascent capitalism in various parts of the world have been. The contributions in this volume explore different parts of this lineage and vivify revolutions for our time.

As the centenary of the first successful revolution against capitalism approached in 2017, few things were less clear than how to commemorate it. The USSR did not complete its 75th year. A quarter-century after its demise, its achievements were a distant memory even among those willing to acknowledge them, and their numbers had long been dwindling amid a splintering left. The First World War had already broken the broad left unity the Second International embodied, and the Russian Revolution had splintered it further. The revolutions it inspired and supported – the Chinese, the Vietnamese and others – led to further divisions.

The Thirty Years' Crisis of capitalist imperialism (1914–45), and the popular upsurges, neatly bookended by the Russian and Chinese revolutions, to which it gave rise, nevertheless issued in broadly progressive outcomes even if they took forms that, while appropriating popular energies, muted their originally far more radical impulses. These outcomes included the actually existing socialisms of Russia, Eastern Europe and China; the welfare states and land reforms on either side of the communist bloc; and decolonisation, which liberated former colonies and restored the policy autonomy they needed to pursue development. The result was a couple of decades of unprecedented popular empowerment, progressive policy and prosperity. However, capital, though chastened and temporarily 'leashed'[1], lived to fight another day. By the 1970s, amid a concatenation of falling profits and productivity, rising wages and prices and Third World assertiveness, it mounted its ferocious neoliberal counter-offensive.

Unable to overcome its historic divisions, however, the left failed either to mount an effective defence of progressive post-war regimes or to develop them further in a progressive direction. Forty years later, the result has been a wave of right-wing and populist mobilisations of the discontents of neoliberalism that should have been the social bases of a reinvigorated left but were mobilised by a populist right instead.

Intellectual retreats of the left

While this outcome was the result of a complex of factors, we are mainly concerned with the intellectual ones. Neoliberalism was but the last of the three counter-revolutionary offensives launched by twentieth-century capitalism. The fascisms of the 1930s and 1940s constituted the first while the containment policies organised by the United States from the 1950s to the 1980s under the rubric of the Cold War, the second.[2] In the first phase, the intellectual contestation between left and right was sharp and the ideas of both socialism and revolution retained considerable popular legitimacy in the West. Hitler took power in Germany, but not without a fight. Between 1918 and 1933, Germany was wracked by bitter class war in which the Communist Party contested power with the Nazis. Likewise, a popular front of the left defended republican democracy against fascism in Spain (1936–39). In France, the Popular Front, with the help of the Communist Party, beat back fascism and won important social and political victories.[3] Nor was revolutionary activity confined to Europe: in El Salvador, the fledgling Communist Party attempted the first communist revolution in the Americas.[4] The story in the next two phases could not have been more different, at least as far as the West was concerned.

Beginning with the Cold War, Western governments, led by the US, mounted a vast ideological campaign against the threat of revolution, and academic theorising about revolution was a critical part of it. Crane Brinton conceived of revolution as pathology.[5] Chalmers Johnson saw it as disrupted equilibrium.[6] Ted Gurr reduced it to violent change.[7] Hannah Arendt viewed revolutions, other than those she designated the 'American' political type leading to moderate constitutional government, as tyrannical.[8] Walt Rostow conceived of modernisation as a way to avoid revolution.[9] These examples, which merely scratch the surface of an enormous corpus of Western writing against revolution, should be enough to demonstrate that Western academics saw revolution itself as basically negative, emphasising instead the need for controlled reform from above. Indeed, there have been three, four or even five generations of theorising about revolution, reflecting changing emphases in the West's concern about a phenomenon which remained alien and threatening.

There were, of course, notable exceptions to this intellectual trend, and nearly all worked in the Marxist tradition, broadly defined. We mention here some of the most prominent. Eric Wolf's *Peasant Wars of the Twentieth Century*[10] demonstrated the ties between the intrusion of capitalism and its effects on peasant communities, depending on local conditions such as the degree of concentration of land holdings, the degree of market penetration and the level and type of taxation, and the great peasant uprisings of the twentieth century.

Barrington Moore[11] showed that, in situations of peasant revolution, the persistence of land-lordism determined whether the outcome of modernisation would be bourgeois democracy, fascism or communism. Theda Skocpol[12] emphasised the link between revolution and agrarian bureaucratic states, underscoring the relative autonomy of the state on the one hand and the potential for revolution on the other, based on the weakness of traditional agriculture and splits between the state and landlord elites. Finally, Charles Tilly, who worked mainly on France, showed that revolutions were the outcome of long-term and deep-seated patterns of popular resistance that differ from nation to nation.[13]

However, not only did these writings remain marginal on the Western intellectual scene, but after the break-up of the Soviet Union, a new tide of scholarship washed over what remained of any positive conception of revolution. It was part of the counter-offensive against Marxist-inspired revolutionary movements of the 1960s and 1970s. Intellectual currents emerged to question Marxist interpretations of the French Revolution, imperialism and colonialism and fascism.[14] A revisionist interpretation of the French Revolution had begun to appear from the 1960s onward to cast doubt on the idea that the Revolution was bourgeois and capitalist. The politically and socially well-connected Oxford historian Alfred Cobban argued instead that the 1789 revolution was led by economically hard-pressed professionals and office-holders who were reluctantly pushed into the abolition of seigneurial dues and feudal privileges by an insurgent peasantry, and that the revolution left the distribution of wealth and power largely unchanged. If anything, it was a revolution against rather than for capitalism. François Furet seconded Cobban's view, despite its theoretical and scholarly weaknesses. Cobban had claimed that the radical Jacobin Republic interrupted the promising development of moderate constitutional government. Furet went on to assert, contrary to the evidence, that this political miscarriage occurred not because of deep material forces but as a result of the subversive teachings of fanatic intellectuals. The parallel with the Bolshevik Revolution was not accidental: Furet was one of the leading anti-communist intellectuals in France at the height of the Cold War. The views of Cobban and Furet, embroidered upon by their epigones, dominated the historiography of the neoliberal period.[15]

Matters were not helped by another intellectual trend. Over the previous century and more, Marxists had questioned Marx's analysis of capitalism as value production on the ground of neoclassical economics and denied the necessity of the link between capitalism and imperialism and the central role of national states in resisting imperialism. This trend, which has become particularly vigorous in the neoliberal decades, was deeply problematic given that the actual record of revolutions to this day has been one of necessarily national revolutions against imperialism outside the homelands of capitalism.[16] In recent years, the trend has led to important parts of the left supporting Western military interventions against this or that Third World 'dictator'.

Thus, on the one hand, neoliberalism led even Marxists to a Schumpeterian celebration of the capitalist economy itself as 'revolutionary', delivering innovation upon destabilising innovation while remaining, theoretically at least, quite innocent of imperialism and, thereby, of revolutions against it. Indeed, the very category of imperialism, which once defined left discourse, suffered a decline in it after the 1970s,[17] and, without it, left and Marxist currents were rendered susceptible to imperialist appeals. On the other hand, in broader discourse, neoliberalism issued in such a comprehensive suspicion of political revolution itself that even that quintessentially bourgeois revolution, the French, now stood in the dock. The neoliberal wisdom that 'there is no alternative' became entrenched: socialism had failed and political revolutions were merely destructive and murderous, with no gains to redeem them.

The post-Cold War conjuncture

Thus, by the time the Berlin Wall fell and the Soviet Union disintegrated into its component national units, the left had been on the intellectual and political back foot for some time. The achievements of the USSR and the reality of a 'revolution from above'[18] organising the transition to capitalism notwithstanding, the neoliberal narrative held sway. Communism had been destroyed by its economic failures and political illegitimacy. Revolution itself was suspect, and Western capitalist triumphalism now had the hubris to claim that history itself had arrived at its terminus: the combination of capitalism and (neo)liberal democracy (as famously proposed by Fukuyama[19]).

No wonder, then, that the centenary of the Russian Revolution was marked, in Russia itself, in muted fashion and with considerable ambivalence by the Putin government,[20] if more fulsomely by small bands of ageing communists. Outside Russia, left currents could muster little more than a desire to 'rethink' revolution, to 'transcend' the Soviet legacy and 'look forward more than back', as one representative volume put it.[21] The leitmotif simply bade good riddance to bad rubbish.

This was the context in which we set about thinking of the most suitable ways to mark the centenary of the Russian Revolution. We were aware of three things: first, that Western triumphalism was far from the end of the story and that the historical file on revolutions was hardly closed. Waves of uprisings, riots and demonstrations had begun rolling across the world stage and have continued to do so: the Occupy Movement, the Arab Spring, and mass upheavals shaking France, Spain, Algeria, Egypt, Sudan, Hong Kong, Venezuela, Chile, Ecuador, Bolivia, Lebanon and still counting.

Secondly, we were aware that the splits and divisions on the left going back to the First World War and the Bolshevik Revolution had only worsened, leaving it unable to diagnose the complex conjuncture that has emerged since the 1990s. Over the course of four decades of neoliberalism and a quarter-century since the fall of the Berlin Wall, the world had not become unipolar, as had been widely expected. Rather, amid the continuing Long Downturn[22] afflicting financialised Western economies, inequality was rising, growth and wages were stagnant, social fabrics were fraying, democracies were being hollowed out and climate change was accelerating. Only the largest corporations and their power had been prospering. Worse, Western economies were losing ground with the rise and assertion of China and other economies, and the world was becoming multipolar – or, as the late Hugo Chavez preferred to say, pluripolar. The left in Western countries, long used to earning its political credentials by underlining the power of Western capitalism, could only be uncomprehending.

Finally, post-Cold War expectations of a 'peace dividend' were also belied. The West, led by the US, had reacted to its sliding power with a new worldwide aggression, military and economic, that was no less murderous for being vain.

As new forms of resistance emerged to contest neoliberalism and imperialism, this time in both the core and the periphery of the world system, taking both class and national forms, splits on the left multiplied further. We realised that we needed to bring revolutions themselves – their actual historical record – out of the fog of mainstream discourse and understand them afresh.

Revolutions and capitalism: two frames

In this context, for those of us at the Geopolitical Economy Research Group planning a conference to mark the centenary of the Russian Revolution, the key was not to think of it alone but to think of revolutions as such, and their relationship with capitalism, in a broadly historical manner. The conference on 'Revolutions' at the University of Manitoba, Winnipeg, from 29 September to 1 October 2017, had two interconnected and equally important frames.

The more proximate frame, considering the century since 1917, was provided by the historical record of revolutions since 1917 and the left's ambiguity about them. Though revolutions had occurred only in backward and underdeveloped countries on Europe's periphery and in the colonial and semi-colonial world, and had taken national forms, political and doctrinal divisions and limitations of the Western left and Marxisms meant that this record could not be intellectually digested and converted into further revolutionary energy. On the one hand, these divisions and limitations had converted the left's internationalism into a blank cosmopolitanism in which nations were at best an irrelevance and at worst politically atavistic cultural forms, much as in the discourses of 'globalisation' and 'empire' to which the left was quite susceptible.[23] On the other, understandings of imperialism and resistance to it, which involve national as well as class resistance, remained contested and ill understood. Today, as revolutionary energies are erupting in the West as well as beyond it, a new understanding of the two and their interrelation is necessary to ground political solidarity across the imperial divide. In this volume, the contributions on the political and geopolitical economy[24] of the Russian, Chinese and Bolivarian revolutions[25] seek to recover and re-examine critical aspects of this historical record of revolutions against imperialism as well as capitalism, which combined class as well as national agency.

The second historical frame is grander and connected to the first. As a form of social production and society, capitalism had a special relationship with revolution. Not only has it taken – and will it take – revolutions to usher capitalism out of history, unless humanity is to descend into barbarism, it took revolutions to usher it into history. This was, quite simply, because capitalism is not natural at all, contrary to pervasive liberal myths turned 'common sense' about capitalism and markets being natural and other social forms involving conscious collective human organisation being artificial. Rather, as it emerges from Marx's analysis, capitalism is the most unnatural manner of organising social production humanity could have chanced on, founded as it was on the 'the separation of free labour from the objective conditions of its realization[,]… from the soil as [our] natural workshop'.[26] This foundational brutality is, as Marx shows, pre-eminently in the *Grundrisse*, the culmination of a long and contested history.

Looked at this way, capitalism is associated with another type of revolution, one we have not recognised as being about capitalism. In addition to the revolutions that ushered capitalism into history, those that that have ushered it out in its peripheries and those that may yet end it in its homelands, there has been the resistance of those threatened by its incursion. It has been undertaken in the name of ancient rights, the land and environment and solidaristic social forms. Such resistance is occurring alongside the more familiar ones since capitalism's birth and, as we know, Marx considered these possibilities positively. Kulchyski and Barkin and Sanchez cover these types of revolutions,[27] giving the idea of permanent revolution a twist. Kees van der Pijl gives it another when he outlines the centuries-long contest between permanent revolution and 'permanent counter-revolution'.[28]

World revolution and counter-revolution: theme and variations

Five keynote addresses gave thematic unity to the conference, taking us from an overall reflection on the dialectic of revolution and counter-revolution in modern times through the Russian and Chinese Revolutions and the Bolivarian revolution in Venezuela to the increasingly manifest revolutionary energies of indigenous peoples today, while other contributions explored related themes.

Kees van der Pijl's[29] panoramic review of the contest between revolution and counter-revolution provided a fitting opening for the conference and this volume. Coining the term 'permanent counter-revolution', he outlines how capitalism has sought to keep revolution at bay since the middle of the nineteenth century, beginning with blunting the radical edge of bourgeois revolutions themselves. Permanent counter-revolution then graduated to opposing the Russian Revolution in alliance with authoritarian and eventually fascist forces (whose early forms also helped defeat the revolutionary wave in Western Europe at the end of the First World War). While counter-revolution failed to defeat the nascent Russian Revolution, it contained and deformed it, van der Pijl argues. In our own times, permanent counter-revolution continues under the leadership of the Anglo-American core of the capitalist world. Having had to defeat fascism when it became a menace to itself, it has now taken to employing para-fascist combinations of covert and overt strategies to pre-empt opposition to capitalism.

Such strategies reached something of a peak in the so-called 'Colour Revolutions' being sponsored by the US and the West in an attempt to roll back popular energies and create an appearance of support for neoliberal capitalism in various parts of the world. The detection of such imperial and counter-revolutionary strategies is also made difficult by confusion on the left on the matter of imperialism. One form it has taken in recent years, particularly since the 2014 confrontation between the West and Russia over Ukraine, is the theory of Russian imperialism and/or the 'clash of two imperialisms', Western and Russian. Ruslan Dzarasov and Viktoria Gritsenko[30] challenge these theses, showing how Russia and the second most important successor state of the USSR, Ukraine, emerged from the Soviet System saddled with oligarchical capitalisms as the Stalinist degeneration of the Soviet system interacted with financialised world capitalism. Russia and Ukraine were relegated to the semi-periphery and periphery, respectively, of world capitalism. This differential placement left Ukraine prey to imperialism while permitting Russia a certain autonomy to resist it and seek to assert influence over the post-Soviet space. This last inevitably put it on a collision course with the West fomenting its Colour Revolutions in Ukraine, there exploiting as well as diverting genuine grievances against Ukraine's comprador oligarchical capitalism.

While the contributions of van der Pijl and Dzarasov and Gritsenko emphasise the degeneration of the USSR, two other contributions redeem it in critical ways. David Lane[31] examines the long-standing contest between positivist and determinist 'scientific' Marxism and its active and creative element which is less concerned with the 'laws' of capitalism and more with the possibilities of human liberation. For Lane, the Russian and Chinese Revolutions, with their iconoclastic understandings of imperialism and people's war, were instances of the latter. Though they were not successful in achieving human liberation to the fullest, they constituted critical advances towards it. Today, as Scientific Marxism keeps taking new forms in response to new developments in capitalism, it is critical to keep alive the active, creative element of Marxism, if we are to progress towards human liberation.

Buzgalin and Bulavka-Buzgalina[32] approach the matter of creativity and revolution from another angle. They conceive creativity philosophically as unalienated human expression and activity that emerges from the cooperation of creators across space and time, in dialogue with the entire cultural – artistic as well as scientific – heritage of humanity. With this fundamental assertion, they go on to show, through an analysis of the insights of three very different figures, Lenin, Bakhtin and Mayakovsky, that the Russian Revolutionaries considered revolution not merely the negation of a previous order but also a dialectical and dialogical co-creation of culture – a new culture, a culture in which masses expressed their essential creativity. The building of this culture was, in an essential sense, communism. This culture therefore is, they argue, universal in its significance, the common heritage of a humankind struggling for its liberation. Their contribution critically overturns the neoliberal equation of revolution with destruction and murder mentioned above.

The umbilical link between the Russian and Chinese Revolutions which bookended the Thirty Years' Crisis of capitalism imperialism (1914–45) and the larger matter of anti-imperialist solidarity is today obscured by the dominant focus on the early mistakes of the Communist International with regard to China, the later Sino–Soviet Split and the general disparagement of the 'national' character of these revolutions. It is a problem that Cheng and Yang[33] address to great effect in their piece on the role of the Communist International in guiding the leadership of the Chinese revolution. Without denying the Comintern's mistakes, particularly in taking a schematic interpretation of the classical Marxist heritage and over-generalising the Russian experience, they emphasise its critical role in forming the Communist Party of China and aiding its theoretical formation and development. They also show how the Communist International's own evolution and theory were influenced by the Chinese Revolution, even as Mao and his colleagues successfully Sinicised Marxism.

The Russian and Chinese Revolutions were as much revolutions against imperialism as they were against capitalism and involved national as much as class struggles as have revolutions since then. If these 'unexpected' elements of revolutions have divided and confused Marxism in the core capitalist countries, a key reason, Desai[34] argues, was intellectual. The incursion of neoclassical economics into Marxism distorted Marx's analysis of capitalism as contradictory value production. The 'Marxist economics' that emerged alleged, falsely, that Marx's analysis suffered from a 'transformation problem' and that it denied or was mistaken about key crisis mechanisms Marx had identified, particularly the paucity of demand and the tendency of the rate of profit to fall. The result was a contradiction-free, worldwide, cosmopolitan capitalism in which states and nations played no role and to which imperialism was 'unnecessary'. Such a Marxism could only fail to understand the history of revolutions over the last century.

Julia Buxton[35] closely examines the Venezuelan Revolution and provides a window into what revolutions of our own time in the poorer parts of the world will look like. Rooted in the mass poverty as well as in the distorted development of the Venezuelan economy, this massive reversal for imperialism, particularly American, demonstrates notable continuities with the pre-revolutionary period thanks to the dominance of the oil industry in the Venezuelan economy. The Bolivarian Revolution's continuing dependence on it has narrowed its political choices. The clear implication is that the survival of the Bolivarian revolution rests on creatively finding ways around this great obstacle, through national and international action.

As it does so, its political legitimacy will be critical. And certainly the Bolivarian process has demonstrated remarkable political creativity in maintaining it. Lee Artz's[36] contribution illuminates a critical aspect of this creativity: how the Bolivarian revolution contested the hegemony of the privately owned media, which still operates in the country and spews vituperation on the Bolivarian government more or less continuously, with a popular media strategy permitting people to create their own, alternative media. This effort was redoubled after the 2002 coup, in which the private media was prominent. The result has been a vibrant alternative media scene, widening popular participation and forming a major front of a counterhegemonic strategy.

The Bolivarian process in Venezuela is anti-imperialist internationally as well as at home, mobilising, in particular, black and indigenous people and communities, drawing attention to the centrality of an anti-imperialist agenda across the Americas. Using Marx's concept of mode of production, Peter Kulchyski[37] theorises the 'bush mode of production', rooted in social and economic equality, which has survived under capitalism and can become a foundation for resistance to the further encroachment of capitalist resource extraction and a vanguard element of the struggle for an ecologically based socialism. For their part, Barkin and Sanchez[38] demonstrate that many indigenous and non-indigenous communities, simply in their existence and functioning – founded on broad communitarian and participatory principles that are ecologically sustainable – constitute a form of resistance, what they call 'r-existence'. Far from passive, it is based on a struggle to conserve and develop ancestral forms of communal being and knowledge. These two contributions recall our second frame, in which revolutions of communities still largely outside capitalism are as much a part of the history of revolutions against capitalism as is the classic image of a working-class revolution against capitalism at its core or peasant revolutions in its peripheries.

In his critique of Susan Buck-Morss's *Hegel, Haiti and Universal History*, Henry Heller[39] shows that Marxism is truly the unsurpassable horizon for an analysis of the global history of the French and Haitian Revolutions. Buck-Morss argues that the Marxist interpretation of Hegel's master–slave dialogue as referring to class struggles in Europe is Eurocentric, and attempts to show instead that it must refer to the Haitian Revolution. In her post-colonial argument, it is the most uncompromising element of the French Revolution in its radical conception of freedom. Against this, Heller argues that the choice of Hegel – anti-Jacobin and Eurocentric – to support the undoubted universalism of the Haitian Revolution is unfortunate, particularly as it is poorly supported by evidence. Heller's analysis reveals that Marxist scholarship remains the soundest guide to the universalism of the Haitian Revolution.

Interest in the history of revolutions and the study of how revolutionary change has been made can be expected to grow as consciousness of the necessity of making revolutionary change increases in all parts of the world, irrespective of the nature and degree of their insertion into capitalism. Such efforts will face historically unprecedented obstacles. Firstly, there will be repression, surveillance, disinformation and counter-revolution, with war and the threat of violence its weapons of choice. Secondly, for every revolutionary Venezuela and Sudan there is a counter-revolutionary Hong Kong or Ukraine, where the possibility of mobilising under the banner of middle-class populism and fascism remains all too real. Thirdly, there is the very different role of the educated classes in politics today. In the century-long cycle of mobilisation against capitalism and imperialism that began in the late nineteenth century, the intellectuals of each country sided with the working and popular classes. Lenin and Kautsky spoke of the proletariat being joined by sections of the bourgeois intelligentsia, while the Fabians, with their characteristically blunt pomposity, spoke of 'brains and numbers'. Today, the relation of the educated classes and the mass of the people is different: they have largely been absorbed into occupations in the private sector whose leading element is the giant corporate sector, or into the neoliberal state. Few of them are left for mass political and revolutionary activity.

Powerful as they are, such obstacles are not guaranteed the last word. The use of force, no matter how determined and well financed, is not always effective, particularly as the world's geopolitical economy becomes more and more pluripolar. This is clear from the long series of imperial failures from Vietnam to Syria. While the threat of fascism is certainly becoming more real in our time, and while the intellectual classes are failing in their duty to reverse it, with the wider spread of education the relation between the intellectual and popular element may itself become a more organic one. Finally, people's war, or the mobilisation of the bodies and consciousness of the masses in new forms – *levée en masse*, urban street-fighting, mass peasant armies, village-based guerilla war – has its own history which is being constantly re-invented, and has been the critical factor in making successful revolutions from 1789 through 1917 and until today.

Disclosure statement

No potential conflict of interest was reported by the authors.

Notes

1. Glyn, *Capitalism Unleashed*.
2. Heller and Desai, "Cold War."
3. Hobsbawm, *Age of Extremes*, 68–9, 130, 147–8, 157–61.
4. Gould and Aldo, *Rise in Darkness*.
5. Brinton, *Anatomy of Revolution*.
6. Johnson, *Revolutionary Change*.
7. Gurr, *Why Men Rebel*.
8. Arendt, *On Revolution*.
9. Rostow, *Stages of Economic Growth*.
10. Wolf, *Peasant Wars*.

11. Moore, *Social Origins of Dictatorship and Democracy*.
12. Skocpol, *States and Social Revolutions*.
13. Tilly, *Collective Violence*.
14. Losurdo, *War and Revolution*.
15. Anderson, "Dégringolade"; "Union Sucrée."
16. Desai, "Marx's Critical Political Economy."
17. Patnaik, "Whatever Has Happened to Imperialism?"
18. Kotz, *Revolution from Above*.
19. Fukuyama, "End of History."
20. Dejevsky, "If Putin Celebrates the Centenary."
21. Panitch and Albo, *Rethinking Revolution*.
22. Brenner, "Economics of Global Turbulence,"; Brenner, "What Is Good for Goldman Sachs."
23. Desai, *Geopolitical Economy*; Desai, "Inadvertence of Benedict Anderson."
24. Desai, *Geopolitical Economy*.
25. Dzarasov and Gritsenko, "Colours of a Revolution"; Cheng and Yang, "Chinese Revolution and the Communist International"; Buxton, "Continuity and Change in Venezuela's Bolivarian Revolution," in this issue.
26. Marx, *Grundrisse*.
27. Barkin and Sánchez, "Communitarian Revolutionary Subject"; and Kulchyski, "Bush/Revolution," both in this issue.
28. van der Pijl, "Russian Revolution at 100," in this issue.
29. Ibid.
30. Dzarasov and Gritsenko, "Colours of a Revolution."
31. Lane, "Building Socialism."
32. Buzgalin and Bulavka-Buzgalina, "Culture and Revolution," in this issue.
33. Cheng and Yang, "Chinese Revolution and the Communist International."
34. Desai, "Marx's Critical Political Economy."
35. Buxton, "Continuity and Change in Venezuela's Bolivarian Revolution," in this issue.
36. Artz, "Political Economy for Social Movements," in this issue.
37. Kulchyski, "Bush/Revolution," in this issue.
38. Barkin and Sánchez, "Communitarian Revolutionary Subject," in this issue.
39. Heller, "Hegel, Haiti and Revolution."

Bibliography

Anderson, Perry. "Dégringolade." *London Review of Books* 26, no. 17 (2004): 3–9.
Anderson, Perry. "Union Sucrée." *London Review of Books* 26, no. 18 (2004): 23.
Arendt, Hannah. *On Revolution*. New York: Viking, 1963.
Artz, Lee. "A Political Economy for Social Movements and Revolution: Popular Media Access, Power and Cultural Hegemony." *Third World Quarterly* (2019): 1–18. doi:10.1080/01436597.2019.1653179.
Barkin, David, and Alejandra Sánchez. "The Communitarian Revolutionary Subject: New Forms of Social Transformation." *Third World Quarterly* (2019): 1–23. doi:10.1080/01436597.2019.1636370.
Brenner, Robert. "The Economics of Global Turbulence." *New Left Review* I, no. 229 (1998): 1–265.
Brenner, Robert. 2009. "What Is Good for Goldman Sachs Is Good for America: The Origins of the Current Crisis." Prologue to the Spanish edition of Brenner 2006. http://www.sscnet.ucla.edu/issr/cstch/papers/BrennerCrisisTodayOctober2009.pdf
Brinton, Crane. *The Anatomy of Revolution*. New York: Vintage Books, 1965.
Buxton, Julia. "Continuity and Change in Venezuela's Bolivarian Revolution." *Third World Quarterly* (2019): 1–17. doi:10.1080/01436597.2019.1653179.
Buzgalin, Aleksandr, and Lyudmila Bulavka-Buzgalina. "Culture and Revolution: Bakhtin, Mayakovsky and Lenin (Disalienation as [Social] Creativity)." *Third World Quarterly* (2019). doi:10.1080/01436597.2019.1700792.

Cheng, Enfu, and Jun Yang. "The Chinese Revolution and the Communist International." *Third World Quarterly* (2020). doi:10.1080/01436597.2020.1763169.

Dejevsky, Mary. "If Putin Celebrates the Centenary of the Russian Revolution, It Could Be Seen as Validating the Idea of State Overthrow." *The Independent*, October 26, 2017. https://www.independent.co.uk/voices/vladimir-putin-russia-centenary-bolshevik-revolution-a8021816.html

Desai, Heller. "Cold War." In *The Palgrave Encyclopedia of Imperialism and Anti-Imperialism*, edited by Immanuel Ness and Zak Cope. London: Palgrave, 2019.

Desai, Radhika. *Geopolitical Economy: After US Hegemony, Globalization and Empire*. London: Pluto Press, 2013.

Desai, Radhika. "The Inadvertence of Benedict Anderson: Engaging *Imagined Communities*." *The Asia-Pacific Journal* 11 (2009): 3085.

Desai, Radhika. "Marx's Critical Political Economy, 'Marxist Economics' and Actually Occurring Revolutions against Capitalism." *Third World Quarterly* (2020). doi:10.1080/01436597.2020.1741346.

Dzarasov, Ruslan, and Viktoria Gritsenko. "Colours of a Revolution. Post-Communist Society, Global Capitalism and the Ukraine Crisis." *Third World Quarterly* (2020). doi:10.1080/01436597.2020.1732202.

Fukuyama, Francis. "The End of History." The National Interest, 1989, Summer.

Glyn, Andrew. *Capitalism Unleashed: Finance Globalization and Welfare*. Oxford: Oxford University Press, 2006.

Gould, Jeffrey L., and Lauria-Santiago Aldo. *To Rise in Darkness: Revolution, Repression, and Memory in El Salvador, 1920–1932*. Durham, NC: Duke University Press, 2008.

Gurr, Ted. *Why Men Rebel*. Princeton: Woodrow Wilson School of Public and International Affairs, Center of International Studies, 1970.

Heller, Henry. "Hegel, Haiti and Revolution: The Post-Colonial Moment." *Third World Quarterly* (2020). doi:10.1080/01436597.2020.1763168.

Hobsbawm, Eric. *The Age of Extremes, a History of the World 1914–91*. London: Penguin, 1994.

Johnson, Chalmers. *Revolutionary Change*. New York: Little Brown & Company, 1966.

Kotz, David M. *Revolution from Above: The Demise of the Soviet System*. London: Routledge, 1997.

Kulchyski, Peter. "Bush/Revolution: Theses on the Challenges That Gatherers and Hunters Pose to Dominant Structures." *Third World Quarterly* (2019). doi:10.1080/01436597.2019.1695115.

Lane, David. "Building Socialism: From 'Scientific' to 'Active' Marxism." *Third World Quarterly* (2020). doi:10.1080/01436597.2020.1724781.

Losurdo, Domenico. *War and Revolution: Rethinking the 20th Century*. London: Verso, 2015.

Marx, Karl. *Grundrisse*. London: Penguin, 1858/1973.

Moore, Barrington. *Social Origins of Dictatorship and Democracy: Lord and Peasant in the Making of the Modern World*. Boston: Beacon Press, 1966.

Panitch, Leo, and Greg Albo. *Rethinking Revolution: Socialist Register 2017*. London: Merlin.

Patnaik, Prabhat. "Whatever Has Happened to Imperialism?" *Social Scientist* 18, no. 6/7 (1990): 73–76. doi:10.2307/3517480.

Rostow, Walter Whitman. *The Stages of Economic Growth: A Non-Communist Manifesto*. Cambridge: Cambridge University Press, 1960.

Skocpol, Theda. *States and Social Revolutions: A Comparative Analysis of France, Russia, and China*. Cambridge, New York: Cambridge University Press, 1979.

Tilly, Charles. *Collective Violence, Contentious Politics, and Social Change: A Charles Tilly Reader*. New York: Routledge, 2017.

van der Pijl, Kees. "The Russian Revolution at 100: The Soviet Experience in the Mirror of Permanent Counter-Revolution." *Third World Quarterly* (2019): 1–17. doi:10.1080/01436597.2019.1665462.

Wolf, Eric. *Peasant Wars of the Twentieth Century*. New York: Harper-Row, 1969.

The Russian Revolution at 100: the Soviet experience in the mirror of permanent counterrevolution

Kees van der Pijl

ABSTRACT
The Russian Revolution is analysed in this paper in the context of a conjuncture dominated by counterrevolution. Beginning with the repression of the 1850s, a process of *permanent counterrevolution* has become the over-determining trend of social-political history. The Russian Revolution was subject to several distinct aspects of this process. First was *external* counterrevolution, the attack on it from the outside. Whilst Anglo-America was the main bulwark organising it, the Nazi/fascist counterrevolution and invasion of the USSR was an example of counterrevolution that ran out of control and ended in a defeat in Europe that was only overcome through a long and risky Cold War. *Internal* counterrevolution affected the Russian Revolution as part of a longer process of adjusting socialist theory to successive defeats. In the Soviet case, Socialism in One Country was the decisive mutation in this respect and must be viewed as the decisive component of the triumph of counterrevolution. After the war, Anglo-America adjusted the counterrevolutionary strategy to surgical excisions of socialist tendencies until the USSR, isolated and ideologically exhausted, collapsed. Even so, several of its legacies continue to be relevant, notably the nationality policy and internationalism. Also, today's information revolution casts a new light on the Soviet planning experience that must be studied now that capitalism is slipping into a systemic crisis.

Introduction

At the centenary of the Russian Revolution there appears little to celebrate. The Soviet Union, the socialist state established by the Bolsheviks once the foreign interventions backing up a contra war had been warded off, collapsed 26 years before the anniversary, exposing its economy to plunder by a class of oligarchs encouraged by Western political supervisors and business partners. Meanwhile North Atlantic Treaty Organization and European Union (NATO) and the EU have advanced to the borders of Russia proper. Civil conflict, well-nigh inevitable as the almost 200 nations, nationalities and national groupings that the USSR inherited from the Tsarist empire (minus Finland and Poland) had to find their place in and across the 15 successor republics into which the union broke up, has further exacerbated the dire situation in many cases. 'Minorities', an unrecognised phenomenon under the Soviet doctrine of internationalism and national autonomy, today create major problems in all successor states, with Russians a minority in 14 of them. The Putin leadership in Russia succeeded in halting the downward slide, but this is no longer part of the history of the October Revolution, because the current government remains committed to privatisation, albeit within a more pronounced state-monitored framework.

In hindsight it would seem that what has long been interpreted as the epoch of the transition of capitalism to socialism that began with the Russian Revolution has been dominated instead by the ability of the capitalist West to snuff out, one after another, attempts at revolutionary transformation. This is not to say that the Russian Revolution was not an existential challenge to Western imperialism and transnational capital. But from around 1848 (and with respect to non-Western revolutions such as the revolt in Haiti, even earlier) the commercially minded, proto-capitalist bourgeoisie had changed sides against further democratisation of society. Over time, the strategic centre of counterrevolution, the Anglo-American, Atlantic ruling class and its offshoots elsewhere, was able to gain control over the disparate reactionary responses to revolution, including the response to the Russian one, and make them part of what I term (inverting Trotsky's notion) *permanent* counter*revolution*. I distinguish between external and internal counterrevolution. *External* refers to the protracted assault on Soviet power, from the intervention fuelling the civil war to the Nazi invasion, and after 1945, the siege by the West. In the process, the *reactionary* aspect of external counterrevolution (the attempt to merely turn back the clock) was gradually eclipsed by the dynamic, forward-looking aspect of which the United States was the standard bearer. This lasted until the late 1960s and early 1970s, when reactionary aspects began to surface again, to the contemporary pre-eminence of high-risk, coercive imperialism reflecting the mindset of speculative capital.

Internal counterrevolution refers to the fact that the revolution itself also adjusted to these defeats by regressively modifying its doctrines and postures, a process that had already begun in Marx and Engels's days after the defeat of the revolution of 1848, after the Paris Commune, and so on. In the case of the Russian Revolution, internal counterrevolution involved the switch from the original attempt to ignite a world revolution to the adoption of a contender state role facing the liberal capitalist heartland, to which it was compelled when from 1924, Western creditors suspended the conditions imposed on Germany at Versailles. This critically contributed to bolstering German capital and its ability to underwrite the rise to power of the Nazis.

After the Axis Powers were vanquished in 1945, ruling class circles in the Atlantic West recognised that a Nazi-style crusade against the Left, entailing the murderous Operation Barbarossa, had come close to dragging down the entire capitalist world with it in the hour of defeat. So, whilst inheriting the mantle of counterrevolution from the Axis, the West switched from fascism run wild to *parafascism*, as I will explain below.

The USSR collapsed from the combined effects of external and internal counterrevolution just before a world-historic transformation, the *information revolution*, had matured to the point where it might have saved the planned economy from the final demise. This I will briefly reflect on in the concluding section.

The rise of the West as a dynamic counterrevolutionary bulwark

The West as we know it emerged out of Mediaeval Europe with the resurgence of towns and a merchant class, fuelled by overseas plunder of people, goods and precious metals. According to Marx its different moments were

> distributed in a more or less chronological order, among Spain, Portugal, Holland, France, and England. *In England they are systematically combined* at the end of the 17th century in the colonial system, the public debt system, the modern tax system, and the system of protection. (*Capital*, vol. 1 [1867], Marx and Engels 1956–1971, xxiii, 779, emphasis added)

Church reform and nationality were interlaced with this process of class formation, contributing to a single, overarching European revolution which Eugen Rosenstock-Huessy, writing in the 1930s, saw as culminating in the Russian Revolution (Rosenstock-Huessy 1993).

In hindsight, however, the English contribution to this process, concluded by the Glorious Revolution of 1688 and the codification of Lockean liberalism in the British Isles and the North American colonies, represents a world-historic rupture that has mortgaged subsequent revolutions to the hegemony of the Anglophone capitalist class which only today shows signs of expiring. The balance between the different, interconnected moments in each modern revolution – class formation, state formation and national unification – and ideological modernisation in its different aspects (legal, religious, philosophical and linguistic) had always been and would always be specific; in England, however, capitalist class formation over-determined the others in every respect.

Crucially, the proto-capitalist bloc regrouped to confront their own lower classes. These were no longer recognised as allies in a continuing process of emancipation; henceforth, repression served to protect the emerging capitalist order from them. In the *Two Treatises of Government*, the bible of the Glorious Revolution, Locke explicitly provided for a state of emergency if private property relations were endangered (Locke 1965, 421, 425; Macpherson 1962). The masses of vagrants driven from common land by the enclosures (privatisation) here for the first time emerged as a proletariat available for exploitation by capital. The number of infractions of property rights punishable by death after 1688 increased four- to fivefold over the next century (Thompson 1968, 237–43; Losurdo 2013, 92). Social cohesion in England suffered as a result because only a powerful force from below, demanding the inclusion of all into a new or renovated political entity, will bring about the integration of all of society into the 'nation'.

The French Revolution, the next instance of the European revolutionary process, in that sense reversed the English priority for private property. It relegated possessive individualism to a secondary status compared to a powerful, inclusive statehood, building on the foundations already laid by royal absolutism (Tocqueville 1988). Hence, ideologues of possessive individualism such as Edmund Burke in his *Reflections on the Revolution in France* warned against a democratisation not properly sealed off from infringing on the private property rights that *economic* liberalism was built around. Only the Anglophone legacy of liberty and diversity fosters a political style that turns 'all change into a subject of compromise, which naturally begets moderation; they produce temperaments, preventing the sore evil of harsh, crude, unqualified reformations, and [renders] all the headlong exertions of arbitrary power … for ever impracticable' (Burke 1887, iii, 277). This compromise, it should be added, is between the different factions of the ruling class, united by property rights; Burke was an ardent supporter of the American secession, in which he recognised the restoration of these rights as codified in the original Lockean liberalism. Indeed, in North America, as Louis Hartz famously wrote, the Lockean state/society complex unfolds to its maximum potential because of the absence of an aristocracy and other feudal remnants, whereas in the Old World, 'it is the continuing pressure of these older forces which renews the doctrinaire passion of European radicalism' (Hartz 1964, 42).

In line with Burke's assessment, England adopted a counterrevolutionary stance towards the French Revolution. By financing the reactionary continental coalition against Napoleon it emerged, in Marx's words, as 'the rock on which the counterrevolution will build its church' ('Sturz des Ministeriums Camphausen' [1848] Marx and Engels 1956–1971, v, 96). Yet, notwithstanding the continuing presence of the aristocracy in social life and the Mediaeval pomp and ceremony of its state institutions, the British ruling class was not a monolithic reactionary bloc. Owing to its access to the colonies and the ruthless exploitation of their and its own domestic (and Irish) workers, it was able to preside, until the 1860s, over an industrial revolution serving the world market; after the Civil War in the United States, British finance provided the investment funds for North American railways and industry. To ensure access, Britain (and later the United States) propagated 'the freedom of other countries – those without factories' (Bauer 1907, 474–5). Or, to cite Marx again, the English turn entire nations into proletarians, simultaneously constituting the rock 'on which the waves of revolution will break' ('Die revolutionäre Bewegung' [1849], Marx and Engels 1956–1971, vi, 149). This combination of counterrevolutionary class instinct with dynamic, forward-looking imperialism, the one conditioning and lending *permanency* to the other, represents the uniqueness of globalising capitalism – as long as it lasts.

Counterrevolution, anti-Revolution, fascism

Under this heading I discuss the set of external constraints imposed on the Russian Revolution. It would be titled 'external counterrevolution' were it not for the necessary distinction between the dynamic, forward-looking imperialism of Anglo-America that underpins permanent counterrevolution, and the mere *anti*-revolutionary response to every revolution. Every revolution provokes a reactionary response, an attempt to defend the old regime and turn back the clock; however, the development of transnational capital across Anglo-America, organising the exploitation of society and nature on a global scale, allowed the Western ruling class to move beyond it to respond through what I call permanent counterrevolution (cf. Mayer 1971, 5–6).

Once the United States joined Britain in underwriting a liberal capitalist world order in the 1820s, this counterrevolutionary capitalist bloc was at the centre of the emerging global political economy, a 'Lockean heartland'. Symbolised in the Monroe Doctrine guaranteeing Latin American independence from Europe, this Anglo-American entente would engender a *transnational* process of liberal class formation of which, in the words of D. G. F. Dufour de Pradt (Napoleon's confessor and one-time ambassador in Warsaw, who betrayed his master in 1814–15), 'England is the head, America the body, and all the enlightened men of Europe, the extended limbs' (De Pradt 1824, 48–9). At the latest in the aftermath of the revolutions of 1848, the bourgeoisie *everywhere* switched sides against the workers, but this did not automatically make them 'the enlightened men of Europe', if only because in the reactionary coalitions with the older ruling classes they were often a minority.

Certainly the 'head and body' in Anglo-America were not in control of the process at a global scale. Indeed, we are looking at a historical epoch in which reactionary *anti*-revolution still largely dominates counterrevolution as I define it here; and the initial external response to the Russian Revolution falls into this first epoch, one in which anti-revolution in the form of fascism/Nazism still prevents the dynamic imperialism of permanent counterrevolution to fully unfold although the modernising aspects are not entirely absent.

The origins of the Russian Revolution go back to the rise of the socialist labour movement at the turn of the twentieth century. The Great War had already been considered useful as a means to destroy the ascendant working class – not just by the atavistic imperialisms of the Central Powers and Russia, but also by Britain itself: its entry into the war, like the Boer War before it, was motivated not least by fear of a civil war in the British Isles (Bosco 2017, 12 and passim; on Imperial Germany, see Fischer 1984, 25 and passim). In Russia, and in the Ottoman and Austro-Hungarian empires too, social compromise was out of reach for the ruling strata altogether. Revolutionary outbreaks in the war's closing stages were partly deflected by national self-determination, but always reflected the brutalisation of 4 years of slaughter in the trenches.

In the initial response to the October Revolution, reactionary, *anti*-revolutionary elements predominated, although in Woodrow Wilson's position the eventual appeal to the enlightened bourgeoisie, necessary to raise the level of confronting socialism to permanent counterrevolution, is already evident. This distinction mattered little in terms of the blows dealt to Soviet power, which as Lenin wrote in his final assessment,

> failed to overthrow the new system created by the revolution, but … did prevent it from at once taking the step forward that would have justified the forecasts of the socialists, that would have enabled the latter to develop all the potentialities which, taken together, would have produced socialism. ('Better Fewer, But Better' [1923], Lenin 1960–1965, xxxiii, 498)

Out of the reactionary elements dominating this first phase and the spasmodic fighting back of the embattled ruling classes against attempts at domestic revolution in Munich, Budapest or Turin, arose fascism and Nazism. These were never *entirely* reactionary, because they pioneered forms of popular mobilisation for counterrevolution, assimilating emotional needs into the anti-/counterrevolutionary project. 'Fascism', writes Barrington Moore, 'was an attempt to make reaction and conservatism popular and plebeian' (Moore 1981, 447). Reaction ultimately was the dominant element: Italian fascism early on destroyed its trade union wing, and the massacre of the plebeian SA leadership by the SS in August 1934 decapitated the Nazi Left wing (Poulantzas 1974, 153; doc. 134 in Kühnl 1980, 242–3). On that basis, Western ruling circles trusted Hitler to destroy the Left, as in the Spanish Civil War, in which he and Mussolini supported Franco's reactionary rebellion against the Republican government.

With the United States still struggling to develop the comprehensive, Fordist response to the 1930s crisis, British appeasers and their counterparts in France were intent on turning Nazi expansion plans against the Soviet Union. Chamberlain and Daladier betrayed Czechoslovakia at the Munich summit in 1938, but they were outmanoeuvred in turn by the Molotov–Ribbentrop Pact a year later. In every respect, the West and the USSR were in a race to try and turn Hitler against the other. After a half-hearted declaration of war in response to the Nazi invasion of Poland, fear of a new Paris Commune among the French ruling class and top brass led to the rout of June 1940, when Hitler unleashed the *Blitzkrieg* on France (Lacroix-Riz 2016).

At the end of the war, the political rift in the 'Anti-Hitler Coalition' again came to the surface. In 1944 Hitler could still gamble on dealing a blow to the Western allies (the December Ardennes offensive) to convince the Anglo-American coalition to join forces against Stalin; it failed, but the massive assault by the Red Army and its breakthrough on the Oder River to relieve the embattled US forces in eastern Belgium brought home the fear that the USSR would defeat the Nazis on its own. In March 1945, Germany had 26 divisions facing the Anglo-American armies as opposed to 170 divisions on the eastern front (Kolko 1968, 372). The Nazi invasion of the Soviet Union all along dwarfed the Western allies' efforts in Europe. However, fascism also had driven far beyond its temporary purpose of neutralising socialist forces and dragged entire countries down with it into the abyss, leaving the USSR in possession of a vastly enlarged, albeit internally weakened, Soviet sphere of influence. The Cold War that had started in 1944–45 would evolve as the attempt to undo this outcome by the combined forces of dynamic imperialism and permanent counterrevolution. It eventually entailed the implosion of the Soviet bloc and the USSR itself, but here, *internal* counterrevolutionary forces outweighed external threats.

Internal counterrevolution

The *internal* weakening of Soviet power, which I see as the dominant element in the set of forces that ultimately condemned it to melt away in the 1980s, is primarily ideological, in the sense of a divorce from revolutionary consciousness. Here, the distinction from anti-revolutionary, reactionary responses may be left aside, because reactionary theories developed in response to Marxism belong to the complex of forces that come under the heading of external counterrevolution (Lukács 1955). The internal counterrevolution can therefore also be labelled *tactical* counterrevolution in distinction from the strategic counterrevolution mounted by the West (Ticktin 1978). If the response to a revolution remains primarily reactionary, 'anti'-revolutionary, the revolutionary theory is least affected; once the dynamic, forward-looking aspect gains ground because the bourgeoisie, which drives forward the development of the productive forces, joins forces with the older ruling classes after 1848 and seeks 'to attain its aims through non-revolutionary means – revolutions "from above"' (Löwy 1981, 5; Gramsci's concept of passive revolution), its corrosive effects on revolutionary theory become far more important.

The essence of Marx's critique is the centrality it assigns to class struggle and the resulting *historicity* of social relations, undermining any attempt to naturalise and eternalise them. The recurrent attempts in the Marxist tradition to codify it as a determinism, as *science*, therefore open the door to ideology, supplanting the live force of the class struggle and revolutionary consciousness by fixed doctrine, Marx-*ism*. 'The shortcoming of Marx's theory is naturally the shortcoming of the revolutionary struggle of the proletariat in his epoch', writes Guy Debord:

> Hence revolutionary theory cannot yet achieve its own, comprehensive existence. The scientific justifications about the future development of the working class [arrived at within the confines of the British Museum], and the organisational practice derived from them, thus would turn

into *obstacles to proletarian consciousness at a more advanced stage.* (Debord 1992, 79, thesis 85, my translation, emphasis added)

We are looking at not only codification per se, but the codification of adjustment to *defeat*, including anticipated difficulties and setbacks preceding actual defeat. Thus, after the defeat of the 1848 revolution, Marx concluded that a dictatorship of the proletariat was necessary to destroy the bourgeois state, which had become a machinery for repression in response to revolutionary challenges ('Der 18te Brumaire des Louis Napoleon' [1852], Marx and Engels 1956–1971, viii, 197). In the Commune of 1871, the Paris workers according to Marx had rightly smashed the existing state and imposed such a dictatorship (letter to Kugelman, 12 April 1871, cited in Lenin, 'The State and Revolution' [1917], Lenin 1960–1965, xxv, 420). Lenin took up this idea in *The State and Revolution* of August 1917, although he also argued, in the same year (in *The Impending Catastrophe and How to Combat it*, of October of that year; both texts in Lenin 1960–1965, xxv), that the immediate conditions for socialism are created by state monopoly capitalism, through state control of the economy. This would turn out to be a major contradiction once the Bolsheviks had taken power.

Even more fundamental was the contrast between two approaches to the nature of working-class power. For Lenin, given the limited political horizon of the immature Russian proletariat, its ingrained economism and its trade unionism, only a vanguard party of professional revolutionaries would be able to overcome these limitations (argued in *What Is to Be Done*, 1902, Lenin 1960–1965, v). This eventually led to the split between the Bolsheviks and Mensheviks. However, when the first workers' uprising occurred in the aftermath of Russia's defeat in the war with Japan in 1905, the revolutionary Russian proletariat organised itself in the *soviets*, councils of workers' delegates. As Trotsky concluded from this experience, the soviets were a novelty in the socialist movement and as organs coordinating the struggle, an authentic democratic form (*Results and Prospects*, here cited from Trotzki 1971, 42). This left the Bolsheviks (which Trotsky would join only later) uneasily perched over and above the soviets. Wouldn't this – the vanguard doctrine, that is – be an instance of Debord's thesis that the codification of a temporary condition as 'theory' turns into an 'obstacle to proletarian consciousness in a more advanced stage'?

Certainly, a vanguard party was necessary to compensate for the imbalance in Russia between the modern proletariat and the peasantry. For, to cite Trotsky again (in *The Permanent Revolution* of 1906),

left to itself, the Russian working class *will inevitably be crushed by the counterrevolution as soon as the peasants turn their back on it*. There will be no alternative but to tie the fate of its political rule and hence the fate of the Russian revolution as such, to the fate of *socialist revolution in Europe*. (Trotzki 1971, 49, emphasis added)

By the mid 1920s, when the international revolution had been defeated, in part by the dynamic, forward-looking counterrevolution in the spirit of Woodrow Wilson, but also by ascendant fascism, this prediction came back to haunt the Bolsheviks. In March 1919, Lenin conceded that as things stood, the revolution would at best progress as a shock-like process reverberating through the existing state system.

There will have to be a series of frightful collisions between the Soviet Republic and the bourgeois states. If the ruling class, the proletariat, wants to hold power, it must, therefore, prove its ability to do so by its military organisation. ('Report of the Central Committee, 8th Congress of the R.C.P. (B)' [1919], Lenin 1960–1965, xxix, 153)

The monopolisation of political representation by the Bolsheviks, backed up by the CheKa secret policy and the Red Army, then led to 'the confiscation of power' (Carrère d'Encausse 1980). Thus, the vanguard in power mutated into a national security state, which first manifested itself when it subdued the rebellion of the Kronstadt sailors. The party itself turned into a state class – the *nomenklatura* – governing revolutionary Russia. At party elections, recommendations from above were henceforth to be followed and the party's repression of factions in 1921 made campaigning for office impossible anyway. In this way the party merged into the confiscatory state (Voslensky 1984, 48–50).

The figure of Stalin would come to personify this state class. As long as the hope for a revolution in Europe remained alive, the Bolsheviks were preoccupied with the international party (the Communist IIIrd International, *Comintern*). When counterrevolution triumphed, Stalin's offices in the domains of nationality policy, the Workers' and Peasants' Inspection, and the party secretariat, became pivotal and the vanguard model was in fact imposed on the Comintern, too, as Gramsci rcognised had occurred at the time (in 1924): 'the statutes of the International give the Russian party de facto hegemony over the world organization' (Gramsci 1978, 194). In other words, instead of the original internationalism (prioritising the fate of the world revolution), the Bolsheviks entrenched behind a sovereign statehood in the hope of gaining time and modernise the state/society complex for the next onslaught.

Stalin's rise, then, was a corollary of the *switch from the world-revolutionary perspective to a contender state posture*, and with him emerged a generation of cadres who had little interest in the niceties of Marxist theory or world revolution. Instead, they were crude and curious, inventive and quick-witted in their own way – brief, real pioneers in the process of building a new society (Deutscher 1966, 335–6). Using this cadre basis, Stalin was able to play off the other leaders against each other, getting rid first of Trotsky, the key exponent of the world revolution that did not happen. In show trials in Moscow in the late 1930s Stalin and his henchmen then decapitated the internationalist Bolshevik party entirely, whilst the national security state degenerated further to a police state (Medvedev 1976). Not unlike the Roundheads and Jacobins before them, the internationalist Bolsheviks turned out to be another vanguard reaching out for a social revolution for which the preconditions were not yet in place. The real preconditions (pockets of modern industry without forward or backward linkages, and a primitive peasant base) then imposed themselves with a vengeance, as a counterrevolution within the revolution (Gramsci 1971, 77). The switch back to a contender role placed all initiative in the state. In the words of Moshe Lewin,

> The state engaged in a hectic, hasty, and compulsive shaping of the social structure, forcing its groups and classes into a mould where the administrative-and-coercive machinery retained its superiority and autonomy. Instead of 'serving' its basis, the state, using the powerful means at its disposal (central planning, modern communications and controlling mechanisms, monopoly of information, freedom to use coercion at will), was able to press the social body into service under its own diktat. (Lewin 1985, 265)

We may add the sequence of retreats and defeats that together, as an internal counterrevolution, reduced the governing doctrine to an ideology ('Marxism–Leninism'). The concepts of the dictatorship of the proletariat, the vanguard party and the outlawing of factions, all codifications of defeat, now merged into a confiscatory state run by a nomenklatura. Its growing remoteness from popular – let alone revolutionary – consciousness required terrorist methods to drive forward social development. With the central, initiating role of the state and the foregrounding of its main task, the industrialisation of the USSR, we also see the recurrence of the economism of Social Democracy (of the type criticised by Marx in the *Critique of the Gotha Programme* [1875] Marx and Engels 1956–1971, xix, 11–32) and stagism (every single state/society has to pass through all historical stages).

At a more fundamental level, Stalinism was based on a relapse of historical materialism to the mechanical, naturalistic materialism of Plekhanov (1969), which Lenin too originally adhered to in *Materialism and Empirio-Criticism* of 1908 (Lenin 1960–1965, xiv). In 1914, however, when he turned to Hegel and other sources of Marxism to understand why the socialists strayed from their anti-war positions, he compiled his *Philosophical Notebooks*, which in key respects resurrected Marx's theoretical revolution (Löwy 1981, 59). Under Stalin, however, it was not these notes but the 1908 tract that attained the status of orthodoxy. This prompted the Dutch Marxist Anton Pannekoek to write his *Lenin as a Philosopher*. In this magisterial booklet of 1927, Pannekoek demonstrates the fatal reduction of Marx's philosophy to a mechanistic materialism in the USSR (Pannekoek 1938, 8, 65).

Counterrevolution after World War II: from fascism to parafascism

The Anglo-American West inherited the anti-Soviet posture of the Nazis, but the gains made by the Red Army and Left liberation movements severely limited the options for a roll-back. As the US-led West was forced to carefully adjust to circumstances where it had to rush in to bail out local ruling classes, counterrevolutionary intervention was inevitably fine-tuned as well. Wholesale assaults on the Left that would take down entire countries with them, as happened to Nazi Germany or Japan, were to be avoided at all costs. The victorious Soviet contender and the political forces around the globe looking up to it this time were in a position to consolidate their gains and build on them, as the Chinese revolution would prove soon after.

In 1944–45, the US and Britain worked through their intelligence agencies, which in turn often collaborated with organised crime, to isolate and repress communist-led trade unions and partisan formations. Yet the organised working class in the West was strong enough to force a class compromise on capital. The fact that decolonisation and new state formation took off in the same period (beginning with India/Pakistan in 1947 and Indonesia in 1949) also limited the projection of power by the liberal heartland. Only in extreme cases, when communists led the decolonisation drive (in Korea after the Japanese occupation ended, or in Vietnam after the defeat of France in 1954), did the West resort to the full deployment of its military might, meanwhile firmly concentrated in the United States.

The counterrevolution in the circumstances obtained a new global cohesion, in which violent repression is coordinated (not necessarily in advance, but at some point) from the centre – that is, the states of the Lockean heartland and in particular, their intelligence services. This is captured by Peter Dale Scott's concept of *parafascism* (Scott 1986). Unlike 1930s fascism, violent repression here is not inscribed in a redistributive mobilisation against imperialist rivals and ultimately against the Anglo-American heartland. Parafascism in the service of the West relies on a distinct covert sphere, which exists in 'a parasitic symbiosis with established power' (Cox 2002, 120; also see Wilson 2009). It is resorted to when strategic elites in the Anglo-American heartland, through their intelligence and media 'sensors', detect signs of class mobilisation potentially endangering positions of the Western ruling class.

After the students' and workers' revolts of 1968–69, an international faction of capital and the capitalist class, abandoning previous national positions, began to regroup along transnational lines (highlighted by the formation of the Trilateral Commission launched by David Rockefeller and his right-hand man, Zbigniew Brzezinski), away from the Cold War bloc confrontation with the USSR. The Commission prescribed, in one of its early reports, rolling back democracy to ensure that economic policy and the social order of possessive individualism remained outside political debate. With respect to the Soviet bloc and sphere of interest, the Trilateral recommendation was to 'devise a global system where the communist philosophy withers and has not new converts' (cited in Gill 1990, 202; cf. Carroll 2010).

The US-led attempt to stamp out communism in the process of decolonisation led to wars of unprecedented destructiveness such as in Korea and Vietnam (involving also Laos and Cambodia), leaving the affected countries with millions of dead and maimed. The targeted assassinations programme was part of the Vietnam War and killed more than 20,000 'suspects' amidst the general destruction but also heralded the parafascist strategy that would resurface in Central America (Valentine 2000). Related to the wars in Indo-China was Anglo-American support for the generals' coup against the Sukarno government in 1965, again entailing a bloodbath on a scale Indonesia had never seen. However, this intervention, like the military coup in Brazil a year earlier, did not rule out 'nationalist' economic policies primarily designed to bolster indigenous ruling class rather than imperialist supervision.

Things were different in Chile in 1973, Uruguay in the same year, and Argentina after 1976. Naomi Klein in her *Shock Doctrine* has compared the violent introduction of market fundamentalism to the use of shock therapy in psychiatry. Her bold thesis throws into relief what was new about these 1970s military dictatorships in Latin America: the unrestrained, violent application of a neoliberal economic model of privatisation, combined with an attack on labour, terminating the very concept of autonomous economic development and any remaining vestige of political liberalism. In both cases, the very memory that things once had been different was eradicated (Klein 2007). Here we see the full political-economic force of Western-centric parafascism at work in ways that was not yet in evidence in the partly self-defeating wars in Indochina. Permanent counterrevolution now had achieved the form in which we still know it today, even if Chile and Argentina were still disparate countermoves against an ongoing tide of progressive reform through the 1970s.

There was one aspect in which post-Pinochet parafascism, counterrevolution in the service of the Lockean heartland rather than potentially ranged against it, still required modification – the issue of reputational damage. Torturing people to death by the thousands cannot be counted on to enthuse a mass public in the West; Operation Condor, the programme of terror squads swarming over all of Latin America to assassinate opponents of the new fascist regimes, caused an uproar when its operatives struck in downtown Washington DC with the connivance of the Central Intelligence Agency (CIA) (Hitchens 2002, 56, 70–5). Hence, when the Italian Communist party, after the Pinochet coup in Chile, decided that a situation of frontal confrontation with the bourgeoisie had to be avoided, and switched to a strategy of 'Historic Compromise' with Christian Democracy (Berlinguer 1976), the parafascist infrastructure in Western Europe and its American masters opted for a new counterrevolutionary strategy.

This strategy aimed to reduce democracy by bracketing the economy (the Trilateral recommendation) *without* a violent seizure of power. Instead, it sought to exploit militant resistance on the extremes of the political spectrum, Left or Right. In the face of terrorist violence from the margins – whether spontaneous or manipulated/provoked by elements of the security infrastructure, 'the deep state' – the political centre would be made to appear rational and moderate by comparison. In 1964 and again in 1970, the mere threat of a Pinochet-style seizure of power by the Italian armed forces worked to sway the (Christian-Democratic) centre from a coalition with the Socialists; and in Greece in 1967, the colonels' regime demonstrated that this was possible in a European NATO country (the same for Turkey at different moments). However, the Historic Compromise threatened to allow the Eurocommunist Italian party to become part of the state and neutralise its repressive apparatus sooner or later. The Strategy of Tension was the answer. It eventually entailed the abduction and assassination of Aldo Moro, a Christian-Democratic politician willing to agree on a national solution to the crisis, in 1978 (Ganser 2005; Tunander 2009). As I have documented elsewhere, this dramatic event, ascribed to the Red Brigades but probably not pulled off by them on their own, allowed the surviving Christian Democrats, many of them complicit in the tragedy, to reinforce state authority in order to move beyond social compromise altogether and effect a sharp neoliberal turn. In several other countries the identification of militant class politics with armed struggle, terrorism and chaos had comparable results (van der Pijl 2006, 143–67).

All along, 'although tactically counterrevolutionary', the USSR under conditions of the competition between the systems was 'compelled to collaborate with social groups and political classes which wish to free themselves from the dominance of American capitalism and imperialism' (Ticktin 1978, 39). However, after the election of Thatcher and Reagan, the counterrevolution switched from passive revolution at home and containment and parafascism abroad to a comprehensive aggressive posture, along with a domestic hard line against labour. The final contest with the Soviet bloc was now launched in earnest, with key Reagan administration officials threatening Moscow with nuclear attack, from Alexander Haig's idea of a nuclear warning shot to Richard Pipes's statement that the 'Soviet leaders would have to choose between peacefully changing their Communist system in the direction followed by the West or going to war' (Garthoff 1994, 11, 12). Certainly, strategic arms control agreements were concluded to limit the arms race, but Reagan in 1982 and 1983 signed three secret National Security Decision Directives: NSDD 32 on neutralising Soviet control over Eastern Europe; NSDD 66 authorising the use of economic sabotage against the USSR itself; and NSDD 75 which made regime change of the USSR official US policy (cited in Schweizer 1994, xiv).

On the basis of a reversal of the US role from a surplus to a deficit country, the world's capitalist ruling classes via several steps signed on to this offensive by financing the US deficit, exporting to and investing in the US, directly and via the City of London. Several transnational counterrevolutionary alliances that are still in operation today, such as that with the Saudi and other Gulf monarchies and their transnational jihadist networks, with the ascendant Far Right in Israel, and with the new Chinese leadership of Deng Xiaoping, came about at this juncture. All were banking on the US capacity to continue to tax the world via the dollar and to defeat all contender formations and open them up for commodification and exploitation (Di Muzio 2007, 531).

From here to the contemporary 'War on Terror' runs an almost straight line (cf. Netanyahu 1986). The Israeli Likud Party, coming to power in the aftermath of the wars that landed the country with occupied Arab territories it could not expect to keep under control on its own, inserted its experience with provoking and suppressing violent resistance (Nederveen Pieterse 1985; Halper 2015).

Russia's fate in the current systemic crisis

Wolfgang Streeck (2013) has analysed the current crisis in terms of an exhaustion of the successive attempts to 'buy time' and thereby postpone the full impact of the crisis of corporate liberalism that began in the late 1960s. For decades the ruling and governing classes in the West succeeded in salvaging a measure of class compromise at home by throwing money into the breaches – using inflation, state debt and private debt. The collapse of 2007–2008 ended that run and left the global political economy in a condition of enduring crisis.

The doubling of the global labour supply to more than 3 billion people in the two decades leading up to the crisis strengthened the hand of transnational capital in organising production across the globe in so-called product or commodity chains (Merk 2011). These chains link labour-intensive, low-paid production notably in Asia to Western markets, but also reduce total demand in the world economy. The ensuing over-accumulation of capital seeking profitable investment as a result encouraged investment in financial assets, assisted by lower taxation (Rasmus 2016, 97–200). If in the 1980s and 1990s, asset-owning middle classes still were part of a class compromise with finance, their savings too have landed in the firing line, narrowing class compromise even further, basically leaving only pockets of organised labour (notably, public sector workers) and an increasingly insecure middle class facing a process of oligarchic enrichment through speculative forays by money-dealing capital.

Like nineteenth-century gunboat diplomacy, Western strategy in the circumstances has become focused on protecting supply routes and the modern equivalents of debt collection such as enforcing conditional International Monetary Fund (IMF) loans. Economic warfare and actual wars for regime change have become commonplace. Indeed, 'the defence of "globalisation" against those who would threaten it should … be placed, along with military threats properly speaking, at the top of the security agenda' (Serfati 2001, 12). Yet the military apparatus to provide for this defence, which is overwhelmingly concentrated in the United States, cannot be legitimated by protecting supply lines and backing up IMF and private credit lines, although the US military is fully literate in this aspect (Klare 2001). That is why Samuel Huntington's thesis of a 'Clash of Civilisations', 2 years after the Soviet collapse, found such fertile ground. It placed Russia and its 'Near Abroad', along with China and 'Islam', outside the boundaries of Western civilisation; the people inhabiting these exoplanets were now cast as existential enemies in the sense of Carl Schmitt (1963).

If we confine ourselves to Russia, it had meanwhile passed under the control of a predatory neoliberal clique around Boris Yeltsin, which executed the radical shock therapy Gorbachev, pressed by the G7 in July 1991, had hesitated to apply (Klein 2007, 219). After the failed coup by Soviet conservatives in August, Yeltsin mounted what David Lane calls an 'effective counter-coup' (Lane 1996, 131). In December, following consultations with the leaders of Belarus and Ukraine, Yeltsin dissolved the Soviet Union and forced Gorbachev to resign. Then, a veritable 'war of manoeuvre' started to remove all social protection. As Richard Sakwa writes, 'the Western-dominated international system itself, particularly in the form of international financial organizations, took on the role of the Comintern of old, exhorting a weak indigenous government to ever more radical acts of liberal domestic economic transformation' (Sakwa 1998, 189).

Across the former USSR, and in Russia on the grandest scale, fortunes were made by selling Soviet stocks of oil and minerals abroad and by the privatisation of state assets in what Misha Glenny calls the 'grandest larceny in history', followed by 'the single biggest flight of capital the world has ever seen' (Glenny 2009, 71, 73; details in Kotz 1997). Whilst the mass of the population faced skyrocketing, liberalised prices for everyday items, the prices of existing stocks of commodities remained frozen at Soviet levels, with world market prices often up to 40 times higher. This spawned huge business empires within a short period. However, 'for the great majority of Russian families, their country has not been in "transition" but in an endless collapse of everything essential to a decent existence' (Cohen 1998, 245). The social drama of predatory enrichment and austerity, played out in slow motion in the West, here was staged all in one go.

After Vladimir Putin took over the presidency in 2000, he re-established a measure of political control over the oligarchs who had plundered post-Soviet Russia's economy, without basically challenging the crony capitalist economic model that had meanwhile taken hold. Political control was aimed at restoring the directive state in the contender tradition. In his *Millennium Manifesto* of 1999, prior to his assumption of the presidency, Putin rightly claimed that 'our state and its institutions and structures have always played an exceptionally important role in the life of the country and its people', adding on another occasion that a strong state should be complemented by *a pliant society*, or as he put it, work was needed for civil society to 'become a full partner of the state' (cited in Lyne 2015, 3, 5). Yet by allowing the oligarchs in control of the most profitable sectors (fuel/energy, metallurgy, food and transport) to continue prioritising exports whilst setting monopoly prices in the domestic market (Dzarasov 2014, 194–5), the Russian government failed to correct the predatory nature of the post-Soviet capitalist economy. Certainly, the commodities boom enabled it to rectify the ravages wrought by the Yeltsin regime and restore public services along with recovering incomes. Also, it was now able to rebuild its armed forces to resist the continued probing of its borders by NATO and act as a stabiliser in areas where the United States was withdrawing, such as the Middle East. But the collapse of oil prices in 2014 forced Moscow to increasingly rely on its reserves to continue to finance its achievements in these domains.

At 100, the Russian Revolution seems an event locked in the distant past with few achievements that have endured. There is no space here to discuss the enduring validity of the theory of internationalism and national autonomy. On the other hand, the study of the Soviet experience has acquired a new topicality as a consequence of the information revolution. Thus, in 1962, still under Khrushchev's leadership, one of many attempts to overcome the stagnation of the USSR's command economy included proposals by key thinkers from the Institute of Cybernetics and the Central Economic Mathematical Institute to construct an 'automated system for economic planning and management on the basis of a nationwide computer network', proposals that were formally submitted in June 1964. However, as Michael Lebowitz relates, in October of that year, Khrushchev was ousted by the Brezhnev/

Kosygin leadership, who instead embarked on a strategy introducing greater enterprise autonomy (Lebowitz 2012, 118–9; cf. Peters 2012). Although the computer planning project was not entirely shelved, its revolutionary potential was not realised. Something comparable happened in Chile, with plans to use surplus telex machines for a cybernetic planning system, Cybersyn, under the socialist Allende government. It too fell victim, to the Pinochet coup (Morozov 2014; Klein 2007, 50).

Now that the information revolution is laying the foundations for a society of an entirely new type, these past experiments must again be studied in depth, as should other aspects of a centrally planned economy. Indeed as Shoshana Zuboff reminds us, Hayek's claim that an economy cannot be planned because of the unknowability of so many of its inner workings is completely superseded by the integral knowledge that Google, Palantir, Axciom and other data giants are obtaining – and continually updating – knowledge eagerly supplied by customers hooked on the Web (Zuboff 2015, 78). In other words, the ideological basis of neoliberal capitalism is being obliterated by the new possibilities of centralising Big Data – except that the first response of a society to such a potential for radical change is to mobilise its defences against it: witness the Khrushchev removal, the Pinochet coup, and today's use of Big Data for spying on the population and perpetual war (Ahmed 2015).

Even so, at the 100th anniversary of the Russian Revolution, a planned economy, eco-socialist in orientation and guided by proper democratic debate and decision-making, need no longer be a chimera. In that light the Soviet experience, both positive and negative, retains its value.

Acknowledgements

Thanks to Radhika Desai and Henry Heller for comments on an earlier draft and to the participants at the Revolutions conference of the Geopolitical Economy Research Centre at the University of Manitoba, October 2017.

Disclosure statement

No potential conflict of interest was reported by the author.

References

Ahmed, Nafeez Mossadeq. "How the CIA Made Google. Inside the Secret Network behind Mass Surveillance, Endless War, and Skynet." Insurge Intelligence, January 22, 2015. Accessed November 29 2017. https://medium.com/insurge-intelligence/how-the-cia-made-google-e836451a959e

Bauer, Otto. 1907. *Die Nationalitätenfrage und die Sozialdemokratie*. Wien: Verlag der Wiener Volksbuchhandlung Ignaz Brand.

Berlinguer, Enrico. 1976. "Gedanken zu Italien nach den Ereignissen in Chile." In *Der historische Kompromiss*, edited by Translated from Rinascita, 28 September 1973 and edited by P. Valenza, 13–67. Hamburg: VSA.

Bosco, Andrea. 2017. *The Round Table Movement and the Fall of the 'Second' British Empire (1909-1919)*. Newcastle: Cambridge Scholars Publishing.

Burke, Edmund. 1887. *The Works of the Right Honourable Edmund Burke*, vols 12. London: John Nimmo.

Carrère d'Encausse, Hélène. 1980. *Le Pouvoir Confisqué. Gouvernants et Gouvernés an U.R.S.S.* Paris: Flammarion.

Carroll, William K. 2010. *The Making of a Transnational Capitalist Class. Corporate Power in the Twenty-First Century*. [with C. Carson, M. Fennema, E. Heemskerk, and J. P. Sapinski]. London: Zed Press.

Cohen, Stephen F. 1998. "Russia: Tragedy or Transition." In *Rethinking the Soviet Collapse. Sovietology, the Death of Communism and the New Russia*, edited by M. E. Cox, 241–250. London: Pinter.

Cox, Robert W. 2002. *The Political Economy of a Plural World. Critical Reflections on Power, Morals and Civilization [with M. G. Schechter]*. London: Routledge.

De Pradt, M. [Dominique G. F. Dufour]. 1824. *L'Europe et l'Amérique en 1822 et 1823*. Paris: Béchet ainé.

Debord, Guy. 1992. [1967]. *La société du spectacle*. Paris: Gallimard.

Deutscher, Isaac. 1966. [1949]. *Stalin. A Political Biography*, rev. ed. Harmondsworth: Penguin.

Di Muzio, Tim. 2007. "The "Art" of Colonisation: Capitalising Sovereign Power and the Ongoing Nature of Primitive Accumulation." *New Political Economy* 12 (4): 517–539. doi:10.1080/13563460701661553.

Dzarasov, Ruslan. 2014. *The Conundrum of Russian Capitalism. The Post-Soviet Economy in the World System*. London: Pluto Books.

Fischer, Fritz. 1984. [1961]. *Griff nach der Weltmacht. Die Kriegszielpolitik des kaiserlichen Deutschland 1914/18*, abridged edition. Düsseldorf: Droste.

Ganser, Daniele. 2005. *NATO's Secret Armies. Operation Gladio and Terrorism in Western Europe*. London: Frank Cass.

Garthoff, Raymond. 1994. *The Great Transition. American-Soviet Relations and the End of the Cold War*. Washington DC: The Brookings Institution.

Gill, Stephen. 1990. *American Hegemony and the Trilateral Commission*. Cambridge: Cambridge University Press.

Glenny, Misha. 2009. *McMafia. Seriously Organised Crime*. London: Vintage.

Gramsci, Antonio. 1971. *Selections from the Prison Notebooks*. Translated and edited by Q. Hoare and G. N. Smith. New York: International Publishers [written 1929-'35].

Gramsci, Antonio. 1978. *Selections from Political Writings 1921-1926*. Translated and edited by Q. Hoare. New York: International Publishers.

Halper, Jeff. 2015. *War against the People. Israel, the Palestinians and Global Pacification*. London: Pluto.

Hartz, Louis, 1964. *The Founding of New Societies. Studies in the History of the United States, Latin America, South Africa, Canada, and Australia* [with K. D. McRae, R. M. Morse, R. N. Rosecrance, and L. M. Thompson]. New York: Harcourt, Brace & World.

Hitchens, Christopher. 2002 [2001]. *The Trial of Henry Kissinger*, rev. ed., London: Verso.

Klare, Michael T. 2001. *Resource Wars. The New Landscape of Global Conflict*. New York: Henry Holt Metropolitan Books.

Klein, Naomi. 2007. *The Shock Doctrine. The Rise of Disaster Capitalism*. Harmondsworth: Penguin.

Kolko, Gabriel. 1968. *The Politics of War. The World and United States Foreign Policy 1943-1945*. New York: Vintage.

Kotz, DavidM. [with F. Weir]. 1997. *Revolution from above. The Demise of the Soviet System*. London: Routledge.

Kühnl, Reinhard, ed. 1980. [1975]. *Der deutsche Faschismus in Quellen und Dokumenten*, rev. ed. Cologne: Pahl-Rugenstein.

Lacroix-Riz, Annie. 2016. *Les élites françaises entre 1940 et 1944. De la collaboration avec l'Allemagne à l'alliance Américaine*. Paris: Armand Colin.

Lane, David. 1996. *The Rise and Fall of State Socialism. Industrial Society and the Socialist State*. Cambridge: Polity Press.

Lebowitz, Michael A. 2012. *The Contradictions of Real Socialism. The Conductor and the Conducted*. New York: Monthly Review Press.

Lenin, V. I. 1960–1965. *Collected Works*. Moscow: Progress.

Lewin, Moshe. 1985. *The Making of the Soviet System. Essays in the Social History of Interwar Russia*. London: Methuen.

Locke, John. 1965. [1690]. *Two Treatises of Government [Intro. P. Laslett]*. New York: Mentor.

Losurdo, Domenico. 2013. [2006]. *Contre-Histoire du Libéralisme*. Translated by B. Chamayou. Paris: La Découverte.

Löwy, Michael. 1981. *The Politics of Combined and Uneven Development. The Theory of Permanent Revolution*. London: Verso.

Lukács, Georg. 1955. [1953]. *Die Zerstörung der Vernunft. Der Weg des Irrationalismus von Schelling bis Hitler*. Berlin: Aufbau-Verlag.

Lyne, Roderic. 2015. "Russia's Changed Outlook on the West: From Convergence to Confrontation." In *The Russian Challenge. [Chatham House Report, June]*, edited by K. Giles, P. Hanson, R. Lyne, J. Nixey, J. Sherr, and A. Wood, 2–13. London: The Institute of International Affairs.

Macpherson, C. B. 1962. *The Political Theory of Possessive Individualism. Hobbes to Locke*. Oxford: Oxford University Press.

Marx, Karl, and Friedrich Engels. 1956–1971. *MEW Marx-Engels Werke*, vols. 35. Berlin: Dietz.

Mayer, Arno J. 1971. *Dynamics of Counterrevolution in Europe, 1870-1956*. New York: Harper & Row.

Medvedev, Roy A. 1976. [1971]. *Let History Judge. The Origins and Consequences of Stalinism*. Translated by C. Taylor and edited by D. Joravsky. London: Spokesman.

Merk, Jeroen. 2011. "Production beyond the Horizon of Consumption: Spatial Fixes and anti-Sweatshop Struggles in the Global Athletic Footwear Industry." *Global Society* 25 (1): 73–95. doi:10.1080/13600826.2010.522984.

Moore, Barrington. Jr. 1981. [1966]. *Social Origins of Dictatorship and Democracy*. Harmondsworth: Penguin.

Morozov, Evgeny. 2014. "The Planning Machine. Project Cybersyn and the origins of the Big Data Nation." *The New Yorker*, 13 October. Accessed January 17, 2018. https://www.newyorker.com/magazine/2014/10/13/planning-machine

Nederveen Pieterse, Jan. 1985. "Israel's Role in the Third World: Exporting West Bank Expertise." *Race & Class* 26 (3): 9–30. doi:10.1177/030639688502600302.

Netanyahu, Benjamin, ed. 1986. *Terrorism. How the West Can Win*. London: Weidenfeld & Nicolson.

Pannekoek, Anton. 1938. [this edition not dated]. *Lenin als filosoof*. Amsterdam: De Vlam.

Peters, Benjamin. 2012. "Normalizing Soviet Cybernetics." *Information & Culture: A Journal of History* 47 (2): 145–175. doi:10.1353/lac.2012.0009.

Plekhanov, G. V. 1969. [1908]. *Fundamental Problems of Marxism*. Translated by J. Katzer and edited by J. S. Allen. New York: International Publishers.

Poulantzas, Nikos. 1974. [1970]. *Fascisme et Dictature*. 2nd ed. Paris: Le Seuil/Maspero.

Rasmus, Jack. 2016. *Systemic Fragility in the Global Economy*. Atlanta, GA: Clarity Press.

Rosenstock-Huessy, Eugen. 1993. [1938]. *Out of Revolution. Autobiography of Western Man [Intro. H.J. Berman]*. Providence, RI: Berg.

Sakwa, Richard. 1998. "Russian Political Evolution: A Structural Approach." In *Rethinking the Soviet Collapse. Sovietology, the Death of Communism and the New Russia*, edited by M. E. Cox, 181–201. London: Pinter.

Schmitt, Carl. 1963. [1932, 1927]. *Der Begriff des Politischen*. 2nd ed. Berlin: Duncker & Humblot.

Schweizer, Peter. 1994. *Victory. The Reagan Administration's Secret Strategy That Hastened the Collapse of the Soviet Union*. New York: Atlantic Monthly Press.

Scott, Peter Dale. 1986. "Transnationalised Repression: Parafascism and the U.S." *Lobster* 12: 1–30.

Serfati, Claude. 2001. *La mondialisation armée. Le déséquilibre de la terreur*. Paris: Textuel.

Streeck, Wolfgang. 2013. *Gekaufte Zeit. Die vertagte Krise des demokratischen Kapitalismus [Frankfurter Adorno-Vorlesungen 2012]*. Frankfurt: Suhrkamp.

Thompson, E. P. 1968. [1963]. *The Making of the English Working Class*. Harmondsworth: Penguin.

Ticktin, Hillel. 1978. "The Relation between Détente and Soviet Economic Reforms." In *Soviet Foreign Policy: Its Social and Economic Conditions*, edited by E. Jahn, 41–56. London: Allison & Busby.

Tocqueville, Alexis de. 1988. [1856]. *L'ancien régime et la révolution,* edited by F. Mélonio. Paris: Flammarion.

Trotzki, Leo. 1971. [1906–1940]. *De permanente of de verraden revolutie*, edited by E. Mandel and translated by H. Hom. Amsterdam: Van Gennep.

Tunander, Ola. 2009. "Democratic State vs. Deep State. Approaching the Dual State of the West." In *Government of the Shadows. Parapolitics and Criminal Sovereignty*, edited by Eric Wilson, 56–72. London: Pluto Press.

Valentine, Douglas. 2000. [1990]. *The Phoenix Program*. New York: William Morrow & Co [Authors Guild Backinprint.com Ed.].

Van der Pijl, Kees. 2006. *Global Rivalries from the Cold War to Iraq*. London: Pluto, and New Delhi: Sage Vistaar.

Voslensky, Michael. 1984. [1980]. *Nomenklatura. Anatomy of the Soviet Ruling Class*. Translated by E. Mosbacher. London: Bodley Head.

Wilson, Eric. 2009. "Deconstructing the Shadows." In *Government of the Shadows. Parapolitics and Criminal Sovereignty*, edited by E. Wilson. London: Pluto Press.

Zuboff, Shoshana. 2015. "Big Other: surveillance Capitalism and the Prospects of an Information Civilization." *Journal of Information Technology* 30 (1): 75–89. doi:10.1057/jit.2015.5.

Colours of a revolution. Post-communist society, global capitalism and the Ukraine crisis

Ruslan Dzarasov and Victoria Gritsenko

ABSTRACT

The Ukraine crisis is usually treated either as Russia's return to the old-style empire-building (the right) or as a clash of two imperialisms (the left). However, the essence of this crisis can be understood only from the dual perspective of the consequences of the Stalinist degeneration of the Russian Revolution and the fate of the modern global capitalism. The most rotten sections of the Soviet bureaucracy moved the society to capitalism. However, this effort could secure only a peripheral (Ukraine) or at best semi-peripheral (Russia) position in the capitalist world-system as a provider of cheap raw materials. Meanwhile, modern capitalism led to world economic crisis. In these conditions, the capital of the core capitalist countries obviously decided to strengthen its control over the periphery, and Russia's aspirations to secure its domination over the former Soviet space were in the way. To thwart them, Western powers decided to provoke a Ukraine crisis, exploiting Ukrainians' justified indignation at the backwardness and corruption inherent in their own peripheral capitalism. Hence, a study of the properties of the post-Soviet societies and their place in the world hierarchy is the key to understanding the Ukraine crisis.

1. Introduction

The Ukraine crisis, which started in late 2013, became the most acute East–West political and military conflict since the end of the Cold War. The right sees it as Russia's return to old-style empire-building in the former Soviet space. The left treats it as a clash of two imperialisms – Russian and Western – for geopolitical domination over Eastern Europe. From the standpoint of the authors, neither account is reasonable, theoretically or empirically.

The existing literature on the Ukraine crisis largely ignores the properties of the new social order established in the post-Soviet societies even though it conditions the relative position of social classes, their development, the nature of the political systems and the foreign alliances of both Ukraine and Russia. The essence of this crisis can be understood only from the dual perspective of degeneration and collapse of the Soviet system and the crisis and decline of the modern global capitalism. The main point of departure to understand both factors is the fate of the Russian Revolution of 1917.

2. The Russian Revolution and its historical legacy

Marx's assertion, that 'The country that is more developed industrially only shows, to the less developed, the image of its own future' is well known.[1] It reflects a linear understanding of historical development according to which societies consistently go through a number of social-economic stages. However, there is evidence that the 'late Marx' supposed that advanced and backward capitalist societies coexist and influence each other's development. Lenin, with his 'law of uneven development' and his teaching about 'the weak link in the chain of imperialism', was more explicit on this point.[2] Trotsky suggested the 'law of uneven and combined development' (UCD),[3] which emphasises two closely interwoven ideas: the unevenness of capitalist development and the coexistence of developed and 'backward' capitalist societies (which creates the 'privilege of backwardness'). From this follows the phenomenon of combined development, which means skipping of stages, as in the fast development of countries like Germany. In Chapter 1 of his masterpiece *The History of the Russian Revolution*,[4] Trotsky depicts Russian capitalism not only as backward, but as dependent on European capitalism and Tsarism. Combined with the remaining shackles of feudalism, this made the Russian capitalist class very reactionary.

As is well known, the so-called Populists (*Narodniks*) believed that the successful development of capitalism in Russia was impossible because its domestic market was weak and the world market was already dominated by advanced capitalist countries. To this, Russian Marxists responded with at least three different answers. The right-wing *Mensheviks* led by Plekhanov took the orthodox position that the Russian big bourgeoisie would lead Russia's transition to capitalism, and the left-wing *Menshevik* internationalists believed that the small and medium bourgeoisie would.[5] Mature Bolshevism, which developed after the 1905 revolution, was a peculiar Marxian Populism. It held that capitalism was impossible in Russia because the Russian bourgeoisie was too reactionary to lead a bourgeois-democratic revolution. Instead, Lenin proposed theories of 'overgrowth of bourgeois-democratic revolution into the socialist one' and Trotsky proposed the theory of the 'permanent revolution'.

In many ways, these debates anticipated the world-systems approach of Braudel, Wallerstein, Frank, Arrighi, Amin and others. All these thinkers saw capitalism as a non-homogeneous world system based on exploitation of its periphery (so-called 'developing nations') by the core (developed countries).[6]

Indeed, industrialisation in Tsarist Russia rested on a semi-feudal exploitation of the peasantry, which benefitted Russian landowners and Russian and European capitalists. The modernisation of Russian society was conditioned by growing competition with Western powers. After the debacle of the Crimean War (1853–1855), former serfs were granted personal freedoms, but not land. This gave rise to semi-feudal semi-bourgeois relations in Russian villages, releasing cheap labour for cities and capitalist industrialisation. However, it was crippled from the very beginning due to a high degree of dependency on European capital.

To attract European technology and investment, the Russian government paid in hard foreign currency or gold rubles which it accumulated from the export of wheat at low prices. Foreign capital accounted for 30–70% of investment in the major Russian industries and extracted profits in gold rubles. In addition, the government also borrowed abroad at extortionate interest rates. Construction of railroads, coal mining, metallurgy, timber production and certain engineering enterprises were developed on the backs of the peasantry and workers whose prices and wages remained low.[7] As a result of this pattern of accumulation in the economy as a whole, accumulation by peasant households was next to nil. Industrial development relied on the systematic degeneration of the Russian peasantry. Mass impoverishment, loss of access to land and periodic hunger became the lot of millions of deprived peasants.

Table 1 presents data comparing the per capita national income of Russia and of selected Western countries for the period of Tsarist industrialisation of 1861–1913.

All figures are in Russian rubles in real terms and the initial Russian level is taken to be 100%. The data demonstrate that between 1861 and 1913, as a result of Tsarist industrialisation, the gap between Russia and the major Western powers increased enormously. In all the other countries, per capita income calculated in 1961 constant prices was greater than in Russia: in Britain by 4.5 times, in the USA by 6.3 times, in Germany by 2.5 times and in France by 2.1 times. In 1913, the corresponding figures were 4.9, 8.7, 3.1 and 2.5. Despite the fact that Russia possessed the greatest population, territory and mineral resources in the group of industrial nations of the time, the gap between Russia and the major Western powers grew enormously. Its share in aggregate world industrial output was only 4.2% at the beginning of the twentieth century.[8] As Peter Gatrell, one of the main writers on the economy and war preparedness of Tsarist Russia, put it, 'Signs of economic progress, including greater integration in the expanding international economy, could not mask the extent of Russia's backwardness relative to its main rivals'.[9]

Such industrial backwardness underlay Tsarist Russia's military inferiority. For instance, in terms of heavy artillery, Russia was behind not only Germany, Britain, France and Italy, but even Romania. The latter had 1.3 cannons per every thousand infantrymen, while Russia had only one. Production of easel machine guns was lower than that of Germany by 13 times, Britain by almost 14 times and France by 5 times. In 1916–1917, Russian industry supplied only about 35% of the demanded quantity of rifles.[10] It is no wonder that Russia suffered military defeat in WWI.[11]

The Russian ruling class also underwent a painful transformation. Big St. Petersburg financial-industrial capital was too reliant on Tsarism and its contracts to lead modernisation as expected by the right Mensheviks. There was some nationally oriented capital, essentially Moscow merchants and industrialists and regional elements (the so-called *Zemtsy*), and

Table 1. Per capita national income (NI) in Russia and some Western countries in 1861–1913.

	1861 г.				1913 г.			
	NI (million rubles, 1913 prices)	Population (million)	Per capita NI (in rubles)	Russia = 100%	NI (million rubles, 1913 prices)	Population (million)	Per capita NI (in rubles)	Russia = 100%
Russia	5269	74	71	100	20,266	171	119	100
Great Britain	6469	20	323	455	20,869	36	580	487
USA	14,405	32	450	634	96,030	93	1033	868
Germany	6313	36	175	246	24,280	65	374	314
France	5554	37	150	211	11,816	39	303	254
Italy	4750	25	183	258	9140	35	261	219
Spain	-	16	-	-	3975	20	199	167

Source: P. Gregory, *Russian National Income, 1885–1913*, Cambridge: Cambridge University Press, 1982, pp. 155–157.

though it did not benefit from government contracts to the same extent, it too was dependent on Tsarism: it could develop only under the umbrella of state protectionist policy. So there was no element of Russian capital that could play any independent role in history.[12] That is why it there are no grounds in history to claim that the revolution prevented Russia from moving to a European type of capitalism or democracy. Nor was it possible, as some have argued, that the Constituent Assembly could have led to 'non-bourgeois' democracy in Russia. However, the Constituent Assembly included bourgeois parties and 'revolutionary democracy'. Their interests were opposed and this remained the arena of their struggle, while the most urgent questions of land and peace were solved by the Second Congress of the Soviets, which effectively made the Constituent Assembly redundant.

As Antonio Gramsci noted in elaborating his concept of 'bourgeois hegemony', there was a difference between dictatorship and democracy under capitalism. The latter creates better conditions for the working-class movement. However, democracy under capitalism has distinct class limits. Bourgeois hegemony is based on socio-economic compromise with subjugated classes. Their interests are partially taken into account. Therefore, while bourgeois-democratic hegemony assumes certain redistribution of the national income in favour of deprived classes, as was done after WWII by the Keynesian 'welfare state', it also involves the so-called 'organic intellectuals' of the ruling class to represent interests of bourgeoisie as 'national' interests. Moreover, even such limited class compromises rely on surplus value from the peripheries of capitalism being redistributed in favour of the developed capitalist countries of the core. In the periphery, by contrast, the dual exploitation of its workers and peasantry means that preconditions for social compromise and bourgeois democracy are much weaker. That is why capital is compelled to rule by undemocratic, authoritative or even dictatorial methods. Russia was one of the first countries to have found the ways to more radical social change in such conditions.

The Bolsheviks clearly understood that the pre-revolutionary Russian bourgeoisie was too exploitative, reactionary and dependent on Western capital and Tsarism to lead a genuine bourgeois-democratic uprising, and based their revolutionary strategy on this understanding. Their insight had a significance far beyond Russia's borders. Lenin's theory of 'overgrowth of a bourgeois-democratic revolution into the socialist revolution' and Trotsky's theory of a 'permanent revolution' refer to the general pattern of social change in conditions of periphery capitalism. Societies where part of the surplus value produced by its toilers is transferred to the West have no preconditions for the sort of social compromise that underlies bourgeois democracy in the West. As a result, the comprador bourgeoisie is unable to lead, hegemonically, any bourgeois-democratic revolution. It has to be led by the working class in an alliance with dispossessed peasantry. Since bourgeoisie cannot rule democratically, victorious workers and peasants will be compelled to move to socialist changes.

This understanding underlay the historical triumph of the Russian Revolution. Russia had broken the bonds of the capitalist world-system. However, due to the isolation of the Russian Revolution in a relatively backward capitalist country, it degenerated into Stalin's oppressive bureaucracy. The internal party strife of the 1920s was the struggle of two opposed systems of values that were already in contention in the 1921–1923 confrontation of Lenin and Stalin.[13]

The essence of the revolution was the interference of the Russian masses in the course of history, while the essence of Stalin's Thermidor was quite the opposite – the subjugation of the masses to the new totalitarian state. The best explanation of Stalinism was provided by

Trotsky in his masterpiece *The Revolution Betrayed*. Despite the officially proclaimed 'socialism in one country', the relative backwardness of Russian society and the absence of victorious socialist revolution in Europe meant that Soviet Russia was simply unable to move to socialism. It could only attempt to do so. This means that it had intertwined elements of socialism and capitalism (not to mention those of traditional society). Trotsky anticipated the impending world war and hoped that it would lead to a new wave of revolutionary struggle in the West. If it succeeded, the Russian masses could overthrow Stalin's bureaucracy to move to a full-fledged socialist society. Otherwise, the Soviet society would slip back to capitalism for reasons that have proved prophetic: While the Soviet bureaucracy has its privileges,

> Privileges have only half their worth, if they cannot be transmitted to one's children. But the right of testament is inseparable from the right of property. It is not enough to be the director of a trust; it is necessary to be a stockholder. The victory of the bureaucracy in this decisive sphere would mean its conversion into a new possessing class. … In reality a backslide to capitalism is wholly possible.[14]

Modern analyses of the end of the USSR confirm this. David Lane, for instance, identifies two major social groups facilitating the demise of the Soviet system:[15] the 'administrative class' (this term is used here in the sense of 'political class'), eager to convert their administrative control over economy into private property rights; and the 'appropriating class' of those possessing professional qualifications and skills, interested in profiting from these assets on a market basis. We would add to these two groups the underground entrepreneurs who had gradually developed in the pores of the Soviet system.[16] As soon as the menace of ideological coercion weakened under Gorbachev's Perestroika, these forces facilitated the shift to capitalism.

It is no wonder, then, that all post-Soviet societies moved to dependent development, with certain important differences: Ukraine demonstrates classical features of a periphery, while Russia is closer to a semi-peripheral status. Ukrainian ruling elite inherited the historical experience of the provincial and, hence, subservient Soviet bureaucracy, which facilitated its subservient position to the West. The Russian nascent capitalist elite inherited the historical experience of the central Soviet bureaucracy, which determined central planning and waged the Cold War. This different 'social capital' conditioned the different social systems. Thus, both the positive legacy of the Russian Revolution and its degeneration determined the nature of post-Soviet societies.

The fate of the other parts of the post-Soviet space is very close to that of Russia and Ukraine. Figure 1 shows that all the former Soviet republics lag behind the USSR in terms of both Human Development Index (HDI) rankings and rankings of per capita gross national income (GNI), except Estonia, which is ahead of Russia in HDI rank and behind in GNI rank.

However, Russia is the only semi-peripheral country in the region. Unlike pure peripheries, semi-peripheral countries are semi-dependent on the core but also able to challenge its domination in some areas. Putin is trying to preserve the semi-peripheral status of Russia, but without any real prospects for achieving the core status. In short, under Putin, Russia is a static semi-peripheral state. As we will see below, in the conditions of the current crisis of global capitalism, Putin's partial and modest resistance to the pressure of the core became untenable for the West. This explains why some countries – like Ukraine and, to a lesser extent, Georgia – became the flashpoints in the confrontation between the West and Russia.

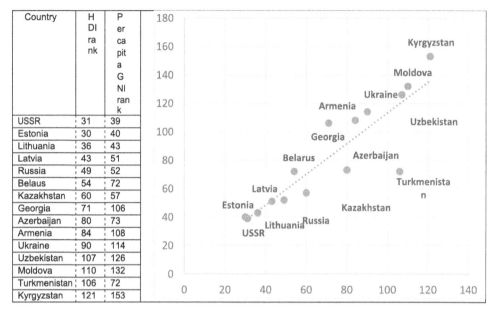

Figure 1. Relationship between international rankings according to the Human Development Index (HDI) and gross national income of the USSR (1987) and the former Soviet republics (2017). Rankings are placed in descending order (first place is the best).
Sources: *Human Development Report 1990*, New York and Oxford, Oxford University Press, 1990, p. 119; UNDP. Human Development Reports. Table 1. Human Development Index and Its Components. Accessed August 11, 2019. http://hdr.undp.org/en/composite/HDI.

In any case, important domestic preconditions with external circumstances – ie North Atlantic Treaty Organization (NATO) and EU enlargement to the East – shaped the Ukraine crisis.

3. Global capitalism and its crisis

Modern global capitalism has developed according to UCD and under the influence of both the USSR up to the early 1990s and thereafter its collapse.

Robert Brenner has argued that the postwar boom in the US was due to the destruction of European and Japanese industry.[17] Stagflation appeared in the 1970s as they recovered and increased competition on the world capitalist market and real wages could not be pushed down due to the Cold War. However, capitalists in the core responded to the problem by starting the Great Shift of production from the Global North to the Global South, taking advantage of the latter's cheap labour.

Thus, a worker from Jamaica earns today two times less than their US colleagues, from Bolivia or India three times less, and from Nigeria four times less.[18] Such deindustrialisation of the core countries led to a shock enlargement of the global workforce. In the 1990s, one and a half billion new workers from China, India and former Soviet republics joined the global labour market, doubling it. In China, industrialisation had led to rapid urbanisation when 300 million people moved to cities in 1995–2007.[19] As a result of the industrialisation of a few developing countries, the share of industrial products in exports from the periphery to the core grew from 20% in 1980 to 80% in 2003.[20] According to some estimates, the drastic expansion of the world labour market during the last two decades led to a decline in the capital/labour ratio by 55–60% (Freeman, 2010).[21] Capitalism was becoming uneven with a vengeance.

The migration of production to the periphery of the world capitalism changed transnational corporations (TNCs) significantly. While traditionally they had focused on owning productive facilities abroad, they now shifted to outsourcing production while keeping key competencies in their own hands. They are able to do this because TNCs operate as monopolies, while producers from the periphery are compelled to compete with each other to become partners of Western corporations. Cutting the price of their services – in fact, cutting the wages of their workers – is the main method of their competition.

All this is reflected in the famous 'flying geese' paradigm.[22] After WWII, Japan was consistently moving from labour-intensive to capital-intensive industries. With every big shift in the Japanese industrial structure, labour-intensive processes moved to other countries in the region, such as South Korea. These 'second-rate states' accepted production processes being abandoned by Japanese capital and they, in turn, moved up the regional industrial ladder, shifting labour-intensive processes down to less developed countries. Value added is distributed among these countries according to their technological position in the hierarchy.

The enormous growth of financial-speculative capital was part and parcel of this process. Global financial markets play an intermediary role in the transfer of incomes created by cheap labour of the periphery to the core. To gain access to the markets of the core, producers from the periphery are compelled to depreciate their national currencies. This implies the transfer of their savings of the reserve currency to the world – ie Western – financial markets. The process of productive capital moving into the financial-speculative sphere was called 'financialisation'. Since it is largely a repercussion of the Global Shift of production, it can be considered another result of UCD.

Such a system inevitably led to the current world economic crisis. The world witnessed the unprecedented expansion of productive capacities in China, India, Brazil, Mexico and other peripheral or semi-peripheral countries. On the other hand, since this process was based on the exploitation of cheap labour, aggregate demand fell consistently short of aggregate supply. Up to a certain moment, this process was alleviated due to the expansion of consumer credit. However, in 2008 it was exactly indebtedness of this kind (chiefly in the US mortgage market) which exploded.

The world economic crisis also implies crisis in the current system of international affairs. Under capitalism, international relations are shaped by core–periphery relations. The structure of the world economy and the structure of international relations are both dependent on the accumulation of capital at a global scale. Great crises of its global regime of accumulation necessarily shake up capitalism's system of international relations. The ruling elite of the core countries is forced to seek ways to shift the burden of crisis to the periphery, which implies its further subordination for greater economic exploitation. On the other hand, a handful of nations belonging to the semi-periphery – BRICS (Brazil, Russia, India, China and South Africa) countries being prominent among them – accumulated economic and political power to challenge this strategy in various ways. This is why, over the last decade, old acute international military-political conflicts have been exacerbated and new ones, such as the Syrian and Ukrainian conflicts, have been initiated.

US strategy in Eurasia traditionally aimed at preventing any power from uniting the peoples and resources of the continent.[23] This largely explains the US ruling class hostility to

Russia: they must prevent it from recovering after the collapse of the USSR. Recently, China has emerged as another power which can aspire to unite Eurasia in the foreseeable future, even as its subjugation becomes critical for the West amid the calamity of the global crisis. In response, China, in particular, seeks to project its power into Eurasia by developing the 'One Belt, One Road' (OBOR) strategy which should secure China land access to Eurasian and world markets, evading US maritime power.

At the same time, Russia has gradually come to aspire to restore its role as a regional power. Post- Communist Russia's concerns have gradually mounted: NATO expansion to the East; a number of 'colour revolutions' bringing to power anti-Russian regimes in a number of the former Soviet republics; NATO involvement in the Balkan civil war against Russia's historical ally, Serbia; plans to install a US anti-missile defence system in Eastern Europe, threatening Russian security; and the so-called EU 'Eastern-European Partnership' pro- grammes, aimed at splitting Russian neighbours from Russia. In 2007, Russian President Vladimir Putin delivered his famous 'Munich speech' to the International Meeting on Security and Cooperation in Europe, with a clear signal that the age of the 'Yes' diplomacy of the 1990s was over. Despite this unambiguous sign of impending confrontation, the West extended invitations to Ukraine and Georgia to join NATO. Their proximity to Russia's heart- land means that they constitute serious military threats to Russia's security, and the Russian ruling class considered these invitations unprovoked acts of aggression. Soon, the new line in Russian foreign policy was put to the test. In August 2008, the pro-American regime of Michael Saakashvili in Georgia invaded the pro-Russian breakaway republic South Ossetia. Russia immediately struck back, effectively putting an end to Saakashvili's venture. This thwarted plans to include Georgia in NATO and was a clear message to the West: further Western advance into the former Soviet space would encounter resistance. It also sent Ukraine a message: Russian military capabilities were largely restored and the US was unable to save its faraway clients.[24] Another Russian response was the Eurasian integration project, involving countries of the former Soviet Union.

Though it has prompted talk of a 'New Cold War', this new Russian foreign policy is a far cry from the Cold War of the Soviet times.[25] Vladimir Putin is not a communist seeking the destruction of capitalism. He is a rather moderate conservative leader following a neoliberal domestic economic course. He has never challenged neoliberal international order or its pivot, US leadership. Instead, he is attempting to compel the West to recognise Russian vital strategic interests in the existing international framework. That is why, even when using military force abroad, Putin carefully avoids full-scale confrontation with the West, targeting only its proxies and always leaving options for compromise. The present authors are not sure that such a strategy is realistic in the long run, but definitely it cannot be seriously considered a New Cold War.

One of the ways to interpret Putin's foreign policy is to consider it as an attempt to find the best possible place between the core and periphery of the current capitalist world-sys- tem. This involves the Russian ruling elite adjusting to operation of the Law of Uneven and Combined Development (LUCD).

This hardly can be dubbed 'imperialism'. It is, rather, a reaction to the failure of neoliber- alism. The Eurasian integration project requires that the ruling circles of Russia, Belarus, Kazakhstan and some other Commonwealth of Independent States (CIS) countries involved in the process at least tacitly recognise the negative results of the radical market reforms undertaken in the 1990s. The project also testifies to the growing awareness among post-Soviet states of their insecurity and vulnerability in conditions of the current world economic crisis and international instability. From this also follows a rejection of what contemporary capitalism has to offer the periphery and semi-periphery. In launching their integration project, these countries sent an unambiguous message that they are determined to develop more independent positions in international policy and economy, annoying Washington. In December 2012, the then US State Secretary Clinton referred to the threat of 're-Sovetisation' of a large part of Eastern Europe and Central Asia.[26]

US strategy not only needs to prevent this, it also requires that Russia join it in thwarting China's OBOR strategy. And if Russia does not, the US strategy of isolating China becomes unrealistic. In this context, as we see below, Ukraine appeared to be the most vulnerable point in the international positions of modern Russia. In its desperation to strengthen its hold over the world economy, and to defend the high profits of its TNCs and financial tycoons through increasing exploitation of the periphery, the US focused on Ukraine. Separating Ukraine off from Russia geo-strategically has been seen as key to preventing Russia's aspirations to great power status. This situation is a far cry from both the Russian imperialism or two imperialisms perspectives.

4. Dialectics of a colour revolution

From our standpoint, understanding the Ukraine crisis requires identifying the social system that emerged after the end of the USSR, placing it in the world system and understanding its ruling classes. Against this backdrop, we can then understand the contest between the two rival visions of the country. It is also important to make a comparison with Russian society to understand the reasons for the West's distinctly different attitudes to the two countries.

As should now be clear, the breakdown of the USSR led not to democracy and market freedoms in the former Soviet republics but to different types of peripheral societies dependent on the core capitalist countries. Two major formative processes shaped them: the degeneration of the Soviet bureaucracy and the influence of the global financialised capitalism. Under their combined influence, rather than rational entrepreneurs of the Weberian type, highly authoritarian, short-term-oriented, rent-seeking oligarchs emerged in these economies. They specialised in rent-seeking and transferring a large part of the incomes created by the labour of the local population to the core capitalist countries, requiring social suppression, an authoritative state. Over the decades, they have presided over deindustrialisation, technological decline and general impoverishment. Since powerful oligarchs save their money in the West, they are extremely dependent on it.[27]

This is more or less the story of all post-Soviet societies. However, there are some important differences between Ukraine and Russia. For example, Russia is semi-peripheral. While it supplies raw materials, purchases manufactured goods on the world market and suffers considerable capital flight, it aspires to an independent role in the world arena and demands that the West treat it as an equal. 'Hands-on governance' of its economy means that oligarchs are, to a certain degree, subjugated to the state and are compelled to invest some of their returns in Russia.

Ukraine, by contrast, has been relegated to the periphery. Its oligarchs are not controlled by the Ukrainian state in any meaningful sense and are instead involved in a constant and often fierce struggle for control over the state, leading them into more myopic strategies, negligible domestic investment and maximum capital flight to the West. Being even more dependent on the proceeds from the export of less-processed goods than Russia, Ukraine is more vulnerable to external shocks, and the performance of its economy is worse. Essentially, Ukraine is today what Russia became in the 1990s. In liberal democratic societies, the ruling elite is assumed to defend national interests and seek social compromise with the subordinated social classes. Ukrainian oligarchs, uncontrolled by the national state, are, by contrast, under strict control of the Western elite (since they keep their money in the West). Their contest for power is a mortal struggle for who will benefit more from betraying national interests and from unlimited exploitation of their fellow Ukrainians. It is far cry from a viable capitalist liberal democracy.

In this context, Maidan was a classic 'colour revolution'. Its essence lies in the exploitation of popular insurrection by external forces pursuing their own interests. Here, local discontent among those disillusioned by Ukraine's periphery capitalism and attracted to possible access to work in the EU definitely played a role. At the same time, undercover Western influence on Maidan was also undeniable. Western influence was not confined to widely publicised facts, as demonstrated by Victoria Nuland, the US State Department deputy who distributed cookies to the protesters, or her discussion with the US Ambassador in Ukraine Geoffrey Payette about who would be the country's prime minister after Yanukovitch was ousted. There is much more to show that the West, primarily the US, took control over all major aspects of social life in Ukraine well before Maidan.

So-called Western 'soft power' appeared in Ukraine from the very beginning of independence. By 2013, about a thousand Western NGOs were operating in Ukraine, tacitly directing its public organisations, mass media and civil institutions.[28] This cost much more than the $5 billion the US spent in 'support of democracy in Ukraine', according to Nuland's famous confession.[29] The main opposition political parties of the country were established under the control and financial support of the West. Tymoshenko and Yatsenuk's Fatherland party[30] and Tiyagnibok's Freedom party[31] were bankrolled by the US government, while Klyatchko's Ukrainian Democratic Alliance for Reforms (UDAR) was funded by Germany.[32] These facts also reveal that, from early on, the US and Germany competed to control events in Ukraine.

According to Alexandr Yakimenko, head of the Ukranian political police under Yanukovitch, the list of the heads of Ukranian law enforcement agencies who became American spies includes the Chairman of the Foreign Intelligence Service from 2005 to 2010, General N. Malomuzh; the Minister of Defence from 2005 to 2007, A. Gritsenko; the head of military intelligence and, after the coup, the head of the Foreign Intelligence Service, V. Gvozd; and the Head of the National Security Service of Ukraine in from 2006 to 2010 and again in 2014–2015, V. Nalivaytchenko.[33] Though Yakimenko's personal involvement in the Maidan events may serve to cast doubt on him, there is strong additional indirect evidence to support his testimony. Just how subservient Ukrainian security officials had become to Western interests was also revealed in the 2008 public scandal when Nalivaytchenko invited the then US Ambassador to Ukraine, William Taylor, to hand out diplomas to graduates at the Academy of Ukrainian Foreign Intelligence Service![34] The office of the Attorney-General even opened a criminal case against Nalivaytchenko for 'providing offices for Central Intelligence Agency (CIA) officers in the Ukrainian Security Service (SBU) headquarters'.[35]

One of the most important aspects of Western countries' covert interference in Ukrainian internal affairs is their support in training militants of right-wing extremist organisations. There is, for instance, the video of the SBU head Nalivaytchenko delivering a speech to militants with Yarosh, the head of the 'Right Sector'.[36] According to some American sources, the secret terrorist network GLADIO (from italian Operazione Gladio, Operation 'Sword'; established by NATO to destabilise the Warsaw Pact countries, but not dissolved after the breakdown of the Berlin Wall), includes Ukrainian nationalists who participated in many 'dirty wars' in the former USSR and beyond.[37] There is evidence that Ukrainian militants were trained in NATO countries such as Poland and the Baltic States.[38]

Thus, long before the Maidan events, the West established its control over all major aspects of Ukrainian society, including powerful oligarchs who keep their money in the West, the main political parties, and the mass media directly through the network of non-governmental organisations (NGOs); and indirectly through dependent oligarchs, the armed forces and secret services and, for good measure, the militants from right-wing extremist organisations. This is nothing less than the infrastructure of a 'colour revolution'. Under such circumstances, it was really up to US diplomats to decide who would run the country weeks before the actual coup succeeded.

Ostensibly, the Kiev 'Maidan' was a kind of bourgeois-democratic uprising, attempting to rid the society of corrupt power and establish European democracy. In reality, it was exploitation of the justified indignation of citizens caused by the inherent properties of a peripheral capitalism by external forces. The present authors do not argue that Maidan can be reduced to Western influence. Of course, there was the powerful gravitational pull of the EU – economically, politically and culturally – on mass consciousness, particularly the consciousness of the youth. However, this gravitation was only the backdrop to the problems engendered by the nature of the peripheral capitalism, and thanks to the near total absence of left forces, it was easily exploited by external forces.

Whatever democratic sentiments inspired Maidan, under Western 'hegemony' it could only further entrench peripheralisation of Ukrainian society. Comprador, the pro-Western Ukrainian capital, is incapable of leading the country to democracy and economic prosperity because it is compelled to sacrifice the interests of the country to Western capital.[39] Just as in Russia a hundred years ago, the bourgeois-democratic Revolution is doomed to failure in contemporary Ukrainian conditions.

The violent takeover of power in Kiev by a pro-Western and anti-Russian, nationalistic regime meant an increase in both social and national oppression for the Russian and pro-Russian population of the southeast of the country.[40] No wonder it engendered a popular uprising there. It started in late February–March 2014, embracing the area from Crimea and Odessa to Kharkov. The police report on events in only one district (*oblast*) of Donetsk depicts a massive grassroots movement: in late March and early April there were about 200 mass events in 33 towns, 148 of them in Donetsk (the district centre) alone. More than 130,000 people participated. This happened in only one district, and in only one month of the so-called 'Russian Spring'.[41]

Probably, the greatest uprising was in Kharkov, the second largest city of the country. According to official information, about 300 anti-Maidan activists were arrested,[42] when, in fact, about 500 people were detained.[43] Hundreds of dramatic mass events with the participation of hundreds of thousands of people swept through Odessa, Crimea, Lugansk, Donetsk, Kherson and Nikolaev districts. In fact, they embraced the whole southeast of the country. The rebels managed to take power where they achieved two immediate goals: disbanding Kiev authorities and capturing weapons in local SBU headquarters. Where they reached the first objective but failed to achieve the second (as in Kharkov), the authorities were able to pick out the ringleaders and take them into custody, thus suppressing the movement. Where the insurrection failed to solve either of the problems (as in Odessa), the carnage was the worst.

At first, the Donbass uprising assumed the form of a national-liberation movement directed against the nationalistic, neo-Banderian regime.[44] However, thanks to the dialectics of the bourgeois-democratic revolution at the periphery considered above, it could not limit itself only to immediate democratic demands. From the very beginning, the movement displayed anti-capitalist sentiments, shared by its patriotic and left elements. They included nationalisation of the oligarchs' property, redistribution of incomes in favour of toilers, introduction of planning and giving power to the people. Thus, the 'Permanent Revolution' approach is arguably the most appropriate for understanding the internal dynamics of the Ukraine crisis.

However, any development of the movement from national liberation with vague democratic slogans in a socialist direction was arrested by none other than Russian authorities. They had good reasons: if such an uprising against periphery capitalism developed a genuine socialist agenda, the movement could well sweep over Russia herself. It is only natural that the Russian semi-comprador ruling elite used all its influence to prevent the movement from going beyond its immediate aims. Deplorable as this fact is, it falsifies both the 'Russian imperialism' and the 'two imperialisms' approaches to this crisis.

Almost the only decisive act of the Russian leadership in the course of this crisis was reunification with Crimea. However, even this is very far from being imperialist in any meaningful sense of this word. Russia was forced to do this in response to the possible NATO attempt to take over Sevastopol – the major Russian naval base in the Black Sea. The reunification of Crimea with Russia put an end to the previously unstoppable NATO movement to the East. However, the reluctance of the Russian ruling elite to cut its strong ties with the West manifested itself in incoherent policy in Donbass. On the one hand, Russia did not allow the military takeover of the pro-Russian Peoples' Republics. On the other hand, it was Russia which prevented the unrecognised republics from radically expanding their sphere of control after the debacle of the Ukrainian military in the late summer of 2014, which refused to officially recognise Donetskaya and Luganskaya People's Republics, imposed on them ambiguous 'Minsk Agreements',[45] and effectively prevented their development towards socialism. All this corresponds to Western interests more than to Russian strategic needs. The ambiguity of Russian strategy in the Ukrainian crisis is conditioned by ambiguity of its social system – semi-peripheral capitalism, caught in persistent contradiction between aspiration to an independent role and the needs of comprador capital.

Conclusion

To sum up, the fate of the Russian Revolution of 1917 created inner preconditions for, and still determines the qualities of, post-Soviet societies. While the Soviet Union transformed the former tsarist empire and made Ukraine and Russia modern industrial societies, the degeneration of the Soviet bureaucracy conditioned their shift to capitalism. On the other hand, while stagflation in the West led to a global shift of production from the North to the South, the collapse of the USSR greatly widened the 'safety zone' of the capitalist world system. In such conditions, the only way of moving to capitalism for the post-Soviet societies was to embrace peripheral (Ukraine) or at best semi-peripheral (Russia) status. This inevitably led to the disappointment of popular expectations in these countries, with their economic inefficiency, corruption, authoritarian states and low living standards. The salient feature of all peripheral societies is their limited sovereignty and dependency of elites on the West.

The failure of the Russian Revolution, which led to the end of the USSR, increased exploitation at the global scale and facilitated the current global crisis, has exacerbated international conflict. The survival of the core requires the semi-periphery to play an auxiliary role, imposing discipline on the periphery and compelling it to increase its services to the core. Rather than doing that, Russia appeared to be asserting itself on the world stage. This was the reason why the West ignited the Ukraine crisis: as a means of putting pressure on Russia.

The failure of Maidan to establish even limited democracy in Ukraine led to popular insurrection in Donbass. While many protesters in Maidan aspired to some form of bourgeois democracy, those in Donbass were definitely in a more socialist mood. However, socialist tendencies there were arrested by the bourgeois, if also semi-peripheral, Russia. This close relation between the inevitable failure of bourgeois democracy and popular insurrection brings Ukrainian events close to the model of a 'permanent revolution' conditioned by UCD. Thus, 100 years after the Russian Revolution triumphed, its legacy still governs the fate of peoples who once embraced it.

Acknowledgements

The authors would like to thank Prof. Radhika Desai (University of Manitoba, Canada) for invaluable help in improving the content and editing the text of this paper.

Disclosure statement

A disclosure statement reporting no conflict of interests has been inserted.

Funding

Ruslan Dzarasov would like to thank the Geopolitical Economy Research Group for financial support provided for the participation in its 2017 Annual Conference. This study was funded by the Russian Foundation for Basic Research, under the grant agreement No. 20-010-00608.

Notes

1. Marx, *Capital*, 91.
2. Lenin, *Collected Works*, 354.
3. Trotsky, *History of the Russian Revolution*, 26–7.
4. Also see the analysis of different Marxian perspectives on UCD law in Van der Linden, "'Law' of Uneven and Combined Development."
5. Tyutyukin, *Menshevism*.
6. See the brilliant account of the modern world capitalism to that effect in the book Amin, *Law of Worldwide Value*.
7. Kagarlitsky, *Empire of the Periphery*; L'achenko, *History of the USSR Economy*.
8. Boffa, *History of the Soviet Union*, 17.
9. Gatrell, "Tsarist Russia at War," 668.
10. Mayevskiy, "To the Issue of Dependency of Russia."
11. Mayevskiy, *Rusian Industry in Conditions*. Sometimes it is argued that Russia did not lose WWI since it formally held the front until the October Revolution. However, the very fact of the domestic upheaval demonstrated its inability to maintain the war effort.
12. Owen, *Capitalism and Politics in Russia*.
13. Levin, *Lenin's Last Struggle*.
14. Trotsky, *Revolution Betrayed*, 191–2.
15. Lane, *Elites and Classes in the Transformation of State Socialism*.
16. Menshikov, *Anatomy of Russian Capitalism*, 81–99.
17. Brenner, *Boom and the Bubble*, 7–47.
18. Rodrick, "Labour Markets."
19. Jagannathan, Kapoor and Schaumburg, "Why Are We in a Recession," 9.
20. Blecker and Razami, *Developing Country Exports of Manufactures*, 45.
21. Freeman, "What Really Ails Europe."
22. Ozawa, *Rise of Asia*, 43–103.
23. Friedman, "Geopolitics of the United States."
24. Friedman, "Perspectives on the Ukrainian Protests."
25. As mentioned above, the Russian Revolution was an insurrection of the periphery against the domination of the core. The existence of the USSR, whether it was truly socialist or not, undermined the domination of imperialism, for instance, supporting the so-called 'socialist orientation in the Third World'. Thus, the West waged the Cold War essentially to prevent autonomous development elsewhere, which refused to complement Western economies' high-value production with low-value production. See Desai, *Geopolitical Economy*, 97–99.
26. Klapper, "Clinton Fears Efforts to 'Re-Sovietize.'"
27. The genesis of the new post-Soviet ruling class in modern Russia and its rent-seeking behaviour as the key element of its mechanism of accumulation of capital in societies of such a type are discussed in details in the book Dzarasov, *Conundrum of Russian Capitalism*.
28. Kovtunenko, "Democratizatory Vseya Ukrainy"; Panov, "'Soft Power' Crushes Ukraine."
29. "Victoria Nuland's Admits."
30. Herszenhorn, "Ukraine's New Premier."
31. Blumenthal, "Is the US Backing Neo-Nazis."
32. "Our Man in Kiev."
33. Popov, "Ex-Glava SBU Nazval Tekh."
34. See discussion and photos in "Ex-Rukovodytel SBU Amerikansky Shpion."
35. Koltsov, "Poroshenko Otkryl Vtoroy."
36. "Nalivaytchenko Sozdaval Praviy Sektor."
37. Engdahl, "Ukraine Secretive Neo-Nazi."

38. See discussion and video shooting in Sapozhnikova, "Otryady Boyevikov, Podzhigavshikh Ukrainu."
39. See an excellent account of relations between Ukrainian oligarchic capitalism and the West in two outstanding Western accounts by Van der Pijl, *Flight MH17*; and Sakwa, *Frontline Ukraine*.
40. Ukraine is a divided nation due to its complicated history. Originally, the core area of the country was predominantly agricultural. Industrial areas of Kharkov and Donbass were included in the Ukraine Soviet Socialist Republic by Bolsheviks to increase workers' presence and facilitate development of the region. Crimea was included in Ukraine only in the 1950s. The population of these regions largely considers itself Russian, not Ukrainian. It is only natural that after the breakdown of the Soviet Union it felt hurt, deprived and abandoned.
41. "MVD Ukrainy zavelo 46 ugolovnykh."
42. "Pochemu molchit Kharkov?"
43. From the personal communication of the present author with Kharkov anti-Maidan activists.
44. Stepan Bandera (1909–1959) was the leader of the Ukrainian nationalists and a Nazi collaborator. The Ukrainian collaborationists became notorious for their atrocities committed against the Jews, Polish, Russians and local communists.
45. Mynsky agreements stopped the successful offensive of the military forces of the breakaway republics and Russian volunteers in summer 2014. This shows the contradictory course of official Russia in the Ukraine crisis. On the one hand, the Russian government provided support in the form of military aid to the people's republics; on the other, it prevented further spread of rebellion, seeking compromise with the West.

Bibliography

Amin, S. *The Law of Worldwide Value*. New York: Monthly Review Press, 2010.

Blecker, R., and A. Razami. *Developing Country Exports of Manufactures: Moving up the Ladder to Escape the Fallacy of Composition?* American University, Department of Economics WP 2006-06, 2006.

Blumenthal, M. "Is the US Backing Neo-Nazis in Ukraine?" *AlterNet*, February 24, 2014. Accessed March 3, 2018. http://www.alternet.org/tea-party-and-right/us-backing-neo-nazis-ukraine

Boffa, J. *Istoriya Sovetskogo Soyuza. V. 1. Ot Revolutsii do Vtoroy Mirovoy Voyni. Lenin I Stalin. 1917–1941 [History of the Soviet Union. V. 1. From Revolution to the WWII. Lenin and Stalin. 1917–1941]*. Moscow: Mejdunarodniyer Otnosheniya, 1994.

Brenner, R. *The Boom and the Bubble. The US and the World Economy*. London & New York: Verso, 2003.

Desai, R. *Geopolitical Economy: US Hegemony, Globalization and Empire*. London: Pluto Press, 2013.

Dzarasov, R. *The Conundrum of Russian Capitalism. The Post-Soviet Economy in the World System*. London: Pluto Press, 2014.

Engdahl W. "Ukraine Secretive Neo-Nazi Military Organization Involved in Euromaidan Sniper Shootings." *Global Research*, March 3, 2014. Accessed March 3, 2018. https://www.globalresearch.ca/ukraine-secretive-neo-nazi-military-organization-involved-in-euromaidan-snyper-shootings/5371611

"Ex-Rukovodytel SBU Amerikansky Shpion?" *Interesniye Novosty*, September 9, 2013. Accessed March 3, 2018. http://internovosti.net/politika/jeks-rukovoditel-sbu-amerikanskij-shpion2013.html

Freeman, R. "What Really Ails Europe (and America): The Doubling of the Global Workforce." *The Globalist*, 5 March 5, 2010. Accessed November 15, 2018. https://www.theglobalist.com/what-really-ails-europe-and-america-the-doubling-of-the-global-workforce/

Friedman G. "Perspectives on the Ukrainian Protests." *Stratfor*, January 28, 2014. Accessed February 5, 2018. http://www.stratfor.eom/weekly/perspectives-ukrainian-protests#axzz-37jewcltX

Friedman, G. "The Geopolitics of the United States. Part 1: The Inevitable Empire." *Stratfor*, July 4, 2014. Accessed February 4, 2018. http://www.stratfor.com/analysis/geopolitics-united-40states-part-l-inevitable-empire#axzz37jewcltX

Gatrell, P. "Tsarist Russia at War: The View from above, 1914–February 1917." *The Journal of Modern History* 87, no. 3 (2015): 668–700. doi:10.1086/682414.

Gregory, P. *Russian National Income, 1885–1913*. Cambridge: Cambridge University Press, 1982. doi:10.1086/ahr/90.2.463.

Herszenhorn, D. "Ukraine's New Premier, the 'Rabbit,' Seems to Be in His Element." *The New York Times*, March 12, 2014.

Jagannathan R., M. Kapoor, and E. Schaumburg. "Why Are We in a Recession? The Financial Crisis Is a Symptom, Not the Disease!"*NBER WP*, 2009. 15404. http://www.nber.org/papers/w15404

Kagarlitsky, B. *Peripheriynaya Imperiya. Rossiya I Mirosystema [Empire of the Periphery. Russia and the World-System]*. Moscow: Ultra. Kultura, 2004.

Klapper, B. "Clinton Fears Efforts to "Re-Sovietize" in Europe." *Associated Press*, December 6, 2012. Accessed February 5, 2018. http://news.yahoo.com/clinton-fcars-cfforts-sovietize-europe-l11645250-politics.html

Koltsov, S. "Poroshenko Otkryl Vtoroy Fron Protiv Agenta CIA." *Vzglyad*, June 17, 2015. Accessed March 3, 2018. http://vz.ru/world/2015/6/17/751041.html

Kovtunenko, S. "Democratizatory Vseya Ukrainy." *Ric.UA*, June 22, 2011. Accessed March 3, 2018. http://ric.ua/index.php?newsid=293

Lane, D. *Elites and Classes in the Transformation of State Socialism*. Abingdon and New York: Routledge, 2017.

L'achenko, P. *Istoriya Narodnogo Khozyaistva SSSR [History of the USSR Economy]*. 4th ed. Vol. 1–2. Moscow: Gospolitizdat, 1956.

Levin, M. *Lenin's Last Struggle*. New York: Random House, 1968.

Lenin, V. *O Lozunge Soyedinennykh Shtatov Evropy . Collected Works*. 5th ed. Vol. 26. Moscow: Izdatel'stvo Politicheskoy Literatury, 1969.

Marx, K. *Capital. Volume I. Translated by Ben Fowkes*. Harmondsworth: Penguin, 1976.

Mayevskiy, I. V. *Ekonomika Russkoi Promyshlennosty v Usloviyakh Pervoy Mirovoy Voiny [Russian Industry in Conditions of the First World War]*. Moscow: Delo, 2003.

Mayevskiy, I. "K voprosu o zavisimosti Rossii v gody Pervoy mirovoy voyni" ["To the Issue of Dependency of Russia in the Years of WWI"]. *Voprosy Istorii* no. 1 (1957): 69–77. Accessed August 8, 2019. https://scepsis.net/library/id_644.html

Menshikov, S. *The Anatomy of Russian Capitalism*. Washington, DC: Executive Intelligence Review News Service, 2007.

"MVD Ukrainy zavelo 46 ugolovnykh del po mitingam v Donetzkoy oblasty." *Vzgl'ad*, 4 April 4, 2014. Accessed March 3, 2018. http://vz.ru/news/2014/4/4/680499.html

"Nalivaytchenko Sozdaval Praviy Sektor, Teper On Glava SBU." YouTube. March 6, 2014. Accessed March 3, 2018. http://www.youtube.com/watch?v=nlINDI7GmAY

Owen, T. *Capitalism and Politics in Russia: A Social History of the Moscow Merchants, 1855–1905*. Cambridge: Cambridge University Press, 1981. doi:10.1086/ahr/89.4.1117-a.

"Our Man in Kiev." German Foreign Policy.com. December 10, 2013. Accessed March 3, 2018. http://www.german-foreign-policy.com/en/fulltext/58705

Ozawa, T. *The Rise of Asia. The "Flying Geese" Theory of Tandem Growth and Regional Agglomeration*. Cheltenham, UK and Northampton, MA: Edward Elgar, 2009.

Panov, V. "'Myagkaya Syla Krushit Ukrainu." ["The 'Soft Power' Crushes Ukraine"]. Stoletiyer. January 31, 2014. Accessed March 3, 2018. http://www.stoletie.ru/politika/magkaja_sila_krushit_ukrainu_325.html

"Pochemu molchit Kharkov?" *Golos Sevastopola*. August 14, 2014. Accessed March 3, 2018. http://voicesevas.ru/news/yugo-vostok/3698-pochemu-molchit-harkov.html

Popov, E. "Ex-Glava SBU Nazval Tekh, Kto Polutchil Pribyl ot Boyny na Maydaner." *Vesti*, 12 March 12, 2014. Accessed March 3, 2018. http://www.vesti.ru/doc.html?id=1368925

Rodrick, D. "Labour Markets: The Unexpected Frontier of Globalization." *The Globalist*, May 31, 2011. Accessed March 3, 2018. http://www.theglobalist.com/printStoryld.aspx?StoryId=9156

Sakwa, R. *Frontline Ukraine. Crisis in the Borderlands*. London, I. B. Taurus, 2015.

Sapozhnikova, G. "Otryady Boyevikov, Podzhigavshikh Ukrainu, Gotovilys v Natovskikh Lageryakh." *Komsomolskaya Pravda*, 11 March 11, 2014. Accessed March 3, 2018. http://www.kp.ru/daily/26203/3090326/.

Trotsky, L. *The History of the Russian Revolution*. Translated by Max Eastma. London: Pluto, 1977.

Trotsky, L. *The Revolution Betrayed*. New York: Dover, 2004.

Tyutyukin, S. *Menshevism: Stranitsy Istorii [Menshevism: Pages of History]*. Moscow: ROSSPAN, 2002.

Van der Linden, M. "The 'Law' of Uneven and Combined Development: Some Underdeveloped Thoughts." *Historical Materialism* 15, no. 1 (2007): 145–165. doi:10.1163/156920607X171627.

Van der Pijl, K. 2018. *Flight MH17. Ukraine and the New Cold War*. Manchester, Manchester University Press, 2018.

"Victoria Nuland's Admits Washington Has Spent \$5 Billion to 'Subvert Ukraine.'" YouTube. – 9 February 9, 2014. Accessed March 3, 2018. https://www.youtube.com/watch?v=U2fYcHLouXY

Building socialism: from 'scientific' to 'active' Marxism

David Lane

ABSTRACT

Historical materialism envisages law-like tendencies ('scientific' Marxism) promoting the development of productive forces and, concurrently, a political praxis ('active' Marxism) requiring human intervention. These positions give rise to conflicting interpretations of Marxism: first to understand society, second to change it – to abolish economic exploitation. The twentieth century witnessed a shift in the locus of the contradictions of capitalism to the economically dependent territories of the imperial powers. Socialist parties, when in power and adopting a Leninist political praxis, furthered modernisation and were successful in reducing economic exploitation. The paper addresses the relationship between the scientific and praxis components of Marxism in contemporary global capitalism. It considers post-Marxist interpretations of the changing class structure, the rise of identity politics and the evolving nature of capital. Forms of domination, oppression and discrimination (bureaucracy, patriarchy, racism, militarism and credentialism) give rise to their own distinctive forms of power relations. It is contended that they should not be equated with Marx's crucial insight into the nature of economic exploitation. Many current Marxist (and 'post-Marxist') writers adopt a 'scientific' position emphasising the inherent contradictions of capitalism. The author claims that without appropriate political praxis, the resolution of such contradictions is unlikely to transcend capitalism.

Marxism has many intellectual and social appeals. As a method of social analysis, it provides a framework for the evolution of societies parallel to that of Darwin's theory of evolution in nature. Marx endorsed a modern society (scientifically based, secular, economically developed and wealthy, politically democratic and socially 'progressive'). But he identified a major fault line, a contradiction, in modern capitalism: it promoted human liberation while practising economic exploitation (Therborn 2008, 68). The labour theory of value is a cornerstone in Marx's approach: its significance is to reveal the illegitimate extraction of surplus value (exploitation) promoting a class contradiction under capitalism. The socialist future visualised by Marx's followers transcended capitalism by destroying the exploitative elements (the domination of capital and market relations) which originally were necessary for progress but which became a fetter on development. Under socialism: psychologically, human beings would fulfil their potential; economically, the economy works for public good, not private gain; and politically, it promotes a real participatory democracy. Socialism has a civilisational as well as a class appeal. Socialism proposes to bring about the emancipatory elements of modernisation while concurrently promoting the development of the productive forces. It promises the birth of a civilisation without economic exploitation, predicated on principles of mutuality and human cooperation.

Followers of Marx have created a world view in which Marxism has three interrelated components: the methods of historical materialism, a socio-economic analysis of capitalism and a politics of class revolution. The first two components give rise to law-like tendencies: capitalism is revealed as having inherent structural contradictions that inevitably lead to a new synthesis: socialism. The unfolding of these contradictions provides the basis for an interpretation of Marx as scientific socialism. Marx, it is contended, devised for the social sciences a paradigm of historical development like that of Darwin in the natural sciences.[1] However, in the third component mentioned above, the process of revolutionary change, Marx recognised the need for human action, for a political praxis. In the politics of revolution, twentieth-century followers of Marx added a fourth component to Marxism: the legitimation of socialist societies which claimed to confirm Marx's critique of capitalism. This paper examines the strategy and outcome of the twentieth-century socialist revolutions before turning to consider the interpretations of twenty-first century capitalism.

Unlike Darwin, for whom change in the natural world was spontaneous, for Marx, human intervention was necessary for history to progress. Only conscious political action could bring about revolution. It is in this respect – how to change the world – that Marx's work has been the most controversial. One has to distinguish between the heritage of Marx as a method of social analysis searching for 'laws' of development, and the praxis of 'active Marxism' (the latter is the process by which theory is realised) which involves recognition of the crucial role of human intervention in history (Gouldner 1980).[2] There are two Marxes: Marx the social scientist, and Marx the socialist activist. There is a tension and sometimes a contradiction between these two components of Marxism.

Varieties of Marxism

The two sides to Marxism consist, firstly, of the changes which take place in the technology of the productive forces, driving the structural collapse of capitalism; secondly and concurrently, of political action, praxis, which furthers the cause of human emancipation which can only occur in the absence of economic exploitation. The scientific elements define the relationships determined by nature, notably the capitalist mode of production; the active elements are those requiring human action to bring about political changes to move to a higher level of productive forces. The extent to which these components in Marx's thought are relied on by commentators and activists determines their economic and social understanding on the one hand and their practical political strategy on the other.

'Scientific' Marxism emphasises the objective conditions of societies, particularly the technological constitution of the forces of production. The laws of development give rise to contradictions between the forces and relations of production, the resolution of which creates a new mode of production. 'The universality towards which [capitalism] is perpetually driving finds limitations in its own nature, which at a certain stage of its development will make it appear as itself the greatest barrier to this tendency, leading thus to its own self-destruction' (Grundrisse 1977, 364). Here, the impersonal laws of development lead to the communist mode of production, which will necessarily evolve out of capitalism. It is essentially a type of economic determinism. Laws have their own logic and are analogous to those of Darwin's paradigm of the physical world. Darwin's world was based on inherent competition in nature, on adaptation to the environment, and change was the accumulation of adaptive variations. For Marx, social change, driven by classes, was progressive; the first form of human society, primitive communism, had no class struggle and no competition. Classes are not therefore inherent in human society; they are a consequence of, and can be eliminated by, human action.

The class relations of production provide the motors of human action in the form of class forces. Political action is necessary to change the world. As Marx famously put it in the Eleventh Thesis on Feuerbach, 'Philosophers have only interpreted the world, in various ways; the point is to change it'.[3] Emancipation can only occur as a consequence of political action which breaks economic exploitation. 'Active Marxism' is the political intervention necessary to bring about the changes which are predicated on the development of productive forces. This approach gives human beings a creative role in history. Thus, 'active Marxism' is the praxis of human action promoting socialism/communism.

As social formations are historically and geographically determined and give rise to various kinds of social structure, capitalism is an institution in perpetual change. Both the scientific and praxis elements are open to interpretation and modification in the light of the changing nature of capitalism. As a scientific method, like Darwin's theory of evolution, Marx's interpretation can and should be developed and, where necessary, corrected. Gareth Stedman Jones considers that 'the Marx constructed in the twentieth century bore only an incidental resemblance to the Marx who lived in the nineteenth' (Stedman Jones 2017, 595). He follows a long line of thinkers who dismiss the contemporary relevance of Marx. Talcott Parsons, in 1965, concluded that Marx 'belongs to a phase of development which has been superseded .... Judging by the standards of the best contemporary social-science ... Marxian theory is obsolete' (Parsons 1967, 3).

Marx indeed generalised on the basis of nineteenth-century capitalism. Interpretations of the dynamics of capitalist development after the nineteenth century will necessarily be different to Marx's views. However, all scientific theories have to be appraised in the light of other theories and empirical findings. One has to consider the development of Marx's approach not only by his early twentieth-century followers such as Lenin, Trotsky, Luxembourg, Bernstein, Lukacs and Gramsci but also by those in the late twentieth century: in the USA, Paul Baran, Paul Sweezy, Harry Braverman, E. O. Wright and Immanuel Wallerstein, and in Europe, Raymond Williams, Victor Kiernan, Tom Bottomore, David McLellan, Ernest Mandel and Eric Hobsbaum, have contributed to an appraisal of Marx (see McLellan 1983). We consider some of these contributions below. The 'scientific' approach is subject to re-evaluation in the light of newly discovered facts. Rather than a Talmudic examination of Marx's original writings, it involves using insights derived from Marx and from other approaches. Without creative destruction and renewal, Marx's own writings become a subject of theology (in this instance an analysis of the language and meaning of Marx's writings).

'Active Marxism'

It is the praxis aspect of Marxism (the human strategy and action necessary to bring about a socialist society) that presents greater difficulties. An active Marxist position opens up divergent and contradictory interpretations. Karl Marx himself brought this out when, in commentating on policies advocated by Jules Guesde in his name, he pronounced: 'what is certain is that I myself am not a Marxist' (Marx and Guesde 1880). To promote political action, opinions can differ about the means to be adopted to move from capitalism to socialism. Here, we turn from a social scientific explanation to an appraisal of political action.

In a scientific sense, in the early twentieth century, the locus of the contradictions of capitalism shifted from the hegemonic Western capitalist countries to countries undergoing early industrialisation. It is here that capitalism broke down when weakened by wars and revolutionary uprisings, many inspired by anti-colonialism and others the consequences of war. Vladimir Lenin is the foremost theorist of active Marxism in the twentieth century:

> The fundamental law of revolution … is as follows: …. It is only when the 'lower classes' do not want to live in the old way and the 'upper classes' cannot carry on in the old way that the revolution can triumph. … [I]n other words: revolution is impossible without a nation-wide crisis (affecting both the exploited and the exploiters). (Lenin 1920)

It was in the dependent territories of the imperial powers that revolution inspired by Marx's ideas of socialism occurred. Following the crises of European wars, the colonial European states had insufficient economic means to maintain their military power and hegemony. However, these societies did not spontaneously mutate into a new mode of production. It is only through political praxis that a revolution can be secured and a new mode of production introduced. Without conscious political action, a national crisis can be followed by collapse and decay. Lenin added political praxis – a movement to take and later consolidate political power – to his analysis of revolution. He shifted the praxis of socialist politics in his proposals for the organisation of a political party of a 'new type' which not only led the revolutionary struggle but also brought 'consciousness' to the working class. Consequently, the seizures of power by Marxist-led parties have called for an evaluation of post-capitalist states founded in Marx's name. In the process of interpretation, intellectuals and political leaders have adapted Marx's ideas to legitimate their ideological or political positions.

The socialist movement in the colonial world was a vehicle for emancipation – a much wider objective than opposition to economic exploitation. These were not revolutions from the economic contradictions in the advanced capitalist countries but were consequent on political and social collapse – features of the wider world economy in which capitalism was embedded. Political movements, such as those which led to the formation of the USSR and the People's Republic of China, broke with the structure of world capitalism. In doing so, unlike reformist European social democracy, they created an alternative to competitive market capitalism. The conditions and consequences were not those formulated in the 'scientific' Marxist approach or contemplated by Marx in the nineteenth century. They were consequences of human effort and political organisation. In these societies, an 'active Marxism' was validated in the sense that a society was built which promoted modernisation without private property and a competitive market. In others, anti-colonialism promoted modernisation and political liberation to further national capitalism. As subjects of imperialism, their economic foundations were at a lower level to, and dependent on, the advanced capitalist countries.

Even among Marxist contemporaries of Lenin, these strategies were open to criticism. The Mensheviks (Julius Martov), Eduard Bernstein and Rosa Luxemburg, contended that the Leninist political party, as an instrument of revolution, undermined the role of the working class (see Luxemburg 1961).[4] Political praxis here is confounded by the principles of scientific Marxism. Such critics evaluate praxis in terms of what Marx wrote rather than whether political policies have resulted in the abolition of exploitation under conditions not antici-pated by Marx. Lenin's argument is that under conditions of imperialism, the crisis of capi-talism shifts its contradictions to developing countries, and consequently political action can break capitalism. Lukacs, for example, makes the point that Lenin's theory of imperialism was connected to 'every political problem of the present epoch, thereby making the eco-nomics of the new phase a guide-line for all concrete action in the resultant decisive con-jecture' (Lukacs 1970, 41). The test of praxis, I contend, is whether it promotes human liberation and breaks the social relationship of economic exploitation.

Evaluation becomes even more controversial when 'Marxism' becomes the official ideol-ogy of a state, sometimes conjoined with Leninism or Mao-Tse-Tung thought. The active Marxist approach would frame Marx's ideas in social and political contexts not anticipated by Marx. Human action, it is contended, can propel societies in the direction of a communist mode of production, quite independently of the 'objective' preconditions for the emergence of a higher mode of production. For example, the leaders of the Soviet Union and China claimed to have constructed the economic basis of socialism while by-passing the capitalist mode of production. Such an evaluation may be at variance with other elements of a cultural or social kind and may differ from political forms that one might expect to find in a socialist society. In other words, existing socialism might combine a progressive movement for human liberation with other regressive features – just as the Enlightenment was conjoined with slavery and colonial domination. State socialism was a different form of modernisation.

Critics of the Marxist–Leninist approach, by focussing on the non-fulfilment and negative features of the society, ignore or diminish the ways in which economic exploitation was abolished. This does not mean that 'exploitation' cannot take other forms such as, for example, the rise of a social stratum which may appropriate unearned income (economically, they may benefit from economic 'rents'). In the socialist countries, such income, unlike that under capitalism which is derived quite legally from ownership of assets, was illegitimate. What we can learn from the Soviet experience is that ruling elites can no longer be differentiated solely in terms of property; account must be taken of positions giving control over resources (both physical and human). Such relations become of considerable importance in societies with state ownership of productive forces, as effective power may reside in a stratum of officials. But this is a form of bureaucratic domination rather than class rule.

The transition to socialism

The formation of the USSR and the People's Republic of China broke the structure of world capitalism. In doing so these countries created an alternative to competitive market capi-talism. But the conditions and consequences were not those formulated in the 'scientific' Marxist approach which envisaged socialism being built on the ashes of advanced capitalism. Socialist regimes were consequences of human effort and political organisation derived from, amongst other things, Lenin's theory of party organisation and Mao's strategy of rev-olutionary war. Active Marxism was validated in the sense that societies were built which advanced modernisation (urbanisation, industrialisation, secularism, universal literacy and education) without economic exploitation. The socialist states fulfilled a major objective of the Communist Manifesto: 'The distinguishing feature of communism is … the abolition of private property'. No other political movement has substantially achieved this goal, even if in doing so other forms of domination continued or were recreated.

The socialist societies pursued new forms of economic and social coordination in the form of economic plans. Under socialism, in 'The Principles of Communism', Engels envisages

> an entirely new organization of society in which production is no longer directed by mutually competing individual industrialists but rather by the whole society operating according to a definite plan and taking account of the needs of all …. Above all, it will have to take the control of industry and of all branches of production out of the hands of mutually competing individuals, and instead institute a system in which all these branches of production are operated by society as a whole – that is, for the common account, according to a common plan, and with the participation of all members of society. (Engels 1987, vol 25)

The objective of national planning is to bring about a coherent pattern of investment, consumption, income distribution and employment. Socialist planning can consider comprehensively the benefits of different developmental proposals and enables social and environmental costs to be calculated and minimised. It provides an alternative framework for economic coordination without private property and private economic exploitation. Under conditions of public ownership, it represents an alternative to market capitalism. Without the need for profit, social costs can play a much greater role in shaping a more ecologically based economy. The exploitation of nature has no costs to corporations in a market economy; there is no economic need to limit natural exploitation. Socialist planning based on public ownership has no propensity for profit maximisation or capital accumulation. Hence, the realisation of ecological values is possible under national planning (Sweezy 1980, 139–151).

The system of planning created in the Soviet Union, and followed in many Third World countries, was successful in promoting modernisation: it achieved rapid industrialisation and significant advances, even surpassing capitalism in such fields as space exploration. Differentials in income and wealth compared to capitalism were significantly reduced. The emancipatory effects of modernisation – a full employment economy, comprehensive education, health care, a secular society, amelioration of the position of women – were important components in policy.

Data collected by the United Nations Development Programme show that for given levels of gross domestic product (GDP), human development in the socialist states was usually significantly higher than their gross national incomes. For instance, the difference in the period 1980 and 1990, between gross national product rank and human development index rank (HDI – life expectancy, adult literacy and educational attainment), was +8 for the USSR, +7 for Czechoslovakia and +21 for Poland; comparative figures are +2 for Japan, and −1 for the USA (see UNDP 1991, 119). In the state socialist countries, national planning had resolved the endemic crises invoked by the cyclical movements of capitalism. The major forms of economic exploitation (rent, interest payments and profits) were abolished and replaced by a state plan. In this sense, the Soviet forms of planning introduced a socialist economic formation. It vindicated 'active Marxism'.

However, state ownership and control did not abolish political domination or social discrimination. Alvin Gouldner is the mouthpiece for many of Marx's critics when he contends that the evolution of a bureaucracy as a new ruling class becomes 'a new, many times worse, domination' than a bourgeois ruling class (Gouldner 1980, 382). This assertion is contentious and unsubstantiated. One should frame the institution of planning in the USSR in the context of a society arising from feudalism. Alec Nove, like many others, noted that 'Russia's past is in many ways more relevant than Marxism to an understanding of the Soviet political and economic structure' (Nove 1979, 42). Rather than transcending capitalism, the socialist states were successful developmental models, which enabled them to catch up to the contemporaneous levels of the forces of production of the capitalist core. This 'catch-up' was achieved without market competition or private property. The extraction of surplus value was utilised for the support of the population, defence and developmental investment.

However, in the latter part of the twentieth century, confronted with the tasks of intensive development in a more advanced and differentiated industrial economy, economic progress declined, and Soviet-type planning was subject to criticism from groups within the political leadership and economic intelligentsia. A major criticism of administrative economic planning is that it is impossible to plan a modern economy efficiently. Competitive markets provide adjustment mechanisms for the regulation of output of goods and services through the price system, regulated by the state. Influential Western critics of planning, such as Alec Nove, and later internal critics, contended that the planning system could not perform these market functions effectively – due to the enormous number of calculations necessary to equate demand and supply at various levels in a modern economy. Thus, planners are able neither to devise output to satisfy consumer demand nor to combine the factors of production efficiently.

Moreover, critics argued that even long-term decisions were subject to the perverse interests of a state bureaucracy which effectively wrote a plan for itself. Though the absence of private ownership and the market ensured that private economic exploitation was limited, bureaucratic domination continued. From this point of view, critics contend that the power of bureaucracy destroys the socialist ideal of a universal plan (Nove 1979, 201, 204). The combination of state ownership and control over the economic mechanism regulates exploitation. Without effective democratic control, critics argued that the state could exert powers of political domination. In an extreme case, it could turn into state capitalism.

What we can learn from the Soviet experience is that ruling elites can no longer be differentiated in terms solely of property; account has to be taken of positions giving control over resources (both physical and human). Such relations become of considerable importance in societies with state ownership of productive forces, as effective power may reside in a stratum of officials. Growing armies of executives, professionals and politicians have significant powers over economic and social life. They are characterised by bureaucratic domination rather than class rule. A shift to capitalism took place after the dismantling of the institutions of state power carried out under Mikhail Gorbachev and Boris Eltsin.

When confronted with declining growth rates in the European socialist countries, the political leadership turned against planning and re-invented the market which, they contended, could augment the system of planning. Such a mixed system, they believed, would solve the 'zastoi' or slowing down of the socialist economies. In China also, reforms were introduced which not only brought markets into the national economy but led to participation in the wider world economy. China's economic system had hybrid features containing segments of 'transition from communism', state socialism and organised capitalism.

In retrospect, the introduction of market relations in the European socialist countries and the privatising of state assets, finally put into effect by radical reformers under Gorbachev, were not successful – at least in the European post-socialist states. In dismantling the system of planning they destroyed what had been the first operational alternative economic system to capitalism. The absence of profit on the one side and the presence of full employment on the other had secured a relatively equal distribution of income and wealth. This was reversed with the reintroduction of the market and private property. The changes are clearly brought out in Figure 1, which marks the proportion of income enjoyed (before tax) by the top 1% of the population before 1917, during and following the Soviet period. By 2006, the proportion of national income enjoyed by the top 1% of the Russian population was even greater than it was before the October Revolution of 1917. The changing pattern of differentials tells its own story. A capitalist class system was instituted following the dismantling of the USSR.

Economic exploitation has reappeared. Yet another assumption of Marx the scientist was negated – socialist societies could 'turn back' to capitalism. It might be argued here that, in a Marxist sense, the 'reversion' to capitalism vindicates the more 'scientific' interpretation of historical materialism; the economic basis was insufficiently advanced to sustain a communist mode of production. The problem with this argument is that it ignores the significant economic advances made in the Soviet Union. At the time of its dismantlement it was behind the USA, but was nevertheless an advanced industrial society with, as noted above, high standards of social development. China also followed a similar developmental trajectory to the Soviet Union; it has adopted market mechanisms but has not abandoned a socialist path. Political leadership (political praxis) must bear considerable responsibility for the destruction of the European socialist societies.

The changing structures of modern capitalism

While Lenin developed an active form of political intervention in the twentieth century, the world economy and geo-political conditions are very different under capitalist globalisation. How, then, can and should 'active Marxism' adapt to the conditions of contemporary capitalism? Six major structural changes have occurred since Marx's day: the technological level of advanced capitalist production and forms of communication; the nature of economic crisis; the geographical spread of capitalism concurrent with the global reach of production enterprises; the transformed class structure; the role of political institutions in managing economic coordination;

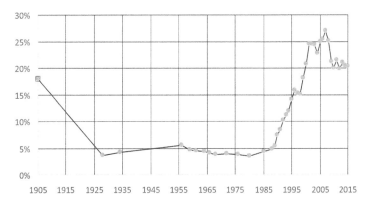

Figure 1. Top 1% income share Russia: Pre-tax income. *Source*: Series on income and wealth inequality (1905–2016) from Novokmet–Piketty–Zucman (2017). Available at https://www.quandl.com/data/PIKETTY-Thomas-Piketty

and the experience of planned socialist societies. Globalisation has created porous borders: the 'Third World' now does not have the same kind of dependency as it had in Lenin's time.

Capitalism is prone to recurring economic cycles giving rise to crises. In 2018, the Governor of the Bank of England, Mark Carney, as well as journalistic commentators such as Paul Mason, praised Marx's economic forecasting. For Carney, it is technology in the form of automation and consequent unemployment that will force down pay because of job losses, thus creating a crisis of capitalism.[5] For Marx, profit was derived from the exploitation of labour; thus, a decline of the labour force would necessarily lead to a reduction in the amount of surplus value and consequently a fall in profit.

Paul Mason emphasises that the technological basis of capitalism will lead to its demise. '[A]utomation coupled with the socialisation of knowledge will present us with the opportunity to liberate ourselves from work'.[6] Following Marx, he argues that capitalism is dependent on profits derived from labour; as the technological level of production advances, it will provide enough products through robotisation and automation to make paid labour unnecessary. The contradiction between economic abundance and people's poverty occurs because the privately owned factors of production produce an abundance of commodities through automation which cannot be bought because of the lack of effective demand caused by unemployment. The technologies which have arisen in the late twentieth and early twenty-first centuries are 'not compatible with capitalism …. Once capitalism can no longer adapt to technological change, postcapitalism becomes necessary' (Mason, p. xiii). Capitalism has 'reached the limits of its capacity to adapt' (Mason, p. xiii). 'When behaviours and organisations adapted to exploiting technological change appear spontaneously, postcapitalism becomes possible' (ibid). For Mason, however, there is not necessarily a transition to socialism.

Alexandr Buzgalin and Andrei Kolganov bring out the ways that market relations are superseded by the extensive redistributive roles of the state, by the rise of business regulation, by the growth of non-profit communitarian enterprise and, perhaps most important of all, by the development of production without direct labour power. All these developments lead to a weakening of the motivation of actors for monetary gain (Buzgalin and Kolganov 2016, 583); they seriously undermine capitalism and provide the 'embryos' of socialism. These views update Marx's ideas of the impending collapse of capitalism from the objective developments in the mode of production.

However, not all of these interpretations are correct. While the political and economic context in which capitalism operates has had important impacts on the forms that political opposition can take, they have not invalidated the processes described by Marx. I consider here only the nature of the class structure.

The changing class structure

The major movers of change for Marx were social classes:

> The owners merely of labour-power, owners of capital, and land-owners, whose respective sources of income are wages, profit and ground-rent, in other words, wage-labourers, capitalists and land-owners, constitute then three big classes of modern society based upon the capitalist mode of production.[7]

This definition captures the simplified social polarity of nineteenth-century England. But it is inadequate for the much more differentiated class structure of the twenty-first century.

As Marx anticipated, capitalism increasingly reduced the numbers of individual producers in agriculture and other forms of self-employment. Capitalism brought all the economically active members of the population into wage labour and subject to his version of the labour theory of value which entailed exploitation:

> In proportion, as the bourgeoisie grows in wealth, the proletariat grows in numbers. For, since the proletarians can be employed only by capital, and since capital extends only through employing labor, it follows that the growth of the proletariat proceeds at precisely the same pace as the growth of capital.
>
> Simultaneously, this process draws members of the bourgeoisie and proletarians together into the great cities where industry can be carried on most profitably, and by thus throwing great masses in one spot it gives to the proletarians a consciousness of their own strength. Moreover, the further this process advances and the more new labor-saving machines are invented, the greater is the pressure exercised by big industry on wages, which, as we have seen, sink to their minimum and therewith render the condition of the proletariat increasingly unbearable. The growing dissatisfaction of the proletariat thus joins with its rising power to prepare a proletarian social revolution.[8]

Marx was correct in identifying the general trends in the labour market. In the USA in 1776, 80% of the non-slave population derived income from their own property and labour; by 1980, 90% of the economically active population was in paid labour. All the industrialised countries have followed this pattern. These developments in the composition of the labour force potentially provide the economic basis for the predicted antagonistic conflict between the bourgeoisie and working class. The higher the number employed in wage labour and the more wages fall, the greater the production of surplus value and the higher the rate of exploitation. Consequently, for Marx, an inexorable rise in (socialist) class consciousness occurred.

However, Marx's prediction was mistaken. As capitalism developed, wage labour increased, but a rising proportion of employees were not creating economic surplus as their labour was not valorised through the market. In the core capitalist countries, a growing number of employees were in receipt of transfer payments from state employment (state workers, such as teachers, civil servants, the police and the military) or from the provision of personal services (eg private security guards, domestic helpers). Such work did not increase surplus value. A further development was that the occupational structure of the working class became more differentiated with the displacement of the manual working class by non-manual occupations. A significant stratum of executive employees has ambiguous class relations: they contribute to economic surplus but concurrently manage labour to extract surplus.

These developments are accepted by writers such as Hardt and Negri, Paul Mason and Alexandr Buzgalin, who propose, misleadingly I believe, that the class structure described by Marx no longer exists. According to this argument, the rise of creative labour or 'immaterial labour' enables production independently of the ownership and control of capital. Immaterial labour, embodied in producing knowledge and communication, becomes dominant in the workforce and replaces the traditional proletariat engaged in manufacturing (Hardt and Negri 2000, 29). Such writers contend that the digital economy enables a collaborative economy to develop outside capitalist relations of production. 'The cooperative aspect of immaterial labour is not imposed or organised from the outside, as it was in previous forms of labour, but rather, cooperation is completely immanent to the labouring activity itself' (Hardt and Negri 2000, 294). Wikipedia is probably the best example such writers have in mind. In post-industrial society, individual creative production gives rise to collective cooperative activity; networks replace and surpass capitalist hierarchies of production relations.

Digital media provide an active network of participants replacing the passive consumers of print technology. Such writers claim that these forms of labour produce use value, not exchange value – hence the term 'post-capitalist'. The internet becomes a creative tool for individual participants. There is a shift in this way of thinking from collective action to spontaneity and autonomy. Political organisation (through parties) is replaced by 'the multitude', and hierarchy by networks. It assumes that the multitude will spontaneously foment a socialist society.

The rise of digital capitalism does not abolish economic exploitation. 'Immaterial' labour involved in information technology performing creative work, rather than in productive work, is still embodied in products which are valorised by media corporations. Neo-liberal capitalism, through the processes of financialization, has enormously widened the scope of market activity and profit making. The state increasingly outsources its activities to private business. Cooperative forms of labour operate in the cracks of capitalism – not at its centre. Media corporations dominate the digital economy. These corporations are capitalist and produce surplus value (see Birkinbine 2017). The digital economy is dominated by the corporate elites controlling profit-maximising companies predicated on neoliberal ideology – to the detriment of democratic control and participation. Contradictions within the technological constitution of capitalism lead to economic crises, not to a challenge to capitalism.

These writers are 'scientific marxists'. The disintegration of capitalism, they claim, is a consequence of the laws of historical materialism. There is an absence of institutional agents to bring about change. Leninist and social-democratic instruments are rejected. Spontaneity and individual autonomy are the sources of revolutionary change. For Antonio Negri, the 'multitude', defined as 'a totality of cooperating singularities', becomes the 'social dynamic' (Negri 2008, 257). And, as Mason (2015, 31) puts it: 'The revolutionary subject is the self'.

In the twenty-first century, in the major capitalist countries, rather than proletarian class consciousness derived from production relations, identity politics was created on the basis of the differentiation of the labour force as well as on social status derived from distinctive forms of consumption. The mass media have promoted individual identities derived from relations of subordination, discrimination and oppression related to ethnicity, caste, gender and age. Such relations also include forms of domination/subordination predating capitalism.

Academia has promoted a concept of class in the context of culture and values. In so doing, an ideological shift has relegated class to a concept similar in standing to gender, caste, race and nationality. This approach moves substantially away from Marx's own paradigm and denies class any revolutionary potential. Drawing on Pierre Bourdieu, writers reconstitute class with an emphasis on its relational and symbolic aspects.[9] Consequently, they move away from the traditional focus on economic relationships to consider 'non-economic capitals' (cultural, social, symbolic) and dwell on how people behave – how they dress, how they live and form identities and how they cope with life in general (Skeggs 2004).

Ernesto Laclau illustrates this shift. He sets the plurality of the social structure in the late twentieth century in a post-Marxist mould:

> For classical Marxism, the possibility of transcending capitalist society depended on the simplification of social structure and the emergence of a privileged agent of social change, while for us, the possibility of a democratic transformation of society depends on a proliferation of new subjects of change. (Laclau 1990, 41)

In my view, such a 'proliferation' of social and political grievances, reflected in ethnic, racial, caste, generational and gender politics, leads to a fragmented form of identity politics – and one which does not challenge capitalism. It is quite erroneous to consider that, in nineteenth-century capitalist societies, oppression based on caste, gender and ethnic origin was unknown to Marx. Quite the contrary: such oppression and subjugation were even greater then than in the twenty-first century. Clearly, these forms of subjugation may have overlapped with and even deepened class division. But the form taken by exploitation and the related class conflict was and is much more important.

The academic deconstruction of class politics has formulated a new critical synthesis in the form of identity protest politics. Identity politics calls for justice and equal rights before the law; worthy causes – but not the transformation of capitalism. It promotes individual liberation which is certainly a form of emancipation, but not the eradication of economic exploitation. This form of 'post Marxism' redefines class as shaped by culture and values. It evades the crucial assertion by Marx that exploitation is the principal contradiction of capitalism. It therefore does not qualify as active Marxism. Moreover, endorsing more equal access to unequal structures of ownership and domination may strengthen, not weaken, the composition of the class system based on property or administrative power. Such politics, predicated on equality of opportunity, do not address the sources of economic exploitation which remains a driving force of capitalism. Marx and Engels, in the Communist Manifesto, noted subordination of different kinds coexisting with class in different modes of production.[10] Such subordination continues under capitalism. Economic exploitation may be associated with, and may even strengthen, other forms of coercion, domination and discrimination which have their own institutional causes.

The changing nature of capital

Transcending capitalism calls for an economic concept of class having not only national but also international scope. Class structures have become globalised. The form of ownership of productive assets has also changed dramatically in major respects compared to nineteenth-century England. In the leading capitalist countries has occurred a depersonalisation of the capitalist class. The global joint-stock corporation has replaced the national capitalist entrepreneur/investor and has led to fragmented non-personal forms of ownership. Financial instruments and funds have displaced the nineteenth-century private shareholder in the national limited joint stock company. The pattern of accumulation has shifted from commodity production to financial channels in which profits accrue through financial instruments, rather than through trade and commodity production (Orhangazi 2008, 864; on financialisation see van der Zwan 2014). 'Capital' takes a more abstract and less personalised form. The geographical spread of productive forces has led to corporations becoming global in ownership and control. Multi-national corporations have replaced national capitalist firms.

The ruling class now includes globalising politicians (notables such as Donald Trump, Tony Blair when Prime Minister of the UK, and Jean-Claude Juncker, President of the European Commission) who manage politics on an international scale. International institutions (the WTO, the IMF, the World Bank) have arisen which coordinate the global economic system. The dominant financial and manufacturing bourgeoisie takes a new global form.

Deterritorialisation also segments the working class which has not declined numerically on a global scale. As international companies seek to reduce labour costs, the greater mobility of capital and cheapening of transport enable manufacturing to be located in areas of low-paid labour. Digital technology through electronic communication facilitates the unrestricted mobility of capital, thus changing the combination of the factors of production in low-income countries. Hence, the focus on class conflict (what Marx described as 'one national class-interest', Manifesto 1958, 35) can no longer be contained within the boundaries of the nation state. A globalised capitalist class replaces, and is distinct from, national class formations.

Advances in technology have led to an enormous increase in the productive forces of capitalism. Despite the cyclical nature of capitalism, workers –even if unemployed in the post-industrial countries – have secured basic subsistence and, helped by the falling prices of manufactured goods and agricultural commodities, consequent on technical advance, have even experienced improvements in living conditions. Consumption becomes more important in people's lives than production. And 'consumerism' arises as an integrating ideology and a focus for individual status and identity. Such conditions, on the one hand, and discrimination against marginalised groups, on the other, are the sociological basis for greater individualisation and concurrently the rise of a politics of identity. The consequence is the absence of a working-class political consciousness which Marx thought would ripen and provide the stimulus for a revolutionary change in the relations to the means of production. This gives rise to quite a different political scenario in the advanced capitalist societies of Western Europe and the USA to that anticipated by Marx and his followers in the nineteenth and early twentieth centuries.

The 'scientific' Marxist would contend that the consequent dismantling of the European state socialist societies in the late twentieth century, and their reversion to private ownership and market coordination, illustrates that the level of productive forces was insufficiently advanced to sustain a communist mode of production. The attempt to move beyond the capitalist mode of production, they claim, was premature. 'Active Marxism' has limits. It can fail. Consequently, one is prompted to consider what socialist structures and processes are needed to supersede capitalism. The challenge of an alternative remains. What lessons are to be learned from the dismantling of the planned economies in the European states in the twenty-first century? If the level of productive forces was not appropriate for a socialist mode of production, does the experience of the socialist countries undermine the strategy of 'active Marxism'? Unlike Alvin Gouldner, I have argued that significant advances were made under the socialist order and that the political leadership, in the terminal stages of the Soviet Union, was faulty and failed to transform the institutions of planning.

Conclusions

I have distinguished between Marx's theorising as a method of social analysis and Marxism as a political strategy, as praxis. Marx's intellectual achievement was an innovative conception of the evolution of societies (an exercise in social Darwinism) and the proposal that the economic processes of capitalism would lead to socialism. For Marx, history promised the introduction of a communist mode of production which accepted the positive aspects of modernisation brought about by capitalist society. Socialism would supersede it by delivering modernisation without economic exploitation. Inherent to Marx's approach is that the dynamics of capitalism would lead to a socialist world economic order. Scientific Marxists envisaged the collapse of capitalism consequent on the resolution of its contradictions.

Marx motivated his followers to change the world in situations not of their own choosing. Adopting a Leninist path, active Marxism in the state socialist societies succeeded in abolishing class-based economic exploitation and became a model in many countries of the Third World. In the context of the level of the productive forces in the socialist countries, the planned economy was a significant advance. However, state socialism as a social formation did not resolve other forms of domination. Capitalism as a world system has not capitulated to socialism. Indeed, the European socialist formations set up in the twentieth century have been dismantled.

All the countries of the world have been drawn into the capitalist order; capitalism has continued to grow and spread, and its developments have confounded Marx's predictions. Its contradictions have been resolved, at least partially, through forms of coordination and control exercised by the state and increasingly by regional and global institutions. The polarisation of class struggle, anticipated by Marx, has been occluded by a much more differentiated occupational system promoting a pluralistic and socially diverse political process. Capitalism has moved from chaotic competition to a more organised form constituted by global financial and non-financial companies and transnational institutions. The cyclical development of capitalism continues. World capitalism has shown a capability for diffusion and adaptation. It is conditioned by variations which exist in different economic and political formations.

'Scientific Marxism', like 'Darwinism' in the physical world, is subject to revision in the light of new facts and theories. Marx's materialist approach has been widely accepted, while many of his political predictions have been discarded. In this respect his work has been absorbed to various degrees by different subjects in the humanities and social sciences; it has influenced political parties and legitimated political leaders; and it remains a fertile but debatable approach to our understanding of world history. Marx made a significant contribution to the understanding of the nineteenth-century class structure of capitalism. His knowledge is limited to the society he knew at the time. To overcome the tendency to reductionism, Marx's approach might be developed with insights from other theories and approaches. Bureaucracy, patriarchy, militarism and credentialism (the exercise of 'expert' knowledge) also constitute forms of political and economic power and have their own laws of development. Social discrimination and political domination should be distinguished from economic exploitation. Such forms of power sometimes overlap with the interests of economic classes, but they are primarily performed by social groups and elites sometimes operating on behalf of nation states or international organisations.

It is mistaken to attribute all the malformations, inadequacies and injustices to inherent faults or contradictions in the class structures of capitalist or socialist regimes. Other problems, such as those concerned with environmental exploitation as well as the consequences of nuclear war, have assumed greater importance in the twenty-first century and were not anticipated by Marx's historical materialism. To understand current international conflict, Thucydides provides a geo-strategic dimension unheeded by Marx. The oppression of marginalised groups has cultural and historical roots. Cultural values are deeply engrained and prove obstinate to change. These dimensions of power might be shaped by, but are not constituent parts of, economic exploitation and should be analysed separately. Moreover, they cannot be equated with economic exploitation – Marx has been vindicated in giving to the ownership of private property and economic surplus obtained through market relationships a qualitatively different level of power than other forms of domination and discrimination.

The digital/post-industrial structures are a more advanced stage of capitalism than that known by Marx. The relations to the means of production in the current world system are driven by corporate capital to expand production and to further profit. The dynamics – the extraction of surplus value – are essentially what Marx described. In the context of such disparities, concerted human action, an 'active' Marxism, is required. The various 'embryos' of change detected by post-capitalist writers will not lead to a spontaneous collapse. The new social movements, the communal non-profit associations, the social and political forms of identity are real enough; but they do not challenge the essential class relations of capitalism.

The legacy of Marx is an important contribution to the analysis of nineteenth-century capitalism, and a major – but not the only – contribution to our understanding of societies in the twenty-first century. As Darwinism has been both modified, developed and sometimes discarded in the physical sciences, so too must Marx's thinking be absorbed into a current critique of capitalism to achieve the goal of human emancipation. In the twenty-first century, Marx's followers, particularly in the West, have addressed the unfolding structural components of capitalist society. They have not, however, devised any instruments of political change to move to socialism; Leninist political praxis has been rejected but has not been replaced.

Disclosure statement

No potential conflict of interest was reported by the author.

Notes

1. The linkage is best known from Friedrich Engels' speech of 1883 in which he explicitly compares Marx's discovery of the law of human history to Darwin's law of the development of nature (Engels F, p.13).
2. Alvin Gouldner distinguished between two Marxisms: scientific and critical.
3. Theses on Feuerbach (written 1845), Marx Engels Archive. Accessed 4 June 2018. Available at https://www.marxists.org/archive/marx/works/1845/theses/theses.htm
4. Luxemburg (1904). Most of the social-democratic parties of Western Europe preferred the course of electoral change predicated on trade union based socialist parties (See Gay P. 1952).
5. Mark Carney, as reported in the *Daily Telegraph*, April 14, 2018.
6. Paul Mason, *New Statesman*, May 4–10, 2018, quotation from p. 31.
7. "Revenues and their Sources," Chapter 52: Classes, in *Capital*, vol. III, part VII. Available at https://www.marxists.org/archive/marx/works/1894-c3/ch52.htm

8. Karl Marx and Frederick Engels, "Manifesto of the Communist Party," section 11.February 1848. Available at https://www.marxists.org/archive/marx/works/download/doc/Manifesto.doc
9. See e.g. F. Devine, M. Savage, J. Scott and R. Crompton. For Russia, a similar position is taken by authors in *Rethinking Class in Russia*, edited by Suvi Salmenniemi, p. 120.
10. See section under 'bourgeoisie and proletarians'.

Bibliography

Birkinbine, B.J. (Eds), et al. 2017. *Global Media Giants*. Routledge: New York and Abingdon.

Buzgalin, A., and A. Kolganov. 2016. "Critical Political Economy: The 'Market-Centric' Model of Economic Theory Must Remain in the past- Notes of the post-Soviet School of Critical Marxism." *Cambridge Journal of Economics* 40 (2): 575–598. doi:10.1093/cje/beu080.

Devine, F., M. Savage, J. Scott and R. Crompton (Eds.). 2005. *Rethinking Class: Culture, Identity and Lifestyle*. Basingstoke: Palgrave.

Engels, F., 1951. *Speech at the Graveside of Karl Marx, Selected Works*. Moscow: Foreign Languages Publishing House, 153.

Engels, F., 1987. "The Principles of Communism." In *Collected Works of Marx and Engels*. Vol. 25. http://www.marxists.org/archive/marx/works/1847/11/prin-com.htm.

Gay, Y. 1952. The Dilemma of Democratic Socialism: Eduard Bernstein's Challenge to Marx. New York: Columbia University Press.

Gouldner, A. 1980. *The Two Marxisms*. Basingstoke: Macmillan.

Grundrisse. 1977. *Selected Writings*, edited by David McLellan, Karl Marx. Oxford: Oxford University Press.

Hardt, M., and A. Negri. 2000. *Empire*. Cambridge, Mass: Harvard University Press.

Laclau, E. 1990. *New Reflections on the Revolution of Our Time*. London: Verso.

Lenin. 1920. http://www.marxists.org/archive/lenin/works/1920/apr/lwc/ch09.htm.

Lukacs, G. 1970. *Lenin (Originally Published 1924)*. London: New Left Books.

Luxemburg, R. 1961. "Leninism or Marxism (1904)." In *The Russian Revolution and Marxism or Leninism*. Ann Arbor: University of Michigan Press.

Manifesto. 1958. *The Communist Manifesto, Marx-Engels Collected Works*. Moscow: FLPH.

Marx, Karl, and Jules Guesde. 1880. The Programme of the Parti Ouvrier. https://www.marxists.org/archive/marx/works/1880/05/parti-ouvrier.htm

Mason, P. 2015. *PostCapitalism: A Guide to Our Future*. London: Allen Lane.

McLellan, D (Ed.). 1983. *Marx: The First 100 Years*. Oxford: Fontana press.

Negri, A. 2008. "Afterword: on the Concept of Revolution." In *Revolution in the Making of the Modern World*, edited by J. Foran, D. Lane and A. Zivkovic, 252–260. London: Routledge.

Nove, A. 1979. *Political Economy and Soviet Socialism*. London: Allen and Unwin.

Orhangazi, O. 2008. "Financialisation and Capital Accumulation in the Non-Financial Corporate Sector: A Theoretical and Empirical Investigation on the US Economy: 1973–2003." *Cambridge Journal of Economics* 32 (6): 863–886. doi:10.1093/cje/ben009.

Parsons, T. 1967. *Sociological Theory and Modern Society*, 109–110. New York: Free Press. Cited by M. Burawoy. Introduction: The Resurgence of Marxism in American Sociology, *American Journal of Sociology*, Vol 88, Supplement (1982). doi:10.1086/649250.

Skeggs, B. 2004. *Class, Self, Culture*. London: Routledge.

Stedman Jones, G. 2017. *Karl Marx*. London: Penguin Books.

Salmenniemi, S. (Ed.). 2012. *Rethinking Class in Russia*. Farnham, Surrey: Ashgate.

Sweezy, P. 1980. *Post-Revolutionary Society*, 139–151. New York: Monthly Review Press. doi:10.14452/MR-032-06-1980-10_1.

Therborn, G. 2008. *From Marxism to Post-Marxism*. London: Verso.

UNDP. 1991. *United Nations, Human Development Report 1991*. New York and Oxford: Oxford University Press.

van der Zwan, N. 2014. "State of the Art: Making Sense of Financialization." *Socio-Economic Review* 12, 1: 99–129. doi:10.1093/ser/mwt020.

Culture and revolution: Bakhtin, Mayakovsky and Lenin (disalienation as [social] creativity)

Aleksandr Buzgalin [iD] and Lyudmila Bulavka-Buzgalina

ABSTRACT

The article shows the dialectic of the relationship of revolution and culture as two sides of creativity - social and art. In a dialogue with the philosophy of Mikhail Bakhtin, the authors reveal culture as the removal of alienation (disalienation) in the process of subject-subjective dialogue, in which a qualitatively new reality is created – Truth, Beauty, Good, a new person is born - a man-creator, and as such, culture is revolutionary. The second side of this connection - the revolution as a culture - is revealed by the authors on the example of the social creativity of revolutionary Russia, the poet of which was Vladimir Mayakovsky. The article gives a panorama of the historical practices of art and social creativity of the 1920s. The authors show that the counterpoint to these practices was the relationship of conformism, bureaucracy and other forms of social alienation which led the Soviet project to the dead end. The authors conclude that disalienation in the social and cultural spheres is possible only to the extent that the sociopolitical revolutionary changes are carried out in unity with the liberation of the cultural potential of the masses, and art creativity is interfaced (united) with social creativity.

Affinities between Bakhtin and Lenin may appear improbable. For most humanitarian intellectuals, and not only in Russia, the first of these is almost a sacred figure, a symbol of spirituality and refined intellect.[1] The second is, for many, a symbol if not of pure evil then at least of political pragmatism, and of destruction, though minorities in Russia and the West evaluate Vladimir Ulyanov-Lenin's contributions to social theory and the progress of society in a more appropriately balanced manner.[2] What of Mayakovsky? Though it may appear that we are inserting him, rather artificially, as a bridge between Bakhtin and Lenin, the figure of this widely admired poet and revolutionary will emerge in a far richer role in what follows.

Today left-wing sentiments are so strong that a report for the US president[3] and an article in the *Economist*[4] speak of them as major threats. Thirty years after 'the end of history'[5] was proclaimed, the *end of the 'end of history'* is upon us. The neoliberal epoch is ending. What is going to replace it?

Admittedly, few today anticipate revolutionary socialist change. However, even 'reformist' demands can make a beginning. But why do we associate our discourse of revolution with culture? Today, Revolution is widely considered the antipode of Culture, as its destruction. At the risk of appearing too ambitious, we hope to demonstrate both that *culture is revolutionary in its essence* and that *revolution is creative, and is successful only when it is cultured*.

These theses may *seem* outrageous. Our task, however, is not to scandalise people, but to conduct a theoretical investigation, though our style may exceed the purely academic. Indeed, we aim, in line with Bakhtin's method, at a *dialogue* with the reader. Let us begin it from first principles, setting out definitions and the socio-philosophical context like pieces on the chess board at the beginning of our game.

1. Culture as revolution: creativity versus alienation. Bakhtin and Lenin

First, the dramatis personae: Mikhail Bakhtin was a Soviet philosopher and literary scholar. Scholars, Western and Soviet, have focused on different aspects of his brief books. We are concerned with two.

First, there is Bakhtin's understanding of the Renaissance as a revolutionary shift in cultural paradigms. In *François Rabelais and the Popular Culture of the Middle Ages and Renaissance*,[6] he appeals to Rabelais and the popular creativity of that epoch. Bakhtin did not see 'Rabelaisianism' as the antithesis of Culture but as a different Culture – new, negating the primarily religious, 'spiritual' 'high' culture and affirming a new, real, earthly culture.

The second important aspect of Bakhtin's thought is his vision of culture as a process, as the result of the co-creativity, a dialogue between co-equal subjects. In the resulting dialectical coupling and negation, there is no object, and no subordination. Taking Dostoevsky's novels as an instance, Bakhtin shows that the author and the literary hero are subjects. The latter breaks free of subordination to the writer and enters into a dialogue with him or her. The person who might seem to be only a puppet in the hands of a puppeteer is transformed into the co-author of the drama.

The real-life analogue to this occurs when a person who breaks free of alienation becomes a subject, not just the slave of objective laws but also their creator, not just a puppet but also the co-author of the drama – which, moreover, is no mere puppet show. Indeed, this co-author is now writing not a play but history, an alternative to the alienated subordination of the human individual to external social forces. We recall the opposition that gripped Hamlet: 'To be, or not to be: that is the question'.

Bakhtin's hero chooses to *be*.[7] The Subject in dialogue with another Subject does not submit to her, nor subordinate her; the two co-create. They carry out *deeds*. They assert the *integrity of being* – that which distinguishes a deed from the movements of a puppet, since a deed is an act that is performed freely. Both aspects are important here. In the first place, action is *free*; becoming cognisant of the laws of being both of Culture and of History, the subject of action chooses what needs to be done in order to realise the imperatives of progress. Second, *action* is free; the subject is not only cognisant of necessity, but he or she acts, carrying out deeds, changing the world in accordance with the laws of development of this world, laws that are known by the person who is carrying out the deeds.

Subjects who carry out deeds break the chains of alienation. They disalienate this world. They create culture and history. Do we not already have here something consonant with the music of Revolution?

This is how the problem must be posed. We cast light on the concepts of 'co-creativity', 'subject-subjective dialogue' and 'deed', using not only Bakhtin but also the critical Soviet scholars Evald Ilyenkov, Nal Zlobin, Genrikh Batishchev, Vadim Mezhuev and others[8] whose works share the concerns of their Western contemporaries such as Bertell Ollman,[9] István Mészáros[10] and Adam Schaff.[11]

The keys to this complex of concepts are alienation/disalienation and co-creation, since what is Revolution if not the removal of relations of social alienation – that is, disalienation? And what is Culture, if it is not co-creation in the unity of its subject (of the person who creates and deobjectifies the phenomenon of culture, and who in the process becomes subjectivised culture, a culture-subject), of its result (the phenomenon of culture, in which the creator reflects the world and himself or herself as the subject of this creation) and of the very process of co-creation, the dialogue of subjects?

Let us begin with the concepts of 'alienation' and 'disalienation'. The content of the first category is well known for Marxists: beginning with Lukács[12] and extending into the 1960s (for a more detailed treatment, see Karl Marx[13] and the above-mentioned works by Bertell Ollman, István Mészáros, Soviet philosophers and in recent times, Marcello Musto[14]).

Alienation emerges here as a class of social relationships within which the genetically universal (to employ a term of Ilyenkov) attributes of the individual as a generic being are 'appropriated' by external forces, and become alien to and dominant over him or her.

However, the reverse process – *disalienation* – is also always present in history, returning to the individual his or her native essence to the degree that person is involved in the process of social creativity. The category of 'disalienation' was first proposed by contemporary Russian scholars and extensively developed by Lyudmila Bulavka-Buzgalina.[15] *Disalienation* refers to *the overcoming of concretely historical forms of alienation through a special type of creative activity that brings into existence not just a certain finished result (a 'thing'), but also a new social relationship that embodies the detailed logic of its co-creation (formation).* In *disalienation*, the main element is the process through which real contradictions are resolved. It emerges in *constructive intentions* (the overcoming of various forms of alienation), runs through their *actual feasibility* (to a new social relationship) and results in the *deed*.

It should be clear by now that we regard disalienation as the process of overcoming alienation by creating culture, new social relations and, thus, history. But what, then, is 'creativity'?

While the puzzle of creativity, though discussed in virtually all fields of scholarship, is still far from solved, we focus here on how Bakhtin and his colleagues conceived of it. For them, creativity is *unalienated cooperation by creators in unlimited social space and time*. Soviet critical Marxism[16] stressed that creativity is always *co*-creativity, a dialogue of all creators. So, scientists, artists and teachers create through (1) their individual activity, and (2) their dialogue with all their teachers and colleagues; with the authors of all the books they have read and the composers of the music they have listened to; with nature, understood in this case as an aesthetic and cognitive value rather than as a source of raw materials; and so forth. It follows, therefore, that the share of creativity contributed by a particular creative worker to a new creative product (which may have a material embodiment such as paper or a CD but whose content is the product of co-creativity) is fundamentally impossible. It also follows that creation is the activity not only of an educated elite, of members of the free professions, but of *all actors. It refers to 'mass' creative activity* – whose protagonists include teachers, doctors, artists, scientists, 'gardeners', social workers, engineers, librarians and so on.

Summing up the argument so far,[17] we can thus identify the following main features of creative activity as opposed to reproductive labour:

- Creativity is not just creating something new. It combines
  - o the dissemination of cultural products,[18] during which they are not consumed (though their physical embodiments might be) and
  - o creating new cultural products in the dialectical materialist sense.[19] Thus, products of creative activity
  - o are unlimited and
  - o are potentially universally accessible, since the costs of replicating cultural goods tend to decline towards zero, at which point they can be disseminated without loss.

- The result of creativity, however, is multifaceted; it is
  - o a cultural product (a work of art, a scientific or design product, a student who has learned something, or people who have become healthier physically and morally), and
  - o new creative qualities of the subject of creativity (in bringing about a new creative result, such a person grows and enriches himself or herself through this activity). As a consequence of the latter, creative activity is characterised
  - o by the property of self-motivation (creative work ceases to be a burden and turns into a need).

- Creative activity is at the same time a special social relation – a subject–subject dialogue[20] of the creator with all other cultural figures in time and space. As a result, creativity is at the same time both

  - o a universal and
  - o a purely individual activity. This dialectic is engaged whenever the creator enters into dialogue, whether in person or through correspondence, with all his or her predecessors and colleagues (that is, when he or she reads a book, listens to music, argues with friends or enjoys nature).
  - o The universality of creative activity determines that it creates a product that is a priori a universal (cultural) value.
  - o For its public recognition, it therefore does not require social and economic mediation (purchase by a market agent or some other person).
  - o Recognition of the value of such a phenomenon occurs exclusively in the process of its distribution through another creative activity (in the process of co-creation).
  - o The purely individual character of creative activity determines that it is unique and 'indispensable' (that is, it cannot be replaced by the functioning of a machine.[21]

These are the main distinctive characteristics of creative activity. At the same time, this is a detailed characterisation of Culture as a phenomenon that revolutionises society and the Individual.

* * *

This is where Lenin comes in. Contrary to contemporary approach, Lenin was not a 'great leader'. Neither before the 1917 revolution nor after its victory did the Bolshevik party have either secretaries or presidents.[22] Rather, Lenin was a leader because the others recognised his talent, not to say genius, as a practical activist and as a theoretician capable of penetrating the essence of historical processes, to pierce the depths of the dialectic of social contradictions, to see objective patterns and to act. He prevailed because he *involved himself simultaneously both in theoretical and in socio-practical creativity.* Lenin the theoretician and Lenin the practical activist were, and will remain, inseparable. He was both creator-scholar (and in this respect, a cultural worker) and creator-practician (and in this sense, a revolutionary).

In these roles, Lenin bears responsibility for defeats as well as victories, tragedies as well as the greatness of the communist emancipation of humanity. Not Lenin alone, but Lenin in the first instance.

We will speak of destruction later. First, we must address Culture as Revolution, or the revolutionary nature of culture. Here it is necessary to add an explanation: *the revolutionary nature of culture is not identical to revolutionary culture, and revolution is not only negation.* Every culture is creativity, and creativity is the creation of the new and the negation of the old, and in this sense it is always revolutionary, for revolution is always a *dialectical* negation, the unity of negation and inheritance. Culture, like revolution, is always *co*-creation, *and* therefore inheritance.

Here, the *importance of integrating the contribution of Mayakovsky* (culture as a revolutionary criticism of the past), *Bakhtin* (emphasis on dialogue, co-creation) *and Lenin* (conjugation of the political and cultural revolution as the inheritance of the entire positive tradition of cultural development and the denial of the entire system of alienation relations) is especially visible.

It is to this counterpoint that all our further analysis will be devoted. But to begin with, culture is *not only* revolutionary. It remains both *endless and uninterrupted in time and space, forming a unity of human existence*, combining the creativity of Confucius and Hesse, Rabelais and Bakhtin, Bach and Einstein. As such, it is an eternal and endless process of co-creation, a dialogue of all with all. It is not revolutionary; in dialectical terms it is the opposite of the qualitative leap, of negation. As such, it is the dialectical (that is, containing in itself unity *as well*) *negation* of revolution.

Why, then, did the greatest revolutionary of the twentieth century (and perhaps of all history up to the present), Vladimir Ulyanov-Lenin, addressing the younger generation of Russian revolutionaries at a congress of the Communist Youth League, tell them that 'You can only become a communist when you have enriched your memory with a knowledge of all the riches that humanity has devised'?[23]

Though there appears to be a pointless hypertrophy in this utterance (to assimilate *all* the cultural wealth of humanity is impossible by definition) it actually refers to the *open character of cultural being*. Entering into dialogue with Pushkin or Goethe, you immerse yourself in the world of ancient mythology, while in reading Bakhtin you unify the irreconcilable, Rabelais and Dostoevsky. When you take delight in Mayakovsky you immerse yourself in a world of astonishing tenderness, and of class struggle …

The 'secret' of Lenin's famous exhortation is simple: when you include yourself in co-creation you assimilate, in a dialogue that is endless, uninterrupted and open in terms of time (we deliberately repeat these concepts) *all* of the wealth of human culture.

That was why Lenin demanded his young followers immerse themselves in culture, adding that 'to renew our state apparatus' study was essential to ensure that 'science does not remain a dead letter or a fashionable phrase (and this, it must be confessed, happens particularly often with us), but that it penetrates into our flesh and blood, and is transformed into a constituent element of our daily lives, fully and genuinely',[24] while in the heat of a bloody struggle for communism.

This is because *the principal mission of revolution is creation*. The principal mission of the communist revolution is the co-creation of communism; and communism, the 'realm of freedom' (Marx, Engels), is nothing other than the world of culture that lies 'beyond material production in the proper sense' (Marx), beyond the 'realm of necessity'. Is this not why another great revolutionary, Karl Liebknecht, formulated his famous aphorism 'communism = culture,[25] while the profound Soviet philosopher of culture Nal Zlobin revealed the dialectic of this association in a brilliant text?[26]

Finally, we can answer the question Why is culture revolutionary? Quite simply because it is co-creation, the creation of that which does not yet exist, and hence the dialectical negation of that which is. That is what revolution is, defined philosophically: the physics of Einstein negates (but does not do away with) the physics of Newton, and the geometry of Lobachevsky, the geometry of Euclid. Romanticism negates classicism, and realism, the romantic .... *All creativity is the dialectics of creation and negation, and here, revolutionary creativity is no exception.*

For precisely this reason, Culture is that which *dialectically* negates revolution.

It is now time to reverse the order our concepts, and to pose the question of Revolution as the *dialectical* negation of culture and insert Mayakovsky into our discourse.

2. Revolution as culture: the Proletkult and/or Soviet culture. Lenin and Mayakovsky

Vladimir Mayakovsky not only won a world reputation, for Soviet citizens he was, and for us he remains, the greatest poet of the Soviet epoch. On the one hand, Mayakovsky was a lyricist of exquisite delicacy ('If the stars catch fire, it's because someone needs it ...', 'Listen to me, violin ...'). On the other hand, he was a poet of *Revolution*, a tribune of the masses ('I want the pen to be like the bayonet ...', 'But if the lowly flock into the party – surrender, enemy, fall and die ...'

Both these sides of Mayakovsky are widely known. It is less widely appreciated that the young Mayakovsky, born into a family of the gentry, had become a Bolshevik revolutionary, and before his sixteenth birthday had been arrested and jailed, before he became a poet. After the victory of the Revolution he did not join the party (the ruling party!), but did more for the revolution than thousands of functionaries, and stated with complete justification: 'I shall raise, like a Bolshevik party card, all hundred volumes of my party booklets'.[27] For us, Mayakovsky personifies the synthesis of Culture and Revolution.

At the age of 36, he committed suicide. Why? Did this deed (and it was unquestionably a *deed*) bear witness to the failure of his attempt at *just this* synthesis?

We need to approach this question with care. The answer emerges out of the contradictory interaction of Revolution and Culture after the revolutionary victory in Russia.

To understand how the contradictions arose and were resolved, we must turn to the historical practices through which the revolutionary masses came to be included in culture, beginning with the most striking example, *the Proletkult*.

Contradictory though it was, the experience of the Proletkult revealed how people have the kind of social being that presupposes not a routine, but a creative relationship with culture, one that guarantees the discovery of their vital strengths. It also revealed how this tie to world culture is 'grounded' in material social interests, since all other ties are at risk of disintegrating when they first encounter reality.

Proletkult was launched in very unpromising circumstances – in the conditions of the Civil War and of the subsequent rebuilding efforts. These very constraints revealed correspondingly starkly the immanent laws governing that interaction, along with its limitations and robustness. They also made the objective necessity of a link between the revolutionary individual and culture all the more manifest. As long as the First World War lasted, the revolutionary development of the proletariat gathered strength, because the ruling class and the intellectual 'elite' seemed unfit to resolve the powerful contradictions that held Russia and the world in their grip. With a stiffening resolve, the proletariat took to the barricades in three revolutions, giving its own answer to the question of power and property. Ultimately, it posed the question Where was the culture for which it had faced death, the culture that would be *About the proletariat, For the proletariat, By the proletariat*?

This is why the question of the 'construction of a new culture' – of a culture permeated by the ideas of socialism – was posed by the advocate of the Proletkult such as the journal *Proletarskaya Kultura* [*Proletarian Culture*] in 1919:

> It is also completely vain and pointless to try to find somewhere an epoch, or an artistic current, out of which one might fish an art for the present-day struggling proletariat. There is no such epoch, and no such artistic current. History does not repeat itself.[28]

So where did the revolutionary class acquire its culture? Alienated from the world cultural heritage by all of its preceding history, the proletariat objectively could not create it, not yet.

So, does the *class* (the intelligentsia prefers the word 'people') that creates the material preconditions not just for the development of culture, but also for the vital activity of its subject, have the right to what it creates?

What matters here is the claim of the proletariat or of ordinary people to the *status of subject* in the world of *culture*. It was a demand for a new type of humanism, oriented towards the creative liberation of genuine relations: '*we shall build our own, our new world*'. The moment the proletariat became the subject of history, of political power, it demanded the kind of culture that expressed its hopes and longings and embodied the kind of artistic vision that would provide workers and artists alike with the possibility of understanding themselves, their social situation and their prospects. As Bakhtin might put it, they could now enter into dialogue with the world of culture and the world of social creativity as subjects. The proletariat demanded a *new* culture that would be bound up with its life and activity.

This call for a *renewal* of culture was made when the objective state in which culture found itself on the eve of the October Revolution was assessed as critical.

On the one hand, it could not cope with the acute social contradictions of the First World War. Its ability to represent everyday life was exhausted, its symbolism hid behind the theatre curtain, and futurism offered only the writhing of fractured form and meaning.

On the other hand, the internal contradictions of culture were locked away as before in old social forms that blocked their development. The essence of this crisis was expressed by Aleksandr Blok in his article "Krushenie gumanizma" ["The Collapse of Humanism"]: 'Creative labour is replaced by joyless toil, and discoveries yield first place to inventions. Everything is multiple, and nothing is unified; the cement needed for cohesion is no longer present. The spirit of music has flown away ....'[29]

Culture had lost its value-orientation, its measure of humanism, its organic creativity, its ethical tension, its universality and its content. Public consciousness of the cultural crisis led directly to the demand for a *new* culture.

On the eve of the October Revolution of 1917, this demand took two forms:

- *ideological*, demanding a proletarian culture that would correspond meaningfully to the interests of the proletariat as the subject of a socialist 'reloading' of the collective being;
- and *cultural*, aimed at the liberation of Culture from the earlier social forms that had fettered it, and that would link it with the main line of social progress that would open up for it a new artistic and social being.

These demands would not be fulfilled as a matter of revolutionary course. Culture is both pervasive and requires constant revolutionary self-renewal.

Lenin responded by stressing the necessity and importance of subordinating matters of culture to the tasks of revolution while also rejecting the idea of proletarian culture as a *special* culture. That would encourage 'theoretically incorrect and effectively harmful ... attempts to concoct one's own special culture, to shut oneself up in one's own isolated organisations'.[30] After all, the task of the proletariat and of the socialist revolution is nothing other than to do away with itself as a class, along with the ending of class society in general.

It should be emphasised that for Lenin the economic and political revolution and the cultural revolution were inseparable, because the purpose of economic and political transformations was to create the prerequisites for the progress of the Human individual, of Culture.[31]

If, however, the proletariat, in heroically and productively realising itself as a subject – that is, as a creator of history – was incapable of being the creator of its own culture, why, then, wage these historic battles? In the name of what? Solely in the name of a crust of bread and political hegemony? If so, what was socialist about the October Revolution?

If not, where were the revolutionary masses to obtain their culture if they could not create it? From the intelligentsia? Would and could it help? Why would it serve interests and tastes other than its own? And if the proletariat could not create 'its own' science and 'its own' art, was the road to creativity not closed to it? After all, culture was hardly the sole field of creativity. That the hard physical labour of the proletariat was rather remote from creativity and would remain so for some time made the matter all the more urgent. Indeed, was it at all possible to end the alienation of the revolutionary masses from culture?

The explosion of social contradictions that was October 1917 left only one course for the dialectical resolution of these questions: the *inclusion of the revolutionary masses in social creativity* through social relations that enabled the resolution of existing contradictions. The revolution needed forms of social development that would permit the development of the individual as a subject of history and culture.

That was how social creativity, as creativity of a new type, resolved the above-mentioned contradiction. When the proletarian individual could not be included in artistic or scientific creativity, social creativity became a universally accessible form in the first place, of the development of the creative potential of the individual, and second, of the realisation of the individual as the subject of creativity.

The masses needed social creativity in the revolutionary period to break out of the economic crisis, out of the collapse of social and political institutions, out of the disintegrating bonds and traditions in the area of culture, out of the heat and violence when the age-old antagonism of inter-class opposition was broken through. These needs arose first from material activity associated with the construction of the new life and with attempts to defend, through bitter struggle, the conquests involved; and second, from the vital need of the individual to understand what his or her real interests and prospects consisted of.

This is why social creativity, as a form of the creation of a fundamentally *new social system*, became a crucially important precondition for the formation of a qualitatively *new* social subject – the *new human individual* (the subject of history and culture).

* * *

This *transformation of Revolution into Culture* became a hugely important problem, and at the same time, a vital conquest of the Revolution. There were only three tests of progress along this path – the path of the development *of the creator*, *of the Revolution* and *of the creator of Culture*.

The first of these tests was the Proletkult itself, a system of relations within whose space the semi-literate worker, soldier or peasant joined clubs in order to begin writing poems, painting pictures or staging plays. Such people also joined technology circles, developed sporting societies, learned to make aeroplanes and dirigibles, learned to *fly* (how much the theme of the sky, of flight, of striving upwards suffused early Soviet society is clear if one walks with head upturned through the entrance hall of the 'Mayakovskaya' metro station).

Did the workers and peasants create works of artistic genius, and did they give birth to technical inventions and scientific discoveries? Very rarely. So why was it, then, that in a half-starved country ruined by the Great War and the Civil War, vast sums were spent on these clubs?

The answer is at once unusually complex and strikingly simple. It is complex, because it was hardly pragmatic: the Proletkult did not yield profits, and did not even 'produce' works of art. It is simple because the Proletkult fulfilled one of the Revolution's primary aims – *giving the revolutionary masses access to culture. The circles and societies of workers, peasants and youth did not create an actual body of Culture; they created new, unalienated relations with regard to the inclusion of working people in Culture. They disalienated the estrangement of the toilers from Culture that had existed for centuries.*[32]

We would like to emphasise once again: the task of the Proletkult was mainly not to make poets from workers, but to create social relations that would make possible dialogue, mutual understanding between the worker and the poet.

Unquestionably, the semi-literate workers wrote primitive plays and were second-rate actors. However, under the Proletkult, they entered into a real dialogue with art, with science and with engineering, alongside the intelligentsia, as equal *subjects of co-creation* (here, these categories of Bakhtin are more than appropriate), and not objects of instruction. Thanks to these dialogues, the semi-literate toilers entered into relationships and activity that enabled them to *de-objectify* the phenomena of culture. In the process, they became co-creators of culture, *dialectically sublating Revolution in Culture.*

The second test of this transformation was *the Leninist plan for cultural revolution*, put into action not long before Lenin's death. It sought a qualitative change in daily life through the development of Culture and of the human individual, a plan for the development of the Revolution through the formation of Culture, through a leap 'to the other side' of the world of cultural deprivation. This was not just about ending illiteracy, or developing professional and technical education. It was to shape a new life, animated by co-creation and with the individual as its subject. This would be a new life in all its manifestations, from inclusion in art and technical creativity to participation by workers in managing their enterprises and the country. Co-creation, as was stressed earlier, is a field of Culture. Once again we witness how Bakhtin, perhaps unconsciously, become a philosopher who perpetuated the thinking and practice of Lenin, however monstrous that might sound to the refined intellectuals who emasculate Bakhtin's heritage, transforming him almost into a precursor of postmodernism.[33]

The third test was the life and creativity of Mayakovsky, the poet who in the very essence of his vital poetic activity was a Revolutionary. That was how he wrote his poems – orienting himself towards the transformation of the world. He did this not only when he was speaking of Lenin, or of his Soviet passport. He wrote *all* his works in that fashion. When he finished one of his most tender and lyrical poems with the words 'We are all horses, a little bit',[34] he was talking of disalienation, of an attitude unalienated to the world. This is also what he was talking about when he saw himself – the town crier, the rowdy, the ring-leader – as a puppy, as a dog-child, affecting, wanting kindness and needing to be protected.

In his satirical plays, Mayakovsky wrote of an alternative to alienation that consisted of vulgar, mean, tedious philistinism. In a surprisingly profound sense he was correct, since the Revolution, along with the USSR to which it had given birth, was ultimately brought down not by imperialist aggressors but by the Pierre Prisypkins. These were the petty-bourgeois Philistines whose unappealing visages, as time went on, were more and more often to crowd out the faces of the revolutionaries – of the people about whom the poet wrote when he dedicated his verses to his comrade Nette, to the steamship and to the man. The latter were the people with whom he talked just as people talk with their comrades, the people whose company he shared as he turned to a portrait of Lenin and affirmed:

'Hellish work
Will be done
And is being done already'

To the degree to which such a dialogue became impossible, as the authorities crossed over increasingly to what the poet detested fiercely ('Like a wolf, I would gnaw out bureaucratism …'), and as the unappealing mug of the petty-bourgeois Philistine began to press down on the revolution, Mayakovsky began to suffocate. He could not live without the air of Revolution and Culture, and took his leave. Of his own will, carrying out the deed …

3. Revolution, that gives birth to culture: the Renaissance, the USSR and the end of the 'end of history'

Social revolution is about transformation, from one state to another; whether it happens slowly or in a flash, however diverse the methods and results, whether the sacrifices are great or not, in the final accounting it represents a transition from an old to a new, more progressive social system.

However, at a time when revolutions are at a discount, when even the progressive results of Europe's bourgeois revolutions in question, how are we to judge the Russian Revolution? Did the qualitative leap that began in 1917 in the Russian Empire, and that affected all humanity during the twentieth century, represent social progress and Revolution? The answer depends on whether one considers 'progress' to be real and not a delusion of the pre-postmodern epoch. If the former, what are its criteria? How do we measure the degree of progressiveness and regressiveness of the 1917 Russian Revolution?

Our own position can be clarified.

Does social progress objectively exist? Yes. Notwithstanding the postmodern attack on 'grand narratives', the line dividing supporters and opponents of progressive reforms within capitalism and supporters and opponents of moving beyond the 'realm of necessity' towards unalienated freedom.

Are there *criteria of social progress*? Here too we can say yes. Practices that are moving humanity slowly, even if circuitously and with setbacks, in the direction of disalienation and of the development of human qualities, of dialogue with nature and so forth, are too numerous to count. The young Bolshevik Ulyanov described this very human striving in his remarks on the draft programme for the Russian Social Democratic Workers Party: not only tending to an increase in well-being, something that even monopoly capitalism might provide, but also to the *free and rounded development of human individuality.*[35] This is a formula that continues and develops the key message of the *Manifesto of the Communist Party*: 'The free development of each, as a condition of the free development of all!'[36]

Was the Revolution of 1917, in the final analysis, socialist and progressive? Yes, Lenin replied to his critics, and he was correct. Despite the most unpropitious material and cultural preconditions, and for all the bloodshed of the Civil War (unleashed only when the counterrevolution was supported by the revolt of the White Czechs and by the intervention of nearly all the antagonists of the First World War who discovered a new unity against the striving of the peoples of Russia for socialism).

On the basis of studying the balance of social creation and destruction, of cultural progress and cultural losses, of progress along the path that led towards the birth of the new human individual and that cost the lives of millions of victims, we say: yes, the revolution in the final analysis was progressive. The balance of alienation and disalienation that bore this revolution within itself, and that continues to bear it, testifies to that, though post-Soviet intellectuals continue to debate this, historical materials and evidence.[37]

Finally, we come to the question of why Revolution gives birth to culture.

Quite simply, because a social-historical rupture is a socialist revolution, a qualitative leap forward along the road of progress, only when it serves as the basis for a flourishing of culture – of science and education, of technical creativity and art (that is, of culture in all its richness), and does so by encompassing a far broader mass of citizens than before.

This follows directly from the Marxist theory of revolution, in which revolution is the dialectical negation of the earlier socio-economic formation and the creation of the preconditions for the development of the new. Revolution is the space-time of direct social creativity, of the liberation of the individual alienation and thus *a festival of the oppressed and the locomotive of history*.

Revolution, through emancipating the broad masses from (earlier) forms of alienation and transforming them into direct participants in social creativity, gives the revolutionary masses an objective interest in their inclusion in cultural co-creation. The latter becomes for them the food and drink craved by people who are hungry and who are tortured by the thirst for culture. They need culture as a weapon for transforming the world. They need it as a tool for transforming the world, as the 'bricks' with which they are to build this world, since what they are creating is a world of culture – a world of co-creation, of the New Human Individual.

The October Revolution provided an impulse for the development of science and education. It provided an impulse for the development and progress of a qualitatively great world culture – Soviet culture. In the final reckoning, tens of millions of people could place *our* above *my*, could live, create, struggle and even die so that the 'realm of freedom' could become a reality, so that 'sky-blue nameless cities' could grow up, so that people could feel their personal responsibility for the future, for the annihilation of fascism, so that the garden city could become real. Listen to these lines of Mayakovsky:

I know there will be a city,

I know that a garden will bloom,

When there are such people

In the Soviet land!

There are such people, new people who overcome alienation in themselves, in the Soviet land. Not were, are. Their historical experience is alive, just as the experience of Garibaldi's followers is alive, or that of the Decembrists …

We remember the sacrifices that pervaded the historical practice of the USSR.[38] But in this text we want to stress that *the socio-economic, political and cultural practices of the USSR and of the other countries of 'real socialism' were permeated by a powerful contradiction between their 'grey' and 'red' lines*. The first, the line of alienation, was drawn by the conformists and the bureaucratic stratum and set out to subordinate the results of the Revolution to their interests. The second, the line of social and cultural creativity, of disalienation, nevertheless remained alive, even though it was closely intertwined with the first. This 'red' line owed its vitality to the Revolution and to the Culture to which it had given birth, both of which continued throughout all those decades.

* * *

It is time to conclude. We have postulated that revolution is not only dialectical negation, but also the dialectical co-creation of culture. The latter is its motivating socio-political impulse. On its basis, we consider that the main argument in favour of the cultural-creative mission of the Revolution that began in Russia in 1917 is the fact that *in the final accounting, the Revolution served as the basis for the rise of a new type of worldwide (that is, becoming the property of the entire world!) culture – Soviet Culture.*

In the USSR, we built culture as communism.

It remains for future generations to complete the project, and to create communism as culture.

Acknowledgements

Thanks are due to the anonymous reviewers and to Andrey Kolganov for providing critical feedback and helpful suggestions, and to Olga Barashkova for help with preparing the article.

Disclosure statement

No potential conflict of interest was reported by the authors.

Notes

1. See Bibler, *M.M. Bakhtin, ili Poetika kul'tury*; Averintsev et al. *M.M. Bakhtin kak filosof*; Emerson, *First Hundred Years of M. Bachtin*; Brandist and Tihanov, *Materializing Bakhtin*; Isupov, "Lessons of M.M. Bakhtin," 7–44.
2. See Buzgalin, Bulavka, and Linke, *Lenin Online*; Budgen, Kouvelakis, and Žižek, *Lenin Reloaded: Toward a Politics of Truth*.
3. Executive Office of the President, "Markets versus Socialism."
4. The Economist, "Rise of Millennial Socialism"; the Economist, "Millennial Socialism."
5. Fukuyama, *End of History and the Last Man*.
6. Bakhtin, *Tvorchestvo Fransua Rable*.
7. It should be noted that in a number of cases Bakhtin is ranked among the forerunners of post-modernism. But the position of both Bakhtin and the authors differs from the postmodern discourse of deconstruction and desubjectivation, for we propose the logic of 'construction', co-creation and actions of the subjects. (For more on criticism of postmodernism, see Jameson, *Postmodernism*.)
8. Ilyenkov, *Filosofiya i Kul'tura*; Zlobin, *Kul'tura i obshchestvennyy progress*; Mezhuev, *Kul'tura i istoriya*; Batishchev, *Vvedenie v dialektiku tvorchestva*.
9. Ollman, *Alienation*.
10. Meszaros, *Marx's Theory of Alienation*.
11. Schaff, *Alienation as a Social Phenomenon*.
12. Lukács, *History and Class Consciousness*.
13. See Marx, "Kapital. Kritika politicheskoy ekonomii," 383–4, 391, 397; Marx, "Teorii pribavochnoy stoimosti," 507, 513, 519, 529.
14. Musto, "Once Again about the Marxian Concept of Alienation."
15. See eg Bulavka, "Practice of the USSR."
16. See Bakhtin, *Problems of Poetics of Dostoevskiy*; Bibler, *Myshlenie kak tvorchestvo*; Batishchev, *Vvedenie v dialektiku tvorchestva*.
17. For more details see Buzgalin, "Creative Economy."
18. Batishchev, "Objective and Discrimination."
19. For more, see Buzgalin and Kolganov, "Global Capital," vol. 2: 85–86, 93, 119–26.
20. For more details see Buzgalin and Kolganov, "Global Capital," vol. 1: 102–4.
21. See Freeman, "Twilight of the Machinocratic Outlook."
22. In the RSFSR Lenin was Chairperson of the Council of People's Commissars, but there were other state leaders as well. The first Secretary of the Central Committee was J. V. Stalin.
23. Lenin, "Tasks of the Unions of Youth," 305.
24. Lenin, "Luchshe men'she, da luchshe," 391.
25. 'In the future there will be no other history of humanity, apart from the history of culture' (Karl Liebknecht, quoted in Zlobin, "Kommunizm kak kul'tura," 2).

REVOLUTIONS 75

26. See Zlobin, "Kommunizm kak kul'tura," 2–26. This thesis was also developed by Zlobin's contemporary Professor Vadim Mezhuev (see Mezhuev, "Sotsializm kak prostranstvo kul'tury.")
27. Mayakovskiy, "Vo ves' golos. 1929–1930."
28. Shoo. "Proletarskaya kul'tura," 19.
29. See Blok, "Krushenie gumanizma," 107.
30. Lenin, "O proletarskoy kul'ture," 337.
31. For more details see Buzgalin, "Political Economy of Revolution."
32. The USSR of the 1920s was characterised by a unique growth of both culture and revolutionary enthusiasm. Space limitations of the article do not allow us to give more examples here, but many such examples are analysed in Bulavka, *Kul'tura. Vlast'. Socializm*; Bulavka, *Fenomen sovetskoj kul'tury*.
33. Emerson, *First Hundred Years of Mikhail Bakhtin*.
34. 'Little child, we all are all horses, a little bit,Each of us, in some way, is a horse'. Mayakovskiy, "Kindness to Horses," 36.
35. See Lenin, "Zamechaniya na vtoroy proekt programmy Plekhanova," 232.
36. Marx and Engels, "Manifest Kommunisticheskoy partii," 447.
37. Slavin and Buzgalin, *Vershina Velikoy revolyutsii*.
38. For more details see Buzgalin et al., *USSR: Optimistic Tragedy*.

ORCID

Aleksandr Buzgalin (iD) http://orcid.org/0000-0003-3923-8385

Bibliography

Averintsev, Sergey S., Yuri N. Davydov, Vladimir N. Turbin, et al. *M.M. Bakhtin kak filosof [M.M. Bakhtin as a Philosopher]*. Moscow: Nauka, 1992.
Bakhtin, Mikhail M. *The Problems of Poetics of Dostoevskiy*. Moscow: Sovetskiy pisatel, 1963.
Bakhtin, Mikhail M. *Tvorchestvo Fransua Rable i narodnaya kul'tura srednevekov'ya i Renessansa [The Creative Work of François Rabelais and the Popular Culture of the Middle Ages and Renaissance]*. 2nd ed. Moscow: Khudozhestvennaya Literatura, 1990.
Batishchev, Genrikh S. 1967. "Objective and Discrimination." In *Philosophical Encyclopedia*, edited by F. V. Konstantinov, 5 vols. Vol. 4, 154–155. Moscow: Soviet Encyclopedia.
Batishchev, Genrikh S. 1997 (1984). *Vvedenie v dialektiku tvorchestva [Introduction to the Dialectic of Creativity]*. St. Petersburg: RHGI.
Bibler, Vladimir S. *M.M. Bakhtin, ili Poetika kul'tury [M.M. Bakhtin, or the Poetics of Culture]*. Moscow: Progress, 1991.
Bibler, Vladimir S. *Myshlenie kak tvorchestvo [Thinking as Creativity]*. Moscow: Politizdat, 1975.
Blok, Aleksandr. "Krushenie gumanizma" ["The Collapse of Humanism"]. In *Sobranie sochineniy. V vos'mi tomakh. Tom 6. Proza 1918–1921 [Collected Works]*, edited by Aleksandr Blok, vol. 6. Prose 19181921, 93–115. Moscow and Leningrad: Hudozhestvennaya literatura, 1962.
Brandist, Craig, and G. Tihanov, eds. *Materializing Bakhtin. The Bakhtin Circle and Social Theory*. Oxford: Macmillan Press, 2000.
Budgen, Sebastian, Stathis Kouvelakis, and Slavoj Žižek, eds. *Lenin Reloaded: Toward a Politics of Truth*. Durham: Duke University Press Books, 2007.
Bulavka, Lyudmila A. *Fenomen sovetskoj kul'tury [The Phenomenon of Soviet Culture]*. Moscow: Cultural Revolution, 2008.
Bulavka, Lyudmila A., ed. *Kul'tura. Vlast'. Socializm. Protivorechiya i vyzovy kul'turnyh praktik SSSR [The Culture. Power. Socialism. Contradictions and Challenges of Cultural Practices of the USSR]*. Moscow: LENAND, 2013.
Bulavka, Lyudmila A. "Practice of the USSR: Challenges to the Present and Future." *Filosofskie nauki* 1 (2012): 47–60.

Buzgalin, Aleksandr V. "Creative Economy: Private Intellectual Property or Ownership by Everybody of Everything?" *Sotsiologicheskie issledovaniya [Sociological Studies]* 7 (2017): 43–53.

Buzgalin, Aleksandr V. "Political Economy of Revolution (Dedicated to the Centenary of the October Revolution of 1917." *Voprosy politicheskoy ekonomii [Questions of Political Economy]* 3 (2017): 10–41.

Buzgalin, Aleksandr V., Lyudmila A. Bulavka, and Peter Linke, eds. *Lenin Online: 13 Professorov o V.I. Ul'yanov-Lenine [Lenin Online: 13 Professors on V.I. Ul'yanov-Lenin]*. Foreword by A.V. Buzgalin. Moscow: LENAND, 2011.

Buzgalin, Aleksandr V., Lyudmila A. Bulavka-Buzgalina, and Andrey I. Kolganov. *USSR: Optimistic Tragedy*. Moscow: Lenand, 2018.

Buzgalin, Aleksandr V., and Andrey I. Kolganov. "Global Capital." In 2 volumes. *Vol. 1. Methodology: Beyond Positivism, Postmodernism and Economic Imperialism (Marx Re-Loaded). Vol. 2. Theory. The Global Hegemony of Capital and Its Limits ('Capital' Re-Loaded)*, 5th ed., 2 vols. Moscow: LENAND, 2019.

Economist, The. "Millennial Socialism: Life, Liberty and the Pursuit of Property." *The Economist* (16 February 2019): 18–22.

Economist, The. "The Rise of Millennial Socialism. A New Kind of Left-Wing Doctrine is Emerging. It is Not the Answer to Capitalism's Problems." *The Economist* (16 February 2019): 11.

Emerson, Caryl. *The First Hundred Years of Mikhail Bakhtin*. Princeton, NJ: Princeton University Press, 1997.

Executive Office of the President. "Markets versus Socialism." In *Executive Office of the President. Economic Report of the President, March 2019: Together with the Annual Report of the Council of Economic Advisers*, 381–426. Lanham, MD: Bernan Press, 2019.

Freeman, Alan. "Twilight of the Machinocratic Outlook: Non-Substitutable Labour and the Future of Production." *Voprosy politicheskoy ekonomii [Questions of Political Economy]* 4, (2016): 37–60.

Fukuyama, Francis. *The End of History and the Last Man*. New York: The Free Press, 1992.doi:10.1086/ahr/97.3.817.

Jameson, Fredric. *Postmodernism, or, the Cultural Logic of Late Capitalism*. Durham: Duke University Press, 1991.

Ilyenkov, Evald V. *Filosofiya i Kul'tura [Philosophy and Culture]*. Moscow: Politizdat, 1991.

Isupov, Konstantin G. Lessons of M.M. Bakhtin." In *Bakhtin M.M.: pro et contra*. Comp., introd. article and comments by K. G. Isupov, chronograph by V. I. Laptun. Vol. I, 7–44. Saint-Petersburg: RKhGI, 2001.

Lenin, Vladimir I. "Zamechaniya na vtoroy proekt programmy Plekhanova" ["Notes on the second draft program of Plekhanov"]. In *Polnoe sobranie sochineniy*, edited by V. I. Lenin, 5th ed., vol. 6, 212–235. Moscow, Gospolitizdat, 1963.

Lenin, Vladimir I. "Luchshe men'she, da luchshe" ["Sooner fewer, but better"]. In *Polnoe sobranie sochineniy [Complete Works]*, edited by V. I. Lenin, 5th ed., vol. 45, 389–406. Moscow: Politizdat, 1970.

Lenin, Vladimir I. "O proletarskoy kul'ture" ["About Proletarian Culture"]. In *Polnoe sobranie sochineniy [Complete Works]*, edited by V. I. Lenin, vol. 41, 336–337. Moscow: Politizdat, 1981.

Lenin, Vladimir I. "The Tasks of the Unions of Youth. Speech to the Third All-Russian Congress of the Russian Communist Union of Youth, 2 October 1920." In *Polnoe sobranie sochineniy [Complete Works]*, edited by V. I. Lenin, 5th ed., vol. 41, 298–318. Moscow: Politizdat, 1981.

Lukács, György. *History and Class Consciousness: Studies in Marxist Dialectics*. Cambridge, MA: The MIT Press, 2000.

Marx, Karl, and Friedrikh, Engels. "Manifest Kommunisticheskoy partii" ["Manifesto of the Communist Party"]. In *Sochineniya [Works]*, edited by K. Marx and F. Engel, 2nd ed., vol. 4, 419–458. Moscow: Gospolitizdat, 1955.

Marx, Karl. "Kapital. Kritika politicheskoy ekonomii. Tom tretiy" ["Capital: A Critique of Political Economy, Vol. 3"]. In *Sochineniya [Works]*, edited by K. Marx and F. Engel, 2nd ed., vol. 25, Part II. Moscow: Gospolitizdat, 1962.

Marx, Karl. "Teorii pribavochnoy stoimosti (IV tom 'Kapitala')" ["Theories of Surplus Value (Volume IV of Capital)"]. In *Sochineniya [Works]*, edited by K. Marx and F. Engel, 2nd ed., vol. 26, Part III. Moscow: Gospolitizdat, 1964.

Mayakovskiy, Vladimir V. "Kindness to horses". In *Mayakovskiy, Vladimir. Poems*. Translated by Dorian Rottenberg, 36. Moscow: Gospolitizdat, 1972.

Mayakovskiy, Vladimir V. "Vo ves' golos. 1929–1930" ["Mayakovskiy. At the Top of My Voice. 1929–1930]. In *Polnoe sobranie sochineniy [Complete Works]*, edited by V. V. Mayakovskiy, vol. 10. Moscow: Gospolitizdat, 1958.

Meszaros, István. *Marx's Theory of Alienation*. London: Merlin Press, 1970.

Mezhuev, Vadim M. *Kul'tura i istoriya. (Problema kul'tury v filosofsko-istoricheskoy teorii marksizma). [Culture and History. (The Problem of Culture in the Philosophical and Historical Theory of Marxism)]*. Moscow: Politizdat, 1977.

Mezhuev, Vadim M. "Sotsializm kak prostranstvo kul'tury" ["Socialism as an Expanse of Culture"]. *Al'ternativy* 2 (1999): 43–102.

Musto, Marcello. "Once Again about the Marxian Concept of Alienation." *Alternatives* 3 (2013): 37–61.

Ollman, Bertell. *Alienation: Marx's Conception of Man in Capitalist Society*. 2nd ed. Cambridge: Cambridge University Press, 1976.

Schaff, Adam. *Alienation as a Social Phenomenon*. Oxford: Pergamon Press, 1980.

Shoo. "Proletarskaya kul'tura" ["Proletarian Culture"]. *Proletarskaya kul'tura (izdanie klubnoy sektsii Odesskogo Proletkul'ta [Proletarian Culture (Publication of the Club Section of the Odessa Proletkult)]* no. 1 (1919): 14–21.

Slavin, Boris F., and Aleksandr V. Buzgalin, eds. *Vershina Velikoy revolyutsii. K 100-letiyu Oktyabrya [The Height of the Great Revolution. Toward the Centenary of October]*. Moscow: Algoritm, 2017.

Zlobin, Nal S. "Kommunizm kak kul'tura" ["Communism as Culture"]. *Al'ternativy* no. 1 (1995): 2–26.

Zlobin, Nal S. *Kul'tura i obshchestvennyy progress [Culture and Social Progress]*. Moscow: Nauka, 1980.

The Chinese Revolution and the Communist International

Enfu Cheng and Jun Yang

ABSTRACT

This article is an intervention in some controversies concerning the role of the Communist International in and outside China. It seeks to tackle the inappropriate denial of its guidance and aid to the Chinese Revolution. In doing so, this paper makes several arguments. First, it argues that the Communist International provided the Chinese Revolution with valuable guidance, support and assistance. These contributed tremendously to the Communist Party of China's birth, development, consolidation and maturation and advanced its theoretical self-consciousness. Second, while the Communist International gave its guidance in the sincere hope that the Chinese Revolution would benefit from correct theories and advanced experiences, it absolutised the theoretical conceptions of the classical Marxists and the Russian experience. This led to mistakes or misjudgments that deserve an accurate evaluation. Third, the Communist International was itself conducting theoretical exploration, and was generally able to adjust its own theories and change its strategies. Fourth, for all the Communist International's guidance, the universal tenets of Marxism had to be integrated with the concrete practice of the Chinese Revolution, and it was the ability of Chinese communists to Sinicise Marxism–Leninism in what amounted to a theoretical revolution under Mao Zedong's leadership that accounts for the revolution's ultimate victory.

Proletarian revolution is an international phenomenon, and revolutionary struggles in an individual country need the support of those in others. For this reason, an international communist organisation needed to be established to lead the international communist movement. After the victory of the October Revolution, the existence of Soviet Russia meant that, for the first time, the international proletarian revolution had a solid base and powerful stronghold. The Bolsheviks, led by Lenin, understood that the law of uneven development of capitalism had made Russia the first country in which a socialist revolution was victorious. However, he also understood that it was merely the prologue, the 'first rung of the ladder', of the world socialist revolution. 'This is the greatest difficulty of the Russian revolution', Lenin explained, 'its greatest historical problem – the need to solve international problems, the need to evoke a world revolution, to effect the transition from our strictly national revolution to the world revolution.'[1] Conscious of the 'ideological and political collapse' of the old proletarian leaderships,[2] and aiming to help the working people, especially of the developed countries of Europe, to build the revolutionary movement, Lenin took the lead in establishing an international league of communist parties and organisations from across the world, the Communist International, in March 1919. The Manifesto of the Communist International drawn up by the body's First Congress and the Twenty-One Conditions adopted at the Second Congress proclaimed the International's strategic objective to be the overthrow of international capital and the establishment of workers' power throughout the world. The communist parties and organisations that joined the International regarded themselves as revolutionary organisations, with the same class position, fundamental interests and ultimate objectives as the proletarian masses of all the countries of the world, and the same view of the Communist International as the fortress and base for combatting the reactionary alliance. Each member organisation also agreed on the definition of proletarian internationalism drawn up by Lenin: that 'the interests of the proletarian struggle in any one country should be subordinated to the interests of that struggle on a worldwide scale' and that 'a nation which is achieving victory over the bourgeoisie should be able and willing to make the greatest national sacrifices for the overthrow of international capital'.[3] It was always possible, of course, that at any given time and place the interests of the proletariat in a particular country might contradict those of the world proletariat. In the long run and fundamentally, however, the two were consistent and could be coordinated based on the general principle of internationalism.

The October Revolution was thus said to have 'erected a bridge between the socialist West and the enslaved East, having created a new front of revolutions against world imperialism, extending from the proletarians of the West, through the Russian Revolution, to the oppressed peoples of the East'.[4] The Chinese Revolution became part of the revolutions occurring around the world. To ally itself with the Chinese national liberation movement and the proletarian revolutionary movement, the Communist International proactively undertook the internationalist duty of guiding, supporting and helping the Chinese Revolution. As an international revolutionary organisation, the Communist International needed to consider the overall state of the revolutionary cause in dozens of countries and regions worldwide. This entailed considerable organisation and coordination of relations between global and local, and it was very difficult to focus exclusively on one particular country and one particular party when circumstances demanded a differentiation between global and local, primary and secondary goals.[5] Meanwhile, Soviet Russia was itself in a difficult position, facing severe financial constraints. Notwithstanding such difficulties, the Communist International provided systematic theoretical and strategic guidance to the Chinese Revolution,[6] as well as various forms of support including supplies, funds and personnel training.[7] As confidential documents have been declassified, this information has become increasingly well known.[8] The Communist Party of China (CPC), along with the other parties and organisations affiliated with the Communist International, were firmly convinced of such principles as the global character of the proletarian class and of the proletarian revolution. The Chinese communists understood the Communist International straightforwardly as 'the Communist Party of many countries', with 'a universal class character'.[9] The International was described by the Chinese communists as having been 'created by Lenin himself', and as devoting 'all its efforts to the emancipation of the working class of the whole world'.[10] Communists in other countries, it was stressed, felt real sympathy for the Chinese communists, and regarded them as brothers.[11] 'They need us', it was declared, 'and we need them'.[12] The First Congress of the Communist Party of China in 1921 proposed 'allying with the Communist International' as a guiding principle, and the party's Second Congress in 1922 passed a resolution calling specifically for joining the International as an affiliated body. The Chinese Revolution and the Communist International thus became connected in a close and profound way.

However, there have been many ill-grounded ideas about the relationship between the Chinese Revolution and the Communist International. They repudiate the history and role of the Communist International. Three major misunderstandings are particularly important:

(1) That, from the perspective of 'national interest' or 'realism', the Communist International was nothing but a disguise for the national interests of the Soviet Union and that it was fundamentally the expression of a kind of selfish nationalism and chauvinism;

(2) That the mistakes of the Communist International were something inherent in it and that, as a result, the Chinese Revolution was a process that was full of subjectivism and dogmatism in its guiding thoughts, sectarianism and exclusionism in its organisational line, and putschism and adventurism in its strategy and principle;

(3) That, alternatively, according to the 'authoritarianism model' and 'power struggle' perspective, the Communist International's guidance of the Chinese Revolution was a history of struggle between Mao Zedong on the one side and Stalin and his agent Wang Ming on the other.

With these controversies in mind, this paper addresses the inappropriate denial of the positive role of the Communist International, the dismissal of the Soviet Union's support in the Chinese Revolution for being motivated by purely selfish Soviet interests and the view that the relationship between the Communist International and the Chinese Revolution was defined by antagonistic relations between the leaders of the CPC and Soviet leaders. We examine the history of the Chinese Revolution and the Communist International, and draw the following conclusions.

1. Mao Zedong was to emphasise in 1945 that 'Without the establishment of the Communist International and its help, the Chinese proletarian political party would not have achieved its present success'.[13] This view is corroborated by our examination of the historical evidence, leading us to conclude that, motivated by the concept of internationalism and the goal of worldwide revolution, the Communist International provided invaluable guidance, support and help to the Chinese Revolution, making significant contributions to the foundation, development, growth and maturation of the CPC and to the theoretical consciousness of its members.

The guidance provided by the Communist International to the Chinese Revolution primarily took the form of ideological instruction aimed at transforming the practice of the Chinese communists. In China, Marxism spread widely after the May 4th Movement in 1919, only two years before the founding of the CPC in 1921. This short interval meant that, during the infancy of the CPC, theoretical preparation and cadre leadership were inadequate. As Liu Shaoqi suggests, 'a prominent weak point of the CPC was that it did not have sufficient ideational preparation and theoretical training, and was relatively naïve'.[14] The party lacked experience and political maturity, just when it needed to confront powerful enemies and a menacing environment. Under such circumstances, the CPC turned to the Communist International as its theoretical source for the basic tenets of Marxism, as well as for the theories of Lenin and Stalin, especially their views on the Chinese Revolution. In particular, at this time, the CPC drew on:

- Lenin's ideas on colonies;
- Lenin and Stalin's ideas on the nature, task, and driving force of the Chinese Revolution, the CPC's cooperation with national bourgeoisie, the future of socialism, and the Chinese proletariat and its party's leadership in the revolution; and
- Stalin's analysis of the division of the Chinese national bourgeoisie into a revolutionary and a compromising sect, the peasants as the most reliable ally of the proletariat, the land-based revolution of peasants as the foundation and content of the bourgeois revolution, and the armed struggle as the characteristic and advantage of the Chinese Revolution.[15]

These ideas were among the most important among those that defined the understanding and practice of the Chinese Revolution. They clarified the direction of the CPC's development, provided ideational guidance for CPC's exploration of the fundamental issues of the New Democratic Revolution[16] and, of course, laid a Marxist theoretical foundation for Mao Zedong's idea of new democracy of the people as opposed to that of bourgeois revolution. The Communist International provided the CPC with invaluable theoretical and policy guidance, which helped it to establish its fundamental positions and concepts. As such, the International helped fulfil the theoretical needs of the Chinese Revolution. Such guidance also had a profound influence on Mao Zedong Thought, both in its initial stages and later, during its development and maturation. Mao Zedong never denied this fact, and it is universally acknowledged by historians of the CPC. The text *Resolution on Several Historical Issues*, for example, notes that 'Comrade Mao Zedong brilliantly developed the theory put forward by Lenin and Stalin on colonial and semi-colonial regions and Stalin's theoretical work on the Chinese revolution'.[17]

In addition to its theoretical and policy guidance, the Communist International played other positive roles. First, the Marxism and Leninism disseminated in China by the Communist International directly guided the foundation of the CPC. Second, the Kuomintang (KMT) was revitalised through the guidance and help it received from the Communist International and went on to lead the vigorous national revolutionary movement and to achieve victory in the Northern Expedition. Third, the Communist International guided and assisted the CPC in formulating the policy of the national united front. Through supporting and educating the KMT and the CPC, the Communist International facilitated the alliance that saw the KMT and the CPC combine in fighting against Japanese imperial invaders during the time of Great Revolution and the National Anti-Japanese War, dramatically improving the situation for the Chinese Revolution and the Chinese Communist Party. Fourth, the Communist International trained a multitude of cadres with specialised skills in various areas. Fifth, the Communist International acknowledged Mao Zedong's capabilities and eventually supported his leadership of the CPC. In fact, the Communist International provided guidance and support throughout the years that saw the main development of the CPC, from the preparations for its founding to the period of the Anti-Japanese War. At the same time, the International influenced the CPC in fundamental areas and on core issues. Without this guidance and help, it is hard to imagine that the Communist Revolution in China, a large and backward country, could have achieved such enormous victories within a relatively short period.

The Communist International and the USSR's support for the KMT must be seen in this context. While the Communist International treated the CPC as a fraternal party, with the same class basis, it saw the KMT as a friend to cooperate with. The Communist International hoped that ultimately the CPC would assume the task of supervising, guiding and transforming the KMT and essentially take the KMT under its wing. However, as long as the CPC and the Chinese working class were smaller and weaker, the Communist International and the Soviet Union gave international recognition to the national government of China as a pragmatic tactic under specific circumstances.

2. In seeking to infuse the Chinese Communists with what they considered the correct theory and advanced experience that would aid their victory, the Communist International based itself on the classical Marxist theoreticians and on the experience of the Russian Revolution. A dogmatic application of these theories and an over-generalisation of the Russian experience led the International into a range of errors, and these need to be analysed in depth.

The guidance provided by the Communist International flowed from a number of basic conceptions. In the first place, the International adhered to the viewpoint, emphasised by Marx and Lenin, that an adequate degree of capitalist development was necessary as the material foundation for socialist revolution. The International's advice for China went along the lines of 'the working-class movement is still weak' and 'still unable to assume the leadership'.[18] Therefore, it must 'forge an alliance with the bourgeoisie within the revolution' and 'comply with the central tasks of the current revolutionary stage'.[19] Second, and proceeding from the fundamental principle that the Communist Party is the vanguard of the working class, the Communist International repeatedly insisted that the CPC, which for many years had been fighting in a rural environment, needed to remain a proletarian party at the same time as it won the leadership of the agrarian movement. As Zhou Enlai once put it, 'In the documents of the Communist International, whenever the question of leadership by the proletarian party came up, it was in connection with the workers movement'.[20] This was because, for the Communist International, the proletariat was the product of large-scale machine production, and communist parties originated from its most progressive members. As the vanguard of the proletariat, the communist party's major task was organising a workers' movement. Third, the Communist International adhered scrupulously to the model provided by the experience of the Russian Revolution. The Chinese Revolution, the International maintained, should set out to mobilise workers in major cities to carry out insurrections, creating a high tide of revolution and achieving victory throughout the country. The International repeatedly demanded that the CPC emphasise in its work the cities where the proletariat was concentrated. Fourth, the Communist International always bore in mind the ultimate nature of the Communists and their historical mission, expecting and longing for the overall outbreak of the worldwide revolution as well as of the revolution in China. Emphatic in the view that the Soviet Union was the fortress of global revolution, and was antagonistic to the capitalist world, the cadres of the International anticipated a general crisis of capitalism. The International interpreted phenomena such as economic crisis, war, social instability and major strikes as signs that the tide of revolution was nearing its peak. The above positions reflected the fact that the Communist International was faithful to the classical theories of Marxism and to the model of the October Revolution, and therefore clung to them strictly, anxious for the CPC to achieve victory in the Chinese Revolution with the guidance of correct theory and advanced experience. This had the effect, on the one hand, of greatly advancing the development of the Chinese Revolution. However, on the other hand, it led to dogmatic mistakes due to a rigid interpretation of Marxism–Leninism and of the Russian experience that took no account of the specific reality in China. For the Communist International, theories of classical Marxist writers on such issues as the material conditions of the proletarian revolution, peasants, revolutions in colonies and backward countries, and the model and experience of the October Revolution, were all universal and had to be followed in all cases. Even when the Chinese Revolution suffered severe setbacks and a sharp decline,[21] the International remained firm in its belief in these basic tenets and models when, in fact, these historical circumstances required careful research and concrete, down-to-earth analysis.

(1) The Communist International emphasised that, in the case of a backward country like China, it was necessary to stress the progressive role of capitalism and, hence, of the capitalist class. This was a principled position that flowed necessarily from a materialist conception of history. Mao Zedong's theory of new democracy rested on this principle, and Mao also used it to criticise populist and agrarian socialist currents within the CPC. However, while the fundamental policy formulated on this issue by the International was correct, the error lay in that the International clung to the established policies on the national democratic revolution and to the experience of the Russian Revolution. In order to apply the Russian experience to China, Stalin compared the Chinese Revolution and the Russian Revolution in July 1927 and proposed the idea of 'three phases' of the Chinese Revolution, which corresponded to the 1905, February 1917 and October revolutions in Russia. The corresponding three phases in the Chinese Revolution were those of the Guangdong Administration in which the CPC cooperated with the KMT, the Wuhan Administration in which the CPC cooperated with the left wing of KMT after the anti-revolution coup of 12 April 1927, and the coming Soviet revolution. At the critical moment after the 12 April coup, the leaders of the Communist International and the Communist Party of the Soviet Union regarded the coup as one conducted by the big bourgeoisie against KMT and its left wing. They believed that it resulted in the removal of the rightists, saboteurs and traitors. However, this transposition of the experience of the Russian Revolution onto the Chinese experience was too schematic.

(2) According to classical Marxism, the Communist Party is supposed to be the political party of the working class, with a solid foundation among working people. The Constitution of the CPC is consistent with this understanding in firmly designating the CPC as the vanguard of the working class. However, after the failure of the First Revolutionary Civil War, the CPC and the movement it led were based for a lengthy period in rural areas. Peasants and other non-proletarian communists made up a majority within the party ranks. It was inevitable, therefore, that the CPC was influenced by non-proletarian thinking. Fearing that the CPC would lose its proletarian nature and become a 'party of the petty bourgeoisie and peasants', the Communist International stressed repeatedly that the CPC needed to maintain close contact with the working class in the cities and with the workers' movement. These theories and perspectives may be correct in principle, and certainly Mao Zedong also thought in these terms. Consider, for instance, his repeated instruction to comrades: 'Do not confuse the party with the peasants …. If we don't believe this, we are not Marxists'.[22] Where the Communist International erred was in being unable to 'form a unified understanding of the leading role of the proletariat and of the role of the peasants as the major force'.[23] The

insistence by the International that the CPC should focus its efforts on propaganda within the working class and on organising workers did not fit the circumstances of the Chinese Revolution. Nor did the specific measures it proposed for resolving the controversy regarding the nature of the CPC – that is, for the party to become mainly working class in its composition, and to include more workers in its leading organs. This criticism does not contradict the recognition of the Communist International's theoretical and policy guidance for CPC. The adherence of the Communist International in the 1920s to workers' struggles in cities was based on its understanding of Marxist tenets and of the experience of the Russian Revolution. This was not wrong in itself. The problem was simply that such experience could not be repeated in China. The new path of the Chinese Revolution that Mao Zedong found through practice did not mean that the perception of the urban working class as the main subject was a mistake, but rather that a detour was needed, ie to accumulate strength in the countryside, followed by the encirclement of the cities with the rural areas.

(3) To rely on a mature industrial proletariat, and to pursue proletarian revolution in cities where modern industry was fully developed, corresponded to the theoretical position of classical Marxism and to the experience of the October Revolution in Russia. However, at the time in question, no precedent existed within the international communist movement for 'enveloping the cities within the rural areas'. Consequently, the Communist International and the CPC agreed on a model of revolution that involved seizing power with armed forces centred in the cities. Mao Zedong's scientific understanding of this issue was, however, gradually taking shape amid the practice of the Chinese Revolution. Specific conditions in China ultimately determined the path that the Chinese Revolution had to take, with its basis in the countryside, reliance on the peasants, gradual accumulation of power and encircling cities with the countryside. Even though the cities are political and economic centres of the country, they are detached and isolated from the countryside, and therefore cannot control what is going on there. At the same time, for the reactionary forces concentrated in the cities, the countryside was the weakest link. All these determined the 'rural-centred' path of the Chinese Revolution. Although Mao proposed that the specific circumstances of the Chinese Revolution required that it first accumulate power in broad rural areas, he emphasised that 'the rural areas at present are only a temporary base; they are not and cannot be the primary base for the whole democratic society of China. Progressing from an agrarian to an industrial base is the task of our revolution'.[24]

(4) The mission of the Communist International was to lead and guide the world revolution; consequently, the cadres of the International were anxious for revolutions to succeed as soon as possible and believed that a peak tide of revolution was in the offing. In the history of the period, such optimism was a common phenomenon. Mao Zedong recognised that the Chinese Revolution would be a 'long and harsh process'; nevertheless, he believed that a rising tide of revolution was 'inevitable', and would 'come very soon'.[25] The Communist International fell into error on this point. As the revolutionary Hu Qiaomu was to note,

> It is easy to make the mistake of unrealistically pursuing quick success, exaggerating the subjective power and political consciousness of the masses, underrating the power of our enemies and exaggerating their difficulties, and consequently, underestimating the difficulties we must confront before the revolutionary victory.[26]

Deng Xiaoping observed that he and his comrades, totally dedicated to the revolution, were liable to be too impetuous. It is true that we have good intentions, that we are eager to see the realization of communism at an early date. But, often our very eagerness has prevented us from making a sober analysis of subjective and objective conditions, and we have therefore acted in contradiction to the laws governing the development of the objective world.[27]

In sum, the above-noted tenets of the Communist International were important and rested on sound foundations. They helped the CPC remain a proletarian political party and to preserve its Marxist character. However, since the Communist International adhered too strictly to the ideas of the classical Marxist theoreticians and to the experiences of the Russian Revolution, while failing to pay sufficient attention to the realities of the situation in China, the strategies for action that the International's representatives proposed and the practical decisions they recommended were not completely suited to the circumstances that Chinese Revolutionaries confronted. These mistakes inevitably hindered or damaged the Chinese Revolution. For example, during the first national revolution from 1924 to 1927, the Communist International stuck rigidly to the established principle of democratic national revolution and to the 'three-phased revolution' based on the experience of the Russian Revolution. Privileging the KMT as the leading force of the revolution compromised the CPC's independence, and it lost opportunities to take resolute actions and countermeasures. During the Agrarian Revolution from 1927 to 1937, the three 'left-leaning errors' of CPC (Qu Qiubai's Putschism from November 1927 to April 1928, Li Lisan's adventurism from June 1930 to September 1930 and Wang Min's dogmatism from January 1931 to January 1935) were mostly the result of guidance by the Communist International. The representative of the Communist International in China insisted on completing the struggle against imperial and feudal power through struggles against the now anti-revolutionary bourgeoisie through armed uprisings in the big cities where the KMT was concentrated, rather than what Mao thought necessary and was doing: establishing revolutionary bases in the countryside far from KMT strongholds. The Communist International was chiefly concerned to stress the antagonism between the Soviet Union as the basis of world revolution and the capitalist world, to the exclusion of nearly everything else. It was waiting for the general crisis of imperialism which, along with social disturbance and workers' strikes, would signal the arrival of the climax of the revolution. Such beliefs, along with its expectation of the success of world revolution as soon as possible, constitute the important causes of the imprudent actions of CPC at this period, most of which consisted in following the Communist International line. This demonstrated that in following the revolutionary road, it is of utmost importance to unify subjectivity and objectivity, theory and the history of actual revolutionary practice.

The task of integrating Marxism with the realities of China needed to be undertaken by Chinese Revolutionaries. It was in this sense that Mao Zedong and Zhou Enlai emphasised that the emergence of dogmatism in the CPC was related to the CPC's immaturity, which led the party to regard instructions coming from the Communist International as invariably correct. For this error, the CPC itself had to take responsibility. Meanwhile, the argument is profoundly correct that the Chinese Revolution could only have achieved substantial victories after Marxism had been 'Sinicised'. The difficulty of Sinicising Marxism lay in the difference of the Chinese conditions from those of the West where Marxism was born and from Russia where Marxism won its first victory. Specifically, China was a backward, semi-feudal and semi-colonised country whose main body was constituted by peasants. The development of its productive forces, economic structure, class relations and major social contradictions were of an entirely different level and character. In such a special country, the proletariat was facing a 'difficult and special task', a 'task that communists around the world had never encountered ... and that cannot be found in any textbook of communism'. Therefore, the CPC had to rely on 'the general theory and practice of communism', while adapting to 'specific conditions such as do not exist in the European countries', and applying such theory and practice 'to conditions in which the bulk of the population are peasants, and in which the task is to wage a struggle against medieval survivals and not against capitalism'.[28]

3. The Communist International also developed its theory while guiding the Chinese Revolution. This meant that it was able to revise its overall theoretical conceptions and change its strategies in line with revolutionary practice. As Zhou Enlai remarked, 'The thinking of Comrade Mao Zedong underwent a process of development. That was also true of comrade Stalin's thinking'.[29]

As the Communist International was guiding the Chinese Revolution, its strategies underwent continuous changes. At the First CPC Congress in 1921, the Communist International advocated that the party dedicate itself directly to socialist revolution, while at the Second Congress in 1922 the International aided the CPC in deciding to lead the democratic revolution first and then the socialist revolution. In May 1923, the Communist International insisted that the land revolution was important but must be advanced under KMT leadership, while at the 7 August meeting in 1927 it shifted its position again and guided the CPC in further specifying its principle of land revolution. The Communist International's position shifted from focussing exclusively on the workers' movement to emphasising the 'revolutionary role' of the peasants, and from considering urban insurrection the only way to the revolution to giving close attention to the construction of Soviets in the countryside and of the red army. The shifts indicate that the International was not entirely rigid in its stance and that Chinese ground realities and practices did influence it. Further, the Communist International also helped the CPC correct certain mistaken policies and guidelines. At important meetings, significant policy adjustments were made under the guidance and influence of the Communist International, while mistaken strategies and approaches were corrected or modified. Such meetings included:

- the West Lake Meeting in 1922, where the decision to build a united front with the KMT was taken;
- the 7 August meeting in 1927, where the general line of the land revolution was adopted;
- the 6th Congress of the CPC in 1928 that ended the tendency to surrender to the right or engage in blindly leftist uprisings against it;
- the Third Plenary Session of the Sixth Central Committee in 1930 that ended Li Lisan's leftist adventurist line, which was prompted by an underestimation of the strength of the enemy and the mistaken belief that revolutionary victory was within sight;
- the Wayaobao Meeting in 1935, which decided on the united national front against the Japanese invasion with new CPC–KMD cooperation; and
- the Sixth Plenary Session of the Sixth Central Committee in 1938 that specified the CPC's role in the national war against the Japanese invasion.

While some of the CPC's errors were corrected without help from the Communist International, the adjustments were made with the International expressing at least a degree of consent. For example, the International accepted the political outcome of the Zunyi Conference, which was held independently by the CPC and affirmed and supported the line of struggle established by the CPC leaders represented by Mao Zedong. This implied that the Communist International supported the CPC resolving its own issues independently, including in instances where the transformation or modification of policies was of great significance for the CPC and the Chinese Revolution. As the Chinese Revolution's victories grew more frequent, Stalin and his colleagues came to recognise more and more that strictly copying the experience of Soviet Russia could lead to errors, and increasingly accepted the validity of China's independent revolutionary road. In a July 1949 conversation with Liu Shaoqi, Stalin acknowledged the initiative and creativity of the Chinese Revolution, in a veiled apology for 'once obstructing' the Chinese Revolution and 'possible wrong expressions'.[30]

4. The general principles of Marxism and Leninism must be integrated with the actual practice of the Chinese Revolution. The ultimate victory of the revolution would, Mao insisted, 'depend on the Chinese comrades' understanding of Chinese conditions'.[31] He led Chinese communists in their first major advance in the Sinicisation of Marxism, and correctly resolved such major issues as how to carry out the central tasks of the Chinese Revolution, how the CPC might remain the vanguard of the working class, and how revolutionary victories might be achieved under the specific circumstances that existed in China.

At the level of fundamentals, any attempt to guide the revolutionary movement in a particular country must set out from that country's actual circumstances, and must rest on a systematic and meticulous understanding of the situations of various social strata and classes. Only in this way can an accurate evaluation of the constantly changing circumstances be made, and an appropriate strategy adopted. From this perspective, attempting to guide the Chinese Revolution through reliance on an international leading centre was indeed problematic, since it was no longer possible for the Communist International to adapt itself to the 'extremely complicated and rapidly changing circumstances'[32] of the Chinese Revolution. It should be noted that during the infancy of the CPC, the party's severe lack of theoretical preparation and practical experience meant that the help and guidance of the Communist International was much needed for dealing with both major and minor issues. For the Second CPC Congress in 1922 to confirm the status of the CPC as a branch of the Communist International was at that time 'a necessary and inevitable choice'.[33] However, as the CPC grew and the Chinese Revolution developed, the functional form of the Communist International no longer met the revolution's requirements. The ultimate victory of the Chinese Revolution required the Chinese communists to 'adopt an attitude of being entirely responsible and highly creative'.[34] In the revolutionary struggle, Mao led the Chinese communists in systematically studying and assimilating the ideas and theories of the Communist International. They acquired a genuine understanding of the Marxist position, viewpoints and method and, analysing the specific issues at play in the Chinese Revolution, summarised the objective laws and lessons they learned from their experience of combatting erroneous trends of subjectivism and dogmatism. Knowledge originates from practice, and it is also on the basis of practice that theory takes shape. Through these processes, Maoism gradually developed and matured. Finding systematic, scientific answers to a series of fundamental questions confronting the Chinese Revolution, it achieved the first leap in the Sinicisation of Marxism.

The key points emphasised by the Communist International – that the Chinese Revolution was national democratic in character, and that the CPC needed to ally itself with the bourgeoisie in the national liberation movement – represented the major theoretical foundation for Mao Zedong's new democratic thinking. Mao summarised and drew on the lessons learned from historical experience, analysing the question of how to handle the struggle and maintain the coalition in the United Front while insisting on the need to preserve the leading role of the proletariat and to adhere to militant struggle as the major form of the struggle in the Chinese Revolution. He forged these concepts into effective weapons through which the CPC could defeat the enemy. To the position of the Communist International that the workers' movement and the revolution in the cities should be the focus of the CPC's work, Mao Zedong responded creatively by proposing that, in the special circumstances of China, the initial focus should be on the rural areas. These could form a strategic base for accumulating and expanding the revolutionary forces of the people, allowing an eventual shift to combat by the Red Army as the main form of struggle in the Chinese Revolution. Meanwhile, Mao stressed repeatedly that, in the rural struggle, the peasants had to be led by the political party of the proletariat. When the time came to seek victories on the scale of China as a whole, the focus needed to shift from the rural areas to the cities, so that the urban movement could direct the fight in the villages. 'Without such a transition, we will pursue a mistaken line', he argued, pointing out that 'without industry and cities, we are doomed to fail'.[35] Mao believed that the role of the CPC as the vanguard of the proletariat, a point stressed by the Communist International, was destined to be one of the key issues in the Chinese Revolution.[36] However, he emphasised that due to the specific configuration of social classes in China, the CPC needed to ensure its status as the vanguard of the proletariat through its guiding ideas and strategies rather than simply on the basis of its class composition. In practice, Mao Zedong developed a uniquely creative approach to party building, one that placed emphasis on ideas. During the period of the Anti-Japanese War, a Rectification Campaign was implemented, aimed at systematically countering petty-bourgeois ideas in the Party. Liu Shaoqi explained the outcome in these terms: 'As we have followed Comrade Mao Zedong's line, we can build, and have already built, a Marxist–Leninist party of the working class, even though the workers in our Party membership do not yet constitute the majority'.[37]

The scientific synthesis achieved by Mao Zedong on the basis of the history and experience of the Communist International provided crucial guidance to the Chinese Revolution. This synthesis involved integrating the fundamental principles of Marxism with Chinese revolutionary practice, proceeding from reality in all the CPC's activity, seeking the truth from facts, and placing emphasis on investigation and study. Guided by Mao Zedong Thought, the power and influence of the CPC were greatly strengthened. Before long, a sweeping victory was achieved in the Anti-Japanese War, and national power was seized.

Disclosure statement

No potential conflict of interest was reported by the author(s).

Notes

1. Lenin, "E gong(bu)di qi ci (jinji)," 439.
2. Lenin, "The Collapse of the Second International", 205–259.
3. Lenin, "Draft Theses on National and Colonial Questions."
4. Stalin, *October Revolution and the National Question*.
5. Zhang, "Wei He Yun'an."
6. From 1923 to 1927, the Communist Party of the Soviet Union convened 122 meetings and passed 738 resolutions – on average, one resolution every two and half days – devoted to Chinese issues. See Li, "Zhong su guanxi de lishi," 2.
7. Yang Kuisong's study on financial aid from the Communist International to the Communist Party of China suggests that such assistance was vital for CPC, especially for its early survival and development. See K. Yang, "Gongchan guoji wei zhonggong."
8. A brief list of such documents includes: Department 1 of the Party History Research Central of CPC Central Committee, *Gong chan guoji*; Institute of Modern History of the Chinese Academy of Social Sciences, *Gongchan guoji youguan zhongguo*; Editorial Committee of the Documents on the History of the International Communist Movement, *Guoji gongchan zhuyi yundong*; Central Bureau of Translation and Compilation, *Guoji gongchan zhuyi yundong*; Georgi Dimitrov, *Ji mi te luo fu riji xuanbian*; and Shen, *Su lian lishi dongan xuanbian*. In addition, journals such as *Zhonggong dangshi yanjiu* [*Studies of the History of the Communist Party of China*], *Dang de wenxian* [*Documents of the Communist Party of China*] and *Zhonggong dangshi ziliao* [*Documents of the History of the Communist Party of China*] have also published many important historical archives.
9. Cai, "Cai Hesen gei Mao Zedong," 132.
10. Mao, "Comintern Has Long Ceased."
11. Mao, "Stalin, Friend of the Chinese People."
12. Mao, "Dui 'guanyu ruogan lishi wenti de jueyi,'" 283.
13. *Ibid.*
14. Liu, "On the Party," 220.
15. See Sun and Cao, *Lie Ning Si*.
16. The New Democratic Revolution refers to the bourgeois revolution in China in which the Chinese proletariat took the leading role, with the goal of overthrowing feudalism, imperialism and the bureaucratic capitalist class. It is the transition period towards socialism in China.
17. Mao, "Fulu," 953.
18. Chuikov, *Mission in China*, 35–6.
19. Pu, "Account of Important Events."
20. Zhou, "Guan yu dang," 178.
21. On 12 April 1927, the new right of the KMT, led by Chiang Kaishek, launched a coup in Shanghai against its own left wing and CPC. In this fatal attack on the CPC Central Committee in Shanghai and its organisations, over 300 people were killed, over 500 were arrested and over 5000 went missing. In July of the same year, the Wang Jingwei group launched another coup in Wuhan with a massacre of CPC members and the revolutionary people, forcing CPC to abandon its legal struggles in cities and turn to the armed struggles and revolution in rural areas.
22. Mao, "Zi zhonguo gongchangdang," 121.
23. Sha, *Mao Zedong sixiang tonglun*, 123.

24. Mao, "Gei Qin Bangxian de xin," 239.
25. Mao, "A Single Spark."
26. Hu, *Collected Works of Hu Qiaomu*, 163.
27. Deng, "Gaige shi zhongguo fazhan."
28. Lenin, "Address to the Second All-Russia Congress."
29. Zhou, "Guan yu dang," 179.
30. Jin, *Lui Shaoqi Zhuan*, 652.
31. Mao, "Oppose Book Worship."
32. Mao, "The Comintern Has Long Ceased."
33. Party History Research Centre of the CPC Central Committee, *Zhongguo gongchandang lishi*, 81–2.
34. Mao, "The Comintern Has Long Ceased."
35. See S. Yang, *Yang Shangkun huiyilu*, 27. This was a talk delivered by Mao Zedong at the Second Plenary Session of the Seventh Central Committee of the Communist Party of China on 5 March 1949.
36. Mao, "Dui 'guanyu ruogan lishi wenti de jueyi,'" 284. For example, Mao Zedong raised this issue on 20 April 1945: 'Our Party grew from 25 thousand to several hundred thousand, with the majority consisting of peasants and petty bourgeois. Without rectification, our Party would have changed its nature, becoming "proletarian" in name only, while being "petty bourgeois" in actuality'.
37. Liu, "On the Party," 330–1.

Bibliography

Cai, Hesen. "Cai Hesen gei Mao Zedong de xin" ["Letters from Cai Hesen to Mao Zedong"] August 31, 1920. In *Xinmin xuehui ziliao [Files of Xinmin Institute]*, edited by the Museum of Hunan Province, 128–132. Beijing: People's Publishing House, 1980.

Central Bureau of Translation and Compilation, ed. *Guoji gongchan zhuyi yundong lishi wenxian [Historical Documents of the International Communist Movement]*, 12 vols. Beijing: Central Translation and Compilation Press, 2011.

Chuikov, V. I. *Mission in China: Notes of a Military Consultant* [在华使命：一个军事顾问的笔记 *Zai hua shi ming: Yi ge jun shi gu wen de bi ji*]. Translated by C. Wan. Beijing: Xinhua Publishing House, 1980. [In Chinese.]

Deng, Xiaoping. "Gaige shi zhongguo fazhan shengchanli de biyou zhi lu" ["Reform Is the Necessary Way for China to Develop Its Productive Forces"]. In *Selected Works of Deng Xiaoping, vol. 3 (1982–1992)*. Beijing: Foreign Languages Press, 1994. https://dengxiaopingworks.wordpress.com/2013/03/18/reform-is-the-only-way-for-china-to-developed-its-productive-forces/

Department 1 of the Party History Research Center of the CPC Central Committee. *Gong chan guoji, liangong (bu) yu zhongguo geming dang'an ziliao congshu [Archive Series on the Communist International, the Communist Party of the Soviet Union (Bolshevik) and the Chinese Revolution]*. 21 vols. Beijing: Library Press and Party History Press, 1997/2012.

Dimitrov, Georgi. *Ji mi te luo fu riji xuanbian [Selected Diaries of Dimitrov]*. Translated by Ma Xipu. Guilin: Guangxi Normal University Press, 2002.

Editorial Committee of the Documents on the History of the International Communist Movement, ed. *Guoji gongchan zhuyi yundong shi wenxian congshu [Book Series on the History of the International Communist Movement]*. 23 vols. Beijing: Renmin University Press, 1986/2001.

Hu, Qiaomu. *Collected Works of Hu Qiaomu*. Beijing: People's Publishing House, 1993. [In Chinese.]

Institute of Modern History of the Chinese Academy of Social Sciences. *Gongchan guoji youguan zhongguo geming de wenxian ziliao [Documents of the Communist International on the Chinese Revolution]*. 3 vols. Beijing: China Social Sciences Press, 1981/1990.

Jin, Chongji. *Liu Shaoqi Zhuan [Biography of Liu Shaoqi]*. Beijing: Social Sciences Academic Press, 1998.

Lenin, V. I. "Address to the Second All-Russia Congress of Communist Organisations of the Peoples of the East." In *Lenin's Collected Works*, vol. 30, 4th English ed., 151–162. Moscow: Progress Publishers, 1965. https://www.marxists.org/archive/lenin/works/1919/nov/22.htm

Lenin, V. I. "Draft Theses on National and Colonial Questions for the Second Congress of the Communist International." In *Lenin's Collected Works*, vol. 31. 2nd English ed., 144–151. Moscow: Progress Publishers, 1920/1965. https://www.marxists.org/archive/lenin/works/1920/jun/05.htm

Lenin, V. I. "E gong (bu)di qi ci (jinji) daibiao dahui wenxian" ["Documents of the 7th (Emergent) Meeting of the RSDLP"]. In *Lenin's Selected Works*, vol. 3, 434–468. Beijing: People's Publishing House, 1918/2012.

Lenin, V. I. "The Collapse of the Second International." In *Lenin Collected Works*, vol. 21, 205–259. Moscow: Progress Publishers, 1974.

Li, Fenglin. "Zhong su guanxi de lishi yu zhong e guanxi de weilai" ["The History of Sino-Soviet Relationship and the Future of the Sino–Russian Relationship"]. In *Preface to Zhong su guanxi shi gang* [*An Outline of the Sino–Soviet Relationship*], edited by Shen Zhihua, 1–8. Beijing: Xinhua Publishing House, 2007.

Liu, Shaoqi. "On the Party." In *Collected Works of Liu Shaoqi*. Beijing: People's Publishing House, 1945/1981. https://www.marxists.org/reference/archive/liu-shaoqi/1945/on-party/ch02.htm

Mao, Zedong. "A Single Spark May Start a Prairie Fire." In *Selected Works of Mao Tse-Tung*, vol. 1. Beijing: Foreign Languages Press, 1930/1954. https://www.marxists.org/reference/archive/mao/selected-works/vol.-1/mswv1_6.htm

Mao, Zedong. "Dui 'guanyu ruogan lishi wenti de jueyi' cao an de shuoming" ["Notes on the Draft of the 'Resolutions on Several Historical Issues'"]. In *Collected Works of Mao Zedong*, vol. 3, 281–284. Beijing: People's Publishing House, 1945/1996.

Mao, Zedong. "Fulu: guanyu ruogan lishi wenti de jueyi" ["Appendix: Resolutions on Several Historical Issues"]. In *Selected Works of Mao Zedong*, vol. 3, 952–1003. Beijing: People's Publishing House, 1945/1991.

Mao, Zedong. "Gei Qin Bangxian de xin" ["Letter to Qin Bangxian"]. In *Selected Letters of Mao Zedong*, 237–239. Beijing: People's Publishing House, 2003.

Mao, Zedong. "Oppose Book Worship." In *Selected Works of Mao Tse-Tung*, vol. 1. Beijing: Foreign Languages Press, 1930/1954. https://www.marxists.org/reference/archive/mao/selected-works/vol.-6/mswv6_11.htm#s6

Mao, Zedong. "Stalin, Friend of the Chinese People." In *Selected Works of Mao Tse-Tung*, vol. 2. Beijing: Foreign Languages Press, 1939. https://www.marxists.org/reference/archive/mao/selected-works/vol.-2/mswv2_24.htm

Mao, Zedong. "The Comintern Has Long Ceased to Meddle in Our Internal Affairs." In *Selected Works of Mao Tse-Tung*, vol. 4. Beijing: Foreign Languages Press, 1943. https://www.marxists.org/reference/archive/mao/selected-works/vol.-6/mswv6_36.htm

Mao, Zedong. "Zai zhongguo gongchandang di qici quanguo daibiao dahui shang de koutou zhengzhi baogao" ["Oral Political Report at the Seventh National Congress of the Communist Party of China"]. In *Collected Report and Speeches of Mao Zedong at the Seventh National Congress of the Communist Party of China*, edited by the Party History Research Center of CPC Central Committee, 104–158. Beijing: CPC History Publishing House, 1995.

Party History Research Center of the CPC Central Committee. *Zhongguo gongchandang lishi* [*The History of the Communist Party of China*], vol. 1. Beijing: CPC History Publishing House, 2011.

Pu, H. "Account of Important Events in the Chinese Revolution in *Dimitrov's Diary*" [<季米特洛夫日记> 中有关中国革命重大事件的记述 'Ji mi te luo fu ri ji' zhong you guan zhong guo ge ming zhong da shi jian de ji shu]. *Study of the History of the Communist Party of China* 5 (2001): 74–84. [In Chinese.]

Sha, Jiansun. *Mao Zedong sixiang tonglun* [*An Overview of Mao Zedong Thought*]. Beijing: People's Publishing House, 2013.

Shen, Zhihua, ed. *Su lian lishi dongan xuanbian* [*Selected Archives of the History of the Soviet Union*]. 34 vols. Beijing: Social Sciences Academic Press, 2002.

Stalin, J. V. *The October Revolution and the National Question. Works*, vol. 4. Moscow: Foreign Languages Publishing House, 1953. https://www.marxists.org/reference/archive/stalin/works/1918/11/19.htm

Sun, Zhongshi, and Baohua Cao. *Lie Ning Si Da Lin lun zhongguo* [*Lenin and Stalin on China*]. Beijing: People's Publishing House, 1950.

Yang, Kuisong. "Gongchan guoji wei zhonggong tigong caizheng yuanzhu zhi kaocha" ["Investigation of the Financial Aids of the Communist International to the Communist Party of China"]. *Social Science Forum*, 2004, no. 4 (2004): 4–24.

Yang, Shangkun. *Yang Shangkun huiyilu* [*Memoirs of Yang Shangkun*]. Beijing: CPC History Publishing House, 2007.

Zhang, Jingru. "Wei He Yun'an suo zhu 'Su e, gongchan guoji yu zhongguo geming' suo zuo de xu." In *Preface to The Soviet Russia, the Communist International and the Chinese Revolution (1919–1923)*, edited by He Yun'an, 1–4. Beijing: Social Sciences Academic Press, 1999.

Zhou, Enlai. "Guan yu dang de liu da de yanjiu" ["A Study of the 6th CPC National Congress"]. In *Selected Works of Zhou Enlai*, vol. 1, 157–187. Beijing: People's Publishing House, 1944/1980.

Marx's critical political economy, 'Marxist economics' and actually occurring revolutions against capitalism

Radhika Desai

ABSTRACT

Most revolutions against capitalism have occurred in 'backward' and Third World societies, and they have divided and disarrayed Marxisms in the West. One key reason, this paper argues, is intellectual. When, long ago, Marxists surrendered to the bourgeois challenge to Marx – neoclassical economics – developing, in place of Marx's critical political economy, a 'Marxist economics', they lost touch with Marx's analysis of capitalism as contradictory value production. That analysis could illuminate how capitalism's contradictions drive its imperialist expansionism and how and why resistance to it must, equally necessarily, take national forms. As a result, major currents of Marxism in the West either have paid attention to imperialism and anti-imperialist resistance but without Marx's analysis of capitalism as contradictory value production or have insisted that their (mistaken) conception of Marx's analysis implies that capitalism has no necessary connection with imperialism. Neither tradition can actually develop Marxism to comprehend the actual historical record of revolutions since Marx's time. Neither can inform new mobilisations against capitalism, whether in or outside its homelands. It is high time we return to Marx's analysis of capitalism as value production and develop it.

Marxism was born of revolution, its first iconic text, *The Manifesto of the Communist Party*, written to orient workers in the revolutions that gathered steam in early 1848. However, their defeat impressed on Marx and Engels the staying power of capitalism and turned Marx to the lifelong engagement with classical political economy that issued in the penetrating (if also incomplete) historical materialist analysis of capitalism as contradictory value production.[1]

Nevertheless, revolution, a transcendence of the social order of capitalism, framed Marx's analysis of capitalism from the outset. It pointed beyond capitalism's anarchy and exploitation – that is, beyond its horizontal contradictions stemming from competition and vertical ones stemming from exploitation[2] – towards 'an association of free men [*Menschen*], working with the means of production held in common, and expending their many and different forms of labour-power in full self-awareness as a single labour force'.[3] It pointed, in other words, towards a consciously organised society of free equals, producing use values and expanding human productive capacities far beyond anything previously imagined. (The alternative was, of course, humanity's destruction). Marx never abandoned this frame. It gave his analysis that unparalleled penetration into the injustices and contradictions that would drive capitalism's history. It has kept new generations going to it like moths to a flame.

However, revolution has not been kind to Marx's followers, at least in Marxism's Western homelands. Here, Marxism has divided and disarrayed over every successful revolution since Marx's time – from the Russian and Chinese through the national and social revolutions in the Third World to Venezuela today. While the specifics disputed naturally varied, there were certain common fault lines. These revolutions did not take place, as expected, in the most advanced capitalist countries as revolutions of an 'internationalist' working class against capitalist exploitation. Rather, they erupted in the 'backward' regions of Europe and then of the Third World. They were revolutions against imperialism as well as capitalism. They featured national as well as class struggles.

While their location in imperialist heartlands undoubtedly threw up obstacles to understanding and assimilating anti-imperialist revolutions to a developing Marxism among Marxists in the West as early as the Second International, as we see below, this paper focuses on a critical intellectual obstacle. To comprehend the historical record of revolutions against capitalism that have actually occurred to date, Marxists need to understand how capitalism's contradictions lead it to be imperialist towards societies outside its core; why such threatened societies must resist in various ways, stronger and weaker (or suffer subjugation); why this resistance must take a national form; and how this dialectic of imperialism and national anti-imperialism has long defined the international relations of the capitalist world and how it has changed over time. In short, Marxists need to understand, as Marx did, how nations have been the material products of the violent dynamic of capitalism, and protagonists within it, just as much as classes. They need to develop an understanding of the 'materiality of nations',[4] as imperialist and anti-imperialist actors, and stop reducing them to cultural phenomena. They need historical analyses of what one writer dubbed 'the worldwide law of value', another capitalism's 'mode of foreign relations' and a third capitalism's 'geopolitical economy',[5] which are oriented to both class and national struggles, and put them in the same historical frame.

This paper argues that, in Western societies, and those intellectually influenced by them, major currents of Marxism have lacked precisely such an understanding. This is because, long ago, they surrendered before the bourgeoisie's challenge to Marxism, neoclassical economics. Born of the so-called Marginalist Revolution circa 1870, this intellectual counterrevolution was fomented against classical political economy, which Marx's critique had recently brought to its culmination. When, after an initial defence (discussed below), Marxists sought to assimilate rather than fight it, they produced a 'Marxist economics' Marx would not have recognised. It forsook Marx's analysis of capitalism as value production, alleging that it suffered from a 'transformation problem' of transforming values into prices. Most Marxist economists also rejected key mechanisms of crisis Marx had identified, particularly capitalism's demand problem and/or the tendency of the rate of profit to fall (hereafter TRPF).

Initially, some Marxist economists, pre-eminently those associated with the US journal *Monthly Review*, for whom imperialism and anti-imperialism were politically important, sought to comprehend them through an eclectic theoretical framework, leaving the terrain of Marx's analysis of capitalism as value production. Later, others, whom we know today as 'Political Marxists', opposed such eclecticism as 'Smithian'. They resorted to a 'pure', 'purely economic' and therefore contradiction-free Ricardian conception of capitalism above any need of state management of its contradictions. Given that, throughout the history of capitalism, such state management of its contradictions, such as its tendency to overproduce commodities and capital, has involved imperialism, this also meant that their conception of capitalism was untainted by imperialism. They denied outright any theoretical relation between capitalism and imperialism, leading to a relative neglect of this nexus at least until 'empire' became prominent in the Bush government's discourse in the 2000s.

No wonder then that, over the past century and more, Marxists have either reduced or denied the revolutionary significance of national struggles against imperialism, or they have articulated solidarity with them only in eclectic Marxist terms. No wonder also that the matter of nations had already split Marxism on the eve of the First World War. These positions have inevitably redounded to the benefit of capitalism's imperial core. Witness, for instance, the support of important parts of the Marxist left in the West for Western military interventions in the Third World in the name of democracy and human rights today.

At a time when capitalism is malingering in its homelands even as it is aggressive abroad; when new and powerful oppositions are growing at home and abroad; when cracks in the post-war unity of the imperialist powers are showing; when resistance from former colonies and semi-colonies, whether capitalist or not, is narrowing imperialist powers' options while making the international order multipolar, we need more than ever to remove the theoretical obstacle constituted by 'Marxist economics' and return to Marx's critique of political economy to develop it for our time to encompass the various forms taken by resistance to it across the world.

In what follows, I first discuss neoclassical economics as the antithesis of Marx's critical development of classical political economy before going on to outline how the neoclassical Trojan horse was wheeled into the Marxist citadel within a generation of Marx's death when, after some initial resistance, major Marxist currents succumbed to it. After briefly recalling how and why imperialism and national resistance to it became politically important to Marxism, I go on to discuss 'Smithian' and Ricardian Marxisms. I conclude by pointing to the possibilities of a properly Marxist understanding of imperialism that the current resurgence of interest in imperialism can exploit.[6]

The neoclassical counterrevolution

Just how intellectually counterrevolutionary and regressive neoclassical economics was is obscured by the tendency, exemplified by Alfred Marshall, to point to continuities between it and classical political economy (though continuities with what Marx called 'vulgar economy' were far stronger) and by the teaching of the history of economics as the 'Whig history' Samuelson openly called for. In it, 'all previous theories must be an inferior form of the present state of knowledge'.[7]

Classical political economy had sought to 'investigate the real internal framework [*Zusammenhang*] of bourgeois relations of production'[8] since capitalism's beginnings. After Physiocracy, it was united in considering labour the source of value. Until Marx, however, classical political economy failed to operationalise this idea to understand how value could be traced to labour when it was not (as in simple commodity production) the predominant input. Smith just gave up. Ricardo wrestled long and unsuccessfully with the problem which was, for him, also connected with how various capitals could receive equal rates of profit when some employed proportionately more labour than others.[9]

Marx carried this tradition forward while knowing that 'insofar as political economy is bourgeois, ie insofar as it views the capitalist order as the absolute and ultimate form of social production ... it can only remain a science while the class struggle remains latent'[10] and that by the mid-nineteenth century, that point had been reached. It 'sounded the knell of scientific bourgeois economics'.[11] While political economy petered out into the vulgarisations of the Mills attempting to 'reconcile the irreconcilable'[12] and the empiricism of the German Historical School, Marx resolved classical political economy's key problems and antinomies. He identified the source of surplus value by distinguishing labour and labour power. He operationalised the law of value by showing how competition pushed values down to their 'socially necessary' level. And he resolved Ricardo's difficulties with labour values, differing proportions of labour and capital and equal profit rates: quite simply, goods in fact did not sell at their values nor did capitals receive equal rates of profit at all times. Exchange at value and profit rate equalisation were outcomes of processes operating over time.[13]

This result was politically problematic for the bourgeoisie. Classical political economy, even in its Ricardian form, had produced socialist currents because Ricardo insisted on the labour origin of value, implying that incomes other than wages were unearned. Marx also exposed the limitations of such Ricardian socialism and, by the late nineteenth century, European working classes were marching under the banner of Marxism. Europe's capitalist classes needed new ideas to justify capitalism and they arrived, as if on cue, systematising what Marx had lambasted and lampooned in *Capital* as 'vulgar economy', prone to the 'fetish character of commodities'. About 1870, three years after the publication of *Capital*, Carl Menger in Austria, Leon Walras in Switzerland and Stanley Jevons in Britain independently distilled the spontaneous consciousness of the bourgeoisie into a systematic apologia for capitalism.

Before proceeding further, we must dispatch an important irony about neoclassical economics. It posited a self-regulating market order which could exist anywhere at any time as a 'system of provision for human needs'.[14] In this form, it catalysed the socialist calculation debate and later discussions of welfare and planning.[15] However, precisely for that reason, it could only fail to penetrate the one historical form of social production that was the farthest thing in human history from a system for provisioning human needs: capitalism.

With regard to capitalism, the 'objective function' of neoclassical economics 'was ... purely apologetic – to justify the capitalist order as more or less inevitable; to justify wages, prices and profits as the result of exchanges carried out on an equal footing'.[16] In performing its ideological role, neoclassical economics has remained implacably opposed to left arguments, particularly in its Austrian and, as Quinn Slobodian has recently argued, 'globalist' Geneva versions.[17]

We may list the key antitheses between Marx's critical political economy and neoclassical economics:

- Classical political economy focused on production (without neglecting exchange), neoclassical economics on consumption and exchange alone.
- In classical political economy, value originated in labour and operated, through competition, to push prices towards the cost of the socially necessary labour commodities embodied. In neoclassical economics, the subjective satisfactions commodities gave individuals, dubbed 'utility' in early versions, determined demand and prices were formed by its interaction with supply.
- Neoclassical economics reached over Marx to Ricardo – not the Ricardo who insisted on the labour origin of value but the Ricardo who accepted Say's Law[18] and conjured up comparative advantage. Accepting Say's Law meant that neoclassical economics denied

capitalism's contradictions and crises tendencies, whether in Walrasian notions of equilibrium or in the sterner Austrian insistence that capitalism's outcomes could not be bettered. It also meant, as Marx and Keynes pointed out, that it conceived exchange as barter, leaving out any consideration of the independent role of money in capitalist society.[19] With Say's Law went comparative advantage. Ricardo may have devised it only 'to support his *theory of value* or to demonstrate that his views on foreign trade are not foreign to it'.[20] However, in claiming that free trade benefitted all nations, it justified colonial patterns of trade.[21] It papered over international tensions that resulted when powerful capitalist countries sought to externalise the consequences of capitalist contradictions, for example by exporting their excess production to colonial or otherwise unprotected markets and undermining prospects for industrial development there. Between them, Say's Law and comparative advantage denied the essential link between capitalism's contradictions and its expansionism or imperialism. For an alternative interpretation of Marx, see Desai, *Geopolitical Economy* and 'Marx, List and the Materiality of Nations' and for Karl Polanyi's astonishingly similar ideas, see Desai, "Commodified Money and Crustacean Nation".[22]

- Classical political economy analysed capitalist society. Neoclassical economics detached something called 'the economy' from it. Max Weber justified this, arguing that modernity separated different spheres of social action and each needed separate study. A wider social scientific division of labour with its various disciplines studying separate spheres of society we know today has grown around it. However, Weber, originally trained as an economist and a partisan of neoclassical economics against German historicism in the Methodenstreit, was concerned above all with the autonomy of the economy. It had an 'especially privileged position': 'However much the institutions abstractly theorised by economics were located historically ... they remained also the supra-historical manifestations of reason and so the universal foundations of a society characterised by its formal rationality, capitalism'.[23]

- Finally, classical political economy's historical approach was replaced by an ahistorical one. Marx's conception of capitalism was doubly historical. First, capitalism was not eternal but a historically specific mode of production. Second, being contradictory, and therefore inherently volatile and unstable, it was historically dynamic, its contradictions hurtling it to its doom. Denying historical change, as neoclassical economics and with it the social sciences generally do (as betrayed in the pervasive use of the simple present tense in them – parties do this, unemployment does that, as if things never change over space and time). They can understand neither capitalism nor its revolutionary historical dynamic.

Marxism and neoclassical economics: from contestation to surrender

Eugen von Böhm-Bawerk may have initiated the encounter between neoclassical economics and Marxism when he criticised Marx in his 1884 *Capital and Interest* and more systematically and frontally in *Karl Marx and the Close of His System*. However, already within a decade of the emergence of neoclassical economics, the new 'subjective' point of view was so 'thoroughly familiar in academic economic circles ... [that] any number of his contemporaries could have produced'[24] a similar critique.

Hilferding defended Marxism against the latter work in 1904, covering Marx's concept of value and his understanding of the equalisation of rates of profit though a process,[25] and challenging the subjectivism of Böhm-Bawerk and neoclassical economics. Bukharin's

Economic Theory of the Leisure Class (finished 1914, published 1919) memorably saw the latter as an 'economic theory of the leisure class' eliminated from production, given to an anomic individualism and psychologism and fearful of revolution.[26] Advocates of the new economics also invoked the opposition between Marx and the new economics: Pareto claimed that Böhm-Bawerk's critique was 'the best reply to Marx's theory of value'.[27]

However, such direct confrontation would soon end. Michael Tugan-Baranovsky, the Russian Legal Marxist, had proposed as early as 1890 that neoclassical economics and Marxism could be reconciled.[28] This 'policy of theoretical conciliation', as Bukharin called it,[29] won the day. With neoclassical economics already pervading the academy, more and more intellectuals would arrive at Marxism already formed by its antithesis, able to approach Marxism only along neoclassical paths.

Just how abrupt this change was is, perhaps, not widely appreciated. The transformation problem is usually traced to Ladislaus Bortkiewicz's attempt to solve it in 1907. However, apart from Marx himself and one superfluous reference to Karl Kautsky, Bortkiewicz cites only Tugan-Baranovsky. Indeed, the three main claims 'Marxist economics' would make against Marx's analysis – that it suffered from a 'transformation problem' of transforming values into prices in a manner compatible with equal profit rates, that it did not consider demand a problem and that profits could not fall because capitalists could hardly want them to – are already present in Tugan-Baranovsky.[30] These were, of course, false problems: the transformation problem was Ricardo's, not Marx's; Marx insisted that 'The ultimate reason for all crises remains the poverty and restricted consumption of the masses'[31]; and the case against the TRPF was a fallacy of composition since Marx had argued precisely that individual rationalities led, at the social level, to this perverse result.[32]

The Russian Legal Marxists (who published legally while the revolutionary Marxists could not) had taken on the Narodnik argument that capitalism could not develop in Russia because its market was too limited, by arguing that capitalism would make its own market as previously self-sufficient peasants demanded more commodities. This view was part of a general denial of capitalism's demand deficit: Tugan-Baranovsky also argued that Marx's criticism of Say's Law was wrong and initiated the trend of using the reproduction schemas of *Capital*, Vol. II, to argue that only disproportions between sectors caused crises in capitalism.[33]

Rosa Luxemburg saw clearly that the Legal Marxists were smuggling in Say's Law through the Vol. II back door. Their victory over the populists, she argued, had been 'rather too thorough':

> In the heat of battle, all three – Struve, Bulgakov and Tugan-Baranovsky – overstated their case. The question was whether capitalism in general, and Russian capitalism in particular, is capable of development; these Marxists, however, proved this capacity to the extent of even offering theoretical proof that capitalism can go on without limits ....[34]

Most Legal Marxists eventually drifted away from Marxism but not before they had shunted Marxism onto the wrong track of 'Marxist economics'. Even though, in the early twentieth century, Hilferding and later Bukharin drew clear lines separating Marxism from neoclassical economics, the waters were already muddied: take two prominent instances.

Luxemburg's argument in *The Accumulation of Capital* that a 'purely capitalist' society consisting only of capitalists and workers could not be self-contained, and needed non-capitalist spheres to export excess production to, relied on considering demand deficits a major contradiction of capitalism. In making her case, she was also clear that those who rejected it and posited a self-contained 'pure' capitalism did so by incorrectly interpreting the reproduction schemas of *Capital*, Vol. II, along Tugan-Baranovsky's lines. However, her arguments were dismissed without 'confronting Luxemburg's theory in its full integrity'[35] because Tugan-Baranovsky's position had become widely shared. Lenin, for instance, declared, even before reading the book, that considering 'the realization of surplus-value ... possible also in a *"purely* capitalist" society' was the 'theoretically correct' position.[36]

The idea of a 'purely capitalist' society, which Luxemburg attacked and Lenin used, was already a neoclassical one. Mandel would remind us, decades later, that not only did the capitalism of *Capital* never refer to any real system, 'pure' capitalism existed nowhere, as Engels pointed out, confidently predicting also that it would not be allowed to since revolutionaries would not 'let it come to that'.[37] We may recall that Lenin relied on the Legal Marxist case in his *Development of Capitalism in Russia* to claim that not only could capitalism develop in the Russian countryside, it was already doing so (a point which was later found to have been greatly exaggerated).[38] Lenin may not have denied underconsumption outright, but he followed Tugan-Baranovsky in seeing disproportionality between, say, producers' goods and consumers' goods arising from the anarchy of capitalist production, as the 'more profound' contradiction.[39]

Secondly, while Hilferding lucidly defended Marx against Böhm-Bawerk, even he proved somewhat open to Tugan-Baranovsky's 'policy of theoretical conciliation' in *Finance Capital*. While criticising Tugan-Baranovsky sharply on many counts – for generalising from English conditions in his work on crises or for assuming that liquidity alone, and not objective conditions, would stimulate recovery after crisis[40] – he takes Tugan-Baranovsky entirely seriously as a Marxist. Noting his 'curious conception of a system of production for production's sake' in which lack of demand could not possibly be a problem,[41] Hilferding nevertheless insists that

> if this is 'madness' there is method in it, and a Marxist one at that, for it is just this analysis of the specific historical structure of capitalist production which is distinctively Marxist. It is Marxism gone mad, but still Marxism.[42]

In calling the notion of 'production for production's sake' Marxist, Hilferding was following the trend, begun by Tugan-Baranovsky, of considering Marx's forte to be his analysis of production and its social relations, one which would gain from being joined to an allegedly superior neoclassical account of circulation. If so, a certain 'Ricardian Marxism', which claimed its Marxist credentials for paying attention to production but supplemented it with an allegedly superior neoclassical view of circulation, was already emerging. Certainly, Zarembka's view of Lenin as 'economist of production'[43] points in that direction; and Henryk Grossman, who also neglected the issue of capitalism's demand deficit and inaugurated the tradition of believing that the TRPF is the only or the most fundamental cause of crisis,[44] could be considered another pioneer. Of course, such a Ricardian Marxism forgot that Marx hardly neglected circulation and that his understanding of it was superior: Marx criticised Say's Law, and consequently paid attention to the role of money and distinguished between asset and commodity prices.

Imperialism and Marxism in the 30 years' crisis of 1914–45

This sort of Marxist economics contributed to the positivistic and economistic turn of the 'Marxism of the Second International'[45] and to its inattention to national questions. Like neoclassical economics, it was prey to the Ricardian fictions, Say's Law and comparative advantage. They denatured Marx's analysis and denied the 'materiality of nations' in managing capitalism's contradictions through domestic and international (imperial) actions. This inattention proved its undoing. The Second International's internationalism collapsed in 1914 because its revolutionary rhetoric could not account for the historical practice of securing working class allegiance through national reforms that gave 'workers … a good deal more to lose than their chains'.[46] Imperial matters were not just ignored; many social democrats also justified colonialism and its 'civilizing mission' because of its material benefits.[47]

To be sure, a starburst of Marxist works on imperialism lit up the intellectual landscape before and during the First World War. However, Hilferding, Bukharin and Lenin focused on the imperial countries and on their competition for colonies and linked it, not to an inherent imperialism of capitalism, but to a specific stage in its development. While their works shed much light on the novelty of this stage – the second industrial revolution, its high capital requirements and greater role of finance (Hilferding), industrial concentration or monopoly (Lenin) and their national organisation (Bukharin) – they reinforced the false impression that the middle decades of the nineteenth century were not imperialist (which was conclusively refuted by Gallagher and Robinson[48]). Moreover, their chief concern was with how this competition resulted in war and with its consequences for the working masses their parties led. While this was an entirely legitimate concern, it is important to note that only Luxemburg paid systematic attention to imperialism's consequences for the colonies.

However, backward Russia could not ignore imperialism so easily. Well before war broke out, Lenin had welcomed Japan's victory over Russia and nationalist ferment in Persia and Turkey in 1905, and spoken of European workers' 'Asian comrades' in 1908. By 1916, his recognition of the centrality of national revolutions against imperialism in the unfolding of world revolution against capital had resulted in the tripartite division of the world into the imperial, backward and colonial and semi-colonial countries, to evolve distinct political strategies for each. Lenin's division prefigured what Alfred Sauvy would later dub the First, Second and Third Worlds.[49]

History soon validated Lenin's intellectual orientation. The failure of revolution in Western Europe after the First World War made national liberation even more important for the Bolsheviks. 'Oppressed nationalities' of the future USSR helped them win the civil war, and national struggles in Asia relieved imperialist pressure on the revolution.[50] At the 1920 Comintern congress, M. N. Roy reversed the Second International's scheme of world revolution, arguing that the reformist west depended on peasants' and workers' revolution in the east, not vice versa. This modified the official position. Imperialist benefits obstructed revolution in the west; communists should support revolutionary bourgeois nationalist movements; and, in certain circumstances, backward countries could achieve communism directly.[51] The Congress of the Peoples of the East later in 1920 brought together representatives of Soviet, Iranian, Turkish, Indian and Chinese nationalist struggles[52] in the first of the gatherings to bespeak the common anti-imperialism of Marxism and the nationalist movements. These developments replaced the Eurocentrism of the Second International with the Third International's focus on imperial and colonial questions, and from here into the 1970s, the comprehensive 'revolt against the West'[53] that defined the twentieth century was faithfully reflected in Marxism.

Post-war 'Smithian' and Keynesian Marxism

So faithfully was it reflected that, as Prabhat Patnaik recalled, until the 1970s, 'imperialism occupied perhaps the most prominent place in any Marxist discussion', particularly in the US. Indeed, 'many European Marxists accused American Marxism of being tainted with "third worldism"', the belief that 'advanced capitalism had manipulated its internal class contradictions to a point where the only effective challenge that could be launched against it …. was in the periphery. *Monthly Review* had a more or less similar position'.[54] However, this attention to imperialism was based on a rather eclectic version of Marxism, blended with Keynesianism, not Marx's analysis of capitalism as value production. Paul Sweezy's intellectual course is exemplary.

In his encyclopaedic introduction to Marx's political economy, *The Theory of Capitalist Development*, in 1941, Sweezy recognised that Marx's oeuvre was different from the neoclassical tradition and also from its later critics. In particular, Sweezy did not dismiss demand problems. Indeed, against the neoclassical stress on consumer choice, he justified Marx's position on the matter of consumer demand on two counts. First, he pointed out that for Marx, 'under capitalism effective demand is only partly a question of consumers' wants. Even more important is the basic question of income distribution'. Second, in this context, 'consumer choice' was 'in itself relatively stable and merely react[ed] to changes elsewhere' and thus had 'a subordinate place in the analytical scheme'.[55]

However, at the same time, Sweezy took a position close to Tugan-Baranovsky's on the falling rate of profit[56] and continued the tradition of regarding Marx's analysis as suffering from a 'transformation' problem. Since, following (the 'bastard') Keynes, Sweezy regarded the demand problem as soluble through demand management,[57] he can be said to have sported, if not a contradiction-free conception of capitalism, one in which its contradictions could be managed. With any self-destruction of capitalism due to its contradictions ruled out, Sweezy believed its demise might occur thanks to the increasing attractive power of a productively superior socialism.[58]

Sweezy's own surrender to neoclassical economics is clear in the introduction he wrote in the volume he edited containing Böhm-Bawerk's attack on Marx, Hilferding's defence and Bortkiewicz's attempt to 'solve' the 'transformation problem'. He worked hard to portray Böhm-Bawerk as a 'dispassionate' critic,[59] arguing that from his 'unhistorical and unsocial standpoint there is only one possible way of regarding economic phenomena'. That was why he naturally assumed that 'Marx must be trying to do the same things' and found Marx wanting. Hilferding, by contrast, argued that 'the defenders of capitalism should look at the system which they consider to be the only possible system, differently from its critics'.[60] This made dialogue between the two systems difficult, Sweezy said, and left it at that: 'I doubt the difficulty can be overcome'.[61] By the time he came to write, with Paul Baran, his most important work, *Monopoly Capital*, Sweezy had simply dispensed with Marx's value analysis and worked with other eclectically devised categories such as 'surplus'.

Monthly Review produced rich and insightful analyses of imperialism – particularly American – of its militarism, its wars, its corporations and surplus transfer, its history and resistance to it. It gave rise to dependency theory and world systems analysis. It informed, and continues to inform, generations of the left and Marxists. However, its analysis dispensed with Marx's analysis of capitalism as value production and was based on a conception of a capitalism which was, if not free of contradictions, at least free of unmanageable ones.

Ricardian Marxism of the neoliberal era

Whereas imperialism had been central to Marxism until the 1970s, it was 'obviously not the case' thereafter, Patniak noted in the early 1990s. The topic had 'virtually disappeared from the pages of Marxist journals, especially of a later vintage', neither 'because anyone has theorised against the concept' nor because 'the world has so changed in the last decade and a half that to talk of imperialism has become an obvious anachronism'. Rather, Patnaik attributed the 'theoretically unself-conscious' silence to 'the very strengthening and consolidation of imperialism' after Vietnam.[62] However, while the concept of imperialism was not challenged theoretically, the conception of capitalism whose development we have been tracking matured to have the same effect as a theoretical challenge.

When, beginning in the 1960s, Marxism in the English-speaking world was revived with *New Left Review* and its publishing house, New Left Books (later Verso), introducing European Marxism into the Anglo-American conversation, the 'transformation problem' was revived, this time in Britain. Prominent English Marxists, such as Maurice Dobb, working on David Ricardo and his twentieth-century follower Piero Sraffa, drew the transformation problem closer to its Ricardian roots. This work, later elaborated by others, pre-eminently Ian Steedman,[63] resulted in an explicitly Ricardian Marxism tracing its roots to an allegedly single 'Ricardo–Marx approach to the problems of value and of distribution'.[64] This Ricardian Marxism was even more prey to the Ricardian fictions, Say's Law and comparative advantage. Whereas Sweezy and his ilk considered the demand problem a manageable one, the Ricardian Marxists did not consider it a problem at all. Implacably opposed to Keynesianism as 'reformist', they can be said to have erected a virtually neoliberal conception of 'pure' 'economic' capitalism without contradictions.

This Ricardian tradition emerged from its early confinement to debates among 'Marxist economists' with Robert Brenner's famous 'The Origins of Capitalist Development' (1977). In it, he accused the *Monthly Review*, dependency and world systems traditions of being 'Smithian'. They had, he felt, trade- and circulation-based understandings of the origin and spread of capitalism which merely replaced Smith's (alleged) optimism with a pessimism about the '"development of underdevelopment" [being] an indispensable condition for capitalist development'.[65]

Soon dubbed 'Political Marxism', this tradition rightly emphasised class relations and struggle, the role of force, and the realm of production. However, it also argued, in a Schumpeterian rather than Marxist vein, that capitalism would develop the forces of production unceasingly. And it aligned neatly with the Ricardo loved by the neoclassical economists, the Ricardo of the twin fictions, Say's Law and comparative advantage. In line with Say's Law, that capitalism had no demand problem, Brenner and Political Marxism held that it did not need imperialism.[66] In line with the idea of comparative advantage, they believed that Third World attempts at autonomous development prompted by theories of underdevelopment were dangerous because they ignored 'the degree to which any significant national development of the productive forces depends today upon a close connection with the international division of labour'.[67]

However, such Ricardian Marxism is an oxymoron, for at least three reasons. First, no one familiar with Marx's advance beyond Ricardo's understanding of value[68] can assimilate the two. Second, all protestations to the contrary, no Ricardian Marxism can have a workable labour theory of value. Ricardo had failed to operationalise it. All the Ricardian Marxists could achieve with each failure to solve the transformation problem they attributed to Marx was to reinforce the false impression that his analysis of capitalism was fundamentally flawed. Finally, and arguably most importantly, it is simply wrong to separate a production-centred 'Ricardian' from a circulation-centred 'Smithian' Marxism. For Marx, capitalism, as generalised commodity production, is the contradictory unity of its production and circulation processes: in it 'the production of surplus value is only the first act … [in] the second act … [t]he total mass of commodities … must be sold'.[69]

Of course, not all Marxists in the West accepted this conception of capitalism. Ernest Mandel[70] rejected and contested all the main claims at issue – the 'transformation problem', the dismissal of demand problems and the TRPF. He particularly contributed to the effort to expose the nullity of the so-called transformation problem.[71] One major result was the Temporal Single System Interpretation (TSSI)[72] of Marx's analysis, which demonstrates that, provided prices and values are seen to constitute a single system and input and output prices as being determined not simultaneously but separated in time, there is no transformation problem. Long ignored, TSSI is now garnering attention and will help those who accepted that Marx had a transformation problem in finding their way to a better understanding of Marx. However, it is as, if not more, important to insist that Marx can and should be read without the distortions neoclassical economics introduces.[73]

The conception of capitalism promoted by Marxist economics is influential far beyond its boundaries thanks to the Weberian social scientific division of labour. It organises academic life, including that of most Marxists, even though it violates Marx's method of analysing society as a whole and doing so in the two historical modes mentioned earlier. Disciplinary Marxisms, themselves unaware of the distance of their partial and ahistorical visions from Marx, have flourished and have tended to take the word of Marxist economists when it comes to understanding Marx's 'economics'.[74]

Ricardian Marxism set back understanding of imperialism, nation states, the dynamic of relations between them and, thus, the record of revolutions against capitalism more surely than had its 'Smithian' counterpart. First, it held that while imperialism 'can and does happen and it does aid capitalist accumulation … it is not required by the logic of capitalism'.[75] Such positions could even lead to the thesis that imperialism was a 'pioneer of capitalism', as Bill Warren[76] put it. Or, in the words of Anthony Brewer,

> Capitalism does not need a subordinated hinterland or periphery, though it will use and profit from it if it exists. … Once industrial capital had taken charge, capitalist conquest could play a progressive (though brutal) role by initiating capitalist industrialization. The origins and rapid development of capitalism in Europe and its slow penetration in Asia were the result of differences in the preceding modes of production in these areas: European domination was a consequence, not a primary cause, of this difference.[77]

The panoply of means through which western productive capacities and living standards are elevated and those in subordinated countries depressed cannot be understood in term of this Ricardian Marxism. They include how surpluses drained from formally or informally subordinated countries have critically aided industrialisation in the core[78]; how expanding markets for imperial products deindustrialised colonies; how imperialism supported the power of unproductive elites incapable of developing productive capacities; how colonies became a labour reserve from which to draw semi-free labour; how constraining Third World consumption relieves upward pressure on commodity prices and secures the value of western monies;[79] and how imperialist countries' monopolies on higher value production are secured and maintained in a wider system of unequal exchange[80] by formally preventing or informally discouraging or preventing countries from improving their productive capacities.[81] The list could go on.

Secondly, Marxists have never asked why nation states have proliferated under capitalism,[82] accepting instead a highly 'culturalist' understanding of nations and nationalism,[83] leaving political economy prey to a blank internationalism akin to what two very different thinkers, Antonio Gramsci[84] and Friedrich List,[85] derided as 'cosmopolitanism'. They are unable to grapple with national and inter-*national* realities of the capitalist world.[86] Either the world economy is considered a single whole in which national economies do not matter, or the core countries are taken to stand in for it. No wonder Marxists in the west have been so credulous of the cosmopolitan ideologies of 'globalisation' and 'empire' which also debilitate Marxist international relations.[87]

Finally, theoretical difficulties with nations and imperialism leave such Marxism with a rather limited, even vague, conception of revolution. Moreover, having dispensed with the notion of contradiction, Western Marxism relies on (western) working-class mobilisation alone to magically overcome a capitalism assumed to be all-powerful, worldwide and eternal. Forsaking the possibility of autonomous national development has also left the western left, ironically, without any plan for building a socialist (and, initially at least, inevitably a national) economy beyond redistribution and democratisation. For it has left the task of developing the forces of production to capitalism on the erroneous Schumpeterian grounds that it alone can do so and, indeed, does so, perpetually and prodigiously. Without a non-capitalist way to build productive capacity, it has shackled itself to capitalism in perpetuity and has, by its own lights, no way out of it. Finally, without an appreciation of the benefits western societies enjoy thanks to their privileged position in the international hierarchy that is the world economy, such a Marxism cannot conceive of how to deal with forsaking them as any socialism must, or with losing them through anti-imperialist advances elsewhere.

Conclusion: from contradictory value production to imperialism and anti-imperialism

Major currents of Marxism have been unable to understand imperialism and national anti-imperialist resistance in consonance with Marx's analysis of capitalism as contradictory value production for more than a century because of a 'policy of theoretical conciliation' between Marx's value analysis and neoclassical economics and the resultant emergence of a 'Marxist Economics'. It treated the necessary connection between capitalism and imperialism in eclectically Marxist or non-Marxist terms or denied it. Both approaches forsook Marxist understanding of how powerful contradictions drive capitalist imperialism and how it is resisted. The opportunity to build intellectually powerful and theoretically consistent understandings of the capitalist world and the key contradictions that drive its international relations, provoking resistance and revolutions, is lost. And large parts of the left had been left susceptible to the dominant discourse of Western imperialism today.

This matters today more than ever. If Patnaik's apprehension that discussions of imperialism among Marxists had declined because imperialism had strengthened in the 1980s is correct, it would follow that they had flourished during the immediate post-war period of decolonisation because imperialism had been weakened. And it is perhaps a sign of its renewed weakening that discussion of imperialism is expanding. After initially doing so in response to the ubiquity of the word 'empire' in the Bush Jr administration's discourse, it now has a critical logic of its own.[88] It is critical that, this time around, we do not forgo the theoretical fruits of an approach to imperialism that is more faithful to Marx's analysis of capitalism as value production.

Acknowledgements

I would like to thank William Carroll, Alan Freeman, Jamie Lawson, Kees van der Pijl, Claude Serfati, Paul Zarembka and two anonymous referees for their insightful comments and suggestions. Length limitations prevented me from taking all of them on board. However, they enriched the argument and deepened my understanding. Remaining faults are my responsibility. I would also like to thank Brendan Devlin for his meticulous help with the formatting and referencing.

Disclosure statement

No potential conflict of interest was reported by the author.

Notes

1. Williams, "Eighteenth Century Brumaire."
2. Desai, "Value of History and the History of Value," classified the main contradictions of capitalism. See also, Desai "Consumption Demand."
3. Marx, *Capital*, Vol. I, 171.
4. Desai, *Geopolitical Economy*, discusses Marx's understanding of classes and nations.
5. Ibid.; Amin, *Law of Worldwide Value*; van der Pijl, *Discipline of Western Supremacy*.
6. No part of this paper suggests wholesale rejection of the writers criticised; they have much to teach. At issue is how neoclassical economics has skewed their work.
7. Freeman, Chick and Kayatekin, "Samuelson's Ghosts," 519.
8. Marx, *Capital*, Vol. I, 174–5n.
9. On the prehistory of conceptions of value, see Dobb, *Theories of Value and Distribution*; Meek, *Studies in the Labour Theory of Value*, 2nd ed.
10. Marx, *Capital*, Vol. I, 96.
11. Ibid., 175n.
12. Ibid., 98.
13. Marx, *Theories*, Vol. II, 197–9. For how Marx resolved the antinomies of classical political economy, see Desai, "Political Economy."
14. Clarke, *Marx, Marginalism and Modern Sociology*, 9.
15. Meek, "Marginalism and Marxism,"; Blackburn, "Fin de Siècle."
16. Mandel, *Marxist Economic Theory*, 717.
17. Slobodian, *Globalists: The End of Empire*.

18. Keynes, *General Theory of Employment*, 32.
19. Regarding Marx and Keynes on Say's Law, see Sardoni, "Keynes and Marx."
20. Marx, *Theories*, Vol. III, 253.
21. For critiques of comparative advantage, see, *inter alia*, U. Patnaik, "Ricardo's Fallacy"; Reinert, *How Rich Countries Got Rich*.
22. Marx, see Desai, *Geopolitical Economy* and 'Marx, List and the Materiality of Nations' and for Karl Polanyi's astonishingly similar ideas, see Desai, "Commodified Money and Crustacean Nation."
23. Clarke, *Marx, Marginalism and Modern Sociology*, 267.
24. Sweezy, "Introduction."
25. Hilferding, "Böhm-Bawerk's Criticism of Marx," 156, 170.
26. Bukharin, *Economic Theory of the Leisure Class*, 29–30.
27. Meek, *Studies in the Labour Theory of Value*, 2nd ed., 243.
28. Kindersley, *First Russian Revisionists*, 53–4.
29. Bukharin, *Economic Theory of the Leisure Class*, 163.
30. For a fuller discussion, see Desai, "Consumption Demand in Marx."
31. Marx, *Capital*, Vol. III, 615.
32. Mandel, "Introduction," in *Capital*, Vol. III, 35–6; and Desai, "Consumption Demand." For an empirical demonstration, see Freeman, "Profit Rate in the Presence of Financial Markets."
33. According to Paul Sweezy, the first to do this. Sweezy, *Theory of Capitalist Development*, 159.
34. Luxemberg, *Accumulation of Capital*, 304.
35. Zarembka, "Rosa Luxemburg's 'Accumulation of Capital,'" 5.
36. Zarembka, "Accumulation of Capital, Its Definition," 218.
37. Mandel, "Introduction," in *Capital*, Vol. II, 68.
38. Lewin, *Russia/USSR/Russia*, 76ff.; Kellogg, *Truth Behind Bars*, ch. 5.
39. Zarembka, "Lenin as Economist of Production," 289.
40. Hilferding, *Finance Capital*, 420n and 421n.
41. On the tiresome persistence of this, see Desai, "Consumption Demand in Marx."
42. Hilferding, *Finance Capital*, 421–2.
43. Zarembka, "Lenin as Economist of Production."
44. Howard and King, *History of Marxian Economics*, 316.
45. Colletti, *From Rousseau to Lenin*.
46. Joll, *Second International*, 114.
47. Eley, *Forging Democracy*, 91, 112.
48. Gallagher and Robinson, "Imperialism of Free Trade."
49. Desai, "From National Bourgeoisies to Rogues."
50. Lenin, "Better Fewer but Better."
51. Claudin, *Communist Movement*, 248, 265.
52. Riddell, *To See the Dawn*.
53. Barraclough, *Introduction to Contemporary History*.
54. Patnaik, "Whatever Happened," 102–6.
55. Sweezy, *Theory of Capitalist Development*, 49, 51.
56. Ibid., 106.
57. Desai, "Keynes Redux," argues that this was not what Keynes believed.
58. Sweezy, *Theory of Capitalist Development*, 362.
59. Sweezy, "Introduction," xiv.
60. Ibid., xxii.
61. Ibid.
62. Patnaik, "Whatever Happened," 103.
63. See particularly Steedman, *Marx after Sraffa*.
64. Dobb, *Theories of Value and Distribution*, 257.
65. Brenner, "Origins of Capitalist Development," 27.
66. Brenner's later work *The Economics of Global Turbulence* places the demand problem centrally in its argument. However, political Marxism does not rely on this work, only on Brenner's "Origins of Capitalist Development."

67. Brenner, "Origins of Capitalist Development," 92.
68. Marx, *Theories*, Vol. I, 164–216.
69. Marx, *Capital*, Vol. III, 352.
70. Mandel was that rare post-war Marxist whose link to the revolutionary working class set him apart from Marxist economics: though he used the term to describe his work, he did not belong to the tradition this essay criticises.
71. Mandel and Freeman, *Ricardo, Marx, Sraffa*.
72. Kliman, *Reclaiming Marx's Capital*; Freeman and Carchedi, *Marx and Non-Equilibrium Economics*.
73. Ferdinand Tönnies's best known work, *Community and Society*, contains a remarkably lucid defence of Marx against the accusation that he could not reconcile average profits with value and thus suffered from the infamous 'transformation problem'. Tönnies, *Community and Society*, 101. See also Desai, "Political Economy."
74. So deeply accepted is the idea that there can be a Marxist sociology or anthropology or political science that the doyen of English Marxism, Perry Anderson, could write elaborate histories of Marxism on their basis: Anderson, *Considerations on Western Marxism*; Anderson, "Components of the National Culture,"; Anderson, "Culture in Contraflow."
75. Zarembka, "Lenin as Economist of Production," 8.
76. Warren, *Imperialism: Pioneer of Capitalism*.
77. Brewer, *Marxist Theories of Imperialism*, 75.
78. U. Patnaik, "Free Lunch."
79. P. Patnaik, *Accumulation and Stability under Capitalism*; P. Patnaik, *The Value of Money*; and P. Patnaik and Patnaik, *A Theory of Imperialism*.
80. Emmanuel, *Unequal Exchange*; and Mandel, *Late Capitalism*.
81. Chang, *Kicking Away the Ladder*.
82. With exceptions, which have, however, their own limitations: Nairn, *Break-up of Britain*; Wood, "Unhappy Families"; and Teschke, *Myth of 1648*.
83. The popularity of Anderson, *Imagined Communities*, is exhibit A here; for a critique see Desai, "Inadvertence of Benedict Anderson."
84. Gramsci, *Selections from the Prison Notebooks*, 274.
85. List, *National Systems of Political Economy*.
86. eg Rosenberg, *Empire of Civil Society*; for a critique see Desai, "Absent Geopolitics of Pure Capitalism."
87. See Desai, *Geopolitical Economy*; and Desai, "Absent Geopolitics of Pure Capitalism."
88. I have in mind works such as P. Patnaik and Patnaik, *A Theory of Imperialism*; Smith, *Imperialism in the Twenty-First Century*; Ness and Cope, *Palgrave Encyclopedia of Imperialism and Anti-Imperialism*; Cope, *Divided World, Divided Class*; and Desai, *Geopolitical Economy*.

Bibliography

Amin, Samir. *The Law of Worldwide Value*. New York: Monthly Review Press, (1978) 2010.
Anderson, Benedict. *Imagined Communities: Reflections on the Origin and Spread of Nationalism*. 2nd ed. London: Verso, (1983) 2006. doi:10.1086/ahr/90.4.903.
Anderson, Perry. "Components of the National Culture." *New Left Review* I/50 (1968): 3–57.
Anderson, Perry. *Considerations on Western Marxism*. London: Verso, 1976.
Anderson, Perry. "Culture in Contraflow." *New Left Review* I/180 (1990): 42–80.
Anderson, Perry. "Culture in Contraflow." *New Left Review* I/182 (1990): 85–138.
Barraclough, Geoffrey. *An Introduction to Contemporary History*. London: Penguin, 1964. doi:10.1086/ahr/71.2.510.
Blackburn, Robin. "Fin de Siècle: Socialism after the Crash." *New Left Review* I/185 (1991): 5–68.
Brenner, Robert. 1998. "The Economics of Global Turbulence." *New Left Review* I/229 May–June: 1–265.
Brenner, Robert. "The Origins of Capitalist Development: A Critique of Neo-Smithian Marxism." *New Left Review* I/104 (1977): 25–93.
Brewer, Anthony. *Marxist Theories of Imperialism: A Critical Survey*. 2nd ed. London: Routledge, 1990.

Bukharin, Nicolai. *The Economic Theory of the Leisure Class*. New York: Monthly Review Press, (1914) 1972.

Chang, Ha-Joon. *Kicking Away the Ladder: Development Strategy in Historical Perspective*. London: Anthem, 2002.

Clarke, Simon. *Marx, Marginalism and Modern Sociology: From Adam Smith to Max Weber*. 2nd ed. Basingstoke: Macmillan Academic and Professional, 1991.

Claudin, Fernando. *The Communist Movement: From Comintern to Cominform*. London: Viking, 1972.

Colletti, Lucio. *From Rousseau to Lenin: Studies in Ideology*. New York: Monthly Review Press, 1972.

Cope, Zak. *Divided World, Divided Class*. Montreal: Kersplebedeb, 2012.

Desai, Radhika. "Commodified Money and Crustacean Nation." In *Karl Polanyi in the Twenty-First Century*, edited by Radhika Desai and Kari Polanyi Levitt, 78–101. Manchester, UK: Manchester University Press, 2020.

Desai, Radhika. "Consumption Demand in Marx and in the Current Crisis." *Research in Political Economy* 26 (2010): 101–141.

Desai, Radhika. "From National Bourgeoisies to Rogues, Failures and Bullies: The Contradictions of 21st Century Imperialism and the Unravelling of the Third World." *Third World Quarterly* 25, no. 1 (2004): 169–185. doi:10.1080/0143659042000185390.

Desai, Radhika. *Geopolitical Economy: After US Hegemony, Globalization and Empire*. London: Pluto Press, 2013.

Desai, Radhika. "Keynes Redux: History Catches Up." In *Bankruptcies and Bailouts*, edited by Wayne Antony and Julie Guard, 123–44. Halifax: Fernwood Publishing, 2009.

Desai, Radhika. "Marx, List and the Materiality of Nations." *Rethinking Marxism* 24, no. 1 (2012): 47–67. doi:10.1080/08935696.2012.635038.

Desai, Radhika. "Political Economy." In *The Bloomsbury Companion to Marx*, edited by Jeff Diamanti, Andrew Pendakis and Imre Szeman. London: Bloomsbury Academic, 2018.

Desai, Radhika. "The Absent Geopolitics of Pure Capitalism." *World Review of Political Economy* 1, no. 3 (2010): 463–484.

Desai, Radhika. "The Inadvertence of Benedict Anderson: Engaging *Imagined Communities*." *The Asia-Pacific Journal* 11 (2009): 1–22.

Desai, Radhika. "The Value of History and the History of Value." In *The Great Meltdown of 2008: Systemic, Conjunctural or Policy-Created?*, edited by Turan Subasat 136–58. Northampton, MA: Edward Elgar Publishing, 2016.

Dobb, Maurice. *Theories of Value and Distribution since Adam Smith: Ideology and Economy Theory*. Cambridge: Cambridge University Press, 1973.

Eley, Geoff. *Forging Democracy: The History of the Left in Europe*. Oxford: Oxford University Press, 2002. doi:10.1086/ahr/108.3.906.

Emmanuel, Arghiri. *Unequal Exchange: A Study in the Imperialism of Trade*. New York: Monthly Review, 1972.

Freeman, Alan. "The Profit Rate in the Presence of Financial Markets: A Necessary Correction." *Journal of Australian Political Economy* 70, no. 70 (2012): 167–192.

Freeman, Alan, and Guglielmo Carchedi. *Marx and Non-Equilibrium Economics*. Cheltenhaum UK: Edward Elgar, 1996.

Freeman, Alan, Victoria Chick, and Serap Kayatekin. "Samuelson's Ghosts: Whig History and the Reinterpretation of Economic Theory." *Cambridge Journal of Economics* 38, no. 3 (2014): 519–529. doi:10.1093/cje/beu017.

Gallagher, John, and Ronald Robinson. "The Imperialism of Free Trade." *The Economic History Review* 6, no. 1 (1953): 1–15. doi:10.2307/2591017.

Gramsci, A. *Selections from the Prison Notebooks*. Edited and translated by Q. Hoare and G. N. Smith. London: Lawrence and Wishart, 1971.

Hilferding, Rudolf. *Finance Capital: A Study of the Latest Phase of Capitalist Development*. London: Routledge & Kegan Paul, (1910) 1981.

Hilferding, Rudolf. *Bohm-Bawerk's Criticism of Marx in Paul Sweezy*, ed. *Karl Marx and the Close of His System by Eugen von Böhm-Bawerk and Bohm-Bawerk's Criticism of Marx by Rudolf Hilferding*, London: The Merlin Press, 1949.

Howard, M. C., and J. E. King. *A History of Marxian Economics*. Vol 1. Basingstoke: Macmillan, 1989.

Joll, James. *The Second International*. London: Routledge and Kegan Paul, 1955.

Kellogg, Paul. *Truth behind Bars: Reflections on the Fate of the Russian Revolution*. Edmonton: Athabasca University Press, 2019.

Keynes, John Maynard. *General Theory of Employment, Interest and Money*. London: Macmillan, (1936) 1967.

Kindersley, Richard. *The First Russian Revisionists: A Study of "Legal Marxism" in Russia*. Oxford: Clarendon Press, 1962.

Kliman, Andrew. *Reclaiming Marx's Capital: A Refutation of the Myth of Inconsistency*. Lanham, MD: Lexington Books, 2007.

Lenin, V. I. "Better Fewer but Better." In *Collected Works*, 2nd ed., Vol. 33, 487–502. Moscow: Progress Publishers, (1923) 1965.

Lewin, Moshe. *Russia/USSR/Russia: The Drive and Drift of a Superstate*. New York: The New Press, 1994.

List, Friedrich. *National System of Political Economy*. Philadelphia: J. B. Lippincott and Co., (1841) 1856.

Luxemburg, Rosa. *The Accumulation of Capital. Routledge Classics*. London: Routledge, (1913) 2003.

Mandel, Ernest. "Introduction." In *Capital*, edited by Karl Marx, Vol. II, 11–79. London: Penguin, 1978.

Mandel, Ernest. "Introduction." In *Capital*, edited by Karl Marx, Vol. III, 9–90. London: Penguin, 1981.

Mandel, Ernest. *Late Capitalism*. London: New Left Books, 1972.

Mandel, Ernest. *Marxist Economic Theory*. London: Merlin Press, 1962.

Mandel, Ernest and Alan Freeman, eds. *Ricardo, Marx, Sraffa: The Langston Memorial Volume*. London: Verso, 1984.

Marx, Karl. *Capital* Vol. I. London: Penguin, (1867) 1977.

Marx, Karl. *Capital* Vol. III. London: Penguin, (1894) 1981.

Marx, Karl. *Theories of Surplus Value* Vol. I. London: Lawrence and Wishart, 1968.

Marx, Karl. *Theories of Surplus Value* Vol. II. Lawrence and Wishart, 1969.

Marx, Karl. *Theories of Surplus Value* Vol. III. London: Lawrence and Wishart, 1972.

Meek, R. "Marginalism and Marxism." *History of Political Economy* 4, no. 2 (1972): 499–511. doi:10.1215/00182702-4-2-499.

Meek, R. *Studies in the Labour Theory of Value*. 1st ed. New York: Monthly Review Press, 1956. doi:10.1086/ahr/81.5.1070-a.

Meek, R. *Studies in the Labour Theory of Value*. 2nd ed. London: Brookings Institution, 1973.

Nairn, Tom. *The Break-up of Britain*. London: New Left Books, 1978.

Ness, Immanuel, and Zak Cope. *The Palgrave Encyclopedia of Imperialism and Anti-Imperialism*. London: Palgrave, 2015.

Patnaik, Prabhat. *Accumulation and Stability under Capitalism*. Oxford: Oxford University Press, 1997.

Patnaik, Prabhat. *The Value of Money*. New York: Columbia University Press, 2009.

Patnaik, Prabhat. Whatever Happened to Imperialsim? in *Whatever Happened to Imperialism and Other Essays*. New Delhi: Tulika, 2003.

Patnaik, Prabhat, and Utsa Patnaik. *A Theory of Imperialism*. New York: Columbia University Press, 2016.

Patnaik, Utsa. "Ricardo's Fallacy: Mutual Benefit from Trade Based on Comparative Costs and Specialization?" in *The Pioneers of Development Economics*, edited by K. S. Jomo, 31–41. London: Zed, 2005.

Patnaik, Utsa. "The Free Lunch – Transfers from the Tropical Colonies and Their Role in Capital Formation in Britain during the Industrial Revolution." In *Globalization under Hegemony*, edited by K. S. Jomo. Delhi: Oxford University Press, 2006.

Reinert, Erik S. *How Rich Countries Got Rich and Why Poor Countries Stay Poor*. London: Constable, 2007.

Riddell, John, ed. *To See the Dawn: Baku 1920, First Congress of the Peoples of the East*. New York: Pathfinder Press, 1993.

Rosenberg, Justin. *The Empire of Civil Society: A Critique of the Realist Theory of International Relations*. London: Verso, 1994.

Sardoni, C. "Keynes and Marx." In *A 'Second Edition' of the General Theory*, edited by G. C. Harcourt and P. Riach, 261–83. London: Routledge, 1997.

Slobodian, Quinn. *Globalists: The End of Empire and the Birth of Neoliberalism*. Cambridge, MA: Harvard University Press, 2018.

Smith, John. *Imperialism in the Twenty-First Century: Globalization, Super-Exploitation, and Capitalism's Final Crisis*. New York: Monthly Review Press, 2016.

Steedman, Ian. *Marx after Sraffa*. London: New Left Books, 1977.

Sweezy, Paul. "Introduction." In *Karl Marx and the Close of His System*, edited by Paul Sweezy. New York: Merlin Press, 1949.

Sweezy, Paul. *The Theory of Capitalist Development: Principles of Marxian Political Economy*. London: Dennis Dobson, (1942) 1946.

Teschke, Benno. *The Myth of 1648: Class, Geopolitics, and the Making of Modern International Relations*. Brooklyn: Verso, 2003.

Tönnies, Ferdinand. *Gemeinschaft und Gesellschaft [Community and Society]*. Oxford, UK: Michigan University Press, (1887) 1957.

van der Pijl, Kees. *The Discipline of Western Supremacy: Modes of Foreign Relations and Political Economy*, Vol. III. London: Pluto Press, 2014.

Warren, Bill. *Imperialism: Pioneer of Capitalism*. London: Verso, 1980.

Williams, G. "Eighteenth Century Brumaire: Karl Marx and Defeat." In *Marx: 100 Years On*, edited by B. Matthews, 11–37. London: Lawrence and Wishart, 1987.

Wood, Ellen Meiksins. "Unhappy Families: Global Capitalism in a World of Nation-States." *Monthly Review* 51, no. 3 (1999): 1–12.

Zarembka, Paul. "Accumulation of Capital, Its Definition: A Century after Lenin and Luxemburg." In *Value, Capitalist Dynamics and Money*, edited by Paul Zarembka, 183–241. Amsterdam and New York: JAI, 2000.

Zarembka, P. "Lenin as Economist of Production: A Ricardian Step Backward." *Science & Society* 67, no. 3 (2003): 276–302. doi:10.1521/siso.67.3.276.21240.

Zarembka, Paul. "Rosa Luxemburg's 'Accumulation of Capital': Critics Try to Bury the Message." *Current Perspectives in Social Theory* 21, no. 3 (2002): 3–45.

ⓐ OPEN ACCESS

Continuity and change in Venezuela's Bolivarian Revolution

Julia Buxton

ABSTRACT
The aims and outcomes of the Bolivarian Revolution in Venezuela are fiercely contested. A sympathetic view sees the possibility of Left revolutionary transformation as destabilised by aggressive US and domestic opposition actions. Detractors trace an authoritarian path from President Hugo Chávez's election in 1998 to an inevitable socialist implosion under his successor Nicolás Maduro two decades later. This article emphasises continuities between the Bolivarian Fifth Republic and the Fourth Republic that the Revolution displaced. These account for the limitations of the transformative process. Historical institutionalism explains the reproduction of rentier practices and centralised state management and political organisation, culminating in cascading crisis across regime types.

Introduction

The election of Hugo Chávez to the Venezuelan presidency in 1998 was a political revolution. It terminated a two-party political system that had controlled the Venezuelan state for 40 years. Chávez's message of national transformation was salient in the context of deep popular alienation from the traditional parties and their record of economic mismanagement and corruption. The crisis of the pre-Chávez years was manifest in electoral abstention, social protest, a see-saw between neoliberal lurches (1989, 1996) and heterodox retrenchment, two military coup attempts (1992), a presidential impeachment (1992) and a banking system collapse (1994). The price per barrel (p/b) of Venezuelan crude, accounting for 95% of export earnings, was at an historic low of $9.40 p/b (1998) when Chávez took office. Reflecting on the legacy of mismanagement that the incoming president inherited, Corrales outlined that

> growth per capita stagnated, unemployment rates surged, and public sector deficits endured despite continuous spending cutbacks. Real wages today are almost 70 percent below what they were 20 years ago [...] More than two-thirds of the population now live below poverty levels.[1]

Two decades after Chávez launched the 'Bolivarian Revolution'[2] Venezuela was again in political and economic turmoil. In January 2019, the second-term presidential inauguration

---

This is an Open Access article distributed under the terms of the Creative Commons Attribution License (http://creativecommons.org/licenses/by/4.0/), which permits unrestricted use, distribution, and reproduction in any medium, provided the original work is properly cited.

of Chávez's successor Nicolás Maduro (2013–) was challenged as illegitimate by the opposition-dominated National Assembly. Assembly president Juan Guaidó was declared 'interim president' on the grounds of Maduro's 'usurpation'. The resulting dual-power situation paralysed governance and projected the armed forces into the political arena as the key powerbroker. Venezuela's internal political conflict assumed international dimensions, with countries aligning behind Maduro or Guaidó depending on their geostrategic interests.

The economy was in severe recession, with successive years of double-digit contraction and hyperinflation that reached an historic high of 2,688,670% at the start of 2019. Oil production had collapsed from 3.3 million barrels of oil per day (b/d) in 1998 to less than 1 million b/d, with output slumping further after the US-imposed sanctions on the oil sector in January 2019. The sanctions deprived the Venezuelan treasury of dollars and revenue for essential imports, and followed punishing sanctions imposed by the US on the Venezuelan financial sector in 2017, which forced a default on $5 billion in interest and principal payments on Venezuela's estimated $110 billion foreign debt. A March 2019 United Nations (UN) document estimated that 3.4 million Venezuelans had left the country, 94% of the population were living in poverty and a quarter required some form of humanitarian assistance.[3]

This article argues that the implosion of Venezuela is due to a deep-rooted, structural crisis of path dependence. This explanatory approach prioritises historical contextualisation over short-term assessments that are based only on interpretation of the Bolivarian period to account for the current crisis. An historical institutionalist perspective emphasises the long-term role of the oil sector in structuring hegemonic and counter-hegemonic struggle for capture and control of the state and national oil sector. Antagonistic poles have duplicated and reproduced the same political strategies of centralisation, institutional politicisation and oil rent distribution to retain power, regardless of ideological orientation, and they share the same organisational characteristics of personalism, corruption, weak accountability and top-down decision-making. The embedding of these practices has led to an accumulation of institutional and economic dysfunction, poverty and inequality over the last half century. Effecting policy and social change requires reversing these practices, but the cost of transformation in political and electoral terms is high, forcing governments back to rent-seeking behaviours. Access to oil export revenues has tempered strategies for path disruption, reinforcing patterns of commodity dependence, boom-and-bust economic cycles and state monopoly capitalism.

Path dependence accounts for frequently overlooked organisational and policy continuities between the Fourth 'liberal democratic' Republic (1958–1998) and Socialism of the Twenty-First Century in the Fifth Republic (1998–). Historical processes continue to shape institutional outcomes in the country, establishing a path dependence that the 'transformative' project of the Bolivarian Revolution ultimately adhered to. Following Mahoney,[4] path dependence is defined as sequences in which 'contingent events set into motion institutional patterns or event chains that have deterministic properties'. Prior institutional choices that pre-date the Bolivarian Revolution restricted later options,[5] and they erode the importance of ideology in understanding the causes of both Venezuela's contemporary crisis and the preceding crisis that galvanised Chávez's electoral success in 1998. The conclusion highlights the persistence of inertia, with early indicators pointing to continuity of exclusionary and centralised practices within the Guaidó interim presidency.[6]

Venezuela's critical juncture

Historical institutionalism emphasises 'critical junctures' that mark the end of a protracted, uninterrupted period, and the move to a new institutional formation that establishes a new path. This path continues to be followed as it produces increased economic or political returns, making path-undermining options less attractive even if it is increasingly dysfunctional.[7]

In the Venezuelan case, 1945 was the critical juncture. The *Trienio* (1945–1948) was formative in setting civilian politics and strategies of state capture and management on a trajectory that has withstood major events and upheaval. It followed from a telescoped process of economic and political change that rendered a century of oligarchic military rule unsustainable and which was driven by the discovery and exploitation of oil resources at the turn of the twentieth century. Over 4000 concessions were granted to largely US oil companies before World War II. By 1928, the historically agricultural society was the world's second largest oil producer, and by 1935 taxes and royalties from the sector accounted for 91% of total export revenues.[8]

Oil exploration and drilling generated enclave patterns of development[9] and an incipient oil nationalism that pressed national government to increase the financial benefits accruing to the Venezuelan state, and for these revenues to be 'sown' across the national economy to promote development.[10] These demands were led by newly emerging intellectual classes, student groups (The Generation of 1928) and party political organisations, most importantly *Acción Democrática* (Democratic Action, AD) formed in 1941.

AD assumed power during the *Trienio* initially as part of a post-coup *junta*. Important for the subsequent path dependence Venezuela assumed, the experience of the AD leadership as an exiled student movement led the party to adopt a centralised and hierarchical structure with dominance by an elite, charismatic leadership. The core constituency of AD was multiclass, this *policlasista* orientation emphasising a meta-narrative of democratisation and oil nationalism above class interests. This positioning distinguished AD from their key rival, the *Partido Comunista de Venezuela* (Venezuelan Communist Party, PCV) founded in 1931, which had gained a strong presence in the labour sector.

In October 1946, the transitionary, AD-led *junta* convened a national constituent assembly to redraft the national constitution, a process that Brewer-Carías argues built on the use of constitution-making processes as 'a *de facto* rejection of the existing constitution, through a coup d'état, a revolution, or a civil war'.[11] The subsequent presidential election of the AD candidate Rómulo Gallegos in December 1947 provided AD with a political dominance that was strengthened by the party's association with the extension of suffrage, labour rights, and rural and social organisation. The reform process alienated the country's social powers, and the AD government was overthrown in a bloodless coup in 1948. A 10-year interlude that saw a return to military control did not lead to a path undermining, with the critical juncture of the *Trienio* establishing institutional and organisational characteristics that informed the return to democracy in 1958.

Path setting

The *Trienio* structured a path dependence in Venezuela that has proved difficult to reverse. Pivotal here were changes to Venezuela's hydrocarbons law during the *Trienio*. The 1910 Mining Code under which oil concessions were granted only levied a ground rent that was paid as contract royalties. The Venezuelan state did not position itself as the owner or beneficiary of the subsoil resources, only as an intermediary that was paid a rent for enabling private sector access to Venezuela's hydrocarbons.

This was revised by the AD government through a 50/50 profit-sharing agreement with oil companies.[12] For Hellinger, the legal revision established 'a mythology of radical nationalism that coloured historical memory of the short lived *Trienio* democracy'.[13] For the AD government, the income enabled a 'sowing' of national wealth with funding for the raft of welfare obligations established in the 1946 constitution. An early blurring of state and party was apparent with the placement of AD loyalists in expanding the state bureaucracy and the use of state monies to sponsor parallel organisations that enabled AD to challenge the PCV's organisational dominance in the labour sector.

Three negative consequences followed from this 'path setting'. Firstly, the Venezuelan state was institutionalised as a landlord, a rentier formation in which the national income was derived from collecting profits from foreign-led activities in the state's hydrocarbon monopoly and not productive activities and investment. Secondly, the sequencing of democratisation and oil nationalist policy configured an association between citizenship and a distributionary state, with rent access mediated by the ruling party. Oil revenues additionally allowed Venezuela to circumvent fiscal policy debates and reconcile seemingly incompatible class demands within a moderate, centrist policy path. Questions of re-distribution in a context of profound inequalities of land, resources and influence inherited from the colonial period were bypassed, with the narrow interests of 'white-gloved' patricians, *hacendados* and powerful business families (the Mendoza, Vollmer, Boulton, Phelps, Blohm and Delfino dynasties)[14] accommodated in what Karl refers to as 'a classic exchange, primarily between AD and the entrepreneurs, of 'the right to rule for the right to make money'.[15]

Puntofijismo and the Fourth Republic

The return to civilian politics after 1958 was made possible by control of ideological, economic, military and political spheres. This was achieved by incorporating a wider constituency into the framework of rentier democracy established during the critical juncture. This included the Christian Democrat COPEI party (*Comité de Organización Política Electoral Independiente*, Independent Electoral Political Organisation Committee), the main union confederation the *Confederación de Trabajadores de Venezuela* (CTV), the private sector, the Roman Catholic Church and the Venezuelan military. The Pact of Puntofijo of 1957 and accompanying agreements were a negotiated convergence between the private sector and business, and between AD and COPEI. The two parties committed to 'coexistence', a 'climate of unity' and an agreement to subsidise co-signatories. *Puntofijismo* was an exclusionary model, with continuity of the PCV's marginalisation. The PCV was not party to the pact, despite playing a pivotal role in the resistance to military dictatorship in the 1950s.

Oil rents lubricated *Venedemocracia*, which was lauded as a model of hemispheric democracy during the brutal period of right-wing dictatorship and anti-communist repression in other Latin American countries.[16] They enabled a succession of national governments to meet the demands of all social classes and avoid distribution- and class-based conflicts. Venezuela nationalised its oil sector in 1975, coinciding with an international oil price boom. Between 1973 and 1977, its gross domestic product (GDP) grew by an extraordinary 31%.

High levels of public spending created a seemingly virtuous growth cycle underpinned by demand-led expansionary policies. This in turn cemented popular loyalty to AD and COPEI and the confidence of elite groups in political arrangements.

Politicisation of institutions was a central element of strategies to retain control of the state. AD and COPEI negotiated and shared powers of appointment and promotion in the judiciary, national election administration, military, public and regional administration and in state corporations.[17] There was also continuity of vertical and centralising tendencies in party political organisation. Expulsions were used to prevent intra-party challenges, most particularly impacting left factions of AD in 1961 and 1963. The closed-block list system that was adopted for national elections empowered the leadership of AD and COPEI to reward loyalists through list placement and punish critics through omission. Regional governors in the nominally federal state were appointed by the ruling party, and AD and COPEI pursued strategies of penetrating and controlling incipient independent organisations as during the *Trienio*.

Left resistance to the class compromise of *Puntofijismo* was taken outside of the limited space of formal politics to rural insurgency in the early 1960s, inspired by the Cuban Revolution. Pacification led to the emergence of a new left party, the Movement to Socialism (*Movimiento al Socialismo*, MAS) founded in 1971, but the influence and electoral appeal of the MAS was circumscribed by the electoral system and by AD and COPEI control of social organisations. A second post-insurgency offshoot, Radical Cause (*La Causa Radical*, LCR) eschewed party political organisation and mobilised around the 'three legs' of arts and culture, labour, and within-community organisations. LCR and PCV were connected to the Revolutionary Bolivarian Movement (*Movimiento Bolivariano Revolucionario 200*, MBR 200) conspiratorial group in the Venezuelan military that was co-founded by Chávez in 1982.

Negative consequences in path retention

Oil export revenues made the Venezuelan state a lazy and profligate landlord with assumed 'magical' characteristics generated by the illusion of oil wealth.[18] The nationalisation of oil in 1975 deepened Venezuela's rentier capitalist profile, with Petróleos de Venezuela, SA (PDVSA) acting only as a holding company for the subsidiaries of the three major international oil companies operating in the country. PDVSA did not engage in exploration and production, and the bulk of refining activities were conducted in the US, the country's largest oil-importing partner.

The state's role in extracting rent from its resource monopoly during the oil price boom accentuated the uncompetitive and increasingly more corrupted characteristics of the state, which became dysfunctional and overextended. Oligopolistic networks of family-owned businesses were privileged over small and medium enterprises (SMEs) in access to credit, contracts, preferential interest rates and commercial information.[19] So systemic was corruption within the network of public sector, private sector and party political interests that case studies filled a three-volume *Diccionario de la Corrupción en Venezuela* (*Dictionary of Corruption in Venezuela*). Transparency International found Venezuela to be the 46th most corrupt country of 52 reviewed for the period 1980–1992.

By the early 1980s, partisan rent distribution was not sustainable amid deteriorating oil prices and economic mismanagement. AD and COPEI governments maintained public spending commitments through international borrowing, currency devaluation, exchange rate manipulation, price and exchange rate controls and raids on PDVSA investment funds. This maintained the illusion of rent extraction capacity, but with the dividends distributed within a diminishing circle of beneficiaries, in turn deepening social inequalities.

Disintegration of the rentier economy ruptured the premise established during the critical juncture of the *Trienio* that the dominant-party political forces represented a unified national interest. Popular alienation from *Venedemocracia* accelerated as the ability to sustain high public spending and finance co-opted networks deteriorated. Nevertheless, the dominant parties retained control of social powers, precluding prospects for political change. The politicisation of state institutions and the engineered exclusion of party-political challengers forced the articulation of political grievance through informal avenues (strikes, abstention and street protests) and regime change conspiratorial networks.[20]

Elite efforts to respond to system atrophy through strategies of path undermining were adopted during the presidency of Carlos Andrés Pérez (1989–1992) and haphazardly by Rafael Caldera, the founder of COPEI in 1946, who was re-elected in 1993 amid evidence of electoral fraud against the candidate of the leftist LCR.[21] Path undermining was intended to transform the rentier state through economic and political liberalisation. There was a dramatic swing to neoliberal stabilisation and adjustment policies, and partial privatisation of PDVSA.

Substantiating historical institutionalist approaches that emphasise the resilience of dysfunctional and inefficient institutions,[22] the reorientation of the rentier state was resisted. Opposition came top down from *Puntofijo* elite groups within state institutions, the AD and COPEI parties, the oligopolistic private sector and affiliated interests,[23] and from the bottom up through grassroots protest against the inequitable social costs of neoliberalism. The latter was exemplified in the *Caracazo* riots of 1989, which were brutally repressed by the security forces.[24]

Electoral reform and initiatives to decentralise political and administrative authority were introduced in 1989. These were subverted by electoral maladministration and fraud, and the reluctance of central authorities in Caracas to decentralise revenues to regional administrations. State recourse to authoritarian measures and violence to sustain *puntofijismo* was reflected in the use of presidential decree powers, recurrent states of emergency, election fraud and rights abuses against independent social movements and popular sectors in the 1990s. This context, and the election of Chávez to the presidency in 1998, represented the opportunity of a new critical juncture and path disruption.

The Bolivarian Revolution: a critical juncture?

Chávez was a political outsider from the middle ranks of the armed forces. He founded the Fifth Republican Movement (*Movimiento V [Quinta] República*, MVR) in 1997 after a period in prison following his leadership of an attempted coup against Andrés Pérez in 1992. Initially an advocate of abstention to galvanise the collapse of *Venedemocracia*, he was converted to electoral competition, but – as detailed by Gott – with limited interest in political party-building and sceptical of bureaucratic party organisation. A bottom-up, horizontal, participatory mass-based movement was emphasised, and contrasted by Chávez with the top-down and centralised organisation of AD and COPEI.

The Bolivarian Revolution promised a participatory democracy, with authority devolved to the lowest level and citizens routinely engaged in decision-making and as protagonists in their own development.[25] While this vision has been claimed as the roots of Socialism of the Twenty-First Century, an ideological direction proclaimed in Chávez's third term (2006–2012), the Bolivarian Revolution did not platform as a socialist project. It mobilised support through a message of democratic rebirth, of sweeping away *Venedemocracia* and replacing the *Puntofijo* state with a new constitutional order, the Fifth Republic. This was a nationalist vision inspired by Independence hero Simón Bolívar (1783–1830), whose ambitions for a politically progressive and integrated continent Chávez saw as betrayed by *puntofijismo*.

Chávez's campaign critiqued neoliberalism, but as part of a broader critique of AD and COPEI's economic mismanagement. His narrative was in line with development paradigms of the post-Washington Consensus period, with Bolivarianism emphasising a 'third way' between market and state. Chávez outlined: 'Our project is not statist. Neither is it extreme neoliberalism. No, we are looking for an intermediate point, as much state as is necessary and as much market as is possible'.[26] The Revolution looked to build a 'social economy', informed by principles of reciprocity, solidarity and exchange, and driven by community-level enterprise.

New path: old mechanisms

While the new Bolivarian government was read by left and right alike as a radical break from Venezuela's neoliberal episode, from the outset there were elements of continuity with the country's longer historical trajectory. This was most immediately evidenced in rhetoric, constitutionalism, domestic oil policy and international diplomacy.

The projection of the Bolivarian Revolution as the articulation of a majority popular and sovereign national interest unified against a corrupt oligarchy echoed the slogans of the early AD party. The Bolivarian project presented itself as a national, not class-based, project, one that defined a new national consensus configured around the interests of grassroots groups, popular sectors and the political left that had been excluded from *puntofijismo* and disarticulated on the grounds of race and class. Bolivarianism was counter-hegemonic in intention, extending to accommodation of private sector interests. Early *Chavismo* sought to engage the confidence of the domestic business sector and private international companies, initially retaining Caldera's finance minister – but, like AD during the Trienio and early *puntofijismo*, on new relationship terms that respected the sovereign interest.

The 1999 Bolivarian Constitution was promoted by the government as a process of democratic participation to legitimise transformative change. A popular referendum on the convening of a constituent assembly was held in April 1999 and approved by 92% of voters. The Bolivarian Constitution was drawn up by a constituent assembly elected in July 1999 that was dominated by the *Chavista* Patriotic Pole (*Polo Patriótico*, PP), which captured 66% of the vote. A second referendum held in December 1999 saw the Bolivarian Constitution approved by 72% of voters, presaging the transition to the Fifth Republic. While contentious for opponents, this marked reproduction of the historical use of constitutional redrafting as declaratory statement of a new political epoch.

The 1999 constitution laid the basis for a reversion to monopoly state capitalism. *Chavismo* was vociferous in objections to the partial privatisation of PDVSA under Caldera, to PDVSA strategies to internationalise operations and increase output (for the perceived benefit of foreign interests), and to the autonomy PDVSA enjoyed *vis-à-vis* the energy ministry. The Bolivarian constitution reasserted national sovereignty of resources (Article 303), and in 2001 this 'new' direction in hydrocarbon policy was set out in a package of 49 decree laws that sought to bring national legislation in line with the 1999 constitution.

This was a re-treading of the oil nationalism of the AD party in the 1940s and the commitment to 'sowing' resource revenues for development. It was read as radical and anti-neoliberal in the 1990s, a period of hemispheric free trade aspirations, and stress on commodity diversification from international financial institutions such as the World Bank and International Monetary Fund,[27] but it marked a reversion to a well-established line of oil policy and state management of resources in the longer context of Venezuela's history.

Historical continuity was further reflected in reorientation back to the hydrocarbon diplomacy of early *puntofijismo*. To contain vulnerability to international oil price falls, Chávez's energy team pursued co-operative relations with other oil-producing countries, in particular through the Organization of Petroleum Exporting Countries (OPEC). Venezuela had been a founding member of OPEC in 1960, an initiative that followed the refusal of the Eisenhower administration to lift import quotas on Venezuelan oil and allow preferential market access. As with the San José Pact of 1980 under which Venezuela and Mexico provided discounted oil to 10 Central American and Caribbean nations, the Chávez government unveiled discounted oil supply and exchange agreements under the umbrella of the 17-country Petrocaribe initiative of 2005.[28] This was intended to support a new Bolivarian vision of regional integration, but was rooted in established tools of Venezuelan oil diplomacy.

The possibility of disruption

Despite these early continuities, the Bolivarian Revolution had the potential for path disruption. The 1999 Constitution set out the requirement that public administration be 'at the service of the citizen … based on the principles of honesty, participation, expeditiousness, efficacy, efficiency, transparency, accountability' (Article 141). Public officials were to serve the state and 'not any partisan interest'. Article 146 set out appointment through 'public competition, based on principles of honesty, capability and efficiency', including in the judiciary and the military, with promotions 'in accordance with merit, hierarchy and vacancies' (Article 331). Institutional restructuring was intended to enhance accountability of the state and public officials, including through the introduction of recall referenda and the creation of new branches of government such as the Citizen's Power, which grouped the ombudsman, fiscal general and comptroller general alongside the judiciary, election council, executive and legislature in a five-fold separation of authority.

In line with ambitions to create a participatory model of democracy, Article 62 of the constitution emphasised 'The participation of the people in forming, carrying out and controlling the management of public affairs … to ensure their complete development, both individual and collective', with mechanisms to transfer economic and public service planning to communities contemplated in Article 184. As the basis of the new social economy, small-scale family business, cooperatives and artisanal associations were to be 'promoted and protected'. The rights of the private sector were upheld in line with the third-way orientation, with Article 299 stating that 'The State, jointly with private initiative, shall promote the harmonious development of the national economy'. The health, welfare and education obligations accruing to the state through the 1999 constitution (and which echoed the ample social provisions of the 1961 constitution) were to be met through tax system reform, anti-corruption mechanisms and responsible fiscal and monetary management (Title VI: Socioeconomic system), including the creation of a macroeconomic stabilisation fund established to set aside windfall oil revenues from higher-than-budgeted oil prices.

With popular approval of the 1999 constitution, the government moved to effect transformative change with the 49 laws of 2001, introduced through executive decree powers as utilised during the neoliberal shift in the 1990s. Land reform was launched under *Plan Zamora*. A new land law taxed and expropriated underused and unused private holdings, capped landholdings and redistributed property to heads of households that petitioned to be part of the programme. New institutions, including the *Instituto Nacional de Tierras* (National Land Institute), the *Instituto Nacional de Desarrollo Rural* (National Rural Development Institute) and the *Corporación de Abastecimiento y Servicios Agrícolas* (Agricultural Corporation of Supplies and Services), were established to determine seizures and eligibility for redistribution, and to provide technical support and marketing assistance to the 65,000 rural workers who benefitted within the first 2 years of the programme.[29]

In line with efforts to build a social economy, 'solidaristic' enterprise was encouraged by new lending frameworks. Credit and banking facilities were made available for traditionally excluded and informal sectors, including a dedicated Women's Bank. By the end of 2005 there were over 83,000 co-operatives that were to be integrated into wider national initiatives such as Social Production Enterprises and Endogenous Development Zones that channelled state contracts, preferential loans and technical support.

New ministries such as the Ministry of Popular Economy (*Ministerio de Economía Popular*, MINEP) served as connectors between the state and communal councils that were given legal status in 2006. The councils were a core element of the Bolivarian vision of popular participation. Based on 200 to 400 households in urban areas, or 20 in more sparsely populated rural areas, the communal councils had responsibility for deliberation, design and delivery of public services, with over 120,000 communal councils established by the end of 2006. State legal and financial support was extended to grassroots initiatives in the *barrios* to build new forms of representation and participation, including through, media, cultural and educational projects. These were intended to craft a new national identity that reflected the racial diversity of the country, and pride in Latin American culture. This was counter-posed with the ethnically white and pro-US orientation of the traditional elite.[30]

A panoply of social policy initiatives, the *misiones*, were rolled out after 2003 to address entrenched problems of inequality, poverty and unemployment, and as rising international oil prices lifted the GDP from a record low of -26.7% in the first quarter of 2003 to an all-time high of 36% in the first quarter of 2004. These delivered health, education, housing, nutritional and employment programmes and sought to build economic inclusion as a prerequisite for meaningful political inclusion.

At the regional level, Venezuela benefitted from the wider political shift of the 'Pink Tide' that brought left governments to power in Brazil, Argentina, Ecuador and Bolivia in the 2000s. These administrations worked with the long-ostracised Cuban government to construct an alternative regional lending and media architecture that excluded the US and exploited economic, social and political complementarities.[31] Venezuela also sought to capitalise on new trade and investment opportunities with China, a strategy that aimed to boost

South–South ties, advance a multipolar global order and reduce bilateral commercial dependence on the US.

The opportunity of the critical juncture was subverted by exogenous pressures. These threatened the government's hold on power and elevated the costs of path deviation. Resistance to the Bolivarian Revolution encouraged the Chávez government to reproduce strategies to control social power and address constituency demands by reverting to the financial expediency of oil rents to build a (counter)hegemonic block. Three key exogenous factors in accelerating path return were opposition disruption, the government's limited constituency base, and the sharp appreciation in the international oil price in the mid-2000s.

From transformation to reproduction

Opposition to the Bolivarian process was initially articulated through organisations and interests that had been protected during *puntofijismo* and which lacked experience of being out of power and influence. Underscoring continuity with the extra-institutional strategies for system change in the 1990s, these groups engaged in strikes and lockouts, an attempted coup in April 2002, and a shut-down of PDVSA operations and oil production in 2002 and 2003 that cost Venezuela 24% of GDP and required a declaration of *force majeure* on unfulfilled oil contracts. The legitimacy of the Bolivarian process was recurrently challenged: in the private sector media; through overseas lobby networks – most saliently in the US; through challenges to the legitimacy of the (pro-government) results of national and regional election process; through a recall referendum on Chávez in 2004, and via strategies of electoral abstention.

Opposition groups were able to sustain disruptive action despite a lack of broad-based support due to the US, which channelled financial assistance to anti-government actors under the rubric of 'democracy promotion'.[32] The US worked to isolate Venezuela through lobbying regional neighbours, the introduction of motions critical of Venezuela in the Organization of American States (OAS), and through the construction of Venezuela as an 'enemy' in the War on Drugs and the War on Terror. There was continuity in this antagonistic policy position across Democrat and Republican administrations, and it began before Chávez had taken office in 1999, with President Clinton's Secretary of State Madeline Albright declining a visa for the then presidential candidate to visit the US.

The Chávez government responded to these efforts to de-legitimise, isolate and displace the Bolivarian project by replicating the strategies pursued during the *Trienio* and Fourth Republic. The strategies chosen were influenced by the government's weak social base, identified as the second key exogenous variable driving path dependence.

From its foundations in the constitutional reform process, the Bolivarian project did not have the popular endorsement implied in Chávez's language of the 'will of the sovereign people'. Chávez had carried half of the country (56%) in the 1998 election, but a sizeable 40% of voters had supported his rival Henrique Salas Römer, and AD won a majority of seats in the 1998 congressional election. Fresh national elections held in July 2000 under the new constitution saw Chávez increase his share of the vote to 59% but on a voter turnout of just 56%. In each of the election processes convened around the 1999 constitution, less than half of the electorate participated – only 44% turned out for the second referendum of December 1999 to approve the new constitution.[33] Subsequent strategies of election boycotts by the opposition provided the Bolivarian project with control of the legislature by default, crafting an artificial and highly vulnerable profile of *Chavista* electoral dominance.

The survival of the Bolivarian Revolution was contingent on the construction of a (counter) hegemonic bloc and consolidation of constituency demands. As the international oil price rose from below $10 p/b when Chávez came to power to $65 p/b by 2006, windfall revenues were redirected away from stabilisation funds and into regional projects and domestic social spending, the latter increasing from 8.2% of GDP in 1998 to 13.6% of GDP in 2006, boosted by PDVSA investment funds of 7.3% of GDP. Real social spending per person was 314% higher in 2006 than in 1998. Going into Chávez's third term, the population living in extreme poverty had fallen to 11% from 20% in 1998, while the number of poor households had declined from 44% in 1998 to 31%.[34] But these social gains were built on fragile institutional ground, with the jettisoning of the initially transformative ambitions of the 1999 Bolivarian Constitution and recourse to rentier practices to telescope change. This shift in the Bolivarian project to one of building Socialism of the Twenty-First Century, with oil as the 'motor of the Revolution', deepened the contradictions and vulnerabilities of the transformative process.

Crisis redux

Socialism of the Twenty-First Century reproduced the problems of rent seeking, misman-agement, corruption, duplication and waste that had characterised *puntofijismo*, the expe-rience of the second half of the 2000s in particular mirroring the boom-and-bust conditions of the 1970s. In response to pressure from pro-government unions and organisations, there was a wave of nationalisation processes affecting over 400 private enterprises. But this was on an *ad hoc* basis, driven by political not economic considerations and without effective integration of the new state-controlled industries into cooperative organisation. The exten-sion of state management generated tensions in relations between the national government and workers' councils that unsuccessfully pressed for control of nationalised industries. The deepening of the state's role in the economy massively overextended the fiscal and technical capacity of the government, which struggled to maintain investment levels in the context of expensive arbitration proceedings from expropriated private owners and as the interna-tional oil price fell back after 2009.

In line with efforts to consolidate its support base, the emphasis of government policy remained on quantity rather than quality of social provision, there was a lack of engagement with technical evaluation or impact assessment, and issues of financial sustainability of social welfare initiatives were not addressed. With patterns of rent dispersal increasingly deter-mined by partisan affiliation, not need, clientelism and corruption became more deeply embedded.[35] The government's reliance on rentier practices extended to cultivating relations with the private sector. After the strikes and lockouts of 2002/2003, the administration pur-sued a compromise with large firms such as Polar Industries to ensure supply and distribution chains, and as efforts to galvanise a social economy failed to improve the availability of goods.

Preferential access to contracts, exchange rates and credit facilities was extended to a new business and financial class connected to the government. The emergence of this *Bolibourgeoisie* reproduced existing structural tendencies towards inefficiency and corrup-tion, while creating new hierarchies of wealth and influence. Exchange rate controls imposed in 2002 became a mechanism for corruption and profit transfer.[36] The retention of price controls, also first introduced in 2002, fuelled hoarding, shortages and growth of the black market. Left critics argued that the Bolivarian Revolution was failing to transform the Fourth Republic state and was uncomfortably 'co-existing' between old and new institutions.[37] There was seen to be limited transformation of the state and economy towards socialist objectives, and oligarchic interests were being nurtured within a model of state monopoly capitalism. Rather than revolutionary, the Bolivarian project was merely reformist.[38] For Ellner: 'if left unchecked, the government's relationship with sectors of the bourgeoisie will solidify and continue to undermine the leadership's socialist commitments.'[39]

Profligacy and opacity in the dispersion of windfall oil revenues and mismanagement of the macro economy were enabled by the weakness of institutional oversight mechanisms. As the government sought to control social power, staffing of the new Bolivarian institutions created by the 1999 constitution was assumed by *Chavista* loyalists, initially appointed under emergency powers by the Constituent Assembly. Institutional politicisation accelerated with the April 2002 coup attempt and PDVSA lockout. These actions led to sweeping purges, and the appointment of pro-government leadership, management and personnel, tasked with reorienting institutions to the Bolivarian mandate and missions. After gaining a supermajority in the national elections as a result of the opposition boycott of 2005, the MVR-dominated National Assembly proceeded to make appointments to state institutions on the basis of partisan loyalty and defence of the revolutionary process.

Party-political centralisation followed from rentier state management and institutional politicisation. Intra-party critiques of the direction of the Bolivarian project from within MVR, relaunched as the Partido Socialista Unido de Venezuela (PSUV) in 2007, were tempered by concerns that the opposition would benefit from dissent and disunity. As with AD and COPEI in the era of *puntofijismo*, the ruling party used expulsion to delimit internal criticism. Sectarianism within the ruling MVR was expressed through competition for institutional control, pitting factions against each other for ministerial positions. With staffing driven by ever-fluctuating government priorities and efforts by Chávez to balance conflicting ideo-logical and sectoral interests within MVR/PSUV, there was constant turnover of senior posi-tions. This further undermined policy oversight, coherence and delivery, as exemplified in the catastrophic deterioration of the security situation in the context of an almost annual change of leadership and staff in the Interior Ministry.

As the government sought to strengthen its social base, emphasis was placed on building parallel organisations, most specifically in the labour sector. This reproduced long-estab-lished practices to contain and control independent social organisation that dated back to the Venezuelan student movement of the 1920s. The shift from a mass-based movement to a more verticalist party-political formation within *Chavismo* divorced Bolivarianism from its grassroots base, and was epitomised in the transformation of MVR and wider pro-govern-ment *Polo Patriótico* (Patriotic Pole) alliance into the PSUV. The centralisation of party and government authority was represented in Chávez's and subsequently Maduro's presidency of both state and party. Ellner noted a constriction of decision-making within the govern-ment and ruling United Socialist Party of Venezuela (*Partido Socialista Unido de Venezuela*, PSUV) and argued that 'Decision-making cannot be the exclusive preserve of the party's national leadership, still less of the president's inner circle.'[40]

The priority of not conceding space to the opposition led the PSUV to duplicate historical AD and COPEI strategies of central leadership determining electoral candidacies and of parachuting senior party figures into national and regional election posts. This ran against the earlier emphasis on empowerment and autonomy of popular sectors. Centralisation and bureaucratisation within a weak and politicised state impeded devolution and local-level initiatives. Communal council and co-operative organisations expressed frustration with the failure of officials to attend meetings and deliver on commitments agreed at the local level. There were complaints that local-level autonomy was undermined by ministerial officials, by centralisation of decision-making at the national level, and by opaque and tardy disbursement of resources. Inefficiencies associated with bureaucratisation, poor communication and the constant turnover of state personnel were a further impediment to programme coherence and the holistic integration of the national and social economy. A trend of partisanisation of communal councils was exacerbated by the refusal of wealthier communities to engage with the council initiative. Within the councils and co-operatives, unforeseen challenges included a lack of popular interest in the constant cycle of participatory schemas, in turn reducing communal control to dedicated activists.[41]

Paralleling the experience of economic deterioration in the 1980s, the response of the government to a fall in the oil price towards the end of Chávez's third term was to artificially maintain its (counter)hegemonic block through international borrowing and increased financial demands on PDVSA. In 2012, PDVSA was required to channel $49 billion in export revenues to the government, rising to $57 billion in 2014. The 'social investment' requirements imposed on PDVSA depleted the company of reinvestment funds.

Falling production stemmed from additional factors of mismanagement and corruption in PDVSA, and a collapse of exploration, drilling and shipping activities that had historically been undertaken by international companies but declined amid ongoing contractual uncertainty. This made forward commitments on oil supplies negotiated by the Chávez and Maduro governments onerous. Over 500,000 b/d was absorbed by China and Russia as repayment of $70 billion lending, while 50,000 b/d was ring-fenced for commitments under oil exchange programmes, most importantly with Cuba. Subsidies on domestic gasoline fed 400,000 b/d to the local market at a retail price of $0.01 per litre,[42] the government having retained a regressive subsidy that overwhelmingly benefitted private car owners.

Conclusion: full circle

The weaknesses in the Bolivarian project were revealed with the death from cancer of Chávez in March 2013 and the succession of Maduro. Personally selected by Chávez as his successor and inaugurated following a thin victory in the presidential elections of April 2013, Maduro lacked connections to grassroots sectors, and was devoid of the political and ideological authority exercised by Chávez. There was a narrowing of influence around the new president, with the elevation of the military faction of the Bolivarian movement to the detriment of the broader base of the traditional *Chavista* movement. Internal party critics were expelled, including former Chávez ministers, as the new president sought to consolidate his political authority.

Maduro inherited a dramatically changed regional landscape, with allies in the Pink Tide governments pushed back by the electoral victories of the political right, falling oil price and production levels, an elevated level of US confrontational posturing by the Trump administration, and an opposition movement increasingly oriented to participation rather than abstention. The eclectic opposition alliance recorded successes in regional elections held in

2008, a strong performance in the 2013 presidential contest, and majority victory in National Assembly elections in 2015.

As during the end days of *puntofijismo* in the 1990s, Maduro sought to retain control of social power by obfuscating challenges and repressing social protest, in turn accelerating system crisis. The judiciary blocked a recall referendum on Maduro in 2016, state governor elections were delayed in 2017, and after the opposition assumed control of the National Assembly, the government devised a circuitous route to bypass the legislature by convening a 'sovereign' Asamblea Nacional Constituyente (ANC) in July 2017. The ANC decreed a forwarding of presidential elections from December to April 2018. Maduro triumphed with 68% of the vote, a victory that was facilitated by a shift back to abstention on the part of leading opposition parties.

Maduro's second-term inauguration in January 2019 met resistance from the National Assembly, which through interpretation of the 1999 Bolivarian Constitution declared a vacuum of power and recognised National Assembly president Juan Guaidó as 'interim president'. The US, Canada, EU countries and right-of-centre Latin American governments recognised Guaidó as the legitimate president, with the US pursuing UN Security Council resolutions crippling sanctions and the freezing of Venezuelan state assets in the US in support of the interim administration. China and Russia continued to recognise Maduro, creating a paralysing situation of dual power and global geopolitical confrontation. While Guaidó was lauded by supporters as leading a democratic revolution in Venezuela, a historical institutionalist perspective calls attention to the interim president's use of meta-narratives of the 'national interest', criticism of a corrupted oligarchy operating against the popular interest, and early trends of exclusion in his decision-making circle to conclude that regime change in Venezuela was unlikely to result in path disruption.

The reproduction of the rentier state, politicised institutions and centralised political organisation during the Bolivarian Revolution has been highlighted and explained through reference to exogenous factors. These elevated the costs of path deviation, leading the Chávez government to adopt strategies pivotal to *puntofijismo* in the construction of the Bolivarian project. While linear trends since the critical juncture of the *Trienio* have been emphasised, bilateral Venezuela–US relations saw continuity but also important change during the Chávez presidency. This explains the severity of Venezuela's contemporary crisis and its global dimensions.

The foreign policy of the Chávez government was a restatement of a long-established tradition of Venezuelan internationalism and foreign policy independence within the US 'sphere of interest'. As with AD and COPEI presidents before him, Chávez pursued South–South ties and strong relations with Middle East oil producer countries, he encouraged and supported regional peace processes, and he identified with 'developing world' concerns of poverty and neo-imperialism.[43] At the same time, and despite anti-US rhetoric, the Chávez presidency saw strong commercial relations maintained with the US, which continued to be Venezuela's principal export market and the geographical hub for the refining of Venezuela's heavy crude oil.

While the US had been consistently 'tolerant' of Venezuela's international adventurism and sovereign foreign policy during the Cold War, this was not the case during the Chávez presidency and in the altered global context of the US War on Terror, the challenge to US unilateralism from China, and following the Pink Tide. The Bolivarian Revolution was read by the US as a challenge to the post-Cold War order that it sought to institutionalise in the hemisphere, of which free trade and liberal democracy were the cornerstones. Even during the moderate and politically centrist phase of path disruption in the first period of the Chávez presidency, the US demonstrated limited tolerance of sovereignty in the hemisphere, unease with unknown national elites, and a negligible capacity to engage with the wider regional backlash against US policy in Latin America.

Through its relations with China, Russia and most particularly Cuba, Venezuela was conceptualised as a threat to the national security interest of the US, in turn leading to ever more severe US sanction. The punitive US response to Venezuelan path disruption efforts led Venezuela back to path dependence as a means of revolutionary defence. The reproduction of domestic historical legacies explains the limited transformation and social and economic crisis of the Bolivarian Revolution, but change in US bilateral policy accounts for the unprecedented severity.

Disclosure statement

No potential conflict of interest was reported by the author.

Notes

1. Corrales, "Venezuela in the 1980s, the 1990s and beyond."
2. Gott, *In the Shadow of the Liberator*.
3. Detailed by *reliefweb*, April 4, 2019, accessed May 9, 2019, https://reliefweb.int/report/venezuela-bolivarian-republic/venezuela-s-humanitarian-emergency-large-scale-un-response
4. Mahoney, "Path Dependence in Historical Sociology," 507.
5. Pierson and Skocpol, "Historical Institutionalism in Contemporary Political Science."
6. Buxton, "Situation Normal in Venezuela."
7. David, "Path Dependence: A Foundational Concept."
8. Tinker Salas, *Enduring Legacy*.
9. Ibid.
10. Uslar Pietri, "Sembrar el petróleo."
11. Brewer-Carías, "1999 Venezuelan Constitution-Making Process," 506.
12. The measure built on legislation from 1943 that established the right of the Venezuelan state to levy tax on profits outside of fixed contract royalties.
13. Hellinger, "Nationalism, Oil Policy and the Party System."
14. See Crist, "Land Tenure Problems in Venezuela"; and Rangel, *La oligarquía del dinero*.
15. Karl, "Petroleum and Political Pacts," 216.
16. Levine, "Transition to Democracy."
17. See contributions in Ellner and Hellinger, *Venezuelan Politics in the Chávez Era*.
18. Coronil, *Magical State*.
19. Coppedge, *Venezuela: Conservative Representation without Conservative Parties*.
20. See for example McCoy and Myers, *Unravelling of Representative Democracy in Venezuela*.

21. Detailed in Buxton, *Failure of Political Reform in Venezuela*, 82–104.
22. Mahoney, "Path Dependence in Historical Sociology," 507.
23. See Di John, *Political Economy of Economic Liberalisation in Venezuela*.
24. López Maya, "The Venezuelan Caracazo of 1989."
25. Cannon, *Hugo Chávez and the Bolivarian Revolution*.
26. Quoted in Spanakos and Pantoulas, "Contribution of Hugo Chávez to an Understanding of Post-Neoliberalism," 42.
27. Svampa, "Commodities Consensus."
28. Hellinger, "Oil and the Chávez Legacy."
29. Maurice Lemoine, "Venezuela: The Promise of Land for the People." *Le Monde Diplomatique*, October 2003.
30. See Fernandes, *Who Can Stop the Drums?*.
31. See Cusack, *Venezuela, ALBA and the Limits of Post-neoliberal Regionalism*.
32. Gollinger, *Chávez Code*.
33. Hetland, "From System Collapse to Chavista Hegemony," 17.
34. Weisbrot and Sandoval, *The Venezuelan Economy in the Chávez Years*.
35. Penfold-Becerra, "Clientelism and Social Funds."
36. See Dachevsky and Kornblihtt, "Reproduction and Crisis of Capitalism in Venezuela."
37. Harneker, "Latin America and Twenty-First Century Socialism."
38. Woods and Sewell, *Venezuelan Revolution: A Marxist Perspective*.
39. Ellner, "Venezuela's Fragile Revolution: From Chávez to Maduro." https://monthlyreview.org/2017/10/01/venezuelas-fragile-revolution/
40. Ibid.
41. See Purcell, "Political Economy of Venezuela's Bolivarian Cooperative Movement"; and García-Guadilla, "Urban Land Committees."
42. Monaldi, "Collapse of the Venezuelan Oil Industry."
43. See for example Ronald Reagan's "Remarks at the Welcoming Ceremony for President Jaime Lusinchi of Venezuela," December 4, 1984, Available at the Ronald Reagan Presidential Library and Museum, accessed March 5, 2019, https://www.reaganlibrary.gov/research/speeches/120484a

Bibliography

Brewer-Carías, A. "The 1999 Venezuelan Constitution-Making Process as an Instrument for Framing the Development of an Authoritarian Political Regime." In *Framing the State in Times of Transition. Case Studies in Constitution Making*, edited by L. Miller, 505–531. Washington, DC: US Institute for Peace, 2010.

Buxton, J. *The Failure of Political Reform in Venezuela*. Aldershot: Ashgate, 2001.

Buxton, J. "Situation Normal in Venezuela: All Fouled Up." *NACLA Report on the Americas* 49, no. 1 (2017): 3–6. doi:10.1080/10714839.2017.1298235.

Cannon, B. *Hugo Chávez and the Bolivarian Revolution*. Manchester: Manchester University Press, 2009.

Coppedge, M. *Venezuela: Conservative Representation without Conservative Parties*. Notre Dame, IN: The Kellogg Institute, 1999.

Coronil, F. *The Magical State: Nature, Money and Modernity in Venezuela*. Chicago: University of Chicago Press, 1997. doi:10.1086/ahr/103.5.1733-a.

Corrales, J. "Venezuela in the 1980s, the 1990s and beyond." *ReVista Fall*, 1999. https://revista.drclas.harvard.edu/book/venezuela-1980s-1990s-and-beyond

Crist, R. "Land Tenure Problems in Venezuela." *American Journal of Economics and Sociology* 1, no. 2 (1942): 143–154. doi:10.1111/j.1536-7150.1942.tb00453.x.

Cusack, A. *Venezuela, ALBA and the Limits of Postneoliberal Regionalism in Latin America and the Caribbean*. London: Palgrave, 2019.

Dachevsky, F., and J. Kornblihtt. "The Reproduction and Crisis of Capitalism in Venezuela under Chavismo." *Latin American Perspectives* 44, no. 1 (2017): 78–93. doi:10.1177/0094582X16673633.

David, P. "Path Dependence: A Foundational Concept for Historical Social Science." *Cliometrica* 1, no. 2 (2007): 91–114. doi:10.1007/s11698-006-0005-x.

Di John, J. *The Political Economy of Economic Liberalisation in Venezuela*. LSE Crisis States Programme. Working Paper no. 46, 2004.

Ellner, S. "Venezuela's Fragile Revolution: From Chávez to Maduro." *Monthly Review*, 69, no. 5 (2017): 1. doi:10.14452/MR-069-05-2017-09_1.

Ellner, S., and D. Hellinger. *Venezuelan Politics in the Chávez Era: Class, Polarization, and Conflict*. Boulder, CO: Lynne Rienner Publishers, 2014.

Fernandes, S. *Who Can Stop the Drums? Urban Social Movements in Chávez's Venezuela*. Durham, NC: Duke University Press, 2010.

García-Guadilla, M. P. "Urban Land Committees: Co-Optation, Autonomy, and Protagonism." In *Venezuela's Bolivarian Democracy: Participation, Politics, and Culture under Chávez*, edited by D. Smilde and D. Hellinger, 80–103. Durham, NC: Duke University Press, 2011.

Gollinger, E. *The Chávez Code: Cracking US Intervention in Venezuela*. Northampton, MA: Olive Branch Press, 2006.

Gott, R. *In the Shadow of the Liberator: Hugo Chávez and the Bolivarian Revolution*. London: Verso, 2011.

Harneker, M. "Latin America and Twenty-First Century Socialism: Inventing to Avoid Mistakes." *Monthly Review* 62, no. 3 (2010): 3.

Hellinger, D. "Nationalism, Oil Policy and the Party System in Venezuela." *Paper presented at the meeting of the Latin American Studies Association*, Miami, March 16–18, 2000.

Hellinger, D. "Oil and the Chávez Legacy." *Latin American Perspectives* 44, no. 1 (2017): 54–77. doi:10.1177/0094582X16651236.

Hetland, G. "From System Collapse to Chavista Hegemony: The Party Question in Bolivarian Venezuela." *Latin American Perspectives* 44, no. 1 (2017): 17–36. doi:10.1177/0094582X16666018.

Karl, T. L. "Petroleum and Political Pacts: The Transition to Democracy in Venezuela." In *Transitions from Authoritarian Rule: Latin America*, edited by G. O'Donnell, P. Schmitter, and L. Whitehead, 196–219. Baltimore, MD: Johns Hopkins University Press, 1986.

Levine, D. "The Transition to Democracy: Are There Lessons from Venezuela?" *Bulletin of Latin American Research* 4, no. 2 (1985): 47–61. doi:10.2307/3338315.

López Maya, M. "The Venezuelan Caracazo of 1989: Popular Protest and Institutional Weakness." *Journal of Latin American Studies* 35, no. 1 (2003): 117–137.

Mahoney, J. "Path Dependence in Historical Sociology." *Theory and Society* 29, no. 4 (2000): 507–548. doi:10.1023/A:1007113830879.

McCoy, J., and D. Myers. *The Unraveling of Representative Democracy in Venezuela*. Baltimore, MD: Johns Hopkins University Press, 2005.

Monaldi, F. "The Collaspe of the Venezuelan Oil Industry and Its Global Consequences." *Atlantic Council*, 2018. https://www.atlanticcouncil.org/images/AC_VENEZUELAOIL_Interactive.pdf

Penfold-Becerra, M. "Clientelism and Social Funds: Evidence from Chávez's Misiones." *Latin American Politics & Society* 49, no. 4 (2007): 63–84. doi:10.1353/lap.2007.0044.

Pierson, P., and T. Skocpol. "Historical Institutionalism in Contemporary Political Science." In *Political Science. The State of the Discipline*, edited by I. Katznelson and H. Milner, 693–721. New York: Norton, 2002.

Purcell, T. "The Political Economy of Venezuela's Bolivarian Cooperative Movement: A Critique." *Science & Society* 75, no. 4 (2011): 567–578. doi:10.1521/siso.2011.75.4.567.

Rangel, D. *La oligarquía del dinero*. Caracas: Editorial Fuentes, 1972.

Spanakos, A., and D. Pantoulas. "The Contribution of Hugo Chávez to an Understanding of Post-Neoliberalism." *Latin American Perspectives* 44, no. 1 (2017): 37–53. doi:10.1177/0094582X16658242.

Svampa, M. "Commodities Consensus: Neoextractivism and Enclosure of the Commons in Latin America." *South Atlantic Quarterly* 114, no. 1 (2015): 65–82. doi:10.1215/00382876-2831290.

Tinker Salas, M. *The Enduring Legacy: Oil, Culture, and Society in Venezuela*. Durham, NC: Duke University Press, 2009.

Uslar Pietri, A. "Sembrar el petróleo." *AHORA* 1, no. 183 (1936). http://hemerotecavirtualsembrarpetroleo.blogspot.com/

Weisbrot, M., and L. Sandoval. *The Venezuelan Economy in the Chávez Years*. Washington, DC: Centre for Economic Policy and Research, 2007. http://cepr.net/documents/publications/venezuela_2007_07.pdf

Woods, A., and R. Sewell. *The Venezuelan Revolution: A Marxist Perspective*. London: Wellred Books, 2005.

A political economy for social movements and revolution: popular media access, power and cultural hegemony

Lee Artz

ABSTRACT

One key marker of mass social movements transitioning to participatory democratic governance is popular media access. This essay argues that democratic media access by public constituencies becomes a site for constructing social revolution and simultaneously a manifest empirical measure of the extent of democratic participation in the production, distribution, and use of communication with new cultural possibilities. The participatory production practices (with citizens producing and hosting their own programs) and the democratic content (of oral histories, local issues, critiques of government and business, and everyday vernacular) reflect the hegemony of emerging 'Bolivarian' twenty-first century socialism expressed as popular participation in media production. Bolstered by constitutional changes and public funding, popular social movements of civil society, indigenous, women, and working class organizations have gained revolutionary ground by securing in practice the right of media production. Findings indicate that public and community media (that move beyond alternative sites of local expression and concerns) provide a startling revolutionary contrast to the commercial media operations in every nation. Popular media constructions suggest a new radically democratic cultural hegemony based on human solidarity with collective, participatory decision-making and cooperation offering real possibilities and experiences for increased equality and social justice.

Social movements and political power in Latin America

In the midst of continent-wide turmoil and conflict at the beginning of the twenty-first century, the sudden increase in the number of governments espousing varieties of socialism and social democracy and enacting programmes to benefit labour, the urban poor and indigenous groups (with an occasional veneer of anti-US intervention rhetoric) became widely known as the 'pink tide'. Pink tide ('Onda Rosa' in Spanish) seems to concisely, albeit insufficiently, characterise the appearance of a generally left political trajectory in Latin American. This was 'pink' rather than 'red', as Larry Rohter of the *New York Times* first opined, pink indicating a lighter tone – not the 'red' of communism, not socialism, but a softer shade of progressive politics. While 'pink tide' cogently labels the leftward trend, more is needed to understand the complexity of what's really taking place in each country and the region as a whole. Only Venezuela and Bolivia explicitly advocate socialism, while the broad commitment to equality and popular participation by other governments open opportunities for more radical social transformation. Although neoliberal capitalism has regrouped across the continent with several electoral victories (as in Brazil and Argentina, as well as the political retreat in Ecuador and Uruguay), lessons for social change can be drawn from the rise of mass social movements from Venezuela and Bolivia to Ecuador and Argentina, among others.

Although three-fourths of Latin American countries have democratically elected progressive left-leaning presidents and legislatures since 1998, the rise of new social democratic and left-populist governments was poorly reported in the world's commercial media. Presenting disconnected and recurring exposés of one or another populist leader, commercial mass media obscured and misrepresented the remarkable historic changes that have occurred in Latin America in the last 15 years. Criticisms by liberal academics, non-government organisations, and some radical commentators[1] further discouraged appreciation of the momentous changes that were occurring.

A broad perspective is needed to analyse and evaluate the 'the extent to which the actors on the left today offer alternatives to neoliberalism' of 'determining to what extent parallelism', mass mobilisations and political initiatives by governments and movements 'go in the direction of ... decreasing inequality between the classes and countries, economic democracy and environmental sustainability'.[2] The impulse for democracy, social justice and social change embedded within social movement actions against privatisation and deregulation of public interest highlights several interrelated conflicts, including the conditions and operations of power, the meaning and practice of democracy, and the interaction of social relations of power that are instrumental in civil society, the government and the market. As the primary means of communication, media are implicated in power, democracy and social movements. In fact, public access to media addresses each of these questions of power – and also indicates the vitality of democracy within each society.

Here, public access does not refer to some amorphous public audience to be served, as with Britain's BBC or other public service broadcasters; public access asserts the right to produce content. Public access media affirms the democratic right to communicate, including the right to have access to production and distribution technologies without restriction by commercial interests or government control. Public, understood in all its complexity, includes the multiple constituencies of each country, including diverse sections of the working class from industrial, service, agricultural and informal workers to those unemployed and underemployed, indigenous nations, ethnic groups, women, youth, community-based organisations, religious, environmental, cooperative and other social, cultural and political collectivities.

Public access media serves as both an indication of the democratic commitment by a political leadership and a means for organising the powers necessary to resist neoliberalism and transform the capitalist order. A primary measure of democracy and social justice accords to the extent to which popular class forces have direct access to and control over their own means of communication. This is a dialectical process: organised social movements affect political power (occasionally securing more direct representation in national governments); the resulting popularly supported government forms and initiatives variously reflect, alter and provide openings for further social movement mobilisation for anti-capitalist advances that may transition to socialism.

The pink tide and more

Referring to the election of left, socialist-leaning and radical popular governments as the pink tide is only a first step to more robust investigations. Radical social movements of indigenous and working classes are organising beyond industrial worksites – portending rising labour conflicts in China and India and across Europe. (Worker protests in China reached record proportions in 2015; in 2016, tens of millions protested neoliberal reforms in India, while mass resistance to austerity has spread across Europe, the Middle East and Africa.)

Latin America is no longer part of the periphery in global production or global politics. Latin America is part of the Global South, but the entire Global South from BRICS (Brazil, Russian, India, China and South Africa) to Mexico, Korea, Nigeria and Eastern Europe can no longer be easily dismissed economically or politically. Industrial, agricultural and financial corporations in Latin America are fully integrated into an emerging transnational capitalist economic and political order. The extraction and production of energy, agriculture, and finished industrial and consumer goods in Latin America, along with their global export, as well as the enormous consumer market that Mexico, Brazil, Argentina, Venezuela and the rest of the nations provide, are an integral part of the global economy.[3]

Unsurprisingly, Latin American alternatives to neoliberal privatisation directly challenge the transnational capitalist system, raising real-life examples that might be emulated and advanced elsewhere. In each case the capitalist state and its social relations survived elections, but a change in governmental power brought new social programmes – to the exact extent that the new government relied on and responded to mass organisation and political mobilisation. Those 'left' governments that blocked mass participation and substituted their own political bureaucracies (as in Argentina, Brazil and Chile) shied away from dedicated social change and instead accommodated the capitalist order, in a vain attempt to compromise and avoid social confrontation. In part, their lack of resistance to neoliberalism contributed to the return of authoritarian electoral tendencies as represented by Bolsonaro in Brazil and Macron in Argentina.

While diverse social programmes of each government reflect the wide range of political agendas by the various 'left' politicians, Venezuela may be the most significant revolutionary project in the last 50 years, and arguably the most important challenge to global capitalism today. Neither Kirchner nor Lula opened doors to power for the working class. In contrast, after the Movement for Socialism (MAS) took national office in 2006, Bolivian national sovereignty took a decidedly egalitarian turn: hydrocarbon resources were nationalised and participatory democracy moved beyond electoral politics to collective self-management of public services.[4]

The political programme and organised actions by each leadership were and are primary determinants of the direction and success of each radical endeavour. Venezuela in particular is marked by widespread and consistent participation by urban working classes in community councils, political formations and parallel institutions organising and mobilising citizens for education, health care, housing, labour rights and media access. Democratic advances in Venezuela, Bolivia and, to some extent, Ecuador have followed the concerted, mobilised efforts of mass social movements in each country.

The constitutional reforms initiated by the 1999 Constituent Assembly in Venezuela, for example, include Article 62 which declares that citizens must 'create, implement, control' all public policies and Article 70 that legalises 'self-management, cooperatives ... based on cooperation and solidarity'. The new constitution included provisions for presidential decrees, which Chavez used in 2001 to enact 49 laws, including land reform, indigenous fishing rights and the nationalisation of some core industries that outraged large property owners and industrial fishing companies. More importantly, initiatives by Chavez were realised by mass participation in institutions that circumvented government bureaucracies. Communal councils and other popular organisations organised 'parallel' institutions through missions: Mission Barrio Adentro (health), Missions Robinson and Rivas (education), Mission Mercal (food distribution), Mission Milagro (eye care) and many others. Although there was no provision on media democracy or public media access in either the constitution or the executive decrees, following the 2002 coup (led in part by RCTV owners with other complicit commercial media), community activists and media workers advocated expanding public media access.

Among the clearest indications of each government's commitment to equality are the changes to media practices; the new laws, regulations and, in some cases, constitutional guarantees affording citizens the democratic right to communication, including access to media production, largely correspond to each 'left' government's orientation and commitment to full democracy. Wherever public access to media production and distribution has increased, it has nourished the communicative and persuasive power and also increased the political power of diverse social movements.

As participation in media production expanded, so too have social movements been able to advocate a new cultural hegemony of participatory democracy, anti-capitalist proposals and cultural expressions of radical national identities and international solidarity – especially across Latin America, as partially demonstrated in the cooperative regional news channel TeleSUR, the ALBA (Bolivarian Alliance for the Peoples of Our America) economic alliance, and the cultural projects of CELAC (the Community of Latin American and Caribbean States).

The trajectory of the political economy of media in Venezuela

The political economy of media is best understood as the complementary interactions of social relations among (1) ownership structures, (2) production practices and (3) media content, including its socio-cultural use. The political economy of media can be only be fully investigated by including each of the components of the social production of media: ownership ~ production practices ~ content for social use.

Media in Venezuela at the end of the twentieth century was similar to media social relations most everywhere, with consolidated private ownership and hierarchical production for profit through advertising-funded entertainment created and distributed to target audiences of consumers, featuring narratives and themes to win consent for capitalist social relations and culture, including passivity, authority and individual consumption.

Venevisión, the Cisneros Group network and the largest media operation in the country, is a major transnational with operations on five continents and in more than 70 countries; it is the leading global exporter of telenovelas to more than 100 countries and 24 languages. The Cisneros Group has investments in Univisión, the largest Spanish network in the United States, DirecTV Latin America, AOL Latin America and Playboy Latin America, as well as beverage and food distribution (Coca-Cola and Pizza Hut in Venezuela, for example), and other cultural productions, including the Los Leones baseball team and the Miss Venezuela

Pageant. Teleleven, owned by the Camero family, is now the second largest broadcaster, airing cartoons, baseball and other entertainment fare. Although Michel Granier's RCTV lost its broadcast license in 2007, in part due to its participation in the 2002 coup against Hugo Chavez, it continued on cable until 2015 and still produces programmes for other Latin American television.

In addition to the large commercial stations, there are a few national specialty broadcasters such as Vale TV (a Catholic, educational channel), Meridiano (a sports channel), La Puma (a music channel) and La Tele (an entertainment channel), and some 30 regional commercial TV and radio stations. Six families own the six largest daily papers, including *El Nacional*, *Tal Cual* and *Ultimas Noticias*. Importantly (with the exception of Venevisión and frequently *Últimas Noticias*), commercial media are sensationalistic, oppositional and at times even rabid in their attacks on the Bolivarian movement.

In 2017, amid the ongoing disinformation, complaints and infrequent accommodations by media elites, (1) the political economy of media in Venezuela (ownership ~ production practices ~ content for social use) remains at least 65% private and commercial and (2) production norms are dedicated to private profits from advertising revenues, with (3) entertainment programming the predominant content. Commercial media in Venezuela still effectively serve the economic and political interests of the Venezuelan capitalist class.

A new, revolutionary political economy of media

Importantly, the 2002 media-instigated coup against the democratically elected Hugo Chavez was only stymied by the outpouring of popular protest and mass demonstrations, including citizens and soldiers surrounding the plotters and demanding the return of the president. Given the crucial role that community radio played in alerting and mobilising citizen action in defense of democracy, media workers initiated conversations and policy proposals to the Chavez government that resulted in new radically democratic laws.

In 2004, following conversations with academics, trade organisations, health, cultural and children's advocacy groups, and social movement organisations, the National Assembly passed the Law on Social Responsibility of Radio and Television establishing the rights of community media and public access to media production and broadcast. The 2004 law establishes the right of 'active participation and oversight of citizens in all the processes of production, distribution, and consumption of media messages … the law anticipates the role of the national independent producers and committees of consumers as specific forms of citizen participation'.[5] As 2004 MINCI (Ministry of Communication and Information) Director Jesse Chacon explains:

> If communication is a social and an individual right, people must be able to practice it … we must privilege the right of communities over private interest. The private media are exerting their right to make a profit, while the organized communities use it as a mechanism for social development.[6]

The Venezuelan National Assembly has promulgated additional laws (2006, 2010, 2012) that further limit private ownership and expand working-class media access and public funding of community social ownership.[7] By 2011, Venezuela was approaching 1200 community media outlets. With government power representing the working-class majority, a public space is assured for popularising democracy, participation and new social relations that are not based on advertising, profits and audience markets. The narrative on community media in Venezuela is above all a prime example of class conflict, highlighting how a socialist-leaning government has used its power to nurture another site of democratic power by establishing and promoting non-state institutions under workers' control for communicating a more human culture. Because the political economy of media in Venezuela reflects the social relations of the larger capitalist society, the incursions against commercial media and the burgeoning parallel community media also reveal the possibilities for the strategy of using government power and working-class citizen action against capitalist state power, of creating a 'state for revolution'. In Venezuela, citizens have the right to *and* the means for media production and distribution.

The consumerist, capitalist character of Venezuelan media has thus been modestly challenged by the appearance of more public television and more community-based media, especially radio. In contrast to commercial media, the parallel political economy of public, community media (ownership ~ production practices ~ content for social use) features (1) public ownership of media broadcasting technology with wide public access to the broadcast spectrum, (2) guaranteed by community and media workers' control of the means of communication, which (3) increasingly created media content with a pro-socialist culture of mutual interest and community-based class solidarity, including discussions and participation by thousands of citizens. Democracy in action appears through organised, engaged, political and cultural communication by masses of working people, youth, women, indigenous and other constituent working-class groups.

The structure and practice of democratic media (the social relations comprising media ownership ~ production practices ~ content for social use) correspond to democratic, participatory production, including democratic decision-making, cultural diversity of producers, open access to technology, training and a maximum distribution of content with an emphasis on social justice and development. With socially owned media, media content can be produced by the working class and its allies, citizens, young and old, men, women, ethnic majority, minority, and indigenous. Media become available for community needs, socialising, educating, entertaining and informing citizens with content enhancing and sharing humanity's diversity with solidarity, humor, drama and meaning.

The arrival of a new structure of social ownership of community media, participatory production practices, and socially progressive programming content parallels the changing social relations throughout the country.[8] There are many examples of new ownership structures, production practices and media content featuring government stations, public broadcasters, and socially owned and directed community media.

Government communication: VTV and TeleSUR

The government-run VTV has a national footprint, primarily broadcasting educational and public service programming. In addition to other news shows, VTV features the weekly 'Alo Presidente!' show, which tours the country with the president and local officials questioned live on issues and topics of the day. VTV also produces the occasional cultural programme such as the 2004 telenovela 'Amores en Barrio Adentro' ('Love in the Neighborhood'), a love story with politics set in changing Venezuela. The narrative had romance, but rather than centring on individual self-interest the story expresses a sense of community and humanity – love in a time of solidarity.

The government also supports TeleSUR (Television of the South), the cooperative satellite television venture of Venezuela, Argentina, Uruguay, Cuba and Bolivia with 12 Latin American bureaus that establishes 'an independent public media space for Latin America'[9] and airs ANTV, the television channel of the National Assembly.

Public access media

The development and expansion of national public broadcasting are easily recognisable changes in the Venezuelan media landscape. The programmes and processes of production underscore how a more democratic political economy frames cultural practice. Three major public broadcasting stations – ViVes, TVes and Avila TV – have been established along with the YVKE Radio Network, with 10 stations providing a parallel public radio system. Public television stations are primarily funded by subsidies from the Social Fund (part of the national budget for social missions and development) and 'advertisements' for national social services. They are each independently run – outside government direction, oversight or even approval – highlighted by several shows highly critical of the government.

The production practices and programming content demonstrate the dialectic of social being determining social consciousness, because by becoming producers, editors, narrators and videographers for the new society, participants become more engaged, vibrant human beings – their social awareness, their life being, is prompted to develop through the explosion in consciousness and awareness of their own creativity, power and lived experience of social contradictions. In dozens of conversations and interviews with producers, directors and technicians (conducted in person in 2005 and 2008, and electronically in 2010–2011 and 2016) expressions of determination and desire for a new society reflected the cumulative experience and democratic participation and decision-making that privileges community, workers, women, indigenous and the average citizen. Witnessing a teenager's apprehension turning to joyful confidence as she begins her first television report is truly inspiring. In Venezuela, public media that broadcast several community-based 15-minute documentaries every day guarantee hundreds of such personal self-realisations and transformations.

Two examples begin to illustrate how a political economy of expanded social ownership and participatory production impact media content and cultural practices.

ViVe

In 2003, Vision Venezuela TV (ViVe) was founded as a Caracas-based public access station under public control. ViVe (or 'vives' (lives), as it is called) is almost exclusively dedicated to community productions as part of its 'Sueño Bolivariano' (Bolivarian Dream) message, which promotes cooperation, solidarity and collective work in place of individual profit and consumerism. Independent, public and cooperatively run, ViVe prohibits advertising. Only 10% of its programming is produced in-house; the remaining 90% of shows come from community producers (eg specials on traditional peasant planting practices, indigenous musical performances, local community cultural activities, and investigative pieces on housing, utilities and even religious events). ViVe programming has included 'Secretos de Familila' (about communication traditions across generations), 'Querencia Andean' (Andean cultural traditions), 'Historias de Vida' (narratives of community organising experiences), 'Cultural de Dia' (arts and crafts expressing contemporary Venezuelan cultural diversity), 'Espacio Musical' (featuring national and international music with artist interviews), 'Real o Medio' (critiques of media from Zulia) and many more (for current programmes, see http://www.vive.gob.ve/programacon). Programming constantly changes to air different experiences and interests, always with participation and production assistance by community videographers. More than 14,000 communities have been featured over the last 10 years, about 30 half-hour shows per week on average.

Due to ViVe's participatory structure and social justice mission, for the first time on national television, women, Afro-Venezuelans and indigenous people are prominent. To ensure quality productions, ViVe organises community-based training for video production through community and workers' councils. The Bolivarian socialist project 'created social missions with health care and education for the poor. ViVe [is] the equivalent for television, where everybody regardless of class, color, or beliefs can take part in the great political debate for socialism and the transformation of this country', says ViVe's Sergio Arriasis.[10]

ViVe is not public service broadcasting as advocated by liberal pluralists or the media reform movement in the United States; it does not strive for impartiality. Rather, ViVe is public *access* broadcasting, with public control and partisan communication for social justice and social change. ViVe even has mobile transmitting stations in working-class and peasant communities in each region of the country, along with courses to teach citizens broadcasting skills. A new social power has emerged as working-class communities and individuals – directly participating and collectively collaborating – produce entertaining solidarity media and democratic cultural experiences. A hard day's work at Vive is invigorating, with energy coming from diverse cultural productions by dozens of community producers. These creative producers represent new human beings, human agents consciously working in and for solidarity among working people and their allies.

Avila TV: hip-hop and the politics of participation

The former Bolivarian mayor of Caracas, Juan Barretto, originally launched Avila TV in 2006 as part of a socialist communication initiative. Close to 400 producers – most under 30 years old – write, produce, edit, film and broadcast edgy, creative programming aimed at urban youth. Avila might be described as a station with hip-hop sensibility and socialist lyrics.[11] A typical Avila broadcast day includes news, music, political talk shows, features on international and community issues, and telenovelas about Caracas working-class families – but no commercials. Their programming decisions are guided by an explicit commitment to a new social order, as expressed by one of the many articulate young producers: 'We aren't trying to sell shampoo or name brand clothes, or any capitalist products for that matter. We are trying to stay true to our principles and combat consumerism'.[12] Watching Avila TV, viewers quickly notice the style, the tone and the structure of programming. At times, even the music feels argumentative, strident.

In 2008, Avila aired a weekly series called 'El Entrompe de Falopio', about women and gender issues in the revolution. A year-long live programme, 'Voice, Face, and Struggle of the People', included one episode titled 'Impunity', where hosts, guests and audience members sharply criticised the government for granting amnesty to the 2002 coup leaders. Even the telenovelas from Avila have political overtones with not-so-subtle barbs at the opposition for undemocratic obstruction and the government for not championing working-class interests and advancing socialism more quickly. High-quality documentaries, professionally and creatively produced, have included the widely acclaimed 2008 *El Golpe* (*The Coup*) and the 2008 feature *200 Years of Caracas: The Insurgent Capital of the Continent*. The young producers at Avila have also aired shows on Afro-Venezuelans, indigenous cultures and homosexuality – all topics ignored or taboo on commercial television. In 2013, Avila launched new programming, including live tours of Caracas's cultural and recreational life, 'Caracas Mision', with 5-minute shorts produced by community videographers, cycling through self-management projects of community councils and missions; 'Political', on location and in studio accounts of social movement democracy in action; 'Desportes Caracas', with reports on professional, amateur and community sports activities; and many more (for commentary and critique, see blog http://avilapendiente.blogspot.com/).

Avila has been an integral part of RED TV (Education for the Revolution and Development of Venezuela), a city-wide educational project to bring classes in screenwriting, playwriting and video production to the working-class communities of Caracas. By 2010, 55 community councils in Caracas had media committees, where community members receive extensive training, mentoring and equipment – cameras, computers and editing software for video production and post-production. Community media committees then have regularly scheduled spots on Avila's daily schedule for airing 10–15-minute video productions.

The Bolivarian government has created laws, provided resources and prepared space for non-commercial, non-capitalist media production. In the vocabulary of the Bolivarian project, new 'protagonists' can now fully participate in creating their own culture and their own stories, and expressing their own interests. While they are making video, making television, making communication, they are also making new human beings. In 2013, two new public stations were announced, one by and for youth, the other TV Obrera (Worker's TV) directed by labour; both appear on the new Open Digital Television system. Lives and experiences of working-class communities and community activists are valuable, valued and shared – informing the nation of how and what new creative human beings can and will be with the revolutionary transformation of society from capitalism to socialism.

Community media: independent and democratic

Complementing (and historically and politically preceding) public broadcasting in Venezuela, community radio and television have a rich tradition of participatory communication. By the 1990s, community media were already appearing across the country: Radio Treat, TV Michelena, Radio Perola, Active Radio La Vega and many more complemented social movements that used street media such as murals, flyers, megaphone 'radio', film clubs and websites like aporrea.org. Today, millions of Venezuelans read, listen to, watch and/or directly involve themselves with community media.

In contrast to the LPFM (Low Power Frequency Modulation) licenses in the US that are limited to 100 watts, the licensing of more powerful broadcast technology allows 'community' media to reach millions of receivers. None of the stations are individually or privately owned; rather, stations are licensed to communities with collective decision-making control. Thus, these are geographically and intimately connected to their members and staff. Community media news reporters in Venezuela see themselves as 'popular communicators' rather than journalists.[13] They rely on the direct capacity of each local community 'to analyze, decide, implement, and evaluate what is relevant to its life'.[14] Communal councils, which operate most community media, are structures of direct democracy by residents, workers and citizens self-organised at the local level. More than 44,000 communal councils have been organised throughout the country, while several thousand workers' councils govern local and national enterprises as social property. As self-representative, direct-democracy constituent assemblies, communes create new power geometry, shaping Venezuela's social–cultural–economic space[15] – towards a new cultural hegemony of participation, democracy, pluralism, social development and social justice. With their own media, communes communicate their preferences for a new social structure of participatory democracy, for a socialist society.

Venezuelan communal councils breathe political and cultural life into community media operations and content, while also challenging the distortions of traditional elite representational politics. As MINCI Director Andrés Izarra oversaw the transformation of Venezuela's media political economy, he understood that a new cultural hegemony depends on persuasion and leadership through mediated communication: 'This is a battle of ideas. Capitalist society is hegemonic in these countries. We have to think about how the socialist values of the collective, the social, and solidarity can predominate over those of capitalism'.[16] An example of Antonio Gramsci's call for a persuasive 'war of position', community media in Venezuela are prime communication means for a new cultural hegemony of direct democracy and solidarity.

Catia TV

A leader in community media is Catia TV in Caracas, the first legal community television network in the country. Catia TV's slogan 'Don't Watch TV, Make TV!' is inscribed on the outside wall of its broadcast studios and is demonstrated daily by collaborative rotating teams of four to seven community producers organised in ECPAIs (Independent Community Audiovisual Production Teams). Each ECPAI decides the topics, formats, aesthetics and content for broadcast programmes, emphasising stories from the barrio, in all their contradictions. Catia TV exemplifies popular education and democratic participation, articulating its television production and programming with assemblies, events and communication guerrillas: muralists, storytellers, oral historians, artisanal creators and puppeteers. Its purpose

> is to act as an organizing tool, where communities build their own audiovisual discourse ... having knowledge of communication; having a critical analysis surrounding the conditions and social context in which an individual or group must live; identifying the cultural and ideological values that effect the group's or collective's vision; developing a understanding of reality and how they act; associating learning with the collective construction of knowledge; and identifying and analyzing [their] own practices.[17]

Catia TV builds collective work for the community's common interest. Working in teams also favours the organised distribution of work and conscious analysis of how to produce material – both activities at odds with the capitalist division of cultural labour based on corporate hierarchy and the alienation and dispossession of media creators from their work. Additionally, media content produced by ECPAIs never has to comply with some profit-driven owner or government oversight. For Catia TV, and other community media workers, the right to media has nothing to do with service or charity, either. The right to produce media forms part of the emerging rights of the Venezuelan working classes to organise themselves, to decide the production of goods and services, and to consciously, collectively determine their own social and cultural norms.

Catia is not a singular example. Dozens of community television stations now broadcast across Venezuela, and not all are successful in integrating community participation with media production. Petaré TV in Caracas, for example, was established without much community input and – despite funding, technology and training – until recently struggled from a lack of collaboration with and an organic connection to residents.

Afro TV

Afro TV, in Balo Vento on the east coast of Venezuela, illustrates the cultural and social potential for community media led by community activists linked to a politically awakening community. About 15% of Venezuela is Afro-Venezuelan, the historic consequence of Spanish slavery and cocoa plantations in the east. Balo Vento had long been neglected by central governments, relegated to continued exploitation by private cocoa growers. Following discussion and ratification of the new constitution that establishes Venezuela as a multiethnic, pluricultural society, the government established a subcommission of African descendants in the National Assembly. The education, health and housing missions were extended to Balo Vento, along with the opportunity for public, independent, community media. Afro TV was the early regional media project launched by a handful of community activists. Their mission includes recovering their African past, expressing their cultural and artistic present, and organising public dialogue on contemporary issues important to Balo Vento, such as land reform, development and workers' control of cocoa production. By 2008, Afro TV was broadcasting 4–5 hours daily on a UHF signal. Afro TV is also available via the Internet. Early programmes included 'Cimmarones', stories of slave rebellion, and 'Que Es Eso', featuring local characters telling their life stories. Afro TV, while modest in its operation, nonetheless illustrates the relationship between media access and community cultural experiences, the dialectical development of becoming new human beings by collaboratively creating their own realities.

Radio: power and access

There are currently more than 100,000 community activists working with hundreds of community radio and television stations with scores of additional broadcasters in various stages of preparation, production, training, licensing and building. Community media have been a national priority for MINCI since 2008, when it unveiled a new strategic plan for funding, training and licensing community media with national broadcast capabilities. Community media now reaches almost two-thirds of the population, the outcome of a continuing dialogue about democratic control over communication and the concerted interaction between government and working-class communities. From officials to teenage producers, socialism for the twenty-first century articulates new social relations, beginning with ownership and control over industry, including media that contribute to a new social consciousness and new social being across classes. Community radio illustrates this dialectical process of protagonist-initiated development of political self-awareness and power.

At Radio 23 de Enero (broadcasting at 3000 watts in Caracas), journalists and producers from the more than 50 social movement collectives broadcast weekly programmes of music, opinion, health, public affairs and news. For decades, community groups in the 23 de Enero neighbourhood have worked on health care, education, sports, housing, security and political organising. Community participation is part of the culture; the local radio station has been broadcasting for years, and community councils and media studios are only the latest manifestations of collaborative participation.

Community assemblies culminated in deciding to start Radio Rebelde in 2003. Neighbourhood producers host shows on local history, natural medicine and the environment. Venezuelan music and culture are emphasised. Regular classes teach newcomers how to start their own programmes. Democratic assemblies of community producers who have equal voice and vote run the station collectively.

Also in Caracas, teens, grandparents, DJs and investigative journalists collectively share the broadcast schedule at Radio Primero Negro, a station with a long history of community organising. Students, mothers, unemployed people and members of community organisations air more than 60 programmes weekly. The station's community activists conduct regular surveys and conversations with neighbourhood residents to assure programmes meet the needs and interests of all, and to continually recruit more participants for the station, offering training and the expertise of station technicians. These 'community' stations reach more than 1 million residents of Caracas – not your typical 'community' broadcaster in the United States or the rest of the North.

Working miners and their Tumeremo community produce their own news and programming on Radio Minero. In Zulia, Maracaibo, the indigenous community broadcasts over Radio Yupa in their native language, with stories and topics drawn from their historic culture and everyday concerns. Radio Negro Primero, Radio Perola, TV Rubio and others existed prior to MINCI, the 2004 Law and SIBCI (Bolivarian Communication and Information System). They have long promoted social change through education and community involvement. Others, like Radio Un Nuevo Dia, Radio Tiuna, and Radio and TV Macarao more closely connect their new access to media with the twenty-first-century Bolivarian socialist project. Each of them thrives under the legality of licensing and community participation and support, and to varying degrees, each continues to demand more from the government. In 2009, more than 3000 media activists held a national day of action for increased public media access and democratic reform.

Democratic media production and distribution

Democratic community media now air inspiring stories by novices facing microphones for the first time and feeling the power of communication, directly experiencing the meaning of democracy and community. Local stations have leaders, directors and specialists on cultural, political and indigenous community issues, creating a 'communication force' for revolutionary change.

Participatory journalism and participatory democratic production at ViVe, Avila, Catia TV, Radio El Negro Primero, Radio Minero and other community media outlets reflect changing social relations. University and professionally trained journalists work alongside community correspondents and participatory journalists, constructing and distributing news and news reports that are accurate and timely, but much more democratic in framing and sourcing because they are not bound by the advertising needs or editorial dictates of market-driven media. New norms of objectivity-with-partisanship serve the information and educational needs of the majority striving for democratic control over their lives.

Community and public media reorganize the practices and functions of media in line with human needs, so that a participatory socially conscious media contributes to the new cultural hegemony of a creative, socialist humanity – against the hegemony of consumerism and neo-liberalism – for a culture of cooperation, solidarity and dedication to creating social justice and solidarity. In this mix, entertainment becomes more varied and journalism of necessity becomes more vibrant, more alive, identifying facts, sources and truths related to the real experience and conditions of the working-class population.[18]

Participation in media creation and broadcast has the ability to transform. As MINCI Alternative and Community Media Director Ana Viloria explained in our 2008 interview,

> Community media visibilises our faces, our voices, so we collectively know what we are doing is connected to humanity. We become protagonists … we make for ourselves the task of learning ideas and tools that are available for the political actor.

For example, in 2013 over 300 community media participants met to discuss and affirm expanding public access to radio and TV. Their political decisions became part of the policy agenda MINCI/SIBCI is currently funding and implementing.

A democratic political economy of media: a revolutionary, participatory culture

The trajectory of public broadcasting, community media and participatory democracy with widespread public access to media delivers a new social function for media. Legalised, funded and supported by the PSUV (United Socialist Party of Venezuela) government, community media entertain and inform – but more importantly, they are revolutionary media striving for a new popular culture, a new humanity. These media air working-class-generated narratives reflecting the collaborative creativity and shared experiences of those who aspire to write their own future history, media that broadcast messages, stories and images of solidarity, collective action, participatory democracy and communities in a struggle for social justice, self-government and working-class leadership of society – from immediate demands for improved water access to global expressions of solidarity with Palestine and Sioux protestors in North Dakota.

This new political economy of media production relies on and forges social relations that challenge capitalism, social relations that build democratic participation by the Venezuelan working and middle classes, women, youth, Afro-Venezuelans, indigenous populations and others previously underserved and excluded, politically, socially and economically. This new democratic political economy of media production and distribution has been facilitated by a government responding to social movement initiatives and using its legislative, executive, financial and rhetorical power to provide resources to advance working-class leadership and democratic social relations in media and other industries.

One-third of media broadcasts in Venezuela are now socially owned, with licensing collectively held by the media users themselves. These democratically run media are nothing like the vertical broadcasting and control prevalent in commercial media. These media do not broadcast to 'receivers' or 'audiences'. These new media function through cooperative relations of production under direct workers' and community control, developing class actions and contributing to a new more democratic social order. State power over communication (including private control and government regulation) is passing to organised workers and their constituents, as community media have both the means and the practices for undermining capitalist social relations, corporate production norms and consumer ideology – as well as challenging and pushing the PSUV government.[19] Community media, in practice, transform individuals, communities and social classes that directly experience their own power to communicate, their power to democratically decide and implement. The burgeoning community media dramatically increase space for public debate and participation by decision-making citizens, especially the working classes.

The struggle for ideological hegemony in everyday life is a precondition for social transformation. Community media in Venezuela contribute to a new, more radically human culture by engaging in an ongoing dialogue and debate with the full participation of the working class, indigenous, peasants, women, youth and other citizens in communities across the country. Murals, posters, graffiti, street radio, puppeteers, newspapers and guerrilla theater complement radio and television broadcasts. Through cooperative interactions, labour, community and media activists are able to develop a collective consciousness and experience a 'moral self-transformation, evidenced by greater self-confidence and feelings of control',[20] transcending the narrow self-interest of entertainment media narratives as a sense of community emerges. The dynamics of a new way of being human are products of each participant's experience within a genuinely democratic practice.

The practices and programmes of ViVe, Avila and Catia TV differ dramatically from commercial media production and content in their democratic, participatory construction, their community origin and creation, their promotion of social development, cooperation and social justice, and their intentional challenge to atomised consumerism and market values. And yet, community media are entertaining. On community radio and television, there are talk shows, educational programs, cultural shows, sports segments, local history programs, children's shows, cooking shows, and a variety of music programs, including salsa, bolero, hip-hop, rock, and llanero (country) music. Community newspapers have editorial pieces and discussion sections with lively debates among contributors. Avila is hip. Catia is edgy. Radio Negro Primero is contemporary. Afro TV links history with future. It seems community media rising from social struggle is vibrant and fun – key attributes of a new cultural leadership.

The expanded right to communicate improves participation, information and decision-making, making for a more democratic society. Simultaneously, community media prepare the working-class majority for the coming unavoidable confrontation with capitalism (within Venezuela and from the United States) by experiencing and communicating in production and programming new norms of class solidarity, collective ownership and democratic practices.

The development, expansion and consolidation of participatory media arise from the contradictory processes of the Venezuelan revolution. The experience and struggles of community media in Venezuela also express the potential (and necessary) function of media as part of the revolutionary process and the relation between social movements, class organisation and political power. The Bolivarian government interactively, dialectally and frequently erratically has led and responded to social movement initiatives. As Ana Viloria, MINCI director in 2008, explained in an interview with me, participatory community media is 'an exquisite contradiction' using the government 'to promote working-class control of media outside and above the state'. To the extent that the PSUV government encourages, allows or follows social movement interests and proposals, the government becomes a means for expanding the revolution and organising, mobilising the working classes and their allies. To the extent that working classes, community organisations and other non-elite social sectors grasp control of factories, schools, city councils and media, they expand their power to enforce their democratic will on the government as they strive to transform society.

Public media access thus is both a measure of democratic participation and a site and means for educating, organising and mobilising working classes towards revolution. Media is not the only or the primary means of political and economic class control, but it is a fulcrum of and for larger class battles.

Media access and social revolution

Public media access with participatory control increases communication among and within communities, social groups and working classes. Participation in deciding, producing and communicating with and for social movements increases the political consciousness of participants, improves political understandings and provides a means for debating and testing tactics and strategies for social change. Media become a vital site for mass agitation and organisation; media allow new political leadership to offer and hone new cultural hegemonies that can represent and incorporate the interests of the majority of society – through music, entertainment and political commentary – as demonstrated by Catia TV, Avila TV and Radio 23 Enero among many other participatory media.

Public media access with participatory control likewise indicates the level of democracy and social power of working classes, women, youth, indigenous groups and other social sectors. Community mass media measures the affiliation and allegiance of various social groups that participate in production and rely on it for information. As a site of mass participation, democratic media production and distribution can be an extraordinary part of a leadership development programme for revolution. And, finally, public access media become an important means for citizen participation and recruitment to action for social change.

While Venezuela has advanced the farthest in mass political consciousness, public policy and public media access, other pink tide nations have emulated the model, reflecting the progress and difficulties of the socio-political dynamics in different contexts.[21] Bolivia has made constitutional amendments requiring a transition to media licensing that provides for one-third commercial, one-third public and one-third community media, including special provisions for indigenous media. The implementation of laws, policies and structures is not as advanced as in Venezuela, but miners, labourers and indigenous have made gains in communication access both rurally and in urban centres.

Likewise, Ecuador, Uruguay and Argentina have legislated and made contradictory attempts at implementing a similar one-third each commercial, public and community media system. None have provided the kind of resources, or the more inclusive, participatory control, that mark Venezuelan community media. In the case of Argentina, Mauricio Macri (elected president in 2015) reversed the democratic media reforms by decree. In Brazil, Chile, Peru and elsewhere – where working-class social movements have not made any concerted efforts towards controlling their own media – there have been no laws or policies for more public media and there remains little democratic access. Indeed, a quick review of the relation between democratic, public media access and the level of political organisation and power of social movements confirms the connection between radical working-class action and organisation and the extent of participatory media control.

The setbacks, challenges and coming class confrontations in Latin America, and the rest of the world (illustrated by US sanctions and interventions in Venezuela, and military actions in Yemen, Syria and elsewhere) represent the continuing assault by transnational capitalism and its neoliberal policies of privatisation and austerity. Even as contradictory and insufficient as they may be by themselves, the successes, gains and struggles by indigenous nations, politically and communally organised working classes, women, youth and subaltern others indicate that working people of the world will not passively accept the deepening capitalist onslaught. Moreover, despite military interventions, coups, defaults and electoral defeats in Latin America, the Middle East, Europe and elsewhere, social movements have not been defeated.

The piquetero motorcyclists may not appear in Shanghai and the indigenous nations in Burma or Indonesia may not occupy highways like the Aymara in Bolivia, but contradictions wrought by wage exploitation and privatisation of public goods will surely prompt new class confrontations in diverse forms. Revolutions everywhere can learn from precedents. Each revolutionary struggle also can contribute further lessons. The experiences of constructing a new political economy of participatory community media suggest that all social movements benefit when they are able to control their own media systems, communicating for and with their revolution.

Disclosure statement

No potential conflict of interest was reported by the author.

Acknowledgements

This work furthers previous observations, presentations and drafts given at several conferences. The author thanks colleagues from the Geopolitical Economy Research Group at the University of Manitoba and the Global Studies Association of North America who provided insights and suggestions to improve this essay.

Notes

1. Katz and Ellner, "Crisis in Venezuela."
2. Rodriguez-Garavito, Barrett, and Chavez, "Utopia Reborn?," 23.
3. Robinson, *Latin America and Global Capitalism*.
4. Tapia, "Bolivia: The Left and the Social Movements," 224–5.
5. Gonzalo Vega, "For a More Engaged Society in Venezuela."
6. Iacobelli and Gironi, "Venezuela Is One of Few Countries."
7. *Venezuela en Noticias*, "Community Media in Venezuela."
8. Another instance of social movement governance is the parliamentary process of 'Legislator Pueblo', where citizens propose laws directly to the National Assembly. In 2011, legislators approved a tenant's movement initiative, the Law on Renting, protecting tenants and small landlords from speculators and poor housing conditions. The National Assembly passed a draft of a media workers' proposal on 'Communications for People's Power' in 2012, to support 1200 community media operations through increased networking, funding and community control.
9. Artz, "TeleSUR."
10. Wynter, "Venezuela: Creating a New Radical Media."
11. Cassel, "Avila TV in Venezuela."
12. Interview with Antonio Mellado at Avila TV, June 2 008.
13. Fernandes, *Who Can Stop the Drums?*, 169.
14. Azzellini, *Communes and Workers Control*, 26.
15. Ibid.
16. Weffer, "Entrevista."
17. Catia TVe Collective, "Catia TVe, Television."
18. Carlos Lujo. Interview at Radio El Primero Negro. Caracas, Venezuela. June 2008.
19. Janicke, "Venezuela Strengthens Community Media."
20. Harnecker, "Workplace Democracy and Collective Consciousness," 512.
21. Artz, *Pink Tide*.

Bibliography

Artz, Lee. *The Pink Tide: Media Access and Political Power in Latin America*. Lanham, MD: Rowman & Littlefield, 2017.

Artz, Lee. "TeleSUR (Television of the South): Discarding Contraflow for Horizontal Communication." *International Journal of Media and Cultural Politics* 2, no. 1 (2006): 225–232.

Azzellini, Dario. *Communes and Workers Control in Venezuela*. Chicago: Haymarket Books, 2018.

Cassel, Lainie. "Avila TV in Venezuela: Revolutionizing Television." *Upside Down World*. June 11, 2009. http://upsidedownworld.org/archives/venezuela/avila-tv-in-venezuela-revolutionizing-television/

Catia TVe Collective. "Catia TVe, Television from, by and for the People." *Venezuelanalysis*. July 19, 2006. https://venezuelanalysis.com/analysis/1843

Fernandes, Sujatha. *Who Can Stop the Drums? Urban Social Movements in Chavez's Venezuela*. Greensboro, NC: Duke University Press, 2010.

Gonzalo Vega, Morelis. "For a More Engaged Society in Venezuela." *Venezuelanalysis*. July 17, 2004. https://venezuelanalysis.com/analysis/590

Harnecker, Piñeiro Camila. "Workplace Democracy and Collective Consciousness: An Empirical Study of Venezuelan Cooperatives." *Monthly Review* 59, no. 6 (2007): 27. http://monthlyreview.org/2007/11/01/workplace-democracy-and-collective-consciousness-an-empirical-study-of-venezuelan-cooperatives/ doi:10.14452/MR-059-06-2007-10_5.

Iacobelli, Donatella, and Raul Grioni. "Venezuela Is One of Few Countries Where Right of Communities to Provide Themselves with Media Is a Reality." *Venezuelanalysis*. February 13, 2004. https://venezuelanalysis.com/analysis/354

Janicke, Kiraz. "Venezuela Strengthens Community Media in 'Battle of Ideas.'" *Venezuelanalysis*. February 14, 2008. http://venezuelanalysis.com/analysis/3158

Katz, Claudio, and Steve Ellner. "The Crisis in Venezuela: The Left and Venezuela." *Socialist Project: The Bullet*. 2017. https://socialistproject.ca/2017/07/b1458/#continue

Robinson, William I. *Latin America and Global Capitalism: A Critical Globalization Perspective*. Baltimore, MD: Johns Hopkins University Press, 2008.

Rodriguez-Garavito, César, Patrick Barrett, and Daniel Chavez. "Utopia Reborn? Introduction to the Study of the New Latin American Left." In *The New Left American Left: Utopia Reborn*, edited by Patrick Barrett, Daniel Chavez, and César Rodriguez-Garavito, 1–41. London: Pluto Press, 2008.

Tapia, Luis. "Bolivia: The Left and the Social Movements." In *The New Left American Left: Utopia Reborn*, edited by Patrick Barrett, Daniel Chavez, and César Rodriguez-Garavito, 215–231. London: Pluto Press, 2008.

Venezuela en Noticias. "Community Media in Venezuela Gets Funding from Telecoms Authority." *Venezuelanalysis*. January 8, 2012. https://venezuelanalysis.com/news/6731

Weffer, Laura. "Entrevista: Andrés Izarra piensa que deben evaluarse todos los operadores de TV." *El Nacional*. January 8, 2007. http://venezuelareal.zoomblog.com/archivo/2007/01/08/entrevista-Andres-Izarra-considera-que.html

Wynter, Carol. "Venezuela: Creating a New Radical Media." *Venezuelanalysis*. May 24, 2010. https://venezuelanalysis.com/analysis/5381

Bush/revolution: theses on the challenges that gatherers and hunters pose to dominant structures

Peter Kulchyski

ABSTRACT
This article argues that bush people deserve greater attention in revolutionary thought and action, both for the strategic value of their struggles against extraction at capital's periphery and the emancipatory social values they continue to embody. But bush struggles cannot be borrowed for other purposes: the agenda of bush people for respect and cultural survival must respected in its own right.

Marx says that revolutions are the locomotives of world history. But perhaps it is quite different. Perhaps revolutions are what happens when the humanity travelling in this train snatches at the emergency brake'. —Walter Benjamin[1]

Search for the emancipatory subject

In the social ferment that characterised the 1960s, mobilisations led by colonised subjects, students, African Americans and feminists led a variety of left thinkers to reimagine the place of the working class as a revolutionary vanguard. The thinking was that some non-working-class element of the population might be the 'real' revolutionary or emancipatory subject of history. This mode of thought is not so distant from the present as might be instinctively presumed: witness the attention, for example, of queer theory to the degree to which transgender, homo-social or non-gendered 'normative' socialities imply a radical, emancipated or emancipatory subject position and are therefore the latest carriers of the torch of revolution, albeit a revolution less interested in state power. Indigenous peoples have also been briefly bathed in the light of this hope; from the actions of the American Indian Movement in the earlier period of ferment to the more recent intensification of struggle in the current historical conjunction at Standing Rock, there have been usually short-lived hopes of an Indigenous-led structural confrontation with capitalism or at least the capitalist state.

This search for an emancipatory subject continues to inflect social thinking. There is a fashion in which many thinkers, when asked about the relevance of their particular social topic, explain in a lucid manner that the question they are studying is the fulcrum, the key, the absolutely essential missing strategic theoretical insight that will unlock the gates of utopia. Dostoevsky, no hero to the left, recognised this tendency in the intellectual and social ferment that gripped late nineteenth century Russia. There is, then, a certain intellectual hubris that often marks left social theory: the desire to be Marx, or, if not Marx, then Benjamin, even if he was never appreciated in his lifetime and demonstrated the truth of his dictum that the dead have a claim on our attention.

Indigenous peoples, or at least the bush peoples with whom I work, value humility. Among Anishnabwe, for example, it is one of the seven 'teachings', a central pillar of their thought. As a scholar in formation, it was contingency, the fact of my own less-than-privileged background, that led me to the study of the bush people I grew up with and around. Apart from their centrality in anthropology, bush people were a marginal social subject, not thought of much by the activist left and only beginning to emerge as a topic of scholarly interest (how dramatically different from the current historical conjunction in Canada when every grant application requires an 'Indigenous' component...). Perhaps it was the influence of Dostoevsky, but I promised myself that I would not repeat the errors or arrogance of my cohort: I would work on a sideshow of politics, a curious but to me compelling social conflict at the margins of the grand worker-feminist-antiracist confrontation unfolding. Always unfolding.

And yet, the current moment demands a reappraisal of the positionality of bush peoples within revolutionary thought and action. In the immediate historical conjuncture, especially in the Americas, bush people have a decidedly critical position in any attempt to account for or bring into being a better world. What follows is an analysis that attempts to be worthy of that insight.

The vexing question of terminology

Almost all of the terms used to describe bush people, even those within the Marxist canon, are flawed inasmuch as they do not account for the difference between hunting and farming peoples. In technical terms, they do not deploy one of the central categories that Marx himself developed as a key to historical materialism: mode of production. Broadly speaking, gathering and hunting peoples (bush peoples) and farming peoples follow entirely distinct ways of life, involving dramatically different social relations, technologies, values, cultural forms, knowledge systems. The gathering and hunting mode of production needs to be understood as entirely distinct from the tributary mode of production, as distinct as the latter is from the capitalist mode of production. Terms such as pre-capitalist social formations, minorities or ethnic minorities, tribal peoples, native peoples, aboriginal peoples, indigenous peoples, traditional cultures, are not up to the task of articulating the former distinction and operate under the assumption that there is the capitalist mode of production and then all the rest, in an indistinct hodgepodge of cultural and social and political economic forms that can be called 'traditional'. While any of these may be used colloquially and many have legal purchase in specific national contexts, they do not belong in a historical materialism that deserves the name.

There is a long tradition in critical thought that focuses on the difference between bush people (hunters) and farmers (the tributary mode). Indeed, from Rousseau's *Origins of Inequality* to Engels' *The Origins of the Family, Private Property, and the State*, itself based on Marx's own, evocative, *Ethnological Notebooks*, to the work of more recent anthropologists such as Eleanor Leacock, Richard Lee and Marshall Sahlins, there is a strain of Marxist theory that centres the distinction.[2] Often, however, the distinction is deployed as an additional club to hit the dominant social order with. Rarely, in the classical Marxist tradition, is it used as a critical tool to be mobilised in the intellectual element of the contemporary struggles of contemporary bush peoples.

In the current historical moment, where colonialism is one of the dominant tools of capitalist hegemony, the failure to address this elision has serious strategic and intellectual consequences whose significance can hardly be underestimated. Effectively, colonised subjects are treated as a block: all the same, suffering from the same form of domination and resisting in the same manner. However, if we accept the most basic point of the intellectual traditions cited above, that bush peoples embody an egalitarian cultural ethos while the tributary mode enacted pernicious forms of social hierarchy including invidious and entrenched forms of patriarchy, does it not make sense to suggest that forms of resistance and forms of domination may have had to reflect these on-the-ground social realities? Frantz Fanon was clearly an enlightenment-influenced thinker in an African context in which a suspicion of the traditions of the colonised subjects he worked with clearly made sense, while his near-colleague Amilcar Cabral found much more inspiration from traditional forms of the sub-Saharan context in which his thought fermented. This might be a matter of intellectual or political temperament, but it seems more likely this difference sprang from the fact that Fanon, working in Algeria, was faced with a substantive (agricultural) tradition that was largely hierarchical and patriarchal in form, while Cabral, working in sub-Saharan Africa, had sustained contact with egalitarian bush people. In an admittedly offhand conversation with a contemporary scholar whose work I admire and who now has turned to Africa as a site of intellectual engagement, I asked Sylvia Federici whether she paid attention to whether her research subjects were hunters or farmers. She looked at me like I was from Mars: 'What possible significance could that have?' This essay is, in effect, my answer.

In what follows the terms enunciated above will be avoided as will the awkward and anthropologically inflected though more accurate terms like 'gatherers' and 'hunters'. This analysis will use the terms 'bush people' and the 'bush mode of production'. In this it reflects the work of the scholar Glen Coulthard,[3] though I myself have also been using the term 'bush' with strong theoretical inflections for 30 years. People in the northern communities that my research and thinking are inspired by and focused on also use the term colloquially. Fortuitous best describes such a terminological conjunction of theoretical rigour and vernacular resonance. There are bush peoples living in all the continents of the world today, still attempting to ensure their cultures, their values, their practices, their communities are passed on to the next generation, struggling to maintain enough of a land base to be able to support themselves. Often they live in contexts where farming peoples also struggle against a common enemy in rapacious colonial capitalism. Anyone who has read Eric Wolf's work – to choose one from a large range of possible activists and thinkers – on peasant revolutions has awareness that the farmers too have a powerful set of grievances and a distinct historical role.[4] This analysis does not want to dismiss the tributary mode of production, but to emphasise the importance of understanding the differences between them and to call attention to the role or positionality of the bush mode of production in contemporary revolutionary thought and practice.

Bush peoples and actually existing socialism

Social democrats, communists, liberals and conservatives have all been remarkably dismissive at minimum, and genocidal at maximum, towards the bush peoples who have inhabited national spaces under their control. No modernist political ideology has given pride of place to bush peoples, and all of the main ideologies that have held the reins of power have had little patience or toleration for bush ways of life. From British and US imperial activities, to the latter's 'Indian wars' and the former's colonial agents' actions, it is patently obvious that leading capitalist countries put bush people, like all other peoples under their sway, far below capital accumulation on their priority list. In those contexts, bush peoples are sometimes not even accorded the basic human rights that capitalist states occasionally, and when convenient, pretend to be guided by in their dealings with their own working people. This much is obvious and need not be rehearsed here. It may as well be noted at this point that some groups of bush people, here and there and now and then, leave or are forced from their bush lives, becoming workers or part of the reserve army of labour: in my analysis these people are a fragment of the working class.

More remarkable is the fact that social democrats and communist countries do not seem to have fared or acted much better, though here and there they may have paid lip service to the 'primitive communist' values of their subject bush peoples. From the Moskito Indians in Nicaragua, to Nenets or Chukchi in Soviet Russia, the Saami in Sweden and Norway, and even, outside of socialist countries, tribal peoples in parts of India or bush 'minorities' in China, the grievances of bush people in what is called 'actually existing socialism' including the developing world bear remarkable similarity to those of bush people in self-affirmed capitalist contexts. The plunder of Africa appears such a wholly generalised affair that blame hardly need be apportioned – though, again, the structure and temporality of the ravenous powers and principled resistances need careful analysis with attention to the distinction that is our central concern here. The priority in land use allocation is always, always, always, the national interest. The nation surpasses any specific minority within it, including bush people. The modern – who does not want to be modern? – demands a surpassing of all forms of the traditional to such an extent that it defines those forms as homogeneous. One can sympathise with a socialism which, beset on all sides by foreign powers eager for an excuse to move in and eager to fund and support fledgling oppositions, must take central control of the various independent state apparatuses to ensure a strong front. And, of course, the nation itself must be deployed in unity in struggle against the enemy. In such a context, no wonder the Moskito are asked for sacrifices, and when they prove unable to make those, when they become recalcitrant, they become enemies of the socialist state. They become amenable to the whispers and the money of Reagan's invidious operatives. The Sandanistas join a long list of socialist countries at war with some of those within its boundaries who best exemplify the very values they hold dear. Perhaps it is a good thing for the revolution at least that in Cuba the bush people and the original farming inhabitants were so nearly destroyed long before Castro, so there can be no such stain on the revolutionary activities ….

Socialism must do a better job of acknowledging the specific social value of bush peoples, both through entrenching rights in constitutional documents and in establishing mechanisms that ensure the rights are enacted. The socialist project must work around bush enclaves that allow them to thrive, while perhaps also learning from them how egalitarian values can continue to circulate in a 'modernist' world order that to date has been marked by sharp and increasing social hierarchy and inequality. Instead of the ownership, control, access and possession principles for dealing with indigenous knowledge (all principles structured around capitalist-inspired values), a set of principles oriented to acknowledgement, respect, appreciation and affirmation can inform relations.

Exploding the notion of nations

There have been, of course, enclaves and socialist-oriented political movements of farming peoples and bush peoples. The example of Bolivia obviously presents itself in the current moment. But the Zapatistas in Chiapas, Mexico, or even more modestly the Pimicikamak Inninew at Cross Lake in Northern Manitoba, represent striking examples of, however compromised, partially autonomous enclaves within the broader totalising capitalist structure and a direct repudiation of the 'there is no outside' orthodoxy of a stream of contemporary critical thinkers.[5] These resistance projects demand and deserve support as bastions where, at the level of community if not institutional leadership, very creative social forms circulate. They sometimes explode or challenge the national cultural imaginaries of their 'host' nations. They point to possibilities within and beyond nations.

When workers travel, at least in the circumstances of the post-war decades, they travel primarily as entitled members of an internationally stratified work force. Rather than identify with the local workers in Cuba, Mexico, Thailand or wherever in the Global South they can afford to spend what little excess income they may have saved, they maintain a racialised and ethnicised zone of privileged difference. The moments of cross-border solidarity are few and fleeting. When bush people or indigenous farmers travel, should they encounter another, the encounter commonly opens up a mutual ethic of questioning that often finds a way to surpass the boundaries of language: What is it like for you now? What food do you eat? What spirits or gods do you thank? What ways do you thank them? What medicines do you have? That is to say, there is an instinctive solidarity across political borders, within and between nations, that continues to circulate for bush peoples, a kind of solidarity that workers, women and other marginalised social subjects within the Global North or self-congratulatory West appear to rarely practice, preferring rather their enclaves of privilege. Upon such a social base it is possible to imagine meaningful bonds of international solidarity based upon actual relationships or the desire for such relationships.

There are a few organisations devoted to international indigenous solidarity: Indigenous Survival International and the Indigenous Peoples and Community Conserved Territories and Areas are among the few that have broad affiliations. The United Nations has several committees devoted to indigenous issues. Among Inuit, the Inuit Circumpolar Conference represents Inuit located in a variety of national contexts. There are also international cultural and sports festivals devoted to indigenous peoples. Perhaps these represent a nascent social structure that deserves attention and support; perhaps these may model a new kind of internationalism oriented around mutual respect rather than condescending paternalisms that inform at least some international solidarities; perhaps these point beyond the borders of nations as a site for revolution. Which is also to say that the alterity of bush people is not so completely incommensurable that nothing can be learned or borrowed from them: modernism has such an eagerness to teach all its 'others' it has forgotten about how to learn.

It is the case that the new information technologies, complicit as they have been in the operations of hegemonic power, do afford strategies of resistance across geographic limits. In the mid-1970s, when I engaged in activism around international solidarity against the Pinochet coup, information from Chile was sparse, very late and sometimes hard to parse. In more recent years when I engaged in solidarity around the judicial harassment of Francisca Linconao in Chile, it was possible to video chat with activists on the ground and get accurate, up-to-date, invaluable and independent information. This made the work much easier and more immediately relevant.

A bush revolution would question the need for borders, would return to the original early twentieth- and late nineteenth-century revolutionary impulse to be resolute about both deploying and challenging national borders: taking them seriously while working across them. National boundaries are fundamentally tools of capital accumulation and capitalist totalisation. Borders in the bush are a matter of the features of the land or substantive cultural differences; the latter shift and retain a porous character. One of the structures that bush revolution insistently questions and sometimes contests, while also deploying, must inevitably be the structure of the nation itself.

Concerning the strategic value of bush peoples to the global socialist project: part 1

In the current historical conjunction, bush peoples are lifting much higher than their revolutionary weight-class: their struggles represent an enormous strategic element of global anti-capitalist contestation. Kees van der Pjil argues, in this special issue, that the 'real', material economy has increasingly less need for labour, but it still as much as ever requires raw materials. In my view, that implies that though there is no doubt that the working class will still have a critical role in revolutionary change, sites of struggle around imperialist extraction (see Foster) or primitive accumulation (see Marx) – that is, around the appropriation of raw materials – have perhaps a growing role in the confrontation with capitalism.[6] Though capital will and does re-scour previously degraded landscapes, it also searches even and ever farther to the periphery of its reach in search of the raw materials essential to its unsustainable drive to accumulation. Many of these geographic reaches involve lands not desired or appropriate for agricultural purposes and previously inaccessible for other purposes. They are the left-over lands that often remain occupied by the bush peoples fortunate enough not to live in a capital friendly terrain: the arctic, much of the subarctic, the desert, the jungle: the bush.

The specific battles over resource extraction draw a growing coalition of social justice activists, environmentalists, socialists and bush peoples. These struggles represent an attempt to 'snatch at the emergency brake'. If multiple sites of these struggles were successful at the same time, it would pose a structural contradiction to capital, choking capital at its source, as it were. If bush peoples are to survive as bush peoples, they must maintain their land base. Thus, in their being, bush peoples challenge the notion of endless growth. Confrontations on the periphery of capitalist so-called development are increasingly at the heart of the struggle with capitalism itself. Bush peoples are on the front lines of many of

Concerning the strategic value of bush peoples to the global socialist project: part 2

There is a second way in which bush peoples embody or represent a strategic significance for global revolution. Bush values are socialist values. Bush peoples' social relations are markedly egalitarian. Bush peoples form communities in which a rough equality circulates even amidst a generally gendered division of labour. Although the latter point deserves an essay of its own, for now suffice it to say that across the gendered division of labour as practiced in the bush, women and men have control over their respective spheres of work, co-own the land as a means of production, and are guided in their relations by the ethic of respect for personal autonomy of the other that is a central ethical principle. The boundary between public and private in bush culture is porous, if it exists at all. Most of the boundaries that social scientists use to understand the structural features of contemporary life are not relevant: work/leisure; culture/economy; community/individual; culture/nature. Bush peoples enact modern examples of a profound and deeply rooted egalitarianism, and can be looked to in order to regain an understanding of how intergenerational communities of production can continue to function. One element of bush communities, as noted above, is the value of respect for personal autonomy, a respect shown between women and men, adults and children, young and old, to any form of sexual/gender difference, to spiritual people of widely divergent practices and views. One wishes that revolutionary cadres had as much internal cohesion and social tolerance. It is not that the context or circumstances make bush egalitarianism easier: social hierarchy is in my view the 'simpler' social form; egalitarianism, whether among bush people or social justice activists, takes work and care and involves much more complex social thinking.

There are actually two implications of this strategic value. First, there is, as noted above, what can be learned by seeing socialist values in practice, embodied and in circulation. This is inspiring, invaluable and, in the world to be remade by revolution, will have an extraordinary significance. Second, revolutionaries are always looking for 'real world' examples of successful revolutionary polities, frequently becoming cynical when the chosen example cannot live up to its socialist billing. Bush peoples represent a 'real world' example that has been around much longer than any other social form. Bush peoples have been here between 60,000 and 200,000 years, and appeared with the emergence of *Homo sapiens*. Agricultural societies have been around 10,000–12,000 years; capitalism a mere few hundred years. From the bush peoples' perspective, social hierarchy is the anomaly, the recent and increasingly unsustainable-looking invention that led to mass misery and ecological destruction. This line of argumentation retains a powerful force of enormous strategic value to revolutionary thought and practice. It is worth noting that Marx long understood this point, from his writings about the insights that 'Cuban savages' had into property in 1842, to his analyses in the *Grundrisse* respecting early forms of production that involve complex social dynamics, to his very late writings on communal forms in nineteenth-century Russia.[7] But the point has largely drifted from the main lines of Marxist thinking, except in anthropology.

Eco-socialism

One time I was visiting a close friend, a socialist thinker of the first rank from Calcutta, India: the sociologist and poet Himani Bannerji. I was showing her photographs of a recent trip to Yellowknife, including some images of the bush. 'How barren', she couldn't help commenting. I was surprised at my own indignant reaction: 'It's lush!' I exclaimed. 'Lush! This is fertile moose, rabbit, muskrat, beaver territory, this is a hunter's paradise!' We laughed as she explained the layers of agricultural labour that enriched the rural landscapes of her native Bengal, and we both recognised that our own reactions performed different ways of seeing.

Each mode of production develops its own symbolic ecology to deploy a form of understanding of what it itself positions in the ontological space conventionally given the name 'nature'. This is no less true of the contemporary moment of capitalism, where the very existence of nature is often questioned or in question, as it is of farmers or fishers who work within presumptions and parameters of their own distinct modes. The notion of wilderness, of territories devoid of human presence that can be bounded as playgrounds and park reserves, is a contemporary echo of the tributary notion of untilled, agriculturally unproductive land. Some version of a 'nature channel' feeds us images of an elsewhere equally devoid of human presence, and we live in the time of lament for the disappearance of these spaces, which itself colours the view of them we hold.

A socialism that foregrounds ecological concerns places near the centre of inquiry a core contradiction of capitalism: the structural demand for unlimited growth in the context of a finite world. This means that at least eco-socialists are positioned to recognise some of the stakes involved in the variety of bush wars taking place at the global margins. But by raising the stature of uninhabited lands or of animal rights, they sometimes do so at the cost of ignoring or even once again devaluing the bush people who rely on and care-take those territories. Who among us in liberal enlightened circles will dare speak on behalf of those vile African poachers?

Many of those African poachers, like the *Inninewug* hunters forced into late-night flashlight hunting in Canada's national parks, are bush people. The bush is not a zone or territory that makes them who they are. They are the communities that make the bush what it is. Bush people construct bush lands, just as farming people construct agricultural lands and just as modernism constructs factory and wilderness spaces. Bush people make changes to the territories they occupy, whether in small ways by building fishing weirs, or in larger ways by using fire to clear the tops of ridges and promote berry growth. But not only do they make the bush as a material landscape, they make the bush as an epistemological, conceptual and symbolic space. The investigation of the forms and content of thought associated with these epistemological insights should be a primary order on the theoretical agenda of an ecosocialism that deserves the name. The corollary to this is that the only way to 'save' the bush, to ensure the continuance of ecological systems outside the logic of capital accumulation, is to develop a strong alliance with the bush people who make them.

Religion and spirituality

A mode of production determines a mode of prayer. Or, at least, to each mode of production is associated a manner of practicing engagement or disengagement with spiritual concerns. In both tributary and capitalist contexts, spirituality is organised into and insistently inscribes hierarchical institutions that partly form secondary structures of surplus extraction. Capitalism, of course, heralds also the possibility of secular society: a disenchanted and spiritually vacant (or in commodified forms spiritually banal) form of refusal of religion, where the newness of the commodity itself stands in for the secondary extraction processes of religion.

Bush peoples are deeply spiritual, but spirituality is structured around and serves to reinforce egalitarian social forms that allow for greater degrees of personal choice. Socialists who want to work with bush people on their own terms would do well to take this to heart, to show respect for a different form of spiritual engagement. The work of Michael Taussig is worth recalling here, not least for attentiveness to the manner in which utopian bush narratives may be read through the lens of a dialectical image-making politics but perhaps also for his insistence on the value of re-enchantment: the bush is an enchanted space, and bush people are the enchanters.[8]

The supplement

A strain of Marxist political economy almost fell over itself in joy in the post-2008 era. The economy, the real, the material, once again proved itself as a motor force of history. And it is true that a strain of cultural studies had come to largely displace historical materialism in the affections of political-minded youth and in the left scholarly community. Class analysis itself waned in the period when so many new social agents jostled for room on the revolutionary agenda. But historical materialist triumphalism over our newfound relevance is unbecoming at best and churlish at worst. It certainly does not advance revolutionary politics or thought.

Derrida has written that 'each advance in politicization obliges one to reconsider, and so reinterpret the very foundations of law such as they had been previously calculated or delimited',[9] and this would appear a better starting point. It could be called the logic of the supplement, the 'and' that overturns what it purports to add to. That, in itself, is a way to think of revolution. Gramsci, it might be noted, had much the same thought:

> every political movement creates a language of its own, that is, it participates in the general development of a distinct language, introducing new terms, enriching existing terms with a new content, creating metaphors, using historical names to facilitate the comprehension and the assessment of particular contemporary political situations, etc., etc.[10]

However much identity politics may be considered a 'detour', it has empowered resistant social subjects, sometimes including subaltern social subjects not previously recognised or acknowledged. To ignore their claims to justice, their specific trajectories of political engagement, their ethical demands, would be to impoverish a revolutionary movement that will require the energies of as many social fragments as can be drawn into its rising tide. Not that 'women', for example, can be seen as a social fragment. Or African Americans. Or the nexus of gay, lesbian, bisexual, transgender people. Each has something to teach to a historical materialism that must desire to learn.

Into this advancing politicisation step the bush people, who were always there. A bush revolution will be a capacious revolution. It will draw upon the bush ethic of respect for the autonomy of the other, and will seek, indeed embrace, the broader horizons and deeper meanings that come along with whatever social groups dare to stand with it and

Culture and historical materialism

The political-economic concept 'mode of production' allows for the possibility of a materialist understanding of culture, certainly of cultural politics. Culture at this level stands in for the platform upon which meanings are constructed, upon which ideas are contested and differences articulated. Each mode of production enacts its own way of embodying time and space, subjectivity and knowledge and language, on which platforms expressive cultures, the cultures of everyday life, are built. The fact of serial organisation of time, for example, allows for the construction of periods called leisure time and, in effect, the very binary opposition of work and leisure. This is as material as the rock we place around the fire we are building.

The bush revolution requires both political economy and a materialist cultural studies for its permutations to be understood. The daily struggle of bush peoples is against capitalism as a totalising social form. Capitalism involves three interrelated totalising forces: the accumulation of capital itself, which drives the whole system; the expansion of the commodity form, which enacts the fullest version of the logic of the system; and the state, which as well as legitimating capital growth, steering the actual development, covering gaps and critical system crises, acts assiduously to build the cultural platform of the system (the organisation of space, time, subjectivity, knowledge and language – the form in which these become recognisable and the principles upon which they are structured: the fact that all actual activities must take place within their logical parameters). Gramsci had some sense of this which he articulated in several places, for example when he wrote:

> every State is ethical in as much as one of its most important functions is to raise the great mass of the population to a particular cultural and moral level, a level (or type) which corresponds to the needs of the productive forces for development, and hence to the interests of the ruling class.[11]

While we might now use the word 'change' rather than 'raise' (and prefer 'type' to 'level'), Gramsci here and elsewhere clearly sees the capitalist state as having a critical role in totalisation, which it inevitably presents as its moral mission: hence, in Canada, residential schools for bush children.

Without an understanding of the logic of capital accumulation, the understanding of why residential schools were built and operated turns upon the moral 'badness' of the colonisers. Without an understanding of material cultural differences across the boundary of mode of production, the particular necessity of residential schools as an institution of forced cultural change is not cognisable.

A general theory of the capitalist state that is not premised to some degree on its role as a totalising agent simply misses or ignores much of the actual activity of that institutional condensation of power. Poulantzas began to see this in the chapter on the nation in his last and best theoretical book.[12] Bush people have known about it for a long time. It is the face of capital that they directly confront. The bush revolution is in solidarity with those of earlier epochs who had enough insight to shoot at the clocks: from a certain perspective, clock time is a part of the logic of the enemy.

The revolution must have poetry

There are other reasons why an effective, or revolutionary, political economy must have attentiveness to cultural studies. It is, after all, in the field of cultural existence that people – working-class people, people of colour, bush people, people across the many lines of difference that may now be articulable – make sense of their positions, their possibilities, their trajectories, their resistances, their collusions. To motivate and move them, to prod them to realise their agency, Mayakovski is needed almost as much as Lenin (and certainly there was a Mayakovski – that is, a poet – inside of Lenin as well).

The problem of bureaucracy, referred to in this volume by Dzarasov, is perhaps another central reason that political economy needs cultural studies. Real-world revolutions have tended, and continue to tend, to fracture between the street-level creative energies of the revolutionary subjects and the real-world determinism of the state functionaries. The former have, so far, always given way to the latter. Or, perhaps, the latter have always found it necessary to restrict the utopian energies of the former. In doing so, though, many of the most promising developments of revolutionary ideals have continually been told to 'wait' for their time until other issues, including the security of the revolution itself, are more firmly established. So far, the waiting never ends. Bureaucracies, once in control, are never oriented to relinquish power. Far from being a representative of universal interest, they assiduously work for the self-interest of the managerial class, wherein creativity and bold decision-making sink to the lowest common denominator and wherein an ethos of doing nothing that will rock the boat, nothing that will arise from a meaningful decision whose lineaments can be allocated to a specific director, is the order of the day. Arendt was right about bureaucracy ('bureaucracy was the result of a responsibility no man can bear for his fellow-man, and no people for another people'[13]), and the problem has only gotten worse. So-called capitalism has not escaped its clutches; a meaningful revolutionary socialism may be the only opening, and that opening must not exist merely in the early years of revolutionary action but must find a way to sustain itself. Bureaucracy and the bush exist in a polar tension: the bush is resolutely anti-bureaucratic, and affords the hope that such a state of affairs is possible.

Bush Paraguay

Sometimes powerful lessons can be packed into short durations. Early in our new millennium, during the decade I think of as the nothings, I travelled for a brief time to Paraguay. In a short visit of a matter of a couple of weeks I could not hope to gain any understanding of the cultural and political complexity of the place, but in short visits to the eastern forest, *caaguasu*, to the western semi-arid *chaco* region, I did see something that stays with me.

Travelling east of Asuncion, in the *caaguasu* I travelled into the jungle. I saw villages with handmade signs that read 'stop the violence'. I saw barefoot children playing in the mid-afternoon sun. I saw a community meeting in which the young men dressed in army fatigues carried carved pieces of wood made to look like AK-47s. I met an elder, who spoke only in a dialect of Guarani, who knew the local medicinal plants, pointed to the ceremonial village building, and had the power of sucking poison from the body of sick people. Here the Guarani (people) were in a complex land struggle. Nearby, mostly Mennonite soybean industrial farmers were bribing poor peasants, *campesinos*, to clear-cut stretches of forest so they could set up a subsistence farm for a few years, gain title, then sell it to the growing, rapacious, industrial farmers. The wood was sold, also through bribes, illegally to logging companies. The giant forest, *caaguasu*, was being eroded and eroded. On the road we passed young campesino children, with shoes and school uniforms, on their way home from schools. The Guarani villages did not have even nursing stations, let alone schools or any outside support.

In the *chaco*, a semi-arid grassland to the north and west of Asuncion, I travelled with an anthropologist. He told me that in the 1930s and 1940s, Mennonite settlers there had relied on the local indigenous peoples, who had saved them many times from starvation. By the 1960s, these Mennonites had established prosperous farms and noticed that their neighbours were steadily losing land. They purchased land and through later decades helped their bush friends establish farms of their own. I met an elder, who showed me his plot. He spoke in Spanish. He wore shoes. He never mentioned healing plants. Later, the kindly anthropologist showing me around pointed to a building as we drove past: here is where the children, when they get beyond elementary school, stay in residences for advanced education. That was when the coin dropped for me: the residential school…

The stark choice in Paraguay for indigenous peoples is of some material well-being, as in the *chaco*, over material impoverishment and cultural wealth in the *caaguasu*. You can have shoes, or your language: this is a choice bush people face worldwide. The bush revolution demands both culture and wealth, egalitarianism and affluence, and will not settle for less.

Form of revolution

What would it mean for theory if each revolutionary transition from a mode of production was unique, a singularity? There is no room for theory in a singularity, and both history and theory would have to content themselves with description. Historical materialism can retrospectively notice what revolutionary struggles changed the political structures in ways conducive to new ownership and technological patterns, and conversely which did not. But there has not been a revolution in the pores of advanced forms of capitalism. And there has not been a bush revolution, though (reading through the pores of history) some attempts have been made.

Across time and distance some elements in revolutionary practices appear consistent: in Livy's account of the overthrow of the Tarquin monarchy in ancient Rome, the establishment of the consuls, for example, involves the revolutionaries seizing control of the city and the army in a manner reminiscent, in broad strokes, of Lenin and Trotsky's strategy in the modern Russian context.[14] Shi Naian's literary account of the justice-seeking bandits in *Outlaws of the Marsh* (perhaps one would want to suggest *Outlaws of the Bush*), also translated as *The Water Margin*, or more historically Sima Qian's account of the fall of the Qin dynasty at the beginning of the dynastic era in China, do not look unlike guerrilla movements in contemporary Mexico, Vietnam or Cuba.[15] Indeed, it might be worth noting that the form of guerrilla warfare itself, theorised and practiced by Amilcar Cabral or Mao Zedong or Vo Nguyen Giap, perhaps draws partial inspiration from the military practices of bush people, with Pontiac being one of the modern forebears of that approach.

The question of where the revolution emerges from – either a core group of elite leaders or a spontaneous mass – remains in theoretical play from Marx's 'Eighteenth Brumaire of Louis Bonaparte' through to Lenin's *What Is to Be Done* and beyond.[16] A bush revolution perhaps accords more with Rancière's recent suggestion of democracy by lot: everyone might be a capable leader; the social whole or bush masses have dispersed abilities to make decisions. The revolution that might be formed out of the bush has, perhaps, one signal feature that marks it from its relatives: it is unrecognisable.

What if a revolution happened and no one noticed?

What if a new global order were being forged, not in New York or Berlin or Beijing? What if the vague traces of its outlines were to be found, as suggested above, in Chiapas, in La Paz, in Pimicikamak? Who would notice? Is the left prepared for this? In the enormous ferment of the Idle No More movement, here in Canada, the left seemed woefully unprepared to seize the moment and support 'someone else's' revolution. Although large numbers of activists turned out for protests, little of the organisational capacity of the left went towards sustaining the moment of that movement. Few were prepared to stand behind a leadership and a set of demands that they were not familiar with.

Where its outlines can be traced in the contemporary historical moment, the bush revolution sits within the pores of a dominant global capitalist set of structures, carving out always-threatened autonomous spaces while implicitly and sometime explicitly wanting, demanding, more. In northern Manitoba, the Inninew of Pimicikamak have passed a first written law and established their own governance structures. The former chief, John Muswagin, once told me that when he would negotiate a funding agreement or some other arrangement with the Canadian federal government, he would come to a close by saying that he would have to get the deal approved by each of the four governing councils. A pause at the other end of the phone. The official invariably would say something like, 'Well, you know, we don't really recognise your system over here…' to which John would just as invariably respond: 'That's fine, that's fine, we don't recognise your system either!' Perhaps the bush revolution looks like that, and too few are willing to look closely enough to see its lineaments unfolding.

Perhaps as well the bush revolution would demand a revolution within the revolution: a revolution in how decisions are made, a revolution in inclusivity, a revolution that embraces a capacious sense of who belongs, a revolution that deploys now, rather than saving for later, the respect for personal autonomy of the other that circulates among bush peoples. In this, the contemporary historical moment, when the vulgarity and stupidity of the ruling elites have reached unparalleled depths amidst an extraordinary increase in the baseline inequality that feeds capitalism, it is easy to despair. One resource for hope is the simple thought that the global revolution needed to put our species on a more just and viable path needs only happen once, we need succeed, fully succeed, but once: at that point the real work of history can begin and the brutality can be left behind. To achieve this will require all the skills and insights of many varieties of peoples, and perhaps many varieties of efforts in effecting change. Resist, rebel and revolt are each a distinctive note in the sweet symphony of social change, in the choreography of social justice.

Disclosure statement

No potential conflict of interest was reported by the author.

Notes

1. U. Marx et al., *Walter Benjamin's Archive*, 47.
2. Rousseau, *Origins of Inequality*; Engels, *Origins of the Family*; Marx, *Ethnological Notebooks*; Leacock, *Myths of Male Dominance*; Leacock and Lee *Politics and History in Band Societies*; Sahlins, *Stone Age Economics*.
3. Coulthard, *Red Skin, White Masks*.
4. Wolf, *Peasant Wars of the Twentieth Century*.
5. Hardt and Negri, *Empire*; Butler, *Gender Trouble*.
6. Foster, *Marx's Ecology*; Marx, *Capital*, Vol. 1.
7. Marx, *Grundrisse*; Marx, "Debates on the Law on Thefts of Wood"; Marx, *The Letters of Karl Marx*.
8. Taussig, *Shamanism, Colonialism, and the Wild Man*.
9. Derrida, "Force of Law," 28.
10. Gramsci, *Prison Notebooks*, vol. 1, 126.
11. Gramsci, *Selections from the Prison Notebooks*, 258.
12. Poulantzas, *State, Power, Socialism*.
13. Arendt, *Origins of Totalitarianism*.
14. Livy, *Early History of Rome*.
15. Naian, *Water Margin: Outlaws of the Marsh*; Qian, *First Emperor*.
16. Marx, "Eighteenth Brumaire of Louis Bonaparte"; Lenin, *What Is to Be Done*.

Bibliography

Arendt, Hannah. *The Origins of Totalitarianism*. New York: Harcourt Brace Jovanovich, 1973.

Butler, Judith. *Gender Trouble*. New York: Routledge, 1990.

Coulthard, Glen. *Red Skin, White Masks*. Minneapolis: University of Minnesota Press, 2014.

Derrida, Jacques. "Force of Law: The 'Mystical' Foundation of Authority." In *Deconstruction and the Possibility of Justice*, edited by D. Cornell, M. Rosenfeld, and D. G. Carlson, 16–30. New York: Routledge, 1992.

Engels, Friedrich. *The Origins of the Family, Private Property and the State*. Harmondsworth, England: Penguin Books, 1986.

Foster, John Bellamy. *Marx's Ecology*. New York: Monthly Review Press, 2000.

Gramsci, Antonio. *Prison Notebooks*, Vol. 1. Translated and edited by Joseph Buttigieg and Antonio Callari. New York: Columbia University Press, 2011.

Gramsci, Antonio. *Selections from the Prison Notebooks*. Translated and edited by Quinton Hoare and Geoffrey Nowell Smith. New York: International Publishers, 1980.

Hardt, Michael, and Antonio Negri. *Empire*. Cambridge, MA: Harvard University Press, 2001.

Leacock, Eleanor. *Myths of Male Dominance*. Chicago: Haymarket Books, 2008.

Leacock, Eleanor and Richard Lee, eds. *Politics and History in Band Societies*. Cambridge, UK: Cambridge University Press, 1982.

Lenin, Vladimir Il'ich. *What Is to Be Done*. Translated and edited by Joe Fineberg and George Hanna. London: Penguin, 1962.

Livy, Titus. *The Early History of Rome*. Translated and edited by Aubrey De Selincourt. Harmondsworth: Penguin Books, 1973.

Marx, Karl. *Capital. Volume 1*. Translated and edited by Ben Fowkes. New York: Random House, 1977.

Marx, Karl. "Debates on the Law on Thefts of Wood." In *Collective Works. Volume 1. Marx:1835–1843*. Edited by Karl Marx and Frederick Engels. New York: International Publishers, 1975.

Marx, Karl. "The Eighteenth Brumaire of Louis Bonaparte." In *Surveys from Exile*. Translated and edited by David Fernbach, 146–249. London: New Left Review, 1973.

Marx, Karl. *The Ethnological Notebooks of Karl Marx*. Translated and edited by L. Krader. Assen: Van Gorcum, 1972.

Marx, Karl. *The Letters of Karl Marx*. Selected and Translated by Saul Padover. New Jersey: Prentice Hall, 1979.

Marx, Karl. *Grundrisse*. Translated and edited by Martin Nicolaus. New York: Random House, 1973.

Marx, Ursula, Gudrun Schwarz, Michael Schwarz, and Erdmut Wizisla, eds. *Walter Benjamin's Archive*. Translated by Esther Leslie. New York: Verso, 2007.

Naian, Shi. *The Water Margin: Outlaws of the Marsh*. Translated and edited by J. H. Jackson. Vermont: Tuttle Publishing, 2010.

Poulantzas, Nicos. *State, Power, Socialism*. Translated and edited by Patrick Camiller. London: Verso, 1980.

Qian, Sima. *The First Emperor*. Translated and edited by Raymond Dawson. Oxford: Oxford University Press, 2009.

Rousseau, Jean-Jacques. *The Basic Political Writings*. Translated and edited by Donald Cress. Indianapolis: Hackett Publishing, 2011.

Sahlins, Marshall. *Stone Age Economics*. Chicago: Aldine-Atherton, 1972.

Taussig, Michael. *Shamanism, Colonialism, and the Wild Man*. Chicago: University of Chicago Press, 1987. doi:10.1086/ahr/95.4.1330.

Wolf, Eric. *Peasant Wars of the Twentieth Century*. New York: Harper & Row, 1969.

The communitarian revolutionary subject: new forms of social transformation

David Barkin (iD) and Alejandra Sánchez

ABSTRACT
The hope for a unique revolutionary actor in the twentieth century evaporated as a result of the weaknesses of social organisations. This paper examines the potential of an almost-forgotten group of revolutionary actors – collectively organised and deliberately involved in processes of social and productive transformation with a legitimate claim to territory – whose present-day activities involve them in concerted processes to consolidate a different constellation of societies on the margins of the global capitalist system. Indigenous and peasant communities throughout the Americas are self-consciously restructuring their organisations and governance structures, taking control of territories they claimed for generations. They are also reorganising production to generate surplus, assembling their members to take advantage of underutilised resources and peoples' energies for improving their ability to raise living standards and assure environmental conservation and restoration. These communities are not operating in isolation. They coordinate activities, share information and build alliances. Hundreds of millions of people are participating in this growing movement; they occupy much more than one-quarter of the world's land area. There is great potential for others to join them, expanding from the substantial areas where they are already operational. Global social networks are ensuring that this dynamic accelerates.

Introduction

The model of a world economic system is promoted to society as the ideal of development and growth to improve well-being and quality of life. This idyllic vision promised equality, justice and freedom through the operation of the globalised capitalist market. From its inception, it was clear that this model of social and productive relations was generating insurmountable contradictions. Grounded in the assumptions of Western ideology and driven by powerful political and economic forces, it is trying to force all peoples and productive systems into a simplified mould conducive to privatised capital accumulation that transforms natural 'resources' and people into commodities. In the process it is attempting to erase the extraordinary diversity of societies and cultures that survived through the centuries and that are attempting to flourish today. The logic of capitalist production is demanding new spaces for the accumulation of capital, generating greater inequality, accentuating the environmental crisis, and threatening the future production of food, the supply of drinking water, and life itself. In this context, it is worth asking: Are there political processes in operation capable of responding to present social and environmental crises? How are processes of social transformation manifesting themselves? And who might be the actors of these revolutions?

Not all societies are deluded by the chimera of progress promised by the high priests of globalisation. Many peoples are searching for alternatives to 'neoliberal' domination, implementing diverse strategies to counteract the adverse effects of the capitalist system. In this contribution, we examine actions of social groups that for generations tried to resist the looting of their resources, their social exclusion and, often worse, the terrible consequences of their integration into capitalism's social and productive institutions. More recently, they are raising their voices, implementing profound processes of socio-economic transformation in diverse spaces. This analysis is firmly rooted in a burgeoning concern for the depths of the environmental crisis that the prevailing model is provoking[1] and the growing recognition that there are myriad indigenous and peasant groups fashioning alternative societies where people can enjoy palpable improvements in their quality of life while taking responsibility for conserving the ecosystems on which we all depend.[2]

Many indigenous and peasant communities, about whom we are reporting, including some with whom we are collaborating, are declaring themselves 'anti-systemic' in the sense that they are generating social and political processes that challenge the logic of capitalism. These communities are important actors in international movements to confront today's economic and environmental crises; their defining characteristic is their relationship to the land. The historical emphasis on the class nature of their struggle[3] and the political identity of their mobilisations[4] are inseparable.[5] Their potential significance may be best illustrated by the fact that these communities occupy an extraordinarily large share of the world's area; considering only part of this population, recent geospatial research shows that 'indigenous Peoples manage or have tenure rights to more than one-quarter of the world's land surface, [which] intersects about 40% of all terrestrial protected areas and ecologically intact landscapes'.[6] By embracing innovative approaches to social (re)organisation, production and environmental management, they offer practical solutions that other social groups in both urban and rural areas can learn from.

While forging their own paths towards social progress, they are demonstrating the fruitfulness of Harvey's plea to learn from both the Marxist analysis of change and the anarchist's call for direct action on the barricades.[7] They are leading the way to open new routes for social progress, formulating strategies to improve their lifestyles, control their productive systems, defend their legitimate claims to significant territories and conserve their natural endowments. These approaches are permitting them to generate surpluses and distribute them for individual and collective benefit, creating a new 'social capacity' that is transforming them into 'collective revolutionary subjects'.

1. The community: the collective basis of the revolutionary subject

The construction of alternatives leads to the possibility of an economic, political, social and ecological transformation. Our analysis is based on the history of many indigenous and peasant societies of Latin America. These societies generally possess worldviews that emerge from their Indo-American roots. These worldviews consist of complex systems of beliefs, values and traditions. Although not exhaustive, we might include the following characteristics: (1) their vision of a balance in relations between society and nature, where the bond with the natural environment entails responsibility; (2) a communitarian view of property, where the care and use of their ecosystem is determined collectively and usufruct rights do not imply the possibility of private property or sale; (3) community work requiring the redefinition of labour, based on non-capitalist values; and (4) participatory democracy, involving unique structures of governance, responsible involvement and collective commitment.[8]

The integration of their worldviews implies a constant redefinition of their identities and a renewed understanding of the significance of their cultural heritage under current conditions.[9] That is, they are peoples who are transcending their historical heritage to redefine their collective identity, with a pluricultural character, that the community is aware of, preserving some characteristics that are functional while discarding those that are not of importance; specifically, the communities decide to enrich their knowledge of the society–nature relationship.[10] The systematisation of this knowledge allows them *to transform themselves as a community* (ie asserting their collective consciousness), generating models that become niches of sustainability and social justice.

Their productive systems are not archaic as conventional economic thinking often presumes. The communities have great capacities (in the logic of their social dynamics based on other rationalities) but these are not recognised by or valued in the globalised market system. In this sense, the production structures implemented by these societies are proving to be important sustainable projects insofar as they combine ancestral knowledge of nature, the use of various technologies, modern productive techniques, and social and moral principles such as environmental and social justice. Intensifying climate change is accelerating the search for improvements in their productive systems and innovative strategies to solve future needs of society.

Guiding this process of moving towards a more resilient society (creating these niches of sustainability) are five principles that we generally find in these communities: (1) autonomy to govern themselves and manage their institutions and territory; (2) solidarity within the community and with other communities involved in similar processes; (3) self-sufficiency, to the degree that it is possible, considering available resources and the ecosystem; (4) productive diversification to provide goods for exchange with other communities to obtain products that cannot be produced locally; and (5) sustainable management of regional resources, that requires collaboration with other communities in the ecosystem.[11]

Their cultural and historical heritages are social resources that contribute to maintaining their existence, as well as to restructuring their internal social processes to respond to current challenges. Their societies are constantly being redefined as a result of interactions with the capitalist system; that is, they are not isolated and must continually interact with the societies of which they are a part. They know and understand their logics, and their community worldviews create the opportunity to maintain non-capitalist economic and social relations and to limit their interactions with the capitalist economic system. In recent decades, these advances have contributed to strengthening their political position, facilitating collective decisions that foster social change. With the recognition of the significance of these developments in the international arena (International Labour Organisation (ILO) Convention 169 and the United Nations Declaration of the Rights of Indigenous Peoples – UNDRIP), their demands are increasingly being accepted as legitimate in national political systems.

The revolutionary subjects are capable of changing their situation, transcending capitalist relations; they are born and reproduced in the community. 'The community is an ethical project that has been proposed for a long time and acts as a guide for social transformations'.[12] The community has fundamental characteristics that give meaning to its construction as collective revolutionary subjects. These include: (1) the community is formed by individuals and recognises them as part of a totality; (2) the community is based on service to advance the common good, a result of the sum of individual contributions in which reciprocity is inherent; (3) the community does not renounce individuality (personal identity) since people find their fulfilment when contributing to the collective (by their own free decision); (4) in the process, it deepens common values respecting plurality and individual values; and (5) the community promotes the growth of social virtues such as solidarity and fraternity, in which a consensual process prevails.[13]

The community is the result of two principal influences: (1) a historical trajectory that includes colonial subjugation and periods of apparent independence under various governance systems (characterised by enslavement, deception, theft, exclusion and inclusion with discrimination); and (2) a worldview founded at the collective level – in which language plays a fundamental role in shaping a different understanding of people's relationship to nature.[14] In other words, we are collaborating with societies historically constituted and developed in the collectivity: the common good prevails over individual interest. The community establishes a social contract (quite different from the Hobbesian social contract of 1651) that defines a political order creating the basis for civilisation, for authority; it is formulated and accepted by the collective in which the individual is subsumed by decisions and the will of the community.[15] This social contract implies unity among the members of society, in sharp contrast to the individuality characteristic of the alternative prevailing in Western societies.

To summarise, the community is a project of collective life, linked to new forms of social and political praxis – other realities, other rationalities.[16] The conjugation of this praxis appears as the creator of new relations of production aimed at improving community and individual welfare. These expressions of organisation are not new; on the contrary, they are the product of generations of resistance during which time values and collective goals were modified and transmitted by tradition and reaffirmed and reconfigured by custom. As part of this evolution, 'being indigenous' has become an important issue for the success of their movements, the acceptance of their social demands, and the forging of alliances, as well as the transformation of their economic, political, social and ecological spaces.

Today, the communities are consolidating societies based on a different logic, in spaces that they occupy within the global system. They are well informed about the epistemological critiques that question the dominant system and its development model; alternative proposals for conducting research and systematising information about their experiences are burgeoning across the globe.[17] Some of their strategies are aimed at understanding and implementing programmes for local and regional progress[18] that take into account their collective visions and environmental justice. This is the context in which the collective revolutionary subject is born.

2. The collective revolutionary subject and transformative action

The potential for social transformation of the collective revolutionary subject is based on its *social capacity* to continually strengthen and deepen its organisation. This social capacity is forged from the intangible resources that communities possess and use for consensual actions to establish strategies to consolidate their well-being.[19] These are the attributes that communities put into practice through their worldviews, including principles of reciprocity, mutual aid and support networks to strengthen social cohesion and community benefit. In this context, we can speak of 'collective attitudes' as 'Dispositions common to the members of a group, [… that …] are expressed in beliefs about society according to preferences, promoting consistent behaviours that [...] involve adherence to certain values and rejection of some situations'.[20]

This social capacity allows the community to mobilise its resources to achieve collectively established goals. On the one hand, these needs are based on the vision of the community and not on those determined by the marketplace, and, on the other hand, they involve the establishment of the economy within society – in other words, an economic process that is subsumed to the needs of society rather than of the market.[21] This entails a rethinking of the notions of progress, development and quality of life, based on the communities' value systems and collective principles; other meanings of well-being are developed, based on qualitative and intangible dimensions (rather than quantitative measures). In this way, this social transformation reflects the consolidation of the communities as governing bodies capable of negotiating with the institutions of the nation state of which they are a part. In the following sections, some elements that are fundamental for this social transformation are examined, elements that create the social capacity of the collective revolutionary subject.

Territorial management of productive systems

The base of the economic sustenance of this type of society is the territory, considered a common good or property; as a result, its appropriation is collective. These societies have a strong attachment to their territory, evident in their special (harmonious) relationship with the natural environment of which they are part. The territory is not conceived as a commodity; it is the giver of life (*Pachamama* or Mother Earth), a place where history, culture, social organisation and nature are encapsulated. Its management has a strong relationship with the construction of collective identity (a socially constructed space). The territory is more than a biophysical space; it is a social, political, cultural, spiritual and economic space that gives meaning to the collective.[22] Productive systems are established by defining a bond with nature, including a commitment to conserve natural endowments and/or promote their restoration. If communities have the capacity to control and manage their territories then they can determine their productive systems, and therefore their social structures.

The territory is an organising structure for the existence of these societies. In many cases, it has been the object of struggles and conflicts for its defence – struggles that have intensified because of the current form of the expansion of capital. In a strict sense, indigenous and peasant communities should have total control over the territory which they inhabit.

However, the state, in complicity with the powerful economic interests, often tries to impose decisions about its use.

In this regard, many new concessions for the exploitation of natural 'resources' are being granted to capital. In some cases, the state has recognised the collective legal ownership of the territory by communities; although in Mexico there are legal figures such as the '*ejido*' and communal property recognised for native peoples, the constitution grants the state the authority to assign all subsoil and water rights. In spite of this, indigenous communities are insisting on their rights, as recognised by the Mexican state with its accession to the ILO Convention 169 that calls for the 'prior, informed consent' of all projects in their areas. As in other countries, this is an important point of contention, that sometimes can be resolved through negotiation, but oftentimes it leads to violence as private interests attempt to impose their might; this is the case, for example, in Ecuador and Brazil, where peoples in the Amazon continue to suffer greatly from invasions and murder, and in Honduras, where a globally recognised leader was brutally assassinated.[23] To prosecute these demands and defend themselves, the communities are developing alliances, support networks, educational processes on legal issues and, above all, political negotiation strategies, to assert effective territorial management for their organisations.[24]

Surplus management

With the consolidation of these new forms of organisation, communities are able to create new activities and identify and mobilise their available resources for their collective benefit. As a result, they are generating increasing volumes of 'economic surplus' that offers them a greater capacity to attend their needs; these new forms of surplus often not only assume a conventional quantitative (monetary) form, but also, and perhaps more importantly, include many material and social resources that are not 'priced' by the market, such as contributions of knowledge, skills, voluntary labour, and shared tools and spaces. Collective management for the production and management of this surplus consolidates the community's social capacity. There is an intangible dimension to this process of generation, appropriation and use that reflects the values and principles of the community, rather than those defined by market dynamics.

From an analytical perspective, this surplus generation begins by discarding the concept of a labour force defined as a commodity in traditional Marxist analysis or in the marketplace. In most communities, this involves mobilising the considerable productive potential of their members through *voluntary or solidarity work* ('*mano vuelta*' and '*tequio*' in some indigenous communities), forms of work not mediated by salary, based on reciprocity and cooperation. To these activities, we might add those of community leadership and administration as well as the tasks of caring (education, health care, social services, etc.) normally attributed exclusively to women that are also often collectively managed; an essential component is the reconsideration of the role of women in society, a factor that has been historically neglected and denigrated in the market.[25] This is akin to tapping the *potential surplus* central to Paul Baran's analysis of economic growth, values that are disregarded in the capitalist organisation of society.[26]

A crucial element in the appropriation of these resources is the exercise of collective ownership and responsibility, involving the assumption of social control of decision-making, on the basis of the same principles of reciprocity and mutual aid. Although part of the surplus is distributed individually to satisfy particular needs and reward individual efforts, the process of collective decision-making about its distribution is one of the pillars on which the communities sustain their autonomy. Generally, we observe that the criteria for generating and distributing surplus are directly evaluated in terms of the strengthening of community life, while responding to diverse social, economic and ecological needs.

This form for the mobilisation of surplus is vital for understanding social change, because it undermines the centrality of the market. In its place, there is a system of production planning, management of surplus funds, and an administrative structure to allocate resources to areas that benefit society. This allows the communities to decide and direct their resources, making decisions an explicit part of the process of community consolidation, and developing alliances with other communities as well as with social and political organisations. Mobilising the surplus also depends on the social capacity to organise work, the productive process, the exchanges and the sustainable management of natural resources. In other words, it is about *political capacity* (autonomy, self-management, bargaining power).

A significant dimension of the use of surplus is its ecological impact. Many strategies have been undertaken to confront environmental challenges. Throughout the Americas (and elsewhere), communities are facing threats created by 'projects of death' (as they are called) such as transnational mega-projects in mining, hydropower and wind power, as well as by land and water grabbing on an international scale. In Mexico, as elsewhere in Latin America, there has been some advance in developing administrative and legislative strategies to strengthen social organisations to defend their territory and ecosystems against such proposals.[27]

Political position

The communities cannot implement programmes for social transformation on their own. Although many have strong historical and cultural roots that are the source of their strength and internal cohesion, their ability to resist the powerful institutions that the nation states have arrayed against them is limited. In the face of this unequal confrontation, many communities throughout the Americas are forging alliances among themselves, with international non-governmental organisations, and some official international bodies to prosecute their demands for self-government and other forms of autonomy. This ability to resist is considerably enhanced by the ratification of international agreements by their governments, such as Convention 169 and the UNDRIP, mentioned above.

The collective revolutionary subject must develop a political position that promotes broader strategies and projects, reinforced by implementing the five principles mentioned above. Considering the limitations on the scope for political action within the capitalist system, the capacity for action of the collective revolutionary subject is based on its ability to exercise an increasing degree of autonomy, through its control over its territories and its surplus. When the state recognises their capacity for self-management (its legal framework), then the communities acquire a greater capacity for social transformation.

The social mobilisations that emerged in Mexico and Latin America in recent decades are playing a crucial role in generating and expanding this capacity. Communities throughout the region are joining in national and international networks to create regional alliances that reinforce their claims as individual communities. In particular, their defence of territory and demands to protect their ecosystems were triggers for these strategies of political organisation. In Mexico, these national groupings include the 'Mexican Network of People Affected by Mining' (REMA – Chiapas, México), 'Movement of People Affected by Dams and in Defence of the Rivers' (MAPDER), 'Civil Society Organization de la Sociedad Civil "Las Abejas De Acteal'" (The Bees of Acteal) and the 'National Indigenous Congress' (CNI).

The collective revolutionary subject is aware of the *power* that it acquires as its social capacity allows it to build an autonomous system of governance, controlling its territory and managing the surplus that it produces. However, these collective revolutionary subjects are not seeking to seize state power (through electoral or violent processes); rather, they are focusing on the exercise of *popular power*[28] and *social power*.[29] The former derives from a collective organisation that exercises its claim for the (expanded) control of the territory; therefore, this type of power is consolidated in indigenous and peasant communities and is quite different from the traditional conception of power centred in the state. This popular power emerges from processes of struggle (both internal and external), sanctioned by the broad support generated in the local assemblies. In contrast, social power results from an emancipatory process to reconstitute and strengthen the social fabric, to restore the natural and planetary environment, and to recuperate and 'modernise' the 'dominated, excluded and exploited cultures of the peripheral worlds [.... It is a] force that emerges independently of and autonomously from civil society, seeking to distance itself from the state and capital'.[30] This social power becomes embodied in alternative projects developed by organised groups that include communities, cooperatives, unions and associations, among others.

The inability of nation states to exercise their sovereignty in the face of international corporate and political pressures to grant investment concessions (for extractive activities or other 'mega-projects') further discredits the possibility for radical social change from within. In contrast, the assertion of the ability and right to govern local spaces is advancing throughout the Americas, reflecting an important step towards the construction of new social relations based on the recognition of human dignity and the abandonment of sub-ordinate relationships. The evolving body of international agreements protecting indigenous rights and their claims as guarantors of biodiversity is proving to be a powerful bulwark against the unfettered incursions of capital during the recent past. This experience is becoming well documented in a growing literature on the concrete experiences of the individual communities and their alliances.[31]

3. Some expressions of the social transformation by the collective revolutionary subject

Today there are many expressions that can be called revolutionary, but their definition is a subject for great debate. The traditional vision of a violent revolution as a reaction against repression by the state is now being reassessed by detailed analyses that document the revolutionary potential in the notion of 'everyday struggles'[32] or political negotiation and reconciliation.[33] The crisis of revolutionary politics has led to new formulations of *resistance* and *rebellion*; these have gained prominence in recent decades,[34] but are more difficult to define with regard to the concept of 'revolutionary'. We consider a *revolutionary expression* to include actions involving important social transformations in defined contexts, including fundamental changes in the social dynamics of social and productive structures, political life, and ecological conservation; these often involve repudiating the initiatives by capital and the state to limit their autonomy or ability to manage their territories. Neil Smith, building on the definition of revolution by the celebrated Trinidadian anticolonial historian, C. L. R.

James, presciently characterised it as coming 'like a thief in the night', adding that 'the thief needs to come with a few tools. Some of these tools are intellectual ideas; others are tools of the imagination about other possible worlds; still others are our human bodies'. In consonance with the thesis of this article, he added: 'most importantly they [require] social and political organization for a more humane future'.[35]

Historically, many analysts characterised Latin American indigenous movements during the 500 years from colonisation to establishment of the neoliberal system as 'resistance'. The perseverance of hundreds of cultures, along with their languages and cosmovisions (belief systems), is transcending this *culture of resistance*,[36] to become a demand for recognition of and support for their inherited lifestyles; in this change in their role in society and on the world scene, these peoples are claiming a new place in the world order and, with it, in the nation states in which they live. These revolutionary subjects are the indigenous, rural and peasant communities involved in formulating strategies to *resist* the economic rationality of globalised market, adding ethical, moral and cultural dimensions of sustainability, demonstrating that their activities are part of processes of social appropriation of nature with social and environmental responsibility,[37] generating surpluses that contribute to their quality of life and the conservation of their ecosystems.

Resistance is related to *rebellion*, assuming many different forms to demonstrate its rejection of the dominant system that implies the *use of power from below*, in contrast to classical revolution that seeks to conquer state power for social transformation. *Rebellion* entails a social organisation to transform the context of those who are below.[38]

But these social movements are going further, recently described as 'r-existence', in Latin America. It offers a new perspective of emancipation and the construction of sustainability. Their struggles are legitimising the rights of peoples to their ancestral territories, in the face of policies to appropriate and transform nature to accelerate the expansion of the global economy. The distribution the benefits of the re-appropriation of nature and technology is not the issue; rather, the 'r-existence' of these traditional populations aims to consolidate renewed social formations and new ways to organise society and assure its respect for nature.[39]

It might appear that indigenous and peasant social movements are simply opposed to capitalist economic expansion. Our formulation suggests that they are going further by finding ways to improve members' quality of life within their social organisations, re-appropriating their cultural identity (language and ancestral knowledge of the past generations) in the process. This 'r-existence' involves recuperating ancestral knowledge and/or reinventing it as well as combining scientific knowledge and new ways to solving problems, in order to remain in their territories while assuring social and ecological balance.[40]

Grounding the analysis

These alternative projects encompass all aspects of life and are creating new social initiatives. The projects combine concerns for protecting the environment and its biodiversity while also enriching inherited skills and knowledge with those acquired in social practice and contacts with others. Water management is a significant area for social mobilisation; in Mexico and elsewhere in Latin America, there is a long history of innovation in resource conservation and use, going back to the irrigation systems constructed in the period before the conquest;[41] even today, new appropriate technologies are evident.[42] Similarly, over the past half-century, peasants' militant actions earned them a worldwide reputation for outstanding forest management practices, combining attention to the health of their trees with strategies for cutting and transformation that contribute to social well-being and cohesion.[43] The diversification of productive activities is increasingly evident as these groups begin to take over activities that were previously the realm of government or the private sector that simply employed their members and encroached on their territories without consideration for benefit-sharing (eg ecological and cultural tourism; handicraft production; agroecological practices).[44]

Perhaps the most far-reaching of the transformations involve the realisation of the significance of biological and cultural diversity as a patrimony to enhance community welfare and improve ecological management. It is increasingly clear that the wealth of knowledge and skills that people in peasant and indigenous communities command are an important potential fount for solving some of the world's pressing ecological, climatic, productive and social problems.[45] For example, a quite spectacular but increasingly contested environmental management system is the Maasai pastoralist practice in Kenya.[46] Like this one, the inherited storehouse from thousands of peoples around the world will be of extraordinary significance in finding ways to increase food production on a scale that assures maintaining the productivity of their ecosystems while making food accessible to the large segments of society that the capitalist organisation is not willing to supply or is not capable of supplying. The world's largest peasant social organisation, with 200 million members, La Vía Campesina, is achieving remarkable advances in pursuing its agenda for food sovereignty using agroecological approaches, in spite of considerable opposition from some international organisations and industrial/commercial agricultural interests.[47] Similarly, the Indigenous and Community Conservation Areas Consortium integrates a network of regional organisations with tens of millions of people in more than 80 countries (https://www.iccaconsortium.org);[48] the New Rural Reconstruction Movement in China is strengthening hundreds of communities, increasing production, and implementing environmental conservation practices for as many as 200 million peasants.[49] Examples abound of other organisations and networks that are also advancing in this direction, such as the Landless Workers' Movement (MST) in Brazil[50] and the Zero-Budget Natural Farming System in India.[51] Two more comprehensive but controversial experiences involve the efforts to create an autonomous region for the Kurdish people[52] and the commune movement in Venezuela (http://orinocotribune.com/), both in the midst of wartime conditions.

As we search for more examples of communities and peoples shaping alternative ways to restructure their societies, a wealth of experiences appears.[53] Two Mexican experiences offer vivid illustrations of these profound transformations. Since 1994, the Zapatista (EZIN) movement has been an enduring process of community construction, reaffirmation of indigenous identities and the consolidation of a diversified productive system. It is guaranteeing palpable improvements in the quality of life of the half-million people living in the hundreds of communities in the region; its commitment to environmental conservation is also remarkable in the present conjuncture of continuing low-intensity aggression from the Mexican state. Although the EZLN steadfastly rejected governmental 'development' programmes, it promoted a national indigenous alliance by participating in the 2018 presidential election; the official system rejected this, leading the group to reaffirm its founding principles: to not remain passive under capitalism, to struggle for power from below and to strengthen collective organisation.[54]

The second example involves the region where about 40,000 indigenous peasants, organised in cooperatives (Tosepan Titataniske) in the mountainous areas of Puebla known for its mineral reserves, are protecting their ecological and cultural diversity. The group developed an effective legal strategy to thwart advances by outsiders while reinforcing its social and productive strategies. The improving quality of life and ecological protection are contributing to consolidating autonomy and local governance institutions.[55]

This essay was written in Mexico, where communities are consolidating their ability to forge autonomous societies from below, capable of implementing the five principles mentioned in the first section. By deepening their political capacity to build alliances and create support networks, they are modifying legal frameworks to facilitate their ability to manage their territories and resources. There are perhaps 20 million people living in these areas, who control as much as one-third of Mexico's territory. Elsewhere in Latin America there are as many as 120 million people engaged in similar activities, increasing their ability to define their collective goals and implement strategies to achieve them. These social organisations offer tangible evidence that there are, indeed, alternatives to development.[56]

4. Marx's revolutionary subject vs the collective revolutionary subject

Marx's theoretical–methodological approach is fundamental to study the revolution and the revolutionary subject. This framework offers diverse postulates that shaped the ideological construction motivating the revolutions of the twentieth century, most of which were peasant revolutions (most analysts recognise that this concept generally also includes indigenous peoples!).[57] In this last section, we examine the distinction between the conceptualisation of Marx's revolutionary subject and our proposal of the collective revolutionary subject.

The Marxist tradition has important elements for understanding present-day social transformations led by communities. In the preface to the Russian version of the Communist Manifesto in 1882, Engels noted that the Russian rural community could be a starting point for a new communist revolution moving from its primitive forms of common property to a superior communist form. This was clear in Marx's letter to Vera Sassulitch in 1881, opening the possibility of different forms of social organisation, such as the Russian peasants' commune, coexisting with the capitalist system.[58]

In this sense, Marxist thought can enrich our understanding of today's dynamics, where the subjects are transforming social reality, reinforcing their unique identities and capacity for change. David Harvey recognised this more than 20 years ago, arguing that it is 'vital to hold fast to the principles that (1) all projects to transform ecological relations are simultaneously projects to transform social relations, and (2) transformative activity (labour) lies at the heart of the whole dialectics of social and environmental change'. He went on to highlight that these social relations must encompass the

> whole spectrum of sociality. Issues of gender, of reproduction activities, of what happens in the living space as well as in the workspace, of group difference, of cultural diversity and of local autonomy deserve careful consideration. A more nuanced view of the interplay between environmental transformations and sociality is seriously called for.[59]

This 'spectrum of sociality' is being enriched by the active participation of the rural peoples, who were left behind in many progressive doctrines of previous decades.

In order to further define our contribution, we compare the Marxist position with our proposal of the revolutionary subject:

- The notion of *social classes*: In the capitalist mode of production, Marx and Engels define two emblematic antagonistic social classes – the proletariat and the bourgeoisie[60] – whose relation is defined by wage labour, which 'masks' exploitation. In our case, we do not propose a social class, but rather *indigenous and peasant communities* that may or may not embody basic capitalist relations (wage labour) – that is, a specific (non-egalitarian) society with particular social dynamics outside the dominant system.
- The *class consciousness* of the proletariat arises as a political consciousness, a knowledge that implies the awareness of its existence and its action – that is, its power of transformation[61] – to later promote the organisation of the working class. In the context of this analysis, this awareness is found in an *explicit collective decision* to not reproduce capitalist dynamics; in many communities this decision stems from an historical peasant/indigenous identity as a referent of their worldview, which motivates its protection and defence.
- The consolidation of the working class into a *political party*, through class consciousness: for Marx, the proletarian organisation starts from small groups that form a single front, until consolidating into a political party that represents them all. From this emerges the fundamental role of the state, where its conquest is the objective of revolution. In our proposal, we suggest a *political position* of the communities that entails a series of negotiation strategies, alliances and agreements to consolidate legal frameworks that allow them to expand their autonomy and territorial and surplus management on the margins of the sphere of state action. The seizing of state power is not an objective of the collective revolutionary subject; rather, these actors seek to create political 'space' to implement their strategies of social and productive reorganisation.
- The conception of *revolution*: the proletariat class, organised and consolidated in a political party, overthrows the bourgeois class and establishes its domination[62] through the political control of the state. As stated above, the revolution in our proposal does not generally assume a violent process, since we show that there are revolutionary expressions such as *resistance*, *rebellion* and *r-existence* that generate the possibilities of forging societies on the margins of the nation state.

These distinctions do not imply an idealistic conception of the collective revolutionary subject. Commonly, when we think of indigenous, rural and peasant communities, our ideas are skewed in many ways, ranging from a romantic vision of the primitive to an outright rejection of traditional social practices as perhaps too fanciful. Whatever the stereotype, outsiders tend to dismiss these communities as not being significant in political terms or relevant as a fount of knowledge for productive or environmental management.

This ready dismissal of their potential ignores the objective reality of today's communities. The transformation by the collective revolutionary subject does not mean going back to the past, because it integrates traditional knowledge with present-day scientific knowledge and technologies, generating mechanisms, procedures and tools that serve to advance towards diverse productive, social and ecological goals of the community; this process is now described as a 'dialogue of knowledge systems'[63] or 'post-normal science'.[64] Within the communities numerous conflicts remain, a product of centuries of adaption and resistance to conquest and the innumerable forms of injustices they suffered;[65] but the remarkable dynamics of conflict resolution is contributing to important advances in collective self-awareness and well-being.

The recent histories of the collective revolutionary subject discussed in this article clearly demonstrate its capacity to effect social change and challenge the power structures of the societies within which these peoples are immersed. They demonstrate consciousness and agency as part of an explicit programme to modify and strengthen their societies and change their relationship with the capitalist world system.[66] When and where possible they are participating in projects of 'national reconstruction', as might have been the case during a short period in Ecuador or in Bolivia, or in ambitious local proposals, such as the Zapatista movement in Mexico.[67] Throughout the Americas, however, myriad groups are restructuring their own relationships with the larger society, as is evident in the flourishing of efforts to implement programmes of environmental justice as they become more steadfast in their opposition to the 'projects of death' proposed by international capital (see eg http://www.ejolt.org).

Although the 'revolutionary' character of these societies remains to be determined, we suggest that the peoples involved in the dynamics described above are clearly cutting new paths for their social and productive organisations that are directly challenging the structure of the state and the capitalist form of social organisation. They are laying the foundations for the convivial society that Ivan Illich wrote about almost a half-century ago.[68] In the face of the substantial threat to human society posed by environmental deterioration and climate change, formulated as the 'Second Contradiction of Capitalist Production',[69] they are at the forefront of the profound transformations that humanity requires. All this makes it essential that we reconsider the significance of these revolutionary forces that are effectively challenging the reign of capital.

5. Conclusions

We suggest that the Marxist aspiration of a revolutionary movement to overthrow the capitalist system as a whole or even in individual states is not a realistic process, in spite of the depths of the economic, social and environmental crises facing humanity. Instead, our analysis suggests that numerous social movements, incorporating hundreds of millions of people, are involved in consolidating social and political institutions as well as productive structures to attend to the well-being of their members and the conservation of their ecosystems.

The search for alternative approaches to achieve these objectives is the most pressing task facing the peasants and indigenous peoples analysed in this article. They are rapidly moving to the margins of their societies because the priorities of the current capitalist system are directed towards the concentration and appropriation of political and economic power, leaving aside the well-being of humanity and planetary equilibrium.[70] The social initiatives to try to change the behaviour of large companies (the main emitters of greenhouse gases globally) are limited by their ability and that of other dominant groups to paralyse transformative initiatives. Instead, the communities are strengthening their autonomy and ability to supply their own needs, directly or through exchanges with others in their networks.

The revolutionary processes with which we are associated or that we offer as examples in this desultory panorama are interacting with the phenomenon of *resilience* of the planetary system. This capacity for resilience is noticed in the collective revolutionary subject that we describe; the revolutionary subject is capable of implementing processes of social reorganisation to face environmental challenges. This interdisciplinary analysis of the revolutionary subject reveals their adaptability in the face of today's multiple social, economic and ecological crises. If we further consider that just the indigenous peoples occupy more than one-quarter of the world's land area[71] – peasants occupy other substantial areas – there is great potential for forging spaces where alternative social organisations can expand from the substantial areas where they are already operational.

In this context, starting from the perspective of an 'ecological economics from below',[72] our proposal involves a collective revolutionary subject, the indigenous and peasant societies that are trying to transcend the capitalist relationship. Their collective political decision not to participate in the logic of capital does not imply that they are isolated societies, outside of capitalism. They were victims of the system and suffered terrible forms of inclusion and exclusion; now they are reconstructing their dynamics and social structures to recuperate valuable parts of their culture, identity and knowledge, linking them with scientific, political, economic and ecological knowledge to manage their territories.

This is the very essence of 'r-existence'. They are creating spaces where they can exercise their autonomy, re-appropriating nature, based principally on their ability to re-invent and control their territories and manage their surplus. This intrinsic capacity of the collective revolutionary subject contributes to diverse dimensions of well-being, such as improvements in working conditions as well as material, social, cultural and environmental conditions including health, education, spirituality and leisure.

The collective revolutionary subject is a social actor that constructs and reconstructs itself, transforming its realities or creating new ones. Although it aims for a virtuous future, it protects its heritage to forge a balanced relation between society and nature, learning from the past and the present to create new alternatives. In sum, the myriad revolutionaries involve different processes according to their contexts, reinforcing the conviction that *other worlds are possible* (and are under construction!).

Disclosure statement

No potential conflict of interest was reported by the authors.

Funding

Funding for this work comes from our university and the fellowship programmes of the National Council of Science and Technology (CONACYT).

Acknowledgements

This paper is a product of a collaborative effort of members of the 'Sustainability Laboratory' in the Department of Economics. We are particularly grateful to the prolonged discussions during its lengthy gestation period; the active members of this group are Wuendy Armenta, Erika Carcaño and Ana Lilia Esquivel. Previous work on this line of research was conducted as part of a European Community Research Program (FP-7) in which we collaborated with colleagues from eight countries on the subject of environmental governance in Latin America; the results are summarised in the book listed in the bibliography (see Barkin and Lemus, in De Castro, Hogenboom, and Baud). We are very grateful for the constructive and comradely comments we received from many colleagues in Mexico and abroad; in particular, we would like to thank Radhika Desai, Maarten de Kadt, Dominick Tuminaro and the members of the University of Zacatecas Seminar in Critical Development Studies. The careful reading and perspicacious comments from the two anonymous readers were quite important for the final revision.

Notes

1. eg Meadows and Meadows, *Limits to Growth*.
2. Berkes, *Sacred Ecology*.
3. Petras and Veltmeyer, "Are Latin American Peasant Movements Still a Force."
4. Esteva, "The Zapatistas and People's Power"; and Alvárez, Dagnino, and Escobar, *Culture of Politics, Politics of Culture*.
5. Bartra and Otero, "Indian Peasant Movements in Mexico."
6. Garnett et al., "A Spatial Overview," 369.
7. Harvey, "'Listen, Anarchist!'"
8. Huanacuni Mamani, *Buen Vivir/Vivir Bien*; and Bengoa, *La emergencia indígena en América Latina*.
9. Barkin and Lemus, "Local Solutions for Environmental Justice."
10. Wolf, *Europe and the People without History*.
11. See Barkin, "Overcoming the Neoliberal Paradigm" for the details of how they are operationalised.
12. Villoro, *De la libertad a la comunidad*, 41–2 (our translation).
13. Ibid.
14. Lenkersdorf, *Cosmovisiones*; and Nations, "Naming the Dragonfly."
15. Villoro, *De la libertad a la comunidad*.
16. Barkin, "Communities Constructing Their Own Alternatives."
17. See Kovach, *Indigenous Methodologies*; Wilson, *Research is Ceremony*; L. T. Smith, *Challenges of Kaupapa Maori Research*; and L. T. Smith, *Decolonizing Methodologies*.
18. Barkin and Lemus, "Local Solutions for Environmental Justice."
19. Barkin et al., "Social Capacity for Surplus Management."
20. Villoro, "Sobre el concepto de revolución," 278 (our translation).
21. Polanyi, *The Great Transformation*.
22. Martínez Luna, *Comunalidad y Desarrollo*.
23. Arsel, Hogenboom, and Pelligrini, "The Extractive Boom in Latin America."
24. Boyce, Narain, and Stanton, *Reclaiming Nature*; Zermeño, *Reconstruir a México en el Siglo XXI*; and Toledo and Ortiz-Espejel, *México, Regiones que caminan hacia la sustentabilidad*.
25. Wrenn and Waller, "Care and the Neoliberal Individual."
26. Baran, *The Political Economy of Growth*; Baran, "On the Evolution of Economic Surplus"; and Gibson-Graham, Cameron, and Healy, *Take Back the Economy*.
27. Carcaño, "Las mujeres indígenas"; Petras and Veltmeyer, *Extractive Imperialism in the Americas*; and Armenta, "Acumulación de capital extra-económica."
28. Vergara-Camus, "The MST and the EZLN Struggle for Land."
29. Toledo, *Ecocidio en México*.
30. Ibid., 144–5 (our translation).

31. See Gonzales and González, "Introduction: Indigenous Peoples and Autonomy."
32. eg Scott, *Weapons of the Weak*.
33. Borrini-Feyerabend et al., *Sharing Power*.
34. Baschet, *Resistencia, Rebelión, Insurrección*.
35. N. Smith, "The Revolutionary Imperative."
36. Bonfil Batalla, *México Profundo*.
37. Barkin, *De La Protesta a La Propuesta*, ch. 27: 485–497.
38. Baschet, *Resistencia, Rebelión, Insurrección*, 7.
39. Porto-Gonçalves and Leff, "Political Ecology in Latin America."
40. Participación de la Comisión Sexta del EZLN, *El Pensamiento Crítico*; Beaucage, "Belleza, placer y sufrimiento"; and Rodríguez, *Defensa comunitaria del territorio*.
41. A. Palerm, *Obras hidráulicas prehispánicas*; and J. Palerm, "A Comparative History."
42. Barkin, *Innovaciones Mexicanas en el Manejo del Agua*.
43. Stevens et al., *Securing Rights, Combating Climate Change*; and Oldekop et al., "Reductions in Deforestation and Poverty."
44. Silva Rivera, del Carmen Vergara Tenorio, and Rodríguez Luna, *Casos Exitosos*; Toledo and Ortiz-Espejel, *México, Regiones que caminan*; and Toledo and Barrera-Bassols, "Political Agroecology in Mexico."
45. Barkin, *De La Protesta a La Propuesta*, ch. 29: 512–38.
46. Farrell, "Snow White and the Wicked Problems of the West"; Ameso et al., "Pastoral Resilience among the Maasai."
47. Desmarais, *La Vía Campesina*; Borras, Edelman, and Kay, *Transnational Agrarian Movements*; Shattuck, Schiavoni, and VanGelder, *The Politics of Food Sovereignty*; SOCLA, "Scaling up Agroecology"; Val et al., "Agroecology and La Vía Campesina I"; Rosset et al., "Agroecology and La Vía Campesina II."
48. CALG, *Defending Commons' Land and ICCAs*.
49. Wen et al., "Ecological Civilization, Indigenous Culture."
50. Borsatto and Souza-Ezquerdo, "MST's Experience in Leveraging Agroecology."
51. Rosset and Khadse, "Zero Budget Natural Farming in India."
52. Saed, "Rojava"; and Fenelon and Hall, "Revitalization and Indigenous Resistance."
53. eg Lönnqvist, *Morral de experiencias*; Pimbert, *Food Sovereignty, Agroecology and Biocultural Diversity*.
54. Enlace Zapatista, "What Is Missing Is yet to Come"; Fitzwater, *Autonomy Is in Our Hearts*.
55. Carcaño, "Las mujeres indígenas"; Serna de la Garza and Martínez Garcés, "Integralidad en la responsabilidad social empresarial"; Armenta, "Acumulación de capital extra-económica"; and Linsalata, "De la defensa del territorio maseual."
56. Lang, König, and Regelmann, *Alternatives in a World of Crisis*; Esteva, Babones, and Babcicky, *The Future of Development*; and Escobar et al., *Pluriverse*.
57. Wolf, *Peasant Wars of the Twentieth Century*.
58. Marx, *Precapitalist Economic Formations*.
59. Harvey, "Marxism, Metaphors, and Ecological Politics," 27.
60. Marx and Engels, *Communist Manifesto*, ch. 1.
61. Caycedo, *The Historical Subject and Its Complexity*.
62. Marx and Engels, *Communist Manifesto*.
63. Barkin and Lemus, "Local Solutions for Environmental Justice"; Anderson et al., *Everyday Experts*.
64. Funtowicz and Ravetz, "Science for the Post-Normal Age."
65. Wolf, *Peasant Wars of the Twentieth Century*; and Wolf, *Europe and the People without History*.
66. Little, "Marx on Peasant Consciousness," in a comment on Engels's comments on Marx's essay, "The Eighteenth Brumaire of Louis Bonaparte."
67. Baronnet, Mora Bayo, and Stahler-Sholk, *Luchas "muy otras"*; Enlace Zapatista, "May the Earth Tremble at Its Core."
68. Illich, *Tools for Conviviality*; and Esteva, "Time to Enclose the Enclosers."
69. O'Connor, "Capitalism, Nature, Socialism."
70. Barkin, *De La Protesta a La Propuesta*, ch. 5: 127–35.

71. Garnett et al., "A Spatial Overview."
72. Barkin, "Radical Ecological Economics."

ORCID

David Barkin (iD) http://orcid.org/0000-0001-5365-7733

Bibliography

Álvarez, S. E., E. Dagnino, and A. Escobar. *Culture of Politics, Politics of Culture: Re-visioning Latin American Social Movements*. Boulder, CO: Westview Press, 1998.

Ameso, E. A., S. A. Bukachi, C. O. Olungah, T. Haller, S. Wandibba, and S. Nangendo. "Pastoral Resilience among the Maasai Pastoralists of Laikipia County, Kenya." *Land* 7 (2018): 78. doi:10.3390/land7020078.

Anderson, C., C. Buchanan, M. Chang, J. Sanchez Rodriguez, and T. Wakeford, eds. *Everyday Experts: How People's Knowledge Can Transform the Food System*. Coventry: Centre for Agroecology, Water and Resilience, Coventry University, 2017.

Armenta, W. "Acumulación de capital extra-económica en el México rural. Cuetzalan del Progreso, Puebla" ["Accumulation of Non-monetary Capital in Rural Mexico"]. PhD diss., Economic Sciences, Universidad Autónoma Metropolitana, 2016.

Arsel, M., B. Hogenboom, and L. Pelligrini, eds. "The Extractive Boom in Latin America." Special Issue. *The Extractive Industries and Society* 3, no. 4 (2016): 880–1129. doi:10.1016/j.exis.2016.10.014.

Baran, P. "On the Evolution of Economic Surplus." [In Spanish.] *El Trimestre Económico* 25, no. 4 (100) (1958): 735–748. https://www.jstor.org/stable/20855461

Baran, P. *The Political Economy of Growth*. New York: Monthly Review, 1957.

Barkin, D. *De La Protesta a La Propuesta: 50 años imaginando y construyendo el futuro [From Protest to Proposal: 50 Years of Imagining and Building the Future]*. México: Siglo XXI Editores, 2018.

Barkin, D. "Communities Constructing Their Own Alternatives in the Face of Crisis." *Mountain Research and Development* 32, (Suppl.) (2012): S12–S22. doi:MRD-JOURNAL-D-11-00088.S1. doi:10.1659/MRD-JOURNAL-D-11-00088.S1.

Barkin, D. *Innovaciones Mexicanas en el Manejo del Agua [Mexican Innovations in Water Management]*. México: Centro de Ecología y Desarrollo, 2001.

Barkin, D. "Overcoming the Neoliberal Paradigm: Sustainable Popular Development." *Journal of Developing Societies* 16, no. 2 (2000): 163–180. doi:10.1163/156852200512030.

Barkin, D. "Radical Ecological Economics," ch. 3.1. In *Imperiled Economies:* 2018, edited by P. Cooney, A. Davis, J. Huato, P. Quick, G. Schneider, R. Vasudevan, and M. Vernengo, 101–113. Boston: Dollars and Sense, 2018. http://www.radicalecologicaldemocracy.org/radical-ecological-economics/

Barkin, D., W. Armenta, D. Cabrera, E. Carcaño, and G. Parra. "Social Capacity for Surplus Management: Building Alternative Societies," 543–557. [In Spanish.] In *La UAM ante la Sucesión Presidencial*, edited by F. Novelo. México: Universidad Autónoma Metropolitana, Unidad Xochimilco, División de Ciencias Sociales y Humanidades, 2011. https://www.researchgate.net/publication/304542041_Capacidad_social_para_la_gestion_del_excedente_la_construccion_de_sociedades_alternativas.

Barkin, D., and B. Lemus. "Local Solutions for Environmental Justice." In *Environmental Governance in Latin America: Conflicts, Projects and Possibilities*, edited by F. De Castro, B. Hogenboom, and M. Baud, 257–286. London: Palgrave Macmillan, 2016. https://link.springer.com/content/pdf/10.1007%2F978-1-137-50572-9_11.pdf

Baronnet, B., M. Mora Bayo, and R. Stahler-Sholk, eds. *Luchas "muy otras": Zapatismo y autonomía en las comunidades indígenas de Chiapas [Other Peoples' Struggles: Zapatismo and Autonomy in the Indigenous Communities of Chiapas]*. México: UAM–Xochimilco, CIESAS y Universidad Autónoma de Chiapas, 2011. https://zapatismoyautonomia.files.wordpress.com/2013/12/luchas-muy-otras-2011.pdf

Bartra, A., and G. Otero. "Indian Peasant Movements in Mexico: The Struggle for Land, Autonomy and Democracy." In *Reclaiming the Land: The Resurgence of Rural Movements in Africa, Asia and Latin*

America, edited by S. Moyo and P. Yeros, 383–409. London: Zed Books, 2005. https://www.sahistory. org.za/sites/default/files/file%20uploads%20/sam_moyo_paris_yeros_reclaiming_the_land_the_ rbookos.org_.pdf

Baschet, J. *Resistencia, Rebelión, Insurrección. Conceptos y fenómenos fundamentales de nuestro tiempo [Resistance, Rebellion, Insurrection. Concepts and Fundamental Phenomena of Our Time]*. México: Universidad Nacional Autónoma de México, Instituto de Investigaciones Sociales, 2012.

Beaucage, P. "Belleza, placer y sufrimiento: reflexiones sobre cuerpo y género entre los nahuas de la Sierra Norte de Puebla." *Culturas y Representaciones Sociales* 6, no. 12 (2012): 165–196. http://www. revistas.unam.mx/index.php/crs/article/download/30479/28292

Bengoa, J. *La emergencia indígena en América Latina [Indigenous Emergence in Latin America]*. 3rd ed. Santiago: Fondo de Cultura Económica, 2016.

Berkes, F. *Sacred Ecology*. 4th ed. Abington: Routledge, 2017.

Bonfil-Batalla, G. *México Profundo: Reclaiming a Civilization*. Austin: University of Texas Press, 1996 [1987].

Borras Jr., S. M., M. Edelman, and C. Kay. *Transnational Agrarian Movements Confronting Globalization*. London: Wiley-Blackwell, 2009.

Borrini-Feyerabend, G., M. Pimbert, T. Farvar, A. Kothari, and Y. Renard. *Sharing Power: Learning by Doing in Co-management of Natural Resources throughout the World*. London: Earthscan, 2007.

Borsatto, R. S., and V. F. Souza-Esquerdo. "MST's Experience in Leveraging Agroecology in Rural Settlements: Lessons, Achievements, and Challenges." *Agroecology and Sustainable Food Systems Online* (2019). doi:10.1080/21683565.2019.1615024.

Boyce, J., S. Narain, and E. Stanton, eds. *Reclaiming Nature: Environmental Justice and Ecological Restoration*. New York: Anthem, 2007.

Carcaño, Valencia, E. "Las mujeres indígenas en la Nueva Ruralidad Comunitaria (NRC) y su implicación en la generación de excedentes. El caso de la organización Masehualsihuamej Monsenyolchicahuanij" ["Women in the New Communitarian Rurality"]. PhD diss., Economic Sciences, Universidad Autónoma Metropolitana, 2013.

Caycedo, J. *The Historical Subject and Its Complexity*. [In Spanish.] Universidad Nacional de Colombia, 1999. http://www.cronicon.net/paginas/Documentos/No.39.pdf.

Coalition Against Land Grabbing (CALG). *Defending Commons' Land and ICCAs*. Palawan, Philippines: CALG, 2018. https://docs.wixstatic.com/ugd/16abfd_c3e762deb8ad41f1a64d139b95ab2e5c.pdf

Desmarais, Annette-Aurélie. *La Vía Campesina: Globalization and the Power of Peasants*. London: Pluto Press. 2007.

Enlace Zapatista. "May the Earth Tremble at Its Core." 2016. http://enlacezapatista.ezln.org. mx/2016/10/18/may-the-earth-tremble-at-its-core/

Enlace Zapatista. "What Is Missing Is yet to Come." 2018. http://enlacezapatista.ezln.org. mx/2018/05/06/whats-missing-is-yet-to-come/

Escobar, A., F. Demaria, A. Kothari, and A. Salleh, eds. *Pluriverse: The Post-Development Dictionary*. Delhi and Chicago: Authors Up Front and University of Chicago Press, 2019.

Esteva, G. "Time to Enclose the Enclosers with Marx and Illich." *The International Journal of Illich Studies* 4, no. 1 (2015): 70–96.

Esteva, G. "The Zapatistas and People's Power." *Capital & Class* 68 (1999): 153–183. doi:10.1177/030981689906800108.

Esteva, G., S. Babones, and P. Babcicky. *The Future of Development: A Radical Manifesto*. Bristol: Policy Press/Bristol University Press, 2013.

Farrell, K. N. "Snow White and the Wicked Problems of the West." *Science, Technology & Human Values* 38, no. 3 (2011): 334–361. doi:10.1177/0162243910385796.

Fenelon, J. V., and T. D. Hall. "Revitalization and Indigenous Resistance to Globalization and Neoliberalism." *American Behavioral Scientist* 51, no. 12 (2008):1867–1901. doi:10.1177/ 0002764208318938.

Fitzwater, D. E. *Autonomy Is in Our Hearts: Zapatista Autonomous Government through the Lens of the Tsotsil Language*. Oakland: PM Press, 2019.

Funtowicz, S. O., and J. Ravetz. "Science for the Post-Normal Age." *Futures* 25 (1993): 739–755. doi:10.1016/0016-3287(93)90022-L.

Garnett, S. T., N. D. Burgess, J. E. Fa, Á. Fernández-Llamazares, Z. Molnár, C. J. Robinson, J. E. M. Watson, et al. "A Spatial Overview of the Global Importance of Indigenous Lands for Conservation." *Nature Sustainability* 1, no. 7 (2018): 369–374. doi:10.1038/s41893-018-0100-6.

Gibson-Graham, J. K., J. Cameron, and S. Healy. *Take Back the Economy: An Ethical Guide for Transforming Our Communities*. Minneapolis: University of Minnesota Press, 2013.

Gonzales, T., and M. González, eds. "Introduction: Indigenous Peoples and Autonomy in Latin America." Special Issue. *Latin American and Caribbean Ethnic Studies* 10, no. 1 (2015): 1–9. doi:10.1080/17442 222.2015.1034437.

Harvey, D. "'Listen, Anarchist!' A Personal Response to Simon Springer's 'Why a Radical Geography Must Be Anarchist.'" *Dialogues in Human Geography* 7, no. 3 (2017): 233–250. doi:10.1177/2043820617732876.

Harvey, D. "Marxism, Metaphors, and Ecological Politics." *Monthly Review* 49, no. 11 (1998): 17–31. doi:10.14452/MR-049-11-1998-04_2.

Huanacuni Mamani, F. *Buen Vivir/Vivir Bien. Filosofía, políticas, estrategias y experiencias regionales andinas* [*Philosophy, Politics, Strategies and Regional Andean Experiences*]. Lima: CAOI, 2010. https://www.escr-net.org/sites/default/files/Libro%20Buen%20Vivir%20y%20Vivir%20Bien_0.pdf

Illich, I. *Tools for Conviviality*. London: Calder and Boyers, 1973.

Kovach, M. *Indigenous Methodologies: Characteristics, Conversations, and Contexts*. Toronto: University of Toronto Press, 2009.

Lang, M., C.-D. König, and A.-C. Regelmann. *Alternatives in a World of Crisis: Seeking Alternatives beyond Development*. Brussels: Rosa-Luxemburg Foundation, 2018. https://www.rosalux.eu/publications/alternatives-in-a-world-of-crisis/

Lenkersdorf, C. *Cosmovisiones* [*Cosmovisions*]. México: Universidad Nacional Autónoma de México, 1998. https://alfarcolectivo.files.wordpress.com/2017/06/cosmovisiones.pdf

Linsalata, L. "De la defensa del territorio maseual a la reinvención comunitario-popular de la política: crónica de una lucha" ["From Maseual Territorial Defense to the Communitarian: Popular Reinvention of Politics"]. *Estudios Latinoamericanos* 40 (2017): 117–136.

Little, D. "Marx on Peasant Consciousness." 2015. http://understandingsociety.blogspot.com/2015/09/marx-on-peasant-consciousness.html

Lönnqvist, L. *Morral de experiencias para la seguridad y soberanía alimentarias: Aprendizajes de organizaciones civiles en el sureste mexicano* [*Handbag of Experiences for Food Security and Sovereignty*]. San Cristobal, Mexico and Santa Cruz, CA: EcoSur/Community Agroecology Network, 2018.

Martínez Luna, J. *Comunalidad y Desarrollo* [*Communality and Development*]. Oaxaca: Conaculta-Culturas Populares e Indígenas y Centro de Apoyo al Movimiento Popular Oaxaqueño, AC, 2003.

Marx, K. *Precapitalist Economic Formations*. 2015. https://www.marxists.org/archive/marx/works/1857/precapitalist/index.htm

Marx, K., and F. Engels. *Communist Manifesto*. 2010. https://www.marxists.org/archive/marx/works/1848/communist-manifesto/ch01.htm#007

Meadows, D., J. Randers, and D. Meadows. *Limits to Growth: The 30-Year Update*. London: Earthscan, 2004.

Nations, J. D. "Naming the Dragonfly: Why Indigenous Languages Matter in the 21st Century." *Langscape* 5, no. 1 (2016): 20–24. https://medium.com/langscape-magazine/naming-the-dragonfly-why-indigenous-languages-matter-in-the-21st-century-885025c8cbc1

O'Connor, J. "Capitalism, Nature, Socialism: A Theoretical Introduction." *Capitalism, Nature, Socialism*, 1, no. 1 (1988): 11–38. http://www.columbia.edu/~lnp3/second_contradiction.htm

Oldekop, J. A., K. Sims, B. Karna, M. Whittingham, and A. Agrawal. "Reductions in Deforestation and Poverty from Decentralized Forest Management in Nepal." *Nature Sustainability* 2 (2019): 421–428. doi:10.1038/s41893-019-0277-3.

Palerm, A. *Obras hidráulicas prehispánicas en el sistema lacustre del Valle de México* [*Prehispanic Waterworks in the Lake System of the Mexico City Valley*]. México: Instituto Nacional de Antropología e Historia, Centro de Investigaciones Superiores, Seminario de Etnohistoria del Valle de México, 1973.

Palerm, J. "A Comparative History, from the 16th to 20th Centuries, of Irrigation Water Management in Spain, Mexico, Chile, Mendoza (Argentina) and Peru." *Water Policy* 12, no. 6 (2010): 779–797. doi:10.2166/wp.2010.110.

Participación de la Comisión Sexta del EZLN. *El Pensamiento Crítico Frente a la Hidra Capitalista, Volumen 1 [Critical Thought in the Face of the Capitalist Hydra, Volume 1].* Mexico: UAM-Xochimilco, 2015.

Petras, J., and H. Veltmeyer. "Are Latin American Peasant Movements Still a Force for Change? Some New Paradigms Revisited." *Journal of Peasant Studies* 28, no. 2 (2001): 83–118. doi:10.1080/03066150108438767.

Petras, J., and H. Veltmeyer, eds. *Extractive Imperialism in the Americas: Capitalism's New Frontier,* Leiden, the Netherlands: Brill, 2014.

Pimbert, M. P. ed. *Food Sovereignty, Agroecology and Biocultural Diversity: Constructing and Contesting Knowledge.* London: Routledge, 2018.

Polanyi, K. *The Great Transformation: The Political and Economic Origins of Our Time.* Boston: Beacon Press, 1944 [2001].

Porto-Gonçalves, C. W., and E. Leff. "Political Ecology in Latin America: The Social Re-Appropriation of Nature, the Reinvention of Territories and the Construction of an Environmental Rationality." *Desenvolvimento e Meio Amiente* 35 (2015): 65–88. http://revistas.ufpr.br/made/article/view-File/43543/27087

Rodríguez-Wallenius, C. A., ed. *Defensa comunitaria del territorio en la zona central de México, Enfoques teóricos y análisis de experiencias [Communitarian Defence of Territory in Central Mexico].* Mexico: Juan Pablos Editor, 2010.

Rosset, P. M., and A. Khadse. "Zero Budget Natural Farming in India – from Inception to Institutionalization." *Agroecology and Sustainable Food Systems Online* (2019). doi:10.1080/2168356 5.2019.1608349.

Rosset, P. M., V. Val, L. Barbosa, and N. McCune. "Agroecology and La Vía Campesina II. Peasant Agroecology Schools and the Formation of a Sociohistorical and Political Subject." *Agroecology and Sustainable Food Systems Online* (2019). doi:10.1080/21683565.2019.1617222.

Saed. "Rojava." *Capitalism Nature Socialism* 26, no. 1 (2015): 1–15. doi:10.1080/10455752.2015.1006948.

Scott, J. C. Weapons of *the Weak: Everyday Forms of Peasant Resistance.* New Haven, CT: Yale University Press, 1985.

Serna de la Garza, M. E., and D. C. Martínez Garcés. "Integralidad en la responsabilidad social empresarial: caso de la cooperativa Tosepan Titataniske." *Otra Economía* 3, no. 4 (2009): 122–139. http://revistas.unisinos.br/index.php/otraeconomia/article/view/1128/307

Shattuck, A., C. Schiavoni, and Z. VanGelder. *The Politics of Food Sovereignty: Concept, Practice and Social Movements.* London: Routledge, 2017.

Silva Rivera, E., M. del Carmen Vergara Tenorio, and E. Rodríguez Luna, eds. *Casos Exitosos en la Construcción de Sociedades Sustentables [Successful Cases in Building Sustainable Societies].* Xalapa, Veracruz: Universidad Veracruzana, 2012.

Smith, L. T. *The Challenges of Kaupapa Maori Research in the 21st Century.* Wellington, NZ: New Zealand Council for Educational Research, 2011. http://www.nzcer.org.nz/system/files/Hui_Procedings__v3_Web_1.pdf

Smith, L. T. *Decolonizing Methodologies: Research and Indigenous Peoples.* 2nd ed. London: Zed Press, 2012.

Smith, N. "The Revolutionary Imperative." *Antipode* 41, no. S1 (2010): 50–65. doi:10.1111/j.1467-8330. 2009.00716.x.

SOCLA (Latin American Scientific Society of Agroecology). "Scaling up Agroecology to Contribute to the Sustainable Development Goals." 2018. https://foodfirst.org/wp-content/uploads/2018/04/Final-2018-Statement-of-The-Latin-American-Scientific-Society-of-Agroecology-SOCLA-regarding-FAO%E2%80%99s-2nd-International-Sympos.pdf

Stevens, C., R. Winterbottom, K. Reytar, and J. Springer. *Securing Rights, Combating Climate Change: How Strengthening Community Forest Rights Mitigates Climate Change.* Washington, DC: World Resources Institute, 2014.

Toledo, V. *Ecocidio en México. La batalla final es por la vida* [*Ecocide in Mexico. The Final Battle Is for Life*]. México: Grijalbo, 2015.

Toledo, V., and N. Barrera-Bassols. "Political Agroecology in Mexico: A Path toward Sustainability." *Sustainability* 9, no. 2 (2017): art. 268. doi:10.3390/su9020268.

Toledo, V., and B. Ortiz-Espejel. *México, Regiones que caminan hacia la sustentabilidad* [*Mexico, Regions that Advance towards Sustainability*]. Puebla: Universidad Iberoamericana, 2014.

Val, V., P. Rosset, C. Zamora Lomeli, O. Giraldo, and D. Rocheleau. "Agroecology and La Vía Campesina I. The Symbolic and Material Construction of Agroecology through the Dispositive of 'Peasant-to-Peasant' Processes." *Agroecology and Sustainable Food Systems Online* (2019). doi:10.1080/21683 565.2019.1600099.

Vergara-Camus, L. "The MST and the EZLN Struggle for Land: New Forms of Peasant Rebellions." *Journal of Agrarian Change* 9, no. 3 (2009): 365–393. doi:10.1111/j.1471-0366.2009.00216.x.

Villoro, L. *De la libertad a la comunidad* [*On the Freedom of Community*]. México: FCE-ITESM. Cuadernos de la Cátedra Alfonso Reyes, 2003.

Villoro, L. "Sobre el concepto de revolución" ["On the Concept of Revolution"]. *Revista del Centro de Estudios Constitucionales,* no. 11 (1992): 277–290. http://www.cepc.gob.es/publicaciones/revistas/revistaselectronicas?IDR=15&IDN=1240&IDA=35439

Wen, T., K. Lau, C. Cheng, J. Qui, and H. He. "Ecological Civilization, Indigenous Culture, and Rural Reconstruction in China." *Monthly Review* 63, no. 9 (2012): 29–44. http://monthlyreview.org/2012/02/01/ecological-civilization-indigenous-culture-and-rural-reconstruction-in-china/

Wilson, S. *Research Is Ceremony*. Halifax, NS: Fernwood Publishing, 2009.

Wolf, E. R. *Europe and the People without History*. Berkeley: University of California Press, 1982.

Wolf, E. R. *Peasant Wars of the Twentieth Century*. New York: Harper & Row, 1969.

Wrenn, M., and W. Waller. "Care and the Neoliberal Individual." *Journal of Economic Issues* 52, no. 2 (2017): 495–502. doi:10.1080/00213624.2017.1321438.

Zermeño, S. *Reconstruir a México en el Siglo XXI: Estrategias para mejorar la calidad de vida y enfrentar la destrucción del medio ambiente* [*Reconstruct Mexico in the 21st Century: Strategies to Improve the Quality of Life and Confront the Destruction of the Environment*]. México: Océano, 2015.

Hegel, Haiti and revolution: the post-colonial moment

Henry Heller

ABSTRACT

Susan Buck-Morss's argument that the Haitian Revolution embodied the most universal aspect of the French Revolution, namely the quest for universal freedom, relies on the supposed references to Haiti in the master–slave dialogue in Hegel's *Phenomenology of Spirit*. The revolution's lodgement at the core of this foundational text of Enlightenment universalism is, for her, about as convincing a demonstration as one can have of the universal significance of the Haitian Revolution. Marxists have opposed her venture, and demonstrated their hostility to post-colonial thinking, principally by claiming that the master–slave is an expression of European class conflict. This paper agrees with Buck-Morss that the Haitian Revolution critically affirmed the principle of universal freedom and, indeed, pushed the revolution in France and Europe in a radical direction. A better affirmation of the universal significance of the Haitian Revolution than the thoughts of Hegel is possible. The latter do not actually provide such affirmation, because racism, Eurocentrism and a hostility to political radicalism are fundamental aspects of Hegel's thought. The alternative affirmation can be found in Marxist analysis. This paper outlines such an analysis, and concludes that post-colonialism of Buck-Morss's sort is no substitute for the perspective provided by historical materialism.

Susan Buck-Morss's *Hegel, Haiti and Universal History* is not an ordinary book. Few could have chosen subjects – those of slavery and the Haitian revolution – that were more centrally in the spotlight at the beginning of the new millennium, particularly in the burgeoning field of post-colonial studies. The Haitian Revolution had anticipated the anti-colonial uprisings of the twentieth century and their challenge to Eurocentrism. Moreover, postmodernist questioning of univeralism having been overcome, the subject of universal history was once again central amid talk of globalisation. Buck-Morss brought these themes together, challenging Eurocentrism and Marxism, through the work of the European philosopher of the universal history of human liberation par excellence, Hegel, for whom universal history was clearly anchored to the emergence of capitalism. In his foundational Jena texts, economic themes, derived from Adam Smith, mingle with political ones of human liberation. Buck-Morss's argument is that the historical referent of the famous master–slave dialectic that eventuates in human liberation was the Haitian Revolution, not class struggle in Europe, as had hitherto been assumed:

Conceptually, the revolutionary struggle of slaves, who overthrow their own servitude and establish a constitutional state, provides the theoretical hinge that takes Hegel's analysis out of the limitlessly expanding colonial economy and onto the plane of world history, which he defines as the realization of freedom – a theoretical solution that was taking place in practice in Haiti at that very moment. The connection seems obvious, *so obvious that the burden of proof would seem to fall on those who wish to argue otherwise*. ... Mutual recognition among equals emerges with logical necessity out of the contradictions of slavery, not the least of which is trading human slaves as, legally, 'things', when they show themselves capable of becoming the active agents of history by struggling against slavery in a 'battle of recognition' under the banner, 'Liberty or Death!'.[1]

However, this paper will demonstrate that while Buck-Morss's analysis may have caught the intellectual wave of the time, it was no substitute for enduring historical understanding. Such understanding shows that Hegel proves a weak reed for connecting universalism, revolution and the Haitian Revolution and that Marxism provides a far more reliable alternative. In this paper we affirm with Buck-Morss that universal history is more than ever necessary and that the Haitian Revolution was critical to it. Indeed, we demonstrate that it forced the French Revolution to assume a more democratic and inclusive form. On the other hand, Buck-Morss's choice of Hegel to affirm her arguments is unfortunate. Her contention that the master–slave dialogue refers to the Haitian Revolution is dubious. We show that it most likely refers to the crisis of feudalism in France and Germany following the French Revolution and the Napoleonic conquest of Germany – the more so as Hegel is demonstrated to be a racist and Eurocentric thinker without sympathy for black people and political radicals. Moreover, her dismissal of Marxist class analysis is demonstrably short-sighted and fails to appreciate that the contemporary conception of the Haitian and French revolutions and of Hegel himself are rooted in it.

The paper opens with a brief exploration of Buck-Morss's distinctive theoretical orientation, which developed in the wake of post-modernism, neoliberalism and post-colonialism. It then criticises Buck-Morss's interpretation of the master–servant dialogue in two ways, firstly as referring to the Haitian Revolution and secondly as proceeding in a distinctively different way from the revolutionary overthrow of slavery. It involved instead the gradual undermining of the lord by the slave or servant engaged in production. It then shows that Haitian events had universal significance especially in helping to radicalise the workers, sans-culottes and peasants in the French Revolution under its economic impact. Hegel, on the other hand, was chiefly concerned with the effects of the revolution in France and his own country, Germany, not Haiti. Indeed, the last part of the paper demonstrates Hegel's Eurocentrism and racism in an argument greatly aided by Tehsale Tibebu's recent treatment of Buck-Morss's arguments and argues that they precluded such a universal viewpoint.

Buck-Morss's Post-Marxist post-colonialism

Susan Buck-Morss's post-Marxist and post-colonialist views stem from her experience of the political failures of the revolutionary students of the United States and West Germany in the 1970s, the collapse of the Soviet Union and the ravages of neoliberalism. Once a revolutionary Marxist, she went over to post-colonialism while retaining some of Marxism's universalism. Her rejection of Eurocentrism stemmed not least from a belief in the West's imminent decline in an emerging world order in which the Global South is set to play the decisive role.

In common with many post-colonialists, she retreats from, if not rejects, the basic categories of Marxism. They will not work in the context of this new order:

> It is true that Marx and many Marxists argue that dialectics is the hinge that turns the critical analysis of the economy into a predictable scenario for the future, but that will not work, not today. I do not think a dialectical analysis of society will discover what Georg Lukács called the 'subject–object of history' – the 'new proletariat' or the necessary one. That is a strained argument to make in the present. The connection is broken.[2] Dialectics is necessary as a method of thought but not in so far as it tries to actualize itself: But it nonetheless seems theory can be beneficial for social change only if theory is attentive to a dialectical method, by which I simply mean a method that can embrace antithetical extremes without insisting that logic eliminate that antithesis. As Adorno said, the antithesis exists in reality. It is a contradictory reality that we cannot wish away in thought. Anytime we think we can, our thought is not capturing the world.[3]

More broadly, she questions the continuing validity of the basic categories of Marxist analysis:

> While it may still be necessary to describe the current economic situation in terms of tendencies in the mode of production (that is, in locating changes in productive forces and productive relations), concepts like surplus value, scarcity, work, the division of labor (particularly the sexual division of labor), class, and the class struggle – are all in need of reassessment.[4]

The proper approach, according to her, is to open oneself to the new world order and its categories, including even religious ones, while not completely closing the door to the insights of Marxism. Her position is today one of a continuing open-mindedness and quietism in the face of the accumulation of recent political failures and the uncertainties of the future.

There is a certain wisdom behind such a political and intellectual position. The premises of Marxist thought must always be open to re-examination. Furthermore, if we have learned anything in recent times, it is that capitalism is mercurial and can dramatically change its form, as it has in the years of neoliberal financialisation. However, its further equally mercurial unfolding now casts new light on Buck-Morss's stance of 2009, making it appear as the product of the period of an uncontested neoliberalism which has now come to an end. We are in a new era of ongoing economic crisis and revolutionary movement in which the categories of Marxism are being renewed and are indispensable to understanding the past and future.[5] In this context, it is important to challenge Buck-Morss's distancing from Marxism, not least because her views still have purchase among academic Marxists.[6]

In *Hegel, Haiti and Universal History*, Susan Buck-Morss rejects not only Eurocentrism, but also what she considers the tired formulas of orthodox Marxism.[7] On the other hand, she is not prepared to fall in with those among the post-colonialists who are content with provincialising Europe and its universalist grand narratives.[8] Rather, she seeks to re-found universal history: 'The task is to reconfigure the enlightenment project of universal history in the context of our too-soon and not-yet global public sphere'.[9] If the old universal history is centred on Europe, her new one is centred on the non-European world and aims to 'unearth certain repressions surrounding the historical origins of modernity'. In this new universal history, Haiti is critical as the first modern black revolution. She asks: 'what happens when, in the spirit of dialectics, we turn the tables, and consider Haiti not as the victim of Europe, but as an agent in Europe's construction?'.[10] For Buck-Morss, liberating the history of Haiti from the thrall of Eurocentricism only takes one so far. She audaciously demands more: that we investigate the question, 'how is it that the revered European-American revolutionary slogan, "Liberty or Death", came to be cordoned off in Western thought and practice from the allegedly infamous tradition of Islamic jihad?'[11] How did it come to be that the Jihadist uprising against the American invasion of Iraq is seen as more irrational than the Virginian gentleman Patrick Henry's celebrated revolutionary outcry against English colonialism, asks Buck-Morss?

In Buck-Morss's work, the distinctiveness of the Western Enlightenment is directly challenged. Based on a scholarship that dates back to C. L. R. James,[12] Buck-Morss argues that, whereas the Europeans of the Enlightenment had more and more loudly bewailed the existence of slavery, it was only when the slaves of Haiti took things into their own hands that slavery was actually abolished:

> For almost a decade, before the violent elimination of whites signalled their deliberate retreat from universalist principles, the black Jacobins of Sainte-Dominique surpassed the metropole in actively realizing the Enlightenment goal of human liberty, seeming to give proof that the French Revolution was not simply a European phenomenon but world-historical in its implications.[13]

It was Toussaint Louverture and his followers who realised the full logic of freedom implicit in the revolution by emancipating themselves: 'and yet only the logic of freedom gave legitimacy to their revolution in the universal terms in which the French saw themselves'.[14]

For Buck-Morss, the Haitians made the French Revolution universal in its geographical scope and in its commitment to social and political equality. Indeed, the French Revolution came to embody a struggle against many ongoing forms of exploitation and oppression – feudal, slave, capitalist and patriarchal. It was universal in the sense of challenging the historic modes of exploitation and oppression in class society as well as in the sense of widening the spaces encompassed by revolutionary change. It was a revolution whose leadership was seized by a capitalist and bourgeois class though its mass base incorporated peasant and artisan revolutionaries, feminists and black slaves. As such, it and the Haitian Revolution prefigured the emancipatory agenda of the future, much as Buck-Morss suggests.[15]

Hegel and Haiti

Many scholars have noted that Hegel, in the *Phenomenology of Spirit*, saw the French Revolution as a universal event. It was universal because the revolution became the moment when absolute spirit or abstract reason attempted to realise itself. However, as abstract reason, it proved extreme and unstable. Unable to produce a stable polity, it actualised itself as a terror.[16]

Buck-Morss's focus is on another section of the *Phenemenology*, namely the master–slave dialogue. However, her view that Hegel was referring to the Haitian Revolution in his master–slave dialogue is untenable. Hegel did philosophise the meaning of the French Revolution. However, insofar as he celebrated revolution, he did so only up to a point. The young Hegel was drawn to the moderate version of the French Revolution espoused by the politics of the Girondins. He rejected the radical and democratic revolution of the Jacobins. Yet it was them and them alone who conceded freedom to the slaves in Haiti.[17] His distaste for the Jacobins in France suggests that he felt the same about the black Jacobins in Haiti. Recent research also makes clear that Hegel's philosophy was premised on Eurocentric and racist assumptions[18] and rules out the possibility that he sympathised with the Haitian Revolution. So, Hegel's universalism was fundamentally limited. Indeed, universalism understood as a global struggle against exploitation of all sorts was beyond Hegel's understanding. Buck-Morss errs in invoking Hegel as proof of the universal significance of the Haitian Revolution and of a revolutionary kind of universalism.

That the significance of the French Revolution was a major preoccupation of Hegel's has long been known. Referring to Hegel's *Phenomenology of Spirit*, Philip Cunliffe notes that:

> Despite Hegel's often maddeningly elliptical language and abstract categories, it is well established that the thrust of his project was an attempt to absorb the impact of modernity by offering a philosophical response to the French Revolution and the unfolding of the modern division of labour.[19]

As David Ciavatta puts it:

> In Hegel's account of the French Revolution … a particular, short-lived and contingent historical event – an event that burst onto the scene abruptly, as if from out of nowhere, and which seemed possible only in the specific socio-political conditions of French society at the time – comes to be transfigured into an autonomous 'shape of spirit'. As such, this event lays claim to having a necessary place within Hegel's systematic, dialectical account of the essential forms of human society.[20]

Buck-Morss herself accepts this view:

> It has long been recognized that Hegel's understanding of politics was modern, based on an interpretation of the events of the France Revolution as a decisive break from the past and that he is even referring to the French Revolution in the *Phenomenology of the Mind*.…[21]

However, Buck-Morss takes this argument further, claiming that Hegel understood the universal meaning not merely of the French Revolution but also of the Haitian self-emancipation from slavery:

> In perhaps the most political expression of his career, he used the sensational events of Haiti as the linchpin in his argument in *The Phenemonology of Spirit*. The actual and successful revolution of Caribbean slaves against their masters is the moment when the dialectical logic of recognition becomes visible as the thematics of world history, the story of the universal realization of freedom.[22]

According to her reading, Hegel finds the situation of master and slave completely opposed initially, i.e. the master has an abundance of necessities and is therefore independent; the slave on the contrary is dependent and exists not for himself but to serve the master. The slave accordingly exists as an object or thing and nothing more. However, as the dialectic evolves, the apparent dominance of the master completely reverses itself as the master becomes conscious of his complete dependence on the slave. The slave is initially responsible for his own lack of freedom by initially choosing life over liberty. He overcomes the state of thingness by demonstrating that he is not a thing but a subject by transforming material nature.[23] Ultimately, according to her reading, the self-liberation of the slave requires risking his own life to obtain freedom through revolution.[24] In the *Phenomenology of Mind*, Hegel insists that freedom cannot be granted to slaves from above. The self-liberation of the slave is required through a 'trial by death' …. The goal of this liberation, out of slavery, cannot be subjugation of the master in turn, but rather, elimination of the institution of slavery altogether.[25]

Buck-Morss concludes that the master–slave dialectic refers to the triumphant revolutionary struggle of the Haitian slaves against their masters. If this interpretation has been ignored, Buck-Morss argues, it is thanks to Marxists. From the time of Marx through most of the twentieth century, the master–slave dialectic has been taken by Marxists as a metaphor for class struggle. According to her, those who took this view included such luminaries as Georg Lukacs, Herbert Marcuse and Alexandre Kojève, and it was the latter who first linked this relationship to the class struggle during the French Revolution.[26] Kojeve appears to have shaped the interpretation of the master–slave dialectic in the French left, and insofar as it was associated with a contemporary event it was linked to the revolution in France rather than that in Haiti.[27]

Buck-Morss claims that it was the class analysis of the Marxists that blocked the consideration of alternatives offered by black historians like C. L. R. James and Eric Williams: With their stagist view of history '(white)' Marxists could only see slavery as a premodern institution. They were the least likely to perceive the dialogue as referring to an actual historical situation namely the Haitian Revolution.[28] She goes on to add: 'there is an element of racism implicit in official Marxism'.[29]

What 'official' Marxism might mean is unclear, especially given how much the history of the French Revolution is contested among Marxists. While undoubtedly some Marxists were hung up on a stagist view of history, others invented the anti-stagist ideas of social formations, uneven and combined development and permanent revolution. It was Daniel Guérin who wrote the history of the French Revolution from the perspective of permanent revolution.[30] Moreover, Marxist class analysis has served the understanding of both the French and Haitian revolutions well.[31] After all, the founding text of modern Haitian historiography is the thoroughly Marxist and universally acclaimed analysis of C. L. R. James's *Black Jacobins* (1938), and class struggle is at its heart: 'from the 1930s until well into the 1980s, the *Black Jacobins* remained the most important book in English on the French Revolution'.[32]

Slavery and the Haitian Revolution

Buck-Morss is right to insist that the Haitian Revolution made the French Revolution a universal event and to insist on the ongoing inter-dependence between events in Europe and the Caribbean. The two revolutions unfolded in parallel with one another. Events in revolutionary Paris directly affected the development of the slave revolt.[33] Furthermore, the revolution in Haiti was based on African traditions of resistance, allowing us to better comprehend its universal dimensions.[34] And the ideals of the French Revolution – liberty, equality and fraternity – appealed to Haitian slaves as much as to French peasants.

In pursuing this chief objective, the emancipation from slavery of his black compatriots, Toussaint Louverture put himself forward as a citizen of a colony of revolutionary France. Article 3 of the first constitution of Haiti – or rather of 'the French colony of Saint-Dominique' – inspired by Toussaint reads, 'there cannot exist slaves on this territory, servitude is therein forever abolished. All men are born, live and die free and French'.[35] It was only when Napoleon attempted to reimpose slavery that Haiti moved to outright independence.

While slavery was illegal in France from at least the sixteenth century, and wage labour and tenancy developed instead, slavery flourished as never before in the French colonies of

Martinique, Guadeloupe and especially Saint-Dominique (later Haiti) in the eighteenth century. On the latter island, there were 15,000 black slaves at the beginning of the eighteenth century and nearly half a million by 1789. Saint-Dominique became the largest sugar producer in America and was known as the 'pearl of the Antilles'. The colony made the fortunes of planters who were tied by marriage into the families of the wealthiest merchants as well as the court nobility of France. The class systems of feudalism in France and of slavery in Haiti were closely tied together.

Throughout the eighteenth century, slavery was justified by racist and ethnocentric arguments and by greed. However, from the middle of the century, French writers, beginning with Montesquieu, began to seriously question the morality and legality of slavery. By the 1770s, a growing number of writers had rejected it in principle. With the works of Condorcet and Jacques-Pierre Brissot in the next decade, the idea of liberty was held to be more important than the notion of property.[36]

The *Société des Amis des Noirs* was founded in 1788 by Brissot and Etienne Clavière with the support of the more powerful English anti-slavery movement. It quickly attracted luminaries like Condorcet, Mirabeau and the Abbé Henri Gregoire. As an elite group it adopted a moderate programme calling for the suppression of the slave trade and the eventual abolition of slavery.

As the revolution developed its influence, it was countered by Caribbean planters and their supporters, organised by Antoine Barnave and the Club Massiac. In the colony, and in France proper in mid-1791, a bitter struggle developed between supporters and opponents of extending citizenship to free coloured proprietors. This ongoing division and strife set the stage for a massive slave uprising in August 1791 in the colony's northern plain, involving about 20,000 slaves and leading to the formation of large bands of rebels. The French authorities lost control. An all-out class struggle developed between masters and slaves, with the latter gaining the upper hand.

Under the control of the Feuillants and then the Girondins, the French National Assembly had done nothing to address the demands of the black population for their freedom.[37] Indeed, many of these moderate revolutionaries had a direct interest in maintaining slavery in Haiti. The deepening of the revolution in Haiti and the Jacobin seizure of power changed the situation. The Jacobins –despised by Hegel – conceded freedom to the black revolutionaries. In an effort to keep hold of the colony, the National Convention in Paris was eventually forced to issue the decree of 16 Pluviose An II (4 February 1794), which abolished slavery throughout the French colonies.

The National Convention was spurred to action by delegates from Saint-Dominique who argued that in the face of the revolt and the threat of foreign invasion, only such a radical step could save the colony by rallying more black insurgents to the side of the revolutionary republic. The National Convention under Jacobin control reluctantly struck down slave property at a time when the pressure of the sans-culottes on that body was at its height. Perhaps only the Jacobins at their most radical could have embraced the policy but, following Robespierre's overthrow in Thermidor, it was sustained by the French Directory until the advent of Napoleon, who attempted to restore slavery.[38] The failure of both the French and, later on, the British to bring back the status quo ante is explained by James:

> … the abolition of slavery was one of the proudest memories of the revolution; and, much more important, the San Domingo blacks had an army and leaders trained to fight in the European

manner. These were no savage tribesmen with spears, against whom European soldiers armed with rifles could win … glory.[39]

Unable to reimpose slavery and the plantation system in Haiti, the new black elite was forced to concede most of the land to small-scale rural coffee producers, contenting itself with the consolidation of a predatory state based on an export-oriented merchant capitalism.[40] In this way, Haitians were able to preserve their liberty by force of arms while the French finally abolished slavery in its colonies in the revolution of 1848.

Slavery in Haiti, although intimately connected to the Old Regime, was also closely bound up with the rise of French capitalism, which grew up in the interstices of the Old Regime during the eighteenth century. Feudalism, capitalism and slavery were tied together in the same social formation prior to the revolution. The profits from the sugar plantations of Haiti fed the expanding textile factories, iron foundries, sugar mills and construction sites of eighteenth-century France. The existence of slavery was compatible with both modes of production: all three were based on the exploitation of labour by a class of seigneurs, masters and capitalists. The French and Haitian revolutions were thus part of a world-historical moment that, in 1789, saw a dramatic transition from the feudal to the capitalist mode of production. In its midst, slavery was overthrown on the island and the Haitian Revolution became a harbinger of the fight for global emancipation from slavery in the nineteenth century.

The historical axis around which these events revolved was, however, the overthrow of feudalism. This was the historical issue in Germany as well as in France, and Marxists have rightly claimed that this was the actual historical referent of Hegel's master–bondsman dialogue. In recent years, revisionists have attempted to deny the anti-feudal and thus bourgeois and capitalist nature of the French Revolution. Scholarly revisionism, including attacks on the Marxist view of the French Revolution, has been an important aspect of the neoliberal and postmodernist period.[41] Undercutting the Marxist perspective helps to occlude the fact that Hegel was preoccupied by the struggle against feudalism and the capitalist transition. It is noteworthy that the Marxist view, with its stress on the struggle against feudalism, has nonetheless regained prominence.[42]

Peasants in revolution

As a result of the late medieval social and economic crisis, most of the French peasantry had gained their personal freedom by the end of the Middle Ages. In other words, they were no longer serfs and could leave the land if they so chose. They could also pass their land on to their heirs. However, until the revolution the lives of peasants were still dominated by the feudal mode of production. Peasants continued to pay rent to their overlords and remained subject to seigneurial exactions and justice. The appropriation of surplus by landlords took the form of labour and money rent and the performance of other menial services.[43] Despite absolutism, the persistence of feudalism was characterized as well by the system of estates marked by privileges and inequality and the continued existence of incomplete rather than full royal sovereignty over local jurisdictions.

The end of serfdom came as part of the overall abolition of feudalism and privilege by the revolution. Under pressure from the Great Fear, the decrees of 5–11 August 1789 abolished feudalism. But redemption payments persisted. The decrees of 18 June 1792 and 17

July 1793 cancelled them in the face of ongoing agrarian unrest.[44] The latter had welled up as a result of the economic crisis which followed the Haitian Revolution.[45]

At the time of the revolution, capitalism had made considerable progress in France. Beginning in the sixteenth century, capitalist tenant farmers renting larger tracts of farmland and employing wage labour established themselves in the north. From the seventeenth century onwards, these rural entrepreneurs maintained profitability by reorganising production and introducing agricultural improvements. Over the same period, there was a great extension of capitalist manufacturing, including the development of factories, especially in the expanding cotton and chemical industries.

These developments continued through the revolutionary period, as did the unification of the national market and the development of a rational monetary and banking system. Petty commodity production progressed and what Lenin described as the American or petty producer road to capitalism was blocked only by the growing burden of capitalist rent following the revolution.[46] The agrarian reform had not gone far enough. Large property controlled by nobles, bourgeoisie and rich peasants remained one of the pillars of the post-revolutionary agrarian order reinforced by the state. Moreover, given the persistence of peasants without land or without sufficient land, rent remained an important component of the social product. The persistence of large property and the burden of rent inhibited a more rapid development of French capitalism.[47]

Wage labour and revolution

The French Revolution was a bourgeois, not a working-class, revolution. Nevertheless, it did bring about a radical transformation in social attitudes towards work, underlining the transition from feudalism to capitalism. Prior to the revolution, all those who had to work to gain their livelihood continued to be cast in a negative light by the upper classes. The nobility and bourgeoisie meanwhile demeaned agricultural and craft labour or work with one's hands, which they did not do. Such attitudes continued to be expressed, but opinions shifted towards a much more positive view of work in the eighteenth century. The upper reaches of society conceded more and more the value of work in keeping order and preserving morality. It was allowed by some commentators that work could inspire a sense of dignity. Although not everyone agreed, work even began to be seen as the source of wealth, happiness and culture.[48] Diderot was notable among those who expressed a positive value towards work. He even questioned the distinction between the mechanical and liberal arts and the supposed superiority of the latter over the former.[49] At the height of the revolution, the value of work was exalted as the revolutionary sans-culottes turned the world upside down. According to them, the worthwhile members of society worked with their hands and produced useful material goods, while the nobility, clergy and speculators parasitically lived off other people's work.[50] These views were largely shared by the radical republican government under the Jacobins.

More and more interest focussed on wage labour and its ever increasing role in the economy as a growing fraction of the population either were made landless or did not have sufficient land to support themselves. Indeed, the problem of begging and vagrancy – a perennial problem – became more acute in the eighteenth century, and episodes of rising bread prices exacerbated the suffering of this population, as did unemployment. Increasingly, work came to be seen as the answer to these problems. In the 1770s, a kingdom-wide system of workhouses was created for the penal incarceration of beggars or vagrants, and an extensive network of *ateliers de charité* was established, intended for the relief of the able-bodied poor. That the crown spent considerable sums on these programmes is an indication of how alarming the problem of mendicity had become in the minds of the authorities. Rather than charity, these institutions offered work in return for wages. Moreover, a strict discipline was imposed in these workhouses in order to maintain or inculcate the habit of work.[51]

These indigent poor were at the bottom of the social scale and regarded with fear and contempt. However, the large and growing number of domestic servants who worked for wages or for their keep were likewise despised by their social betters. Even craftsmen and journeymen close to the bottom of the social hierarchy regarded them with contempt as essentially unproductive. Furthermore, they were viewed as suffering from a degrading personal dependence on their employers which was close to slavery. On the contrary, the work of artisans and journeymen, it was claimed, was honest and free. On the other hand, the situation of domestics may have been disliked even more by craftsmen and journeymen because it reminded them that wage labour was, in the final analysis, itself a kind of dependence or slavery.[52] Moreover, insofar as the guild system remained intact, masters attempted to keep workers dependent by insisting on a paternalistic right to control them.

Wage labour's importance in the eighteenth-century economy was second only to that of the work of peasants. Indeed, in the countryside many poor peasants were employed part time as wage labourers or did piece-work in the burgeoning rural cloth-manufactures. However, many others in both town and country worked for wages full time. On the other hand, historians have denied that these still largely disorganised and fragmented producers were actually a proletariat. Ernest Labrousse, for example, while recognising the growing significance of wage labour, was reluctant to acknowledge the existence of a proletariat given the lack of a sense of class consciousness and the fact that many workers also had access to supplementary means of subsistence. Nonetheless, he concluded that some 60% of the French population were day labourers or cottagers who, to a greater or lesser degree, were dependent on wages.[53]

Likewise, Albert Soboul recognised the economic importance of wage labour in manufacture while also stressing the subordination of craft workers to their masters, as reflected in the sans-culottes movement. According to Soboul, urban workers for the most part lacked the capacity to develop a consciousness of their own interests or act independently of their employers.[54] While acknowledging that the consciousness of workers was not fully differentiated from that of their masters – that, indeed, many workers aspired to become masters – it is important to underscore that the very idea of a revolution based on capitalism requires acknowledgement of the important and growing role of wage work as the basis of profits in the economy. Moreover, Labrousse and Soboul underestimated the degree of workers' self-awareness and their capacity to act in their own interest. They failed to take into account the widespread working-class unrest of the pre-revolutionary and revolutionary period. Stephen Lawrence Kaplan has recently argued that the widespread working-class unrest, both urban and rural, in fact represented the birth of modern working-class politics.[55]

Contemporaries were aware of the growing importance of wage work. The Physiocrats, the most important economic school of the eighteenth century, regarded agricultural wage work as the source of economic value. Labour unrest including strikes played an important role prior to and during the French Revolution. Most importantly in the course of the revolution, there was a serious questioning of the very legitimacy of wage labour:

Nothing engaged the *Physiocrats* and other eighteenth-century French economists more than the theory of wages. Yet this preoccupation with wages in eighteenth-century French economic thought is seldom acknowledged. It was a reflection of the French economists' preoccupation with the extraction of surplus value in the agricultural sector already marked by capitalist relations of production.[56] It is notable that Marx refers to the Physiocrats as the 'first systematic spokesmen of capital' who happened to 'consider rent-yielding, or agricultural, capital to be the only capital producing surplus-value, and the agricultural labour set in motion by it, the only labour producing surplus-value, which from a capitalist viewpoint is quite properly considered the only productive labour'.[57]

The Physiocrats were not without their critics. Jean-Joseph-Louis Graslin and Emmanuel-Joseph Sieyès rejected as too limited the idea that land was the only source of wealth. On the contrary, they asserted that it was labour which was the real source of wealth and that labour in both manufacture and agriculture produced value.[58] Their views were confirmed by Adam Smith, whose works gained currency in the years leading up to the revolution.[59] The increased plausibility of Smith's views in French public opinion was reinforced by his unconditional endorsement of laissez-faire and the growing importance of textile and chemical manufacturing and mining in France.

As an Enlightenment thinker Hegel had a very positive view of work. While enslaving the bondsman, it helps him develop his sense of himself, as the master–servant dialogue suggests. Hegel, who had read Adam Smith, likewise saw wage workers as an integral albeit subordinate part of the future emerging realm of civic freedom. Their lot could further be improved by the intervention of the state.[60]

Haiti radicalises France

The Haitian upheaval radicalised the revolution in France. Its impact went beyond ideas. Haitian slavery formed a vital part of the commercial and manufacturing economy of Paris and the whole French Atlantic littoral. Its collapse following the Haitian Revolution set off a crisis critical to the onset of the radical and democratic phase of the revolution. It brought down the constitutional monarchy and put the Jacobins in power. The republic established in place of the monarchy was based on universal male suffrage and frequent elections at the local level. In the face of ongoing peasant demands, the Jacobins furthermore eliminated the last vestiges of feudalism and made possible a partial redistribution of the land in favour of the poor. Faced with counter-revolutionary threats, the need to mobilise the economy for war, and ongoing shortages of bread, the Jacobin government abandoned laissez-faire and brought the economy under state control. It was the Jacobins – execrated by Hegel – who abolished New World slavery. It was under the Jacobins that the role of women in society was actively discussed and that women for the first time enthusiastically participated in politics at the local level. The mobilisation and democratisation of the economy under control of the state stimulated discussion of the possibilities of socialism and led to the eventual emergence of the conspiracy of Babeuf – the first attempt to organise a new political order based on the working class. In an effort to break the stranglehold that the loss of Haiti and the economic blockade imposed on the French economy, the Jacobins pursued the foreign wars initiated by their Girondin predecessors, turning them into wars against feudalism and absolutism not only in France but in Germany and beyond.

However, raising the issue of the French intrusion into Germany leads us to the question of Hegel's attitude towards the social and political situation in Germany – something that very much concerned him and which Buck-Morss does not discuss. And here we find evidence that the master–slave dialectic might refer to something besides Haiti. Hegel, one recalls, was a German living in the wake of the French Revolution and the advent of Napoleon. Sympathetic to the revolution, in 1806 he expressed admiration for Napoleon as a world-historical figure who embodied the French Revolution which was destined to transform Germany for the better.[61] At that time, Napoleon had just defeated Prussia, and all Germany lay at his feet. Indeed, Napoleon proceeded to re-organise and consolidate many of the German states into the Confederation of the Rhine. Meanwhile, a humiliated Prussia embarked on its own programme of reform. An essential feature of both these German developments was the abolition of serfdom or the granting of freedom to the enserfed peasantry. As a result, in subsequent years many former serfs became workers on the estates of the landlords.[62] These changes are rightly considered by Marxists the initial steps in the development of capitalism in Germany.

Hegel's early political writings distilled the economic and political aspects of these developments. Most of it was concerned with the disarray of a divided Germany faced with French power. We would argue that it was primarily the new situation created by the French Revolution and Napoleon that Hegel must have had in the back of his mind in what became his master–servant dialogue.[63] In fact, in the original German version of the master–servant dialogue, he refers to the bondsman or serf rather than the slave.[64] In footnotes Buck-Morss acknowledges these references to bondsmen, but she fails to discuss the German situation as an alternative to her thesis.[65]

The master–slave dialogue and its historical referent

What is the actual evidence that Buck-Morss provides connecting Hegel to the Haitian Revolution? According to her, Hegel knew all about the slave revolt in Haiti because he read contemporary journals and newspapers:

> No one has dared to suggest that the idea for the dialectic of lordship and bondage came to Hegel in Jena in the years 1803–5 from reading the press-journals and newspapers. And yet this selfsame Hegel, in this very Jena period during which the master–slave dialectic was first conceived, made the following notation: 'Reading the newspaper in the early morning is a kind of realistic morning prayer'.[66]

Certainly, Hegel read the papers and journals, some of which were in French and English. However, Buck-Morss gives no direct evidence that he followed events in Haiti closely. There is none. Buck-Morss is not deterred:

> We are left with two alternatives. Either Hegel was the blindest of all the blind philosophers of Freedom in Enlightenment Europe ... or Hegel knew about real slaves revolting successfully against real masters, and he elaborated his dialectic of lordship and bondage deliberately within this contemporary context.[67]

However, in a note she admits that Hegel does not mention Haiti in the key text *The Phenomenology of Spirit* (1806), though she adds somewhat disingenuously that he does not mention the French Revolution either.[68] However, we point out that instead of referring to the French Revolution directly under the title 'The Enlightenment', he discusses eighteenth-century thought, and in the course of this overview he names the principal foes of reason as the priests allied with the tyrants.[69] The next section, entitled 'Absolute Freedom and Terror', considers the philosophical implications of the revolution, especially its radical phase.[70] In it, Hegel asserts that absolute freedom as idea realises itself in the world as terror and death:

> In this its characteristic *work*, absolute freedom becomes explicitly objective to itself, and self-consciousness learns what absolute freedom in effect is. *In itself*, it is just this *abstract self-consciousness*, which effaces all distinction and all continuance of distinction within it. It is as such that it is objective to itself; the *terror* of death is the vision of this negative nature of itself.[71]

The French Revolution is clearly the focal point of this discussion and especially the Terror. In the form of the realisation of absolute freedom, it embodied an abstract conception of freedom which would allow no restriction and could not consolidate itself in stable institutions, but instead led to the destruction of the regime of the Terror.

Hegel may not have mentioned the French Revolution directly in the *Phenomenology*, but its presence in the text is palpable. There is no comparable discussion of the Haitian Revolution. Hegel was in fact preoccupied by the excesses of the French revolutionary Terror and its historical role. James Schmidt has documented Hegel's correspondence and reading on the revolution between 1794 and 1806. When, for instance, Jacques Carrier, perhaps the most notorious agent on mission during the Terror, was put on trial for his misdeeds and executed, Hegel wrote to Schelling indignantly: 'you probably know that Carrier has been guillotined. Do you still read the French papers? This trial is very important and has revealed the complete infamy of the Robespierrists'.[72] The tyranny of Robespierre may have been horrifying but, by the time he wrote the *Phenomenology*, Hegel came to consider it a necessity: 'And thus in the French Revolution, a fearful force sustained the state. This force is not despotism but tyranny, pure horrifying domination. Yet it is necessary and just, insofar as it sustains the state as this actual individual'.[73] Robespierre was dealt with in this way: he became powerful when his terror was necessary to sustain the state. His power left him when it was no longer necessary. That which is necessary happens, but necessity comes to be allotted at different points to different individuals.[74]

Until his death, the French Revolution remained a major preoccupation for Hegel. It is obvious that Hegel's views were closest to those of the moderate revolutionaries and were hostile to the Jacobins. Moreover, we know that the former were opposed to the revolutionary overthrow of slavery in Haiti. One wonders, then, why Buck-Morss would think that Hegel would have been favourable to the Black Jacobins of Haiti. Citing Kant, she recalls how the French Revolution inspired the public with the idea of self-rule. She then insists that Hegel was similarly inspired by the Haitian Revolution: That such enthusiasm characterized the young Hegel's reception of the Saint-Domingue Revolution, is the claim of 'Hegel and Haiti …. Hegel achieved glimpses of a global perspective, viewing the uprising of the slaves of Saint-Domingue as a manifestation of universal freedom, the realization of which he saw as the very structure and meaning of history.[75]

Hegel and racism

However, the recent publication of the work of the African historian Teshale Tibebu, entitled *Hegel and the Third World: The Making of Eurocentrism in World History* (2011), throws Buck-Morss's core thesis into serious question. In the first place, Tibebebu takes note as we have done of Buck-Morss's inability to present direct evidence that Hegel knew of the Haitian Revolution. Saying that he read the newspapers and periodicals conscientiously is not good enough, Tibebubu suggests.[76]

He makes two further points. Hegel was an ardent admirer of Napoleon Bonaparte. It was this same Napoleon, 'this world soul', who reinstated slavery in the French colonies of the Caribbean, including Haiti, in 1802. Haiti stood up to and defeated Napoleon's forces. Hegel wrote the *Phenomenology* in 1806, four years after the reimposition of slavery in the French Caribbean islands minus Haiti. Tibebu asks, why did Hegel not revise his views about Napoleon and call him the enemy of freedom, considering that Napoleon had extinguished the flame of freedom in most of the French colonies and revived the threat of slavery in Haiti? Didn't Hegel read about such events in his morning newspapers? Buck-Morss's Hegel simply could not have it both ways: admiration for Napoleon and enthusiasm for the success of the enslaved in Haiti. Another issue is that Hegel was never a revolutionary when it came to the abolition of slavery. He was more a reformist. Like other liberals, Feuillants and Girondins, he advised the gradual phasing out of slavery.[77]

However, Tibebu's charge against Buck-Morss's view of Hegel is not based simply on these details. Tibebu is deeply steeped in the basic texts of Hegel's philosophy, including the *Phenomenology*. He demonstrates that Hegel's notorious later Eurocentrism and racism, especially against Africans, is rooted in the fundamental premises of his early philosophic works. Reason realises itself progressively as a result of the spirit conquering nature. The essence of humanity is self-conscious spirit, which realises itself by overcoming unconscious nature through labour.[78] In the light of these assumptions, Hegel concluded that Africans, by dint of geography and culture, are excluded from this development. Permanently confined to the state of nature, they are doomed to remain imprisoned in an animal-like existence. In the light of this analysis, Buck-Morss's thesis that Hegel was inspired by the black Jacobins of Haiti seems improbable.

The devastating implications of Tibebu's careful, systematic analysis of Hegel's thought are reflected in a review by Christian Davis:

> For Hegel, freedom is the goal of history – 'world history is the progress of the consciousness of freedom', he insisted – but freedom is only possible in the context of a political, religious, and socio-economic system that allows for self-knowledge through independent self-reflection, one that permits 'the subject to follow its own conscience and morality' and to recognize the universal dignity of all humankind. According to Hegel, this system had its antecedent in classical Greece and found its modern expression in the bourgeois capitalist order of Protestant Prussia. As Tibebu demonstrates with remarkable detail, Hegel deemed the world outside the European West as permanently incapable of generating such a system from within.[79]

Davis pays particular attention to Tibebu's emphasis on Hegel's dismissive view of Africans:

> [Tibebu] shows how Hegel relegated the populations of what he called 'Africa proper' – Africans outside Egypt and beyond the reach of the Mediterranean – to the lowest ranks of humanity: as slaves to nature who live by instinct and as cruel, inhumane brutes who lack self-control.

Indeed, Hegel designated the true African as an 'animal man', without an awareness of God, morality, or law, and Tibebu attributes great significance to the fact that he reserved this label for Africans alone.[80]

Moreover, Tibebu challenges Buck-Morss's reading of the master–slave dialogue. The latter assumes that the slave actually challenges the master through revolutionary action. Tibebu acknowledges that, according to Hegel, the slave is revolutionary, but not by virtue of directly challenging the master: "*the resistance of the servant against the master*" is a theme Hegel did not incorporate in his dialectic of mastery and servitude.[81] A close examination of Buck-Morss's analysis of the master–slave dialectic fails to confirm the idea that it demands a revolution against the master. Rather, the slave is revolutionary because he transforms nature through his work. The servant's valour is directed not against the master but against nature. His victory is not over his master but over nature. The servant is master of nature; the master remains master of the servant. The class system remains intact.[82]

However, it also makes the servant the real subject of the historical process, marking him off from the master. The servant transforms nature in the urge to satisfy his needs. Hegel's view is the precursor to Marx's anthropology of labour. The significance of Hegel's emphasis on the role of the servant is pointed out in Marx's *Economic and Philosophical Manuscripts of 1844*:

> The outstanding achievement of Hegel's *Phenomenology* and its final outcome, the dialectic of negativity as the moving and generating principle, is thus first that Hegel conceives the self-creation of man as a process, conceives objectification as loss of the object, as alienation and as transcendence of this alienation, that he thus grasps the essence of labor and comprehends objective man … as the outcome of man's *own labor*.[83]

It is true that later on in the *Philosophy of the Subjective Spirit*, Hegel did concede that in Haiti a Christian commonwealth had been established. However, citing this passage, as Buck-Morss does in a completely de-contextualised way,[84] in support of her thesis is not convincing because it occurs in a viciously racist paragraph which emphasises the incapacity of Africans and blacks:

> Negroes, uninterested and lacking in interest, in a state of undisturbed naivety, are to be regarded as a nation of children. They are sold and allow themselves to be sold without any reflection as to the rights or wrongs of it. There is something childish about their religion. They fail to hold fast to their more sublime sentiments, this sublimity being, with them, merely a passing thought, which they make into their fetish by transferring to the first likely stone. If it fails to help them, this fetish is then abandoned. Completely good-natured and inoffensive when calm, they commit the most frightful atrocities when suddenly aroused. They cannot be said to be ineducable, for not only have they occasionally received Christianity with the greatest thankfulness and spoke movingly of the freedom they have gained from it after prolonged spiritual servitude, but in Haiti they have even formed a state based on Christian principles. They show no inner tendency to culture however. In their homeland the most shocking despotism prevails; there, they have no feeling for the personality of man, their spirit is quite dormant, remains sunk within itself, makes no progress, and so corresponds to the compact and undifferentiated mass of the African terrain.[85]

Is this the stuff of recognising the universality of the revolution in Haiti? Hardly.

Tibebu does concede that the master–servant dialectic can be applied to all sorts of exploitative and oppressive relations:

We can apply this dialectic to understand all historical situations of mastery and servitude or lordship and bondage, including slavery, feudalism, colonialism, racism, and so on. In short, all forms of oppressive social relations, those not based on freedom for all, can be subsumed under the dialectical relation of mastery and servitude and can be scrutinized from this vantage point.[86]

However, given the deep-seated Eurocentrism of his overall philosophy and the overt racism evident in his works, the idea that Hegel would be inspired by the Black Jacobins of Haiti is far-fetched.

Hegel's master–servant dialectic referred to the end of feudalism in France and Germany. While it can be used to study slavery and other forms of oppression, Hegel was not a revolutionary when it came to slavery or capitalism. Indeed, he would have no sympathy for the revolutionary current which emerged among workers during the French Revolution.

The universalism of the French Revolution is affirmed by its overthrow of feudalism and its socialist movements as well as by the Haitian Revolution against slavery, which advanced the revolution and radicalized it at critical points. It is reflected also in its women's movement, with which, given Hegel's view of women, he could not possibly have sympathised.[87] Hegel's Euro- and phallo-centric universalism fell short, though there is a striving within it towards a universal view of the meaning of history. It was from this perspective that he analysed the French Revolution. In his imperfect way, Hegel's approach anticipated that of Marx. On the other hand, his Eurocentric, racial and patriarchal assumptions make it unsurprising that he was unable to achieve such a global perspective.

Disclosure statement

No potential conflict of interest was reported by the author(s).

Notes

1. Buck-Morss, *Hegel, Haiti and Universal History*, 10–12.
2. Mansour, "Postcolonialism or Postmodernism."
3. Ibid.
4. Buck-Morss, "Theorizing Today: The Post-Soviet Condition," 27.
5. Bellamy-Foster, "Marx's Open-Ended Critique"; Musto, *Marx Revival*.
6. Buck-Morss, *Revolution Today*.
7. Buck-Morss, *Hegel, Haiti and Universal History*, 107–8.
8. Ibid., ix.
9. Ibid., 79.
10. Ibid., 80.
11. Ibid., 143.
12. James, *Black Jacobins*; cf. Taber, "Navigating Haiti's History."

13. Buck-Morss, *Hegel, Haiti and Universal History*, 39.
14. Ibid., 42.
15. Ibid., 146–7.
16. Norris, "Disappearance of the French Revolution"; Ciavetta, "Event of Absolute Freedom."
17. Schmidt, "Cabbage Heads and Gulps of Water," 4–32.
18. Tibebu, *Hegel and the Third World*.
19. Cunliffe, "Susan Buck-Morss."
20. Ciavetta, "Event of Absolute Freedom," 577–8.
21. Buck-Morss, *Hegel, Haiti and Universal History*, 59.
22. Ibid., 60.
23. Ibid., 54.
24. Ibid., 55–6.
25. Ibid., 55.
26. Kojeve, *Introduction to the Reading of Hegel*, 44, 57, 69.
27. Arthur, "Hegel's Master–Slave Dialectic," 67–8.
28. Buck-Morss, *Hegel, Haiti and Universal History*, 57.
29. Ibid., 57.
30. Guérin, *Lutte de Classes*.
31. Blackburn, *Overthrow of Colonial Slavery*; Fick, *Making of Haiti*.
32. Sepinwall, "Beyond 'the Black Jacobins,'" 5.
33. Popkin, *Facing Racial Revolution*, 43, 53, 112, 128, 130.
34. Fick, *Making of Haiti*.
35. Louverture, "Louverture Project."
36. Ehrard, "Aspects de l'Idée du Travail dans l'Encyclopédie," 110–20.
37. Geggus, *Haitian Revolutionary Studies*, 153.
38. Blackburn, "Haiti, Slavery and the Age of the Democratic Revolution," 646, Losurdo, *Liberalism: A Counter-History*, 35–66.
39. James, *Black Jacobins*, 70.
40. Trouillot, *Haiti: State against Nation*, 43–50.
41. Losurdo, *War and Revolution*.
42. Heller, *Bourgeois Revolution in France*; Heller, "Bankers, Finance Capital."
43. Ado, *Paysans en Révolution*, 42, Lemarchand, *Paysans et Seigneurs*, 50–51, 253, 256, 260.
44. Bressan, "Un Épisode Importante"; Lemarchand, "Thierry Bressan"; Lemarchand, *Paysans et Seigneurs*, 321.
45. Heller, *Bourgeois Revolution in France*, 134.
46. On the development of capitalism in France before and during the French Revolution see Heller, *Bourgeois Revolution in France*; and Heller, *French Revolution and Historical Materialism*.
47. Mcphee, "French Revolution, Peasants and Capitalism," 1273–4.
48. Koepp, "Order of Work," 16, 20; Truant, "Independent and Insolent," 255–7.
49. Ehrard, "Aspects de l'Idée du Travail dans l'Encyclopédie."
50. Sewell, *Work and Revolution in France*, 110–1.
51. Olejniczak, "Working the Body of the Poor," Conchon, "Charity Workshops in the Last Decades," 20.
52. Koepp, "Order of Work," 317–8, 366, 374.
53. Labrousse, *Derniers Temps de l'Âge Seigneurial*, 495–6.
54. Soboul, *Sans-Culottes de l'An II*, 427–31, 451–3.
55. Kaplan, *Fin des Corporations*, 449–50, 546, 550, 564.
56. Gehrke and Kurz, "Karl Marx on Physiocracy," 56, 61; Viaggi, "Role of Profits in Physiocratic Economics."
57. Marx and Engels, *Pre-Capitalist Socio-Economic Formations*, 194.
58. Faccarello, "Enigmatic Mr. Graslin," 8; Staum, *Minerva's Message*, 201; Von Eggers, N., "Toward A Materialist Conception."
59. Carpenter, *Disseminaton of the Wealth of Nations*; Whatmore, "Adam Smith's Role in the French Revolution," 66–7, 80–83; Dorigny, "Les courants des libeerálisme française," 29.
60. Ashton, "Hegel & Labour."

61. Lukacs, *Young Hegel*, 305, 309–11.
62. Eddie, *Freedom's Price*, 17–23; Simon, *Failure of the Prussian Reform Movement*, 104.
63. Comay, *Mourning Sickness*, 138, 140.
64. Hegel, "Phänomenologie des Geistes," 150–1.
65. Buck-Morss, *Hegel, Haiti and Universal History*, 52, n. 60, 62.
66. Ibid., 49.
67. Ibid., 50.
68. Ibid., 50, n. 83.
69. Hegel, *Phenomenology of Spirit*, 542.
70. Ibid., 582-95.
71. Ibid., 592 (emphasis in original).
72. Hegel, *The Letters* quoted in Schmidt, "Cabbage Heads," 5.
73. Hegel, *Gesammelte Werke* 8: 258 quoted in Schmidt, "Cabbage Heads and Gulps of Water," 18.
74. Hegel, *Gesammelte Werke* 8: 260 quoted in Schmidt, "Cabbage Heads and Gulps of Water," 18.
75. Buck-Morss, *Hegel, Haiti and Universal History*, 115.
76. Tibebu, *Hegel and the Third World*, 46.
77. Ibid., 47.
78. Ibid., 29.
79. Davis, "*Hegel and the Third World*," 227–8.
80. Ibid., 228–9.
81. Tibebu, *Hegel and the Third World*, 62.
82. Ibid., 62.
83. Marx, *Economic and Philosophic Manuscripts*, 177; Tibebu, *Hegel and the Third World*, 56.
84. Buck-Morss, *Hegel, Haiti and Universal History*, 62.
85. Hegel, *Philosophy of the Subjective Spirit*, quoted in Tibebu, *Hegel and the Third World*, 83.
86. Tibebu, *Hegel and the Third World*, 43.
87. Godineau, *Women of Paris*; Stafford, "Feminist Critique of Hegel on Women and the Family."

Bibliography

Ado, Anatoli. *Paysans en Révolution: Terre, Pouvoir et Jacquerie, 1789–1794*. Paris: Société des études robespierristes, 1996.

Arthur, Chris. "Hegel's Master–Slave Dialectic and a Myth of Marxology." *New Left Review* 142 (1983): 67–76.

Ashton, Paul. "Hegel & Labour." Legacy of Hegel' Seminar, University of Melbourne, February 5, 1999. https://www.marxists.org/reference/archive/hegel/txt/ashton.htm

Bellamy-Foster, John. "Marx's Open-Ended Critique." *Monthly Review* 70, no. 1 (2018). https://monthlyreview.org/2018/05/01/marxs-open-ended-critique/

Blackburn, Robin. "Haiti, Slavery and the Age of the Democratic Revolution." *William and Mary Quarterly* 63, no. 4 (2006): 643–674.

Blackburn, Robin. *The Overthrow of Colonial Slavery, 1776–1848*. New York: Verso, 1988.

Bressan, Thierry. "Un Épisode Important et Méconnu du Procès du Régime Seigneurial en France: l'édit D'août 1779 Contre Les Survivances Serviles." *Histoire, Économie et Société* 15, no. 4 (1996): 571–599.

Buck-Morss, Susan. *Hegel, Haiti and Universal History*. Pittsburgh: University of Pittsburgh Press, 2009.

Buck-Morss, Susan. "Theorizing Today: The Post-Soviet Condition." *Log* no. 11 (2008): 23–31.

Buck-Morss, Susan. *Revolution Today*. Chicago: Haymarket, 2019.

Carpenter, Kenneth. *The Disseminaton of the Wealth of Nations in French and in France 1776–1843*. New York: The Bibliographical Society of America, 2002.

Ciavetta, David. "The Event of Absolute Freedom: Hegel on the French Revolution and Its Calendar." *Philosophy and Social Criticism* 40, no. 6 (2014): 577–605.

Comay, Rebecca. *Mourning Sickness: Hegel and the French Revolution*. Stanford, CA:Stanford University Press, 2011.

Conchon, Anne. "Charity Workshops in the Last Decades of the 18th Century, Mélanges de L'École Française de Rome." *Italie et Méditerranée* 123, no. 1 (2011): 173–180.

Cunliffe, Philip. "Susan Buck-Morss, *Hegel, Haiti and Universal History.*" *Marx and Philosophy Review of Books*, 2010. https://marxandphilosophy.org.uk/reviews/7584_hegel-haiti-and-universal-history-review-by-philip-cunliffe/

Davis, Christian S. "Hegel and the Third World: The Making of Eurocentrism in World History by Teshale Tibebu (review)." *Northeast African Studies* 13, no. 1 (2013): 227–231.

Dorigny, Marcel, "Les courants des libéeralisme française á la fin de l"Ancien Régime et aux débuts de la Révolution Française: Quesnay ou Smith?" In *Französchise Revolution und Politizche Oeconomie*, edited by M. Barzen, 26–36. Trier: Karl-Marx-Haus, 1989.

Eddie, S. A. *Freedom's Price: Serfdom, Subjection, and Reform in Prussia, 1648–1848*. Oxford: Oxford University Press, 2013.

Ehrard, Jean. "Aspects de l'Idée du Travail Dans l'Encyclopédie." In *L'età Dei Lumi: Studi Storici Sul Settetcento Europeo in Onore di Franco Venturi*, 285–300. Naples: editore Jovene, 1985.

Faccarello, Gilbert. "The Enigmatic Mr. Graslin: A Rousseauist Bedrock for Classical Economics?" *The European Journal of the History of Economic Thought* 16, no. 1 (2009): 1–40. doi:10.1080/09672560802707399.

Fick, Caroline E. *The Making of Haiti: The Saint Domingue Revolution from Below*. Knoxville: University of Tennessee Press, 1990.

Geggus, David Patrick. *Haitian Revolutionary Studies*. Bloomington: Indiana University Press, 2002.

Gehrke, Christian, and Heinz D. Kurz. "Karl Marx on Physiocracy." *The European Journal of the History of Economic Thought* 2, no. 1 (1995): 53–90. doi:10.1080/10427719500000095.

Godineau, Dominique. *The Women of Paris and Their French Revolution*. Berkeley, CA: University of California Press, 1998.

Guérin, Daniel. *La Lutte de Classes Sous la Première République, 1793–1797*. 2 vols. Paris: Gallimard, 1968.

Hegel, G. W F. "Phänomenologie Des Geistes." In *Werke. Vollständige Ausgabe Durch Einen Verein Von Freunden Des Verewigten*, edited by Philipp Marheineke, 45. Berlin: Duncker und Humblot, 1832.

Hegel, G. W F. *Phenomenology of the Spirit*. Trans. A. V. Miller. Oxford: Oxford University Press, 1977.

Heller, Henry. "Bankers, Finance Capital and the French Revolutionary Terror." In *The French Revolution and Historical Materialism: Selected Essays*, 165–237. Leiden: Brill, 2017.

Heller, Henry. *The Bourgeois Revolution in France 1789–1815*. New York: Berghahn Books, 2006.

Heller, Henry. *The French Revolution and Historical Materialism: Selected Essays*. Leiden: Brill, 2017.

James, C. L. R. *The Black Jacobins*. London: Secker & Warburg, 1938. 2nd ed. New York: Vintage, 1989.

Kaplan, Steven. *La Fin Des Corporations*. Paris: Fayard, 2001.

Koepp, Cynthia J. "The Order of Work: Ideas, Attitudes and Representations in Eighteenth-Century France." PhD diss., Cornell University, 1992.

Kojeve, Alexander. *Introduction to the Reading of Hegel*. Translated by James H. Nichols. New York: Basic Books, 1969.

Labrousse, Ernest. *Des Derniers Temps de l'Âge Seigneurial Aux Préludes de L'âge Industriel (1660–1789)*, Vol. 2, Histoire Économique et Sociale de la France, edited by Fernand Braudel Labrousse, 4 vols. Paris: PUF, 1975.

Lemarchand, Guy. *Paysans et Seigneurs en Europe: Une Histoire Comparée, XVIe–XIXe Siècle*. Rennes: Presses universitaires de Rennes, 2011.

Lemarchand, Guy. "Thierry Bressan, Serfs et Mainmortables en France au XVIIIe Siècle, la Fin D'un Archaïsme Seigneurial." *Annales Historiques de la Révolution Française* 354, no. 4 (2008): 223–225.

Losurdo, Domenico. *Liberalism: A Counter-History*. London: Verso, 2011.

Losurdo, Domenico. *War and Revolution: Rethinking the Twentieth Century*. London: Verso, 2015.

Louverture, Toussaint. "The Louverture Project, Text of Toussaint's Constitution (English) 1801." http://thelouvertureproject.org/index.php?title=Haitian_Constitution_of_1801

Lukacs, György. *The Young Hegel: Studies in the Relations between Dialectics and Economics*. Cambridge, MA: MIT Press, 1976.

Marx, Karl. *Economic and Philosophical Manuscripts*. Moscow: Progress Books, 1959.

Marx, Karl, and Friedrich Engels. *Pre-Capitalist Socio-Economic Formations*. Moscow: Progress, 1979.

Mansour, Chris. "Postcolonialism or Postmodernism? An Interview with Susan Buck-Morss." Platypus Review, no. 34, 2011, April. https://platypus1917.org/2011/04/02/postcolonialism-or-postmodernism-an-interview-with-susan-buck-morss/

McPhee, Peter. "The French Revolution, Peasants and Capitalism." *The American Historical Review* 94, no. 5 (1989): 1265–1280. doi:10.2307/1906350.

Musto, Marcello. *The Marx Revival: Key Concepts and New Critical Interpretations*. New York: Cambridge University Press, 2020. doi:10.1086/ahr/99.1.192.

Norris, Andrew. "The Disappearance of the French Revolution in Hegel's Phenomenology of Spirit." *APSA 2011 Annual Meeting Paper*, August, 2011. https://papers.ssrn.com/sol3/papers.cfm?abstract_id=1900559

Olejniczak, William. "Working the Body of the Poor: The Ateliers de Charité in Late Eighteenth-Century France." *Journal of Social History* 24, no. 1 (1990): 87–107. doi:10.1353/jsh/24.1.87.

Popkin, Jeremy D. *Facing Racial Revolution: Eyewitness Accounts of the Haitian Insurrection*. Chicago, IL: University of Chicago Press, 2007.

Schmidt, James. "Cabbage Heads and Gulps of Water: Hegel on the Terror." *Political Theory* 26, no. 1 (1998): 4–32. doi:10.1177/0090591798026001002.

Sepinwall, Alyssa Goldstein. "Beyond 'the Black Jacobins': Haitian Revolutionary Historiography Comes of Age." *Journal of Haitian Studies* 23, no. 1 (2017): 4–34. doi:10.1353/jhs.2017.0000.

Sewell, William Hamilton. *Work and Revolution in France: The Language of Labor from the Old Regime to 1848*. Cambridge: Cambridge University Press, 1980.

Simon, Walter. *The Failure of the Prussian Reform Movement, 1807–1819*. Ithaca, NY: Cornell University Press, 1955.

Soboul, Albert. *Les Sans-Culottes de L'An II*. Paris: Clavreuil, 1958.

Stafford, Antoinette M. "The Feminist Critique of Hegel on Women and the Family." *Animus* 2 (1997): 64–92.

Staum, Martin S. *Minerva's Message: Stabilizing the French Revolution*. Montreal: McGill-Queen's University Press, 1996.

Taber, Robert D. "Navigating Haiti's History: Saint-Domingue and the Haitian Revolution." *History Compass* 13, no. 5 (2015): 235–250. doi:10.1111/hic3.12233.

Tibebu, Teshale. *Hegel and the Third World: The Making of Eurocentrism in World History*. Syracuse: Syracuse University Press, 2011.

Trouillot, Michel-Rolph. *Haiti: State against Nation: The Origins and Legacy of Duvalierism*. New York: Monthly Review Press, 1990.

Truant, Cynthia M. "Independent and Insolent: Journeymen and Their 'Rites' in the Old Regime Workplace." In *Work in France: Representations, Meaning, Organization, and Practice*, edited by Kaplan and Koepp, 131–173. Ithaca, NY: Cornell University Press, 1986.

Viaggi, Gianni. "The Role of Profits in Physiocratic Economics." *History of Political Economy* 17, no. 3 (1985): 367–384.

Von Eggers, N. "Toward a Materialist Conception of Constituent Power: Reinterpreting the Constitutional Theory of Sieyes." *History of Political Thought* 39, no. 2 (2018): 325–356.

Whatmore, Richard. "Adam Smith's Role in the French Revolution." *Past & Present* 175, no. 1 (2002): 65–109. doi:10.1093/past/175.1.65.

Index

absolute freedom 194
Academia 56
Acción Democrática (Democratic Action, AD)
    113, 115
active Marxism 47, 48–50, 58
Afro TV 138
Albright, Madeline 120
alienation 73; *vs.* creativity 63–7; forms of 72; in
    Venedemocracia 116
American Indian Movement 146
Anglo-America 15–16, 20–1
animal rights 153
Anishnabwe 147
"Anti-Hitler Coalition" 17
anti-imperialism 94, 104
anti-revolution 15–16
Arab Spring 4
Arendt, Hannah 2, 156
Artz, Lee 7–8, 128
Asamblea Nacional Constituyente (ANC) 124
autonomy 163
Avila TV 135–6, 139, 141

Babeuf conspiracy 192
Bakhtin, Mikhail 7, 62; culture as revolution 63–7
Balo Vento, Venezuela 138
Baran, Paul 48, 101, 166
Barkin, David 5, 8, 161
Barnave, Antoine 188
Barretto, Juan 135
Batishchev, Genrikh 64
Bees of Acteal 168
Berlin Wall, fall of 4, 39
Bernstein, Eduard 49
Big data 25
Black Jacobins (James) 187
Blair, Tony 57
Blok, Aleksandr 68
Bolivarian Revolution 7–8; critical
    juncture 116–20; disruption 118–20;
    new path and old mechanisms 117–
    18; survival of 121; transformation to
    reproduction 120–3; transformative project
    of 112; in Venezuela 6, 111
Bolívar, Simón 117

Bolshevik Revolution 3, 4
Bolsheviks 18–19, 32, 78, 100
Bortkiewicz, Ladislaus 98, 101
Bottomore, Tom 48
Bourdieu, Pierre 56
bourgeois-democratic revolution 3, 30, 32, 39–
    40, 41, 81
bourgeois hegemony 32
bourgeois social class 172
Braverman, Harry 48
Brenner, Robert 34, 102
Brewer, Anthony 103
Brewer-Carías, A. 113
BRICS (Brazil, Russia, India, China and South
    Africa) countries 35, 130
Brinton, Crane 2
Brissot, Jacques-Pierre 188
Buck-Morss, Susan 8, 182, 194; master–slave
    dialect 183, 185; post-Marxist/post-
    colonialism view of 183–5
Bukharin, Nicolai 97–8, 100
Bulavka-Buzgalina, Lyudmila 7, 62, 64
bureaucracy 156
Burke, Edmund 14–15
bush minorities, in China 149
bush peoples 147; cultural and historical
    heritages 163; and existing socialism 149–
    50; mode of production 147–8, 153; social
    relations 152; spirituality of 153–4; strategic
    value 151–2; working class 151–2
Bush Revolution: attentiveness to
    cultural studies 155–6; culture and
    historical materialism 155; eco-
    socialism 153; form of revolution 157; *nations*
    notion 150–1; Paraguay 156–7; religion
    and spirituality 153–4; strategic value of
    bush peoples 151–2; struggle against
    capitalism 155; supplement 154; unnoticed
    revolution 158
Buxton, Julia 7, 111
Buzgalin, Alexandr 7, 54, 55, 62

caaguasu, Paraguay 156
Cabral, Amilcar 148
Caldera, Rafael 116

capital accumulation 23, 51, 98, 155, 162
capitalism 190; international
  relations 35; Marx's analysis of 3; nature of 57–
  8; as non-homogeneous world system 30; and
  revolution 5; socio-economic analysis of 47;
  structures of 53–4; transition to socialism 50–
  3; uneven 35; as value production 93–4, 101
capitalist imperialism, crisis of 1, 7
capitalist state 155
Caracazo riots, of 1989 116
Carney, Mark 54
Carrier, Jacques 194
Catia TV 137–8, 139, 141
Central Intelligence Agency (CIA) 38
Chacon, Jesse 132
chaco, Paraguay 157
Chávez, Hugo 4, 111, 115, 123–4, 132
Chavista movement 117, 121, 123
Cheng, Enfu 7, 78
Chile 21, 151
China: bush minorities in 149;
  industrialisation in 34; labour conflicts in 130;
  New Rural Reconstruction Movement in 170;
  OBOR strategy 36; and Russia 123; spread of
  Marxism 80
Chinese Revolution 7; and Communist
  International 79–80; militant
  struggle 88; rural-centred path of 84;
  Sinicising Marxism 85–6; Stalin about 87
Christian democracy 22
Christian Democrat COPEI party 114
Ciavatta, David 186
Cisneros Group 131
class conflicts 58, 133
class consciousness 172
class formation 14
classical political economy 95–7
class revolution, politics of 47
Clavière, Etienne 188
Clinton, Hillary 37
Club Massiac 188
Cobban, Alfred 3
co-creation 63–4, 71
Cold War 2, 4, 17, 124
collective attitudes 165
collective identity 163, 165
collective management 166
Colour Revolutions 6, 37–40
commercial media, in Venezuela 132
Commonwealth of Independent States (CIS)
  countries 36
communism 4, 67; primitive communism 48
Communist International: and Chinese
  Revolution 79–80; land revolution 86;
  revolutionary role of peasants 86
Communist Party of China (CPC) 79–81;
  dogmatism in 85; left-leaning errors 85
community: collective basis of revolutionary
  subject 163–5; consolidation 167;
  fundamental characteristics 164

community media, in Venezuela 133, 136–7;
  Afro TV 138; Catia TV 137–8, 139, 141
community radio, in Venezuela 138–9
Condorcet 188
Constituent Assembly in Venezuela 130
consumerism 58
core-periphery relations 30, 35
corporate liberalism 23
cosmopolitanism 104
Coulthard, Glen 148
counter-revolution 15–17; intellectual 94;
  neoclassical 95–7; *vs.* world revolution 5, 6–9;
  after World War II 20–3
creative activity 65
creative labour 55, 68–9
creativity *vs.* alienation 63–7
Crimean War 30
critical junctures, in Venezuela 113–15
cultural revolution 70–1
culture: as co-creativity 7, 63; and historical
  materialism 155; as revolution 63–7
Cunliffe, Philip 186
Cybersyn project 25

Darwin, Charles 47
Davis, Christian 195
Debord, Guy 17
decision-making 166–7
democracy: promotion 120; and social
  movements 129
democratic media 133; production and
  distribution 139–40; revolutionary/
  participatory culture 140–2
de Pradt, D. G. F. Dufour 15
Derrida, Jacques 154
Desai, Radhika 1, 7, 93
deterritorialisation 58
"dialogue of knowledge systems" 172
digital capitalism 56
digital media 56
disalienation 64, 73
Dobb, Maurice 102
dogmatism 85
Donbass uprising 40, 41
Dostoevsky, F. 63, 147
Dzarasov, Ruslan 6, 29, 156

Eastern-European Partnership programmes 36
economic exploitation 47–8, 53, 57
economic liberalism 14
eco-socialism 153
ECPAIs (Independent Community Audiovisual
  Production Teams) 137
Ellner, S. 122
El Salvador, communist revolution in 2
Eltsin, Boris 52
emancipatory subjects, search for 146–7
end of the "end of history" 62, 71
Engels, Frederick 51, 57, 93, 171
England, social cohesion in 14

Enlai, Zhou 82, 85–6
Enlightenment 50, 148, 185, 194
environmental crisis 162
environmental justice 163, 165
Eurocentrism 182
external counterrevolution 13, 15, 17

Fanon, Frantz 148
fascism 16; to parafascism 20–3; threat of 9
Federici, Sylvia 148
feudalism 189
financialisation 35
First World War 4
flying geese paradigm 35
Fourth Republic, in Venezuela: and *Puntofijismo* model 114–15, 120
France 2; and Haiti 188, 192–3
fraternity 164
French Revolution 3, 14, 183, 185, 190
Furet, François 3

Gallegos, Rómulo 113
Gatrell, Peter 31
geopolitical economy 5, 9, 94
Germany: fascism in 2; French intrusion into 193
GLADIO secret terrorist network 39
Glenny, Misha 24
global capitalism, and crisis 34–7
globalisation 23, 54
global socialist project 151–2
Glorious Revolution of 1688 14
Gorbachev, Mikhail 23–4, 52; Perestroika 33
Gouldner, Alvin 51, 58
Gramsci, Antonio 19, 32, 104, 137, 154, 155
Granier, Michel 132
Graslin, Jean-Joseph-Louis 192
Gregoire, Abbé Henri 188
Gritsenko, A. 38
Gritsenko, Victoria 6, 29
Grossman, Henryk 99
gross national income (GNI) 33, *34*
Grundrisse (Marx) 5, 152
Guaidó, Juan 112, 124
Guérin, Daniel 187
Guesde, Jules 49
Gurr, Ted 2
Gvozd, V. 38

Haig, Alexander 22
Haiti: and France 188, 192–3; and Hegel 185–7; slavery in 187–9
Haitian Revolution 8, 13, 182, 184; connecting Hegel to 193; and slavery 187–9
Hardt, M. 55
Hartz, Louis 15
Harvey, David 171
Hegel, G. W. F. 183; connection to Haitian Revolution 193; and Haiti 185–7; *Phenomenology of Spirit* 185–6, 194, 195; and racism 195–7; universalism 186

Hegel, Haiti and Universal History (Buck-Morss) 8, 182, 184
Heller, Henry 1, 8, 182
Hellinger, D. 114
Henry, Patrick 185
Hilferding, Rudolf 98–101
Himani Bannerji 153
historical heritage 163
historical materialism 47, 147, 154; and culture 155
historical trajectory principle 164
Historic Compromise strategy 22
History of the Russian Revolution, The (Trotsky) 30
Hitler, Adolf 2, 16–17
Hobsbaum, Eric 48
Homo sapiens 152
Human Development Index (HDI) 33, *34*
human intervention, role of 47
hunters/gatherers *see* bush peoples
Huntington, Samuel 23
Hu Qiaomu 84
hydropower 167

identity politics 57, 154
Idle No More movement 158
Ilyenkov, Evald 64
immaterial labour 55–6
imperialism 3, 94–5, 102, 104; and Marxism 99–100
India, Zero-Budget Natural Farming System in 170
indigenous peoples 147
industrialisation, in China 34
information revolution 13
Inninewug hunters 153
intellectual counterrevolution 94
internal counterrevolution 13, 17–20
International labour organisation (ILO) Convention 169 164, 167
International Monetary Fund (IMF) loans 23
Inuit Circumpolar Conference 150
Izarra, Andrés 137

James, C. L. R. 168–9, 185, 187
Jevons, Stanley 96
Johnson, Chalmers 2
Jones, Gareth Stedman 48
Juncker, Jean-Claude 57

Kaplan, Stephen Lawrence 191
Karl, T. L. 114
Kautsky, Karl 8, 98
Kenya, Maasai pastoralist practice in 170
Keynesian Marxism 100–1
Keynes, John Maynard 97
Kharkov uprising 39
Khrushchev, N. 24–5
Kiernan, Victor 48
Klein, Naomi 21
Klyatchko, V. 38

KMT *see* Kuomintang (KMT)
Kojève, Alexandre 187
Kolganov, Andrei 54
Kulchyski, Peter 5, 8, 146
Kuomintang (KMT) 81–2

labour force 166
Labrousse, Ernest 191
Laclau, Ernesto 56
land holdings 2
Landless Workers' Movement (MST) 170
Lane, David 6, 23–4, 33, 46
Latin America: government
    communication 133–4; social movements
    and political power in 128–9
La Vía Campesina 170
law of uneven development 30, 78–9
Leacock, Eleanor 148
Lebowitz, Michael 24
Lee, Richard 148
leisure time 155
Lenin as a Philosopher (Pannekoek) 20
Lenin, Vladimir Ulyanov 16, 18,
    49, 100; active Marxism 49, 53;
    contributions to social theory 62; culture
    as revolution 63–7; democratic revolution
    into socialist revolution 32; law of uneven
    development 30, 78–9
Lewin, Moshe 19
Liebknecht, Karl 67
Li Lisan 85, 86
Linconao, Francisca: judicial harassment of 151
List, Friedrich 104
Liu Shaoqi 80, 87–8
Livy, Titus 157
Lockean liberalism 15; codification of 14
Louverture, Toussaint 185, 187
Lukács, G. 50, 64, 187
Luxemburg, Rosa 49, 98

Macri, Mauricio 143
Maduro, Nicolás 112, 123–4
Mahoney, J. 112
Maidan events 38–9, 41
Malomuzh, N. 38
Mandel, Ernest 48, 99
The Manifesto of the Communist Party 72, 93
Mao-Tse-Tung 50
Mao Zedong 7, 80–1, 85–6, 88; new democracy
    theory 83
Marcuse, Herbert 187
Marginalist Revolution (1870) 94
market dynamics 166
Marshall, Alfred 95
Martov, Julius 49
Marxism 46; active 47, 48–50; and imperialism
    99–100; and neoclassical economics 97–9
Marxist Economics 7, 94–5, 98, 104
Marx, Karl 47, 57; analysis of
    capitalism 7, 93–4, 101; changing

nature of capitalism 57–8; class
    structure 54–7; *vs.* collective revolutionary
    subject 171–3; *Grundrisse* 5, 152;
    letter to Vera Sassulitch 171; mode of
    production concept 8; resolving classical
    political economy 95–6; structures of
    capitalism 53–4
Mason, Paul 54, 55, 56
mass creative activity 65
mass media 56
master–slave dialogue 183, 185, 193–4
materiality, of nations 94, 100
Mature Bolshevism 30
Mayakovsky, Vladimir 7, 62, 66, 67
McLellan, David 48
Menger, Carl 96
Mensheviks 18, 30, 49
Mészáros, István 64
Mexican Network of People Affected by Mining
    (REMA–Chiapas) 167–8
Mexico: national groupings 167–8; Zapatista
    (EZIN) 170, 173
Mezhuev, Vadim 64
Millennium Manifesto 24
MINCI (Ministry of Communication and
    Information) 132, 139
Mining Code (1910) 113
Minsk Agreements 40, 43*n*45
mode of production 155; of bush peoples 147–
    8, 153; concept by Marx 8
modern capitalism 46; changing structures
    of 53–4
modernisation, ideological 14
Molotov–Ribbentrop Pact 16
Monroe doctrine 15
Moore, Barrington 3, 16
Moro, Aldo 22
Moskito Indians, in Nicaragua 149
Mother Earth 165
Movement for Socialism (MAS) 115, 130
Movement of People Affected by Dams and in
    Defence of the Rivers (MAPDER) 168
Mussolini, B. 16
Musto, Marcello 64
Muswagin, John 158

Naian, Shi 157
Nalivaytchenko, V. 38
Napoleon 193, 195
Narodniks (Populists) 30
National Convention 188
National Indigenous Congress (CNI) 168
national reconstruction 173
National Security decision directives 22
national unification 14
nations 150–1
natural resources, exploitation of 166
Negri, A. 55, 56
Nenets/Chukchi, in Soviet Russia 149
neoclassical counterrevolution 95–7

neoclassical economics 94, 97; and Marxism 97–9; objective function of 96
neoliberal capitalism 25, 56, 129
neoliberalism 2
New democratic Revolution 81
New Rural Reconstruction Movement (China) 170
North Atlantic Treaty Organization (NATO) 12, 34
Nove, Alec 51–2
Nuland, Victoria 38

OBOR strategy *see* One Belt, One Road (OBOR) strategy
Occupy Movement 4
October Revolution 13, 53, 68–9; anti-revolutionary elements 16; bridge between West and East 79; development of Soviet culture 73
official Marxism 187
Ollman, Bertell 64
One Belt, One Road (OBOR) strategy 36
Open digital Television system 136
Organization of American States (OAS) 120
Organization of Petroleum Exporting Countries (OPEC) 118

Pachamama (Mother Earth) 165
Pact of Puntofijo, of 1957 114
Pannekoek, Anton 20
parafascism 13, 20–3
Pareto, J. 98
Paris Commune 13, 16–18
Parsons, Talcott 48
Partido Comunista de Venezuela (Venezuelan Communist Party, PCV) 113
Partido Socialista Unido de Venezuela (PSUV) 122
path dependence, in Venezuela 112, 113–14; negative consequences 115–16
Patnaik, Prabhat 100–2, 104
Payette, Geoffrey 38
peasants, in revolution 189–90
Peasant Wars of the Twentieth Century (Wolf) 2
Pérez, Carlos Andrés 116
permanent counterrevolution 5, 6, 13, 21
permanent revolution 30, 40
Petaré TV 138
Petróleos de Venezuela, SA (PDVSA) 115, 117, 123
Phenomenology of Spirit (Hegel) 185–6, 194, 195
Physiocrats 192
"pink tide" 128
Pinochet coup, in Chile 21, 25, 151
Pipes, Richard 22
Plan Zamora 119
Plekhanov, G. V. 20, 30
Polanyi, Karl 97
Polar Industries 121

political economy 95–7; democratic media 140–2; of media in Venezuela 131–3
Political Marxism 94, 102
popular power, exercising 168
Populists (*Narodniks*) 30
possessive individualism 14
post-normal science 172
Poulantzas, Nicos 155
primitive communism 48
The Principles of Communism (Engels) 51
Prisypkins, Pierre 71
product/commodity chains 23
productive diversification 163
productive systems, territorial management of 165–6
proletarian revolution 78, 84
pro-letariat social class 172
Proletkult 68, 70
public access media 129, 134–6; Avila TV 135–6, 139, 141; expanding 131; and social revolution 142–3; Vision Venezuela TV (ViVe) 134, 139, 141
Puntofijismo model, in Venezuela: and Fourth Republic 114–15, 120
pure capitalism 98–9
Putin, Vladimir 13, 24, 33; Munich speech 36

Qian, Sima 157
Qu Qiubai 85

Rabelais, François 63
Radio Negro Primero 139, 141
Reagan administration 22
rebellion 169, 172
Red Brigades 22
Red TV 136
Reflections on the Revolution in France (Burke) 14
religion, and spirituality 153–4
Renaissance 63, 71
resilience 173
resistance 169, 172
re-Sovetisation 37
revolution: and agrarian bureaucratic states 3; and capitalism 5; *vs.* counter revolution 6–9; as culture 67–71; experts' view of 2; form of 157; giving birth to new culture 71–3; history of 8; Paraguay 156–7; peasants in 189–90; post-Cold War conjuncture 4; unnoticed 158; and wage labour 190–2; *see also specific Revolutions*
revolutionary expression 168
revolutionary subject: collective basis of 163–5; Marx *vs.* collective 171–3; social transformation expressions 168–71; and transformative action 165–8
Revolution Betrayed, The (Trotsky) 32–3
r-existence 8, 169, 172, 174
Ricardian Marxism 101–4
Ricardo, David 95–7, 102
Robespierre, M. 194

Rohter, Larry 128
Römer, Henrique Salas 120
Rosenstock-huessy, Eugen 14
Rostow, Walt 2
Rousseau, Jean-Jacques 147
royal absolutism 14
Roy, M. N. 100
Russia: and China 123; semi-peripheral status of 33; systemic crisis in 23–5; Tsarist 30–1, *31*; and Ukraine 6
Russian capitalism 30
Russian peasantry 30–1
Russian Revolution 4, 71–2; anti-revolution 15–17; counterrevolution after World War II 15–17, 20–3; failure of 41; fascism 15–17; historical legacy of 30–4; internal counterrevolution 17–20; permanent counterrevolution of Soviet in 12; West as dynamic counter-revolution 14–15
Russian Spring 39

Saakashvili, Michael 36
Saami, in Sweden 149
Sahlins, Marshall 148
Saint-Dominique *see* Haiti
Sakwa, Richard 24
Sánchez, Alejandra 5, 8, 161
San José Pact of 1980 118
Sassulitch, Vera 171
Say's Law 97, 99
Schaff, Adam 64
Schmidt, James 194
Schmitt, Carl 23
scientific Marxism 6, 47–8, 59
scientific socialism 47
Scott, Peter Dale 20
Second Contradiction of Capitalist Production 173
Second International 99–100
self-sufficiency 163
Shock Doctrine (Klein) 21
shock therapy, in psychiatry 21
SIBCI (Bolivarian Communication and Information System) 139
Sieyès, Emmanuel-Joseph 192
Skocpol, Theda 3
slavery, and Haitian Revolution 187–9
Slobodian, Quinn 96
Smith, Adam 95, 182, 192
Smithian Marxism 100–1, 102
Smith, Neil 168
Soboul, Albert 191
social capacity 162, 165
social classes 172
social contract 164
social creativity 69–70
social democracy 20
social formations 48
socialism 46, 58, 149–50; transition from capitalism 50–3

socialist planning 51
sociality spectrum 171
social justice 129, 163
social mobilisations 167, 169
social movements, and political power in Latin America 128–9
social power 168
social progress 72
social relations 140
social revolution 71; and media access 142–3
social transformation 161
socio-economic analysis of capitalism 47
solidarity 150, 163, 164
Soviet bureaucracy 33
Spain, fascism in 2
spirituality, and religion 153–4
Stalin, J. 19, 32, 80
state formation 14, 20
state socialism 50
Streeck, Wolfgang 23
surplus management 166–7
sustainable management 163
Sweezy, Paul 48, 101

taxation 2
Taylor, William 38
technology 54, 58, 133
TeleSUR 134
Temporal Single System Interpretation (TSSI) 103
tendency of rate of profit to fall (TRPF) 94, 98, 103
territorial management, of productive systems 165–6
theoretical conciliation policy 98
Third International 100
Thucydides 59
Tibebu, Teshale 195, 197
Tilly, Charles 3
Tosepan Titataniske 171
transformation problem 103
transformative action, and revolutionary subject: political position 167–8, 172; surplus management 166–7; territorial management of productive systems 165–6
transnational corporations (TNCs) 35
transnational mega-projects, in mining 167
tribal peoples, in India 149
Trienio period 113
Trotsky, L. 18; law of uneven and combined development (UCD) 30; permanent revolution theory 30, 31; *Revolution Betrayed, The* 32–3
Trump, Donald 57
Tsarist Russia 40; industrialisation of 30–1, *31*
Tugan-Baranovsky, Michael 98–9, 101
Two Treatises of Government 14
Tymoshenko, Y. 38

Ukraine 37, 43*n*40; Colour Revolutions in 6; Western soft power 38
Ukraine Crisis 29; colour revolution dialectics 37–40; global capitalism

and 34–7; Russian Revolution and historical legacy 30–4
Ukrainian Democratic Alliance for Reforms (UDAR) 38
Ukrainian Security Service (SBU) 38
uneven capitalism 35
United Nations (UN) 112; committees for indigenous issues 150
United Nations Declaration of the Rights of Indigenous Peoples (UNDRIP) 164
United Nations Development Programme (UNDP) 51
universal history 183
USSR 71, 73; collapse of 13, 36, 40; formation of 49, 50; industrialisation of 20; support for Kuomintang (KMT) 82

van der Pijl, Kees 5, 6, 12, 151
Venedemocracia 114; collapse of 116
Venevisión 131
Venezuela: Bolivarian Revolution 116–20; commercial media in 132; crisis 121–3; critical juncture 113–15; government communication 133–4; hydrocarbons law 113; negative consequences in path retention 115–16; path setting 113–14; *Puntofijismo* and Fourth Republic 114–15, 120; social movements 130
Venezuelan National Assembly 132
Venezuelan Revolution 7, 141
Vietnam War 21
Viloria, Ana 140, 142
Vision Venezuela TV (ViVe) 134, 139, 141
von Böhm-Bawerk, Eugen 97, 99, 101

VTV 133
vulgar economy 95–6

wage labour, and revolution 190–2
Wallerstein, Immanuel 48
Walras, Leon 96
Wang Ming 80, 85
Warren, Bill 103
water management 169
Wayaobao Meeting 86
Weber, Max 97
West, as dynamic counter-revolution 14–15
Western triumphalism 4
Williams, Eric 187
Williams, Raymond 48
Wilson, Woodrow 16, 18
wind power 167
Wolf, Eric 2, 148
worldview 164
Wright, E. O. 48

Xiaoping, Deng 22, 84–5

Yakimenko, A. 38
Yang, Jun 7, 78
Yanukovitch 38
Yatsenuk, A. 38
Yeltsin, Boris 23–4

Zapatista (EZlN) 170, 173
Zarembka, Paul 99
Zemtsy 31
Zero-Budget Natural Farming System (India) 170
Zlobin, Nal 64, 67
Zuboff, Shoshana 25